Collins

INCLUDES PICTURE ROUNDS

ULTIMATE PUB QUIZ

500
QUIZZES

Published by Collins
An imprint of HarperCollins Publishers
Westerhill Road
Bishopbriggs
Glasgow G64 2QT

HarperCollins Publishers
1st Floor, Watermarque Building,
Ringsend Road, Dublin 4, Ireland

First Edition 2020

10 9 8 7 6 5 4 3 2

© HarperCollins Publishers 2020
All quizzes copyright Puzzler Media – www.puzzler.com

ISBN 978-0-00-840622-6

Collins® is a registered trademark of HarperCollins Publishers Limited

www.harpercollins.co.uk

Typeset by Puzzler Media

Printed and bound by CPI Group (UK) Ltd, Croydon, CR0 4YY

A catalogue record for this book is available from the British Library.

If you would like to comment on any aspect of this book, please contact us at the
above address or online.
E-mail: puzzles@harpercollins.co.uk

Introduction

What makes a good quiz? A witty and amusing host and a choice of interesting categories are good places to start.

You could combine the hosting talents of Alexander Armstrong and Jeremy Paxman but you need a great set of questions too.

That's where *Collins Ultimate Pub Quiz* comes in. We've taken the hassle out of creating the perfect quiz by providing around 10,000 questions, including 30 picture quizzes, on all manner of subjects in an easy-to-use format.

There's something on offer for everyone, too, from easy questions for those taking their first tentative steps from quizzing base camp right up to super-tricky testers for those experienced trivia travellers heading for the highest peaks of general knowledge.

Let's get going.

The quizzes

The book is divided into two parts, each with 250 quizzes. Half of the quizzes are based on themes ranging from animals to art, food to football, science to sitcoms and a whole host of subjects in between. The rest of the quizzes are pot luck and contain a little bit of everything.

The quizzes in each part of the book are grouped together depending on how tricky we think they are. The easy ones come first, followed by medium and finally hard.

Easy

With a wide range of themes on offer in our easy section, you're bound to find some questions and quizzes easy and others a bit harder. It's not all straightforward in this section though: watch out for a few themes that aren't quite as obvious as the title suggests. Quiz 251 marks the start of the second easy section.

Medium

You'll get a good general knowledge workout when you tackle our medium quizzes. Classic themes that appeared in the easy section are repeated here, but you'll most likely need some extra thinking time to complete the quizzes at this level. The second medium section starts at Quiz 401.

Hard

You'll really need to work those little grey cells when you venture into our hard quiz section, so set aside plenty of time. An enthusiast's knowledge would be a definite advantage on some of the themed quizzes. When you've toiled your way through the first section, the second hard section begins at Quiz 476.

The answers

Each quiz header tells you where the answers are printed. They're mostly just a couple of pages away, for example the answers to Quiz 1 appear at the bottom of Quiz 3. The exceptions are the last two quizzes in each part of the book, which appear at the bottom of the first two quizzes in that part.

Running a quiz

When you're running a quiz night, there's a great sense of satisfaction to be had in doing a job well, and a little bit of effort beforehand will go a long way to making sure that your quiz goes without a hitch.

❖ Plan: consider how many questions you want to ask in the time available, making sure you leave enough thinking time between questions. Once you've done that, pick a good range of subjects so that there's something for everyone.

❖ Rehearse: Go through all the questions you're going to be asking beforehand, checking any potentially tricky pronunciations and making sure your timings work. Note down all the questions (notes look better in a quiz environment than reading from a book) and answers. Every effort has been made to ensure that all the answers in *Collins Ultimate Pub Quiz* are correct. Despite our best endeavours, mistakes may still appear. If you see an answer you're not sure is right, or if you think there's more than one possible answer, then do check.

❖ Paper and writing implements: make sure you prepare enough sheets of paper for everyone to write on, including scrap paper, and have plenty of pens to hand for those who need them.

❖ Prizes: everyone likes a prize. No matter how small, it's best to have one on offer.

Good luck! We hope you enjoy *Collins Ultimate Pub Quiz*.

Contents

Easy Quizzes

Easy Quizzes

Photo credits

120. Authors
1. Sir Terry Pratchett – Michal Kalasek
2. JK Rowling – JStone
3. David Walliams – Featureflash Photo Agency
4. Jeffrey Archer – Featureflash Photo Agency
6. Neil Gaiman – lev radin
7. George RR Martin – Kathy Hutchins
8. Fern Britton – Featureflash Photo Agency
9. Stephen King – Everett Collection

150. Rock Bands
1. U2 – Featureflash Photo Agency
2. Coldplay – s_bukley
3. The Rolling Stones – JStone
4. Aerosmith – JStone
5. Foo Fighters – DFree
6. ZZ Top – Fabio Diena
7. Muse – Photo Works
8. Guns N' Roses – A.PAES

180. British Olympic gold medallists
1. Max Whitlock – Stockphotovideo
2. Alistair Brownlee – Stefan Holm
3. Dame Kelly Holmes – Featureflash Photo Agency
4. Adam Peaty – Maxisport
5. Dame Katherine Grainger –landmarkmedia
6. Greg Rutherford – Ron Adar
7. Nicola Adams – Featureflash Photo Agency
8. Justin Rose – Mitch Gunn
9. Geraint Thomas – Huw Fairclough

210. Comedians
1. Ellie Taylor – Featureflash Photo Agency
2. Kevin Bridges – Featureflash Photo Agency
3. Adil Ray – Urbanbuzz
4. Russell Howard – Featureflash Photo Agency
5. Sara Pascoe – Featureflash Photo Agency
6. Rhod Gilbert – Featureflash Photo Agency
7. Aisling Bea – DFree
8. Geoff Norcott – Terry Murden
9. Shappi Khorsandi – Featureflash Photo Agency

236. Cabinet Ministers
1. Kenneth Baker (Baron Baker of Dorking) – David Calvert
2. Justine Greening – Twocoms
3. Danny Alexander – Twocoms
4. William Waldegrave (Baron Waldegrave of North Hill) – David Fowler
5. Virginia Bottomley – David Fowler
6. Peter Lilley – David Fowler
7. David Gauke – Bart Lenoir
8. Esther McVey – Twocoms
9. Chris Patten (Baron Patten of Barnes) – David Fowler

264. Multiple Oscar-winning Actors
1. Denzel Washington – DFree
2. Meryl Streep – JStone
3. Tom Hanks – Featureflash Photo Agency
4. Dame Elizabeth Taylor – Featureflash Photo Agency
5. Mahershala Ali – DFree
6. Sally Field – s_bukley
7. Sean Penn – Andrea Raffin
8. Jodie Foster – DFree
9. Jack Nicholson – 360b

294. Cars
1. Citroën 2CV – Martin Charles Hatch
2. Ford Capri – Martin Charles Hatch
3. De Lorean DMC – amophoto_au
4. VW Beetle – mattxfoto
5. BMW Mini – Manu Padilla
6. Jaguar E-type – Nadezda Murmakova
7. Lotus Elan – Martin Charles Hatch
8. Morris Minor – Kevin Cole 44

312. Chefs and Cooks
1. John Torode – Featureflash Photo Agency
2. Nigella Lawson – Landmarkmedia
3. Gordon Ramsay – DFree
4. Lorraine Pascale – Featureflash Photo Agency
5. Prue Leith – Featureflash Photo Agency
6. Mary Berry – Featureflash Photo Agency
7. Jamie Oliver – Featureflash Photo Agency
8. Nadiya Hussain – Twocoms
9. Dave Myers – Featureflash Photo Agency

400. TV Presenters
1. Fiona Bruce – Featureflash Photo Agency
2. Naga Munchetty – Twocoms
3. Adrian Chiles – Featureflash Photo Agency
4. Richard Hammond – Ink Drop
5. Steve Backshall – John Gomez
6. Gabby Logan – Featureflash Photo Agency
7. Matt Baker – Featureflash Photo Agency
8. Liz Bonnin – Featureflash Photo Agency
9. Ore Oduba – Featureflash Photo Agency

460. Guitarists
1. PJ Harvey – Christian Bertrand
2. Eddie Van Halen – Debby Wong
3. Eric Clapton – JStone
4. Carlos Santana – Anthony Ricci
5. BB King – Randy Miramontez
6. Jimmy Page – robin jason
7. Orianthi – CarlaVanWagoner
8. Joe Perry – JStone
9. KT Tunstall – Clive Watkins

486. New York Landmarks
1. Central Synagogue – DW labs Incorporated
2. Grand Central Terminal – TTstudio
3. Flatiron Building – Quick Shot
4. St Patrick's Cathedral – Karyna Bila
5. The Eldorado (apartments) – Beketoff
6. The Met Life Tower – Andrew F. Kazmierski
7. The Plaza Hotel – MISHELLA
8. The Woolworth Building – Felix Lipov

QUIZ 1 – Pot Luck

ANSWERS ON PAGE 3

1   What type of boat shares its name with a currency unit previously used in the Republic of Ireland?

2   In which month does the full moon known as a "strawberry moon" occur?

3   What gesture is an anagram of "aligns"?

4   A pacemaker regulates which organ of the body?

5   The character of Duchess and her three kittens feature in which 1970 animated film?

6   Which rapper had a 2018 hit with *Yikes*?

7   What nationality was the inventor Thomas Edison?

8   In February 2020, which English player became the most successful wicket-taker in the history of the Women's T20 World Cup?

9   What colour are mistletoe berries?

10 What is the name of Danny Dyer's *EastEnders* character?

11 In which English county is the town of Congleton situated?

12 What word can mean both a protective part of a car and "very large"?

13 A melodica is what type of musical instrument?

14 Who wrote the 2018 memoir *Becoming*?

15 Which is the second-smallest planet in the solar system?

16 What term is given to the rubber or plastic covering on an electric wire that prevents it causing electric shocks?

17 Which type of dog has breeds including Bearded, Rough and Smooth?

18 In the nursery rhyme *Sing a Song of Sixpence*, what is the pocket full of?

19 Which children's author wrote *The Tale of Ginger and Pickles*?

20 What shape of gemstone shares its name with a bakery product?

Answers to QUIZ 249 – Pot Luck

1	José	11	Tilda Swinton
2	Idaho	12	2008
3	Lichfield	13	Giancarlo Baghetti
4	David Hume	14	One thousand million
5	The Aegean Sea	15	Ola Rapace
6	*Tennō*	16	Ganymede
7	They are self-taught	17	Cusco
8	Culture Beat	18	Shiva
9	Venezuela	19	May
10	*Thank You for the Music* (ABBA)	20	1880s (1884)

1

Easy

1. The Lyell Centre features in which crime drama series?

2. By what name is the BFI Southbank also known?

3. The Taj Mahal is clad in what type of stone?

4. In what type of building was the 2020 *Back in Time...* series set?

5. Miami Beach in Florida is particularly noted for an area of buildings in which architectural style?

6. Thomas Bruce, 7th Earl of Elgin, famously removed a frieze from which ancient Athenian building?

7. Which device originated in mills, allowing bags of grain to pass up through floors and not fall back down?

8. In which US city is the concert venue Carnegie Hall?

9. The Temple of Zeus at Olympia was an example of which order of Greek architecture?

10. In what type of building would you find a nave and a transept?

Medium

11. To the nearest hundred, how many steps are there between Whitby Abbey and the town?

12. The Bling Bling building is located in which UK city centre?

13. The National Trust property of Ham House lies on the River Thames just south of which town?

14. In which decade was the Space Needle in Seattle built?

15. Which is the largest inhabited castle in England?

16. The Pompidou Centre lies in which European capital city?

17. How many stainless steel spheres are there on the Atomium in Brussels?

18. What is the name of the London building that houses both the House of Commons and the House of Lords?

19. A proscenium is found in what type of building?

20. The 2020 TV series *Secrets of the Museum* featured which London institution?

Hard

Answers to QUIZ 250 – Geography

1	Syracuse	11	Mongolia
2	Pico de Orizaba, also called Citlaltépetl	12	Argentina
3	Ticino	13	St Kilda
4	New Zealand	14	The Ohio River
5	4,655 miles	15	Georgia
6	The Greater Sunda Islands	16	Colombia
7	Russia	17	Barra
8	Denmark	18	Lake Yamanaka
9	Himachal Pradesh	19	Tuvalu
10	Baku (Azerbaijan)	20	New Hampshire

1 What is the English term for the work of art the French call *La Joconde*?

2 Which sign of the Zodiac has the shortest name?

3 To the nearest ten miles, how long is the Channel Tunnel?

4 Which group had a 1979 hit with *He's the Greatest Dancer*?

5 Which Spanish-named storm followed Storm Dennis in February 2020?

6 Who hosted the 2020 Radio 4 series *Nature Table*?

7 In which country is the province of British Columbia?

8 Which weather occurrence might be described as "forked"?

9 Which two words that sound the same but are spelt differently mean "labyrinth" and "corn"?

10 What is the fourth colour of the rainbow?

11 By what name is the character of T'Challa known in the title of a 2018 film?

12 What was the name of the video cassette format developed by Sony in the 1970s, that lost out to VHS?

13 Which member of the spurge family of plants, known for its red or pink bracts, is particularly popular at Christmas?

14 In which country is the ancient site of Karnak?

15 The Red Ensign is the flag of which organisation?

16 In which month does the Edinburgh Festival Fringe take place?

17 What title was shared by a 2019 comedy series by Aisling Bea and a 1989-90 sketch show by Brian Conley?

18 Which event of 1969 was described as "three days of peace and music"?

19 Actor Michael Sheen was born in which country of the UK?

20 In the story of the Three Little Pigs, from what did the second pig build his house?

Easy

Medium

Hard

Answers to QUIZ 1 – Pot Luck

1	Punt	11	Cheshire
2	June	12	Bumper
3	Signal	13	A wind instrument
4	The heart	14	Michelle Obama
5	*The Aristocats*	15	Mars
6	Kanye West	16	Insulation
7	American	17	Collie
8	Anya Shrubsole	18	Rye
9	White	19	Beatrix Potter
10	Mick Carter	20	Baguette

Easy

1. The internet subscription service Spotify offers which product?
2. Is nickel magnetic?
3. Which electronics company produces the Xperia line of smartphones and tablets?
4. What does an antiemetic drug prevent?
5. The SE, X and 11 are models of which electronic gadget?
6. In the human heart what name is given to either of the top two chambers?
7. How many adenoids are there in the human body?
8. What is the name of Apple's tablet computer?
9. The Large Hadron Collider lies under the border of which two European countries?
10. The surname of which electrical engineer (d.2013) is synonymous with the noise-reduction systems he pioneered?

Medium

11. Galileo first observed the rings of which planet in 1610?
12. What is the name of the chief muscle used in breathing?
13. Which letter on a computer keyboard is used for the paste command?
14. Photovoltaics is concerned with which form of energy?
15. What is the name of Google's cloud-based file service?
16. What name is shared by a highly ionised gas and a constituent of blood?
17. In which part of the human body does most digestion of food take place?
18. As of 2020, how many planets are there in the solar system?
19. Which creature features in the logo of Twitter™?
20. What name is given to the equivalent of an earthquake on the Earth's natural satellite?

Hard

Answers to QUIZ 2 – Buildings

1	Silent Witness	11	200 (199)
2	National Film Theatre	12	Liverpool
3	Marble	13	Richmond
4	A corner shop	14	1960s (1962)
5	Art Deco	15	Windsor Castle
6	The Parthenon	16	Paris
7	Trapdoor	17	Nine
8	New York	18	The Palace of Westminster
9	Doric	19	A theatre
10	A church	20	The V&A Museum

1   What are the two main colours seen on a UK fire engine?

2   Johnny Sexton re-signed for which rugby union team in 2015, having previously played there from 2006 to 2013?

3   The letter Q is in which position in the alphabet?

4   The octane rating system is used for which everyday product?

5   What is the first name of Helen George's character in *Call the Midwife*?

6   The Carpathian mountain range lies on which continent?

7   In terms of population, what is the largest city in Scotland?

8   With which band did Gwen Stefani sing?

9   What nationality is comedian Desiree Burch?

10   Keble College is part of which university?

11   The word "tantalising" is derived from a figure in which branch of mythology?

12   Which music genre of the 1970s was associated with safety pins?

13   Did Neil Armstrong first step on the moon with his left foot or his right foot?

14   Who provided the voice of Queen Lillian in the Shrek films?

15   Which three colours mark the numbers on a traditional roulette wheel?

16   How many wings do bees have?

17   Pugilism is another name for which sport?

18   Who co-starred with Cary Grant in the 1955 film *To Catch a Thief*?

19   What type of metal is used to make most drinks cans?

20   How many masts are there on a brigantine?

Easy

Medium

Hard

Answers to QUIZ 3 – Pot Luck

1	The *Mona Lisa*	11	*Black Panther*
2	Leo	12	Betamax
3	30 miles (31.35)	13	Poinsettia
4	Sister Sledge	14	Egypt
5	Storm Jorge	15	British Merchant Navy
6	Sue Perkins	16	August
7	Canada	17	*This Way Up*
8	Lightning	18	Woodstock
9	Maze and maize	19	Wales
10	Green	20	Sticks

1   Neapolitan food originates from which Italian city?

2   The name of which drink is an anagram of "nastier"?

3   Which type of canapes take their name from the Italian for "little crusts"?

4   The Spanish town of Buñol is famed for an annual festival in which participants throw which food item?

5   The tangerine takes its name from which African city?

6   Serrano ham is produced in which country?

7   Which fish is traditionally used in kedgeree?

8   In bread-making, what is the term given to the period where the dough is left to rise before baking?

9   What type of vegetable can be cooked in a manner known as "duchesse"?

10   Which food is nicknamed "Welsh caviar"?

11   What type of drink may be ruby or tawny?

12   What food group does fish belong to?

13   On which continent did the pineapple originate?

14   What colour is the flesh of a butternut squash?

15   According to the proverb, eating what a day keeps the doctor away?

16   *Cerveza* is the Spanish name for which drink?

17   How is food cooked if it is served as tempura?

18   The name "roulade" is taken from "to roll" in which language?

19   *Daucus carota* is the Latin name for what vegetable?

20   Purple sprouting is a variety of which vegetable?

Answers to QUIZ 4 – Science and Technology

1	Music	11	Saturn
2	Yes	12	The diaphragm
3	Sony	13	V
4	Nausea and vomiting	14	Solar energy
5	iPhone	15	Google Drive
6	Atrium	16	Plasma
7	Two	17	The small intestine
8	iPad	18	Eight
9	France and Switzerland	19	A bird
10	(Ray) Dolby	20	Moonquake

QUIZ 7 – Pot Luck

ANSWERS ON PAGE 9

1   What type of vehicle is Mater in the Cars animated series of films?

2   Which singer joined *The Voice UK* as a coach for the 2020 series?

3   If you ordered a *bistecca* in an Italian restaurant, what would you eat?

4   Which word meaning "something that is not true" becomes a discord with the addition of one letter?

5   Which mineral is the proverbial opposite of cheese?

6   How many deliveries does each side bowl in a 20/20 cricket match?

7   What are Helvetica, Lucida and Times?

8   Which liquid measure is synonymous with cowboy hats?

9   How is the International Criminal Police Organization more commonly known?

10 Which word can mean both a woman's close-fitting bodice and describe a region of Spain?

11 Lance Armstrong was stripped of how many Tour de France titles?

12 Silken and firm are types of which food?

13 In which 2002 film did Keira Knightley play a footballer?

14 In Hindu society, which animal is honoured as a symbol of unselfish giving?

15 Which clergyman coined the phrase "The Rainbow Nation" about South Africa?

16 What two colours are on the top of a fly agaric mushroom?

17 Which is the only continent with no cities?

18 The symbol for infinity looks like which numeral on its side?

19 Who played Eva Perón in the original stage production of *Evita*?

20 What name links a cartoon lasagne-loving cat and a US president?

Answers to QUIZ 5 – Pot Luck

1	Red and yellow	11	Greek (Tantalus)
2	Leinster	12	Punk
3	17th	13	His left foot
4	Petrol	14	Dame Julie Andrews
5	Trixie	15	Red, black and green
6	Europe	16	Four
7	Glasgow	17	Boxing
8	No Doubt	18	Grace Kelly
9	American	19	Aluminum
10	Oxford	20	Two

1 In which country of the UK was the miniseries *Deadwater Fell* set?

2 What is the name of Ralf Little's detective inspector in *Death in Paradise*?

3 Who was the original presenter of *The Generation Game*?

4 Jasmine Harman is best known for co-presenting which Channel 4 property programme?

5 Who was the main presenter of *Antiques Roadshow* in the 1990s?

6 Waleed Zuaiter starred as a former police inspector in which 2020 series shown on Channel 4?

7 The TV series *My Family and the Galapagos* features which marine biologist?

8 Which actor co-starred with Nick Mohammed in the 2020 TV comedy series *Intelligence*?

9 The TV series *Holby City* was first aired in which decade?

10 Jimmy Corkhill was a character in which long-running series?

11 What is the first name of Sir Derek Jacobi's character in *Last Tango in Halifax*?

12 What type of programmes does Mark Pougatch present?

13 In the TV series *Game of Thrones*, to which house did Bran belong?

14 Which drama series, first broadcast in 2018, features sisters Hannah, Nina and Rose?

15 What is the name of Adam Rickitt's *Hollyoaks* character?

16 What was the subtitle of the 2020 series of *Strike Back*?

17 In which US state did the 2020 series *Win the Wilderness* take place?

18 Which historian presents the *Biggest Fibs* TV series?

19 Which ballet dancer appeared on *The Muppet Show* in 1978?

20 Who presented the 2020 series *Rough Guide to the Future*?

Answers to QUIZ 6 – Food and Drink

1	Naples	11	Port
2	Retsina	12	Proteins
3	Crostini	13	South America
4	Tomatoes	14	Yellowish-orange
5	Tangier	15	An apple
6	Spain	16	Beer
7	Smoked haddock	17	Coated in batter and deep-fried
8	Proving	18	French
9	Potato	19	Carrot
10	Laverbread	20	Broccoli

1 Which marsupial lends its name to a trick of feigning death?

2 What colour is tartrazine, also known as E102?

3 Which 1950s radio comedy show featured the characters Moriarty, Neddie Seagoon and Major Bloodnok?

4 In which UK city were the Commonwealth Games held in 1986?

5 Which is the correct spelling of the skin complaint: exsema, eczema or excema?

6 Which company created the first waterproof wristwatch, the Oyster, in 1926?

7 The father of which TV cook was Chancellor of the Exchequer as part of Baroness Margaret Thatcher's cabinet?

8 Who played bass on most songs by The Beatles?

9 If a boat is sailing "with the Sun", is it travelling from left to right or from right to left?

10 On which part of your body might you be said to have a chip if you are holding a grudge?

11 Which historical figure has been played on screen by Heath Ledger and Sir Mick Jagger?

12 The Aztecs were located in which Latin American nation?

13 *Good Girl Gone Bad* was a 2007 album released by which singer?

14 The Huguenots were Protestants from which country?

15 The Slow Food movement began in which country in 1986?

16 Which soft drink is used as the mixer in a Moscow Mule cocktail?

17 How many Shakespeare plays have the name Henry in the title?

18 On the pH scale, pure water is neutral. What is its pH number?

19 What type of cross features on the St John Ambulance's logo?

20 How many players in a netball team are allowed to shoot?

Easy

Medium

Hard

Answers to QUIZ 7 – Pot Luck

1	A breakdown truck	11	Seven
2	Meghan Trainor	12	Tofu
3	Steak	13	*Bend it Like Beckham*
4	Fiction (Friction)	14	Cow
5	Chalk	15	Archbishop Desmond Tutu
6	120	16	Red and white
7	Typefaces	17	Antarctica
8	Gallon	18	8
9	Interpol	19	Elaine Page
10	Basque	20	Garfield (Andrew Garfield)

Easy

1 Which is the only country in the world that has a name beginning with "Q"?

2 Which is the largest lake in Italy?

3 Miami, Florida and San Juan in Costa Rica make up two of the three points in which "triangle"?

4 The city of Montego Bay lies in which country?

5 Mount Everest lies in which two countries?

6 In which hemisphere is Australia located?

7 Which country is the biggest by area: Australia, Brazil or Chile?

8 How many of the world's largest 20 deserts lie in Europe?

9 In the 2011 census, which was the largest city in India, by population?

10 The Summer Palace is a UNESCO World Heritage site in which Asian city?

Medium

11 Which city has been called Constantinople and Byzantium?

12 The Golden Gate strait is in which US state?

13 Which two cities united in 1872 to become what is now the capital of Hungary?

14 Which two celestial symbols are on the Turkish flag?

15 Niagara Falls is in the Canadian province of Ontario and which US state?

16 Which two European countries have borders on both the Mediterranean and the Atlantic?

17 In which sea does the Isle of Man lie?

18 Jakarta is the capital of which country?

19 The African state of Tanganyika is now part of which modern republic?

20 In which city are the Bellagio Fountains?

Hard

1   Which singer published the autobiographies *Step Inside* (1985) and *What's It All About* (2003)?

2   Which vegetables complete the saying "Fine words butter no ___" ?

3   The name of which bone originates from the Greek for "chest"?

4   Which former footballer has a fragrance range that includes *Instinct* and *Intimately*?

5   What is the surname of the title character in the TV series *Vera*?

6   Cider, rice and sherry are forms of which common foodstuff?

7   What is the name of the evil doll in the Child's Play series of films?

8   Which ailment is sometimes called "the kissing disease"?

9   What type of facial feature is a goatee?

10   What type of creature is a meadow pipit?

11   In which year did Barack Obama become US president?

12   Which of Shakespeare's plays is set in Rome and Egypt?

13   *Get on Up* is a biopic about which famous musician?

14   Eric Bana and Edward Norton have both played which superhero?

15   Who plays Julia Harris in the Horrible Bosses films?

16   The Japanese Shimano company makes parts for which form of transport?

17   Which is the biggest: a sheet of A4, A3 or A2 paper?

18   In the Bible, what are chapters divided into?

19   Which UK travel company went into liquidation in September 2019?

20   Which is the only US state with a one-syllable name?

Easy

Medium

Hard

Answers to QUIZ 9 – Pot Luck

1	Possum (playing possum)	11	Ned Kelly
2	Yellow	12	Mexico
3	*The Goon Show*	13	Rihanna
4	Edinburgh	14	France
5	Eczema	15	Italy
6	Rolex	16	Ginger beer
7	Nigella Lawson	17	Seven
8	Sir Paul McCartney	18	pH 7
9	From left to right	19	Maltese Cross
10	Your shoulder	20	Two

Easy

1   What colour is the lid on a jar of Marmite®?

2   In which year did Thomson Airways announce that the company was to rebrand as TUI Airways?

3   Swarovski has its headquarters in which European country?

4   Which animal is depicted on a tin of Colman's Mustard?

5   In which decade did Heinz introduce the octagonal ketchup bottle?

6   Which creature appears on the label of a bottle of Bacardi®?

7   Which US company bought the UK supermarket chain ASDA in 1999?

8   The retailer Dunelm sells what type of product?

9   Which brand of drinks was advertised with the slogan "It's frothy, man!"?

10 Which famous toy brand featured in the title of a 2013 Ed Sheeran hit?

11 The TAG Heuer company produces which items?

12 Which mountain features on the packaging of Toblerone™ chocolate?

13 What type of nuts are used to make the brand of chocolate spread Nutella?

14 The Laughing Cow is a brand of which snack food?

Medium

15 Which iconic Kodak camera was first introduced in 1900?

16 What is the most common colour of Lambrusco wine?

17 The Ferrari logo features three coloured stripes: red, white, and which other colour?

18 Which company produces the Flake chocolate bar?

19 Steinway & Sons is famous for the production of which musical instrument?

20 In which decade was the Spirograph® toy originally produced?

Hard

Answers to QUIZ 10 – Geography

1	Qatar	11	Istanbul
2	Lake Garda	12	California
3	The Bermuda Triangle	13	Buda and Pest
4	Jamaica	14	Moon and star
5	Nepal and China	15	New York
6	Southern hemisphere	16	France and Spain
7	Brazil	17	The Irish Sea
8	None	18	Indonesia
9	Mumbai (12.4 million)	19	Tanzania
10	Beijing	20	Las Vegas

1   Which medieval sporting contest was played between two people on horseback, both carrying lances?

2   Which Italian city's airport has VRN as its code?

3   In which sitcom, first shown in 2018, does Nicola Coughlan play a character called Clare?

4   What type of animals would originally have been housed in a mews?

5   Who directed the 2019 film *The Irishman*?

6   When using a keyboard, on which keys should your index fingers initially be positioned in order to touch type?

7   What is a shoe mould called?

8   Father Time is usually depicted carrying which two items?

9   According to superstition, how many years of bad luck result from breaking a mirror?

10   Which Latin term, meaning "fostering mother", is used to describe a person's former school or university?

11   What colour is the gemstone peridot?

12   London's Drury Lane is associated with which field of the arts?

13   What sport is played by the New Zealand team the Black Caps?

14   What is the name of the handle fitted to a rudder?

15   A cochlear implant helps people with what type of impairment?

16   What animal appears on the badge of Leicester City FC?

17   Which is the longest word in the radio phonetic alphabet?

18   King George V opened which royal garden in 1932 as part of Scotland's National Garden Scheme?

19   What is calculated by dividing a person's weight by their height squared?

20   What type of equipment is manufactured by Massey Ferguson?

Easy

Medium

Hard

Answers to QUIZ 11 – Pot Luck

1	Cilla Black	11	2009
2	Parsnips	12	*Antony and Cleopatra*
3	The sternum	13	James Brown
4	David Beckham	14	Hulk
5	Stanhope	15	Jennifer Aniston
6	Vinegar	16	Bicycles
7	Chucky	17	A2
8	Glandular fever	18	Verses
9	A beard	19	Thomas Cook
10	A bird	20	Maine

What are the names of these birds?

Easy

1

2

3

Medium

4

5

6

7

8

9

Hard

Answers to QUIZ 12 – Brands

1	Yellow	11	Watches
2	2015	12	Matterhorn
3	Austria	13	Hazelnuts
4	A bull	14	(Spreadable) cheese
5	1890s (1889)	15	Brownie
6	A bat	16	(Italian) red wine
7	Walmart	17	Green
8	Home furnishings	18	Cadbury
9	Cresta	19	Pianos
10	Lego®	20	1960s (1965)

1   Which gland is affected by goitre?

2   Good King Wenceslas and his page brave the cold weather on the feast day of which saint?

3   A joiner works with what substance?

4   In Roman numerals, which symbol has the highest value?

5   What type of creature is a common whitethroat?

6   In which 2014 film does Ben Affleck play the husband of a missing woman?

7   As at the end of 2019, which was the only element in the periodic table with a name beginning with "U"?

8   What is the name of Fred Thursday's wife in the TV series *Endeavour*?

9   Flat-leaf, or Italian, are types of which herb?

10 What type of structure is the Washington Monument?

11 How many prime ministers did Australia have in 2013?

12 What ailment is caused by the rhinovirus?

13 Which is the older horse race, the Victoria Derby or Melbourne Cup?

14 What does "kara" mean in the words karaoke and karate?

15 Li Na (b.1982) is a former champion in which sport?

16 In the Bible, who was the first baby to be born?

17 The J-type approach is a method used in which athletic event?

18 *Two Ton Tessie from Tennessee* was the signature song of which entertainer?

19 Which fruit links stories about Sir Isaac Newton and William Tell?

20 Which popular pink confection was invented in 1928 by accountant Walter Diemer?

Answers to QUIZ 13 – Pot Luck

1	Jousting	11	Green
2	Verona	12	Theatre
3	*Derry Girls*	13	Cricket
4	Horses (stables)	14	Tiller
5	Martin Scorsese	15	Hearing impairment
6	F and J	16	A fox
7	A last	17	November
8	An hourglass and scythe	18	Balmoral
9	Seven	19	BMI (Body Mass Index)
10	*Alma mater*	20	Agricultural equipment

Easy

Medium

Hard

Easy

1 Who won the Male Solo Artist Brit award in 2020?

2 Which Beatles album was the top-selling UK album of the 1960s?

3 The Village People single *Go West* was covered by which duo in 1993?

4 Which duo released the 1970 song *Cecilia*?

5 What was the title of Phil Collins' first UK no.1 hit, originally recorded by The Supremes in 1966?

6 Which singer-songwriter topped the charts in 2020 with *Blinding Lights*?

7 "There lived a certain man in Russia long ago" is a lyric from which hit song?

8 Céline Dion was born in which country?

9 Which classic Queen song famously featured in the film *Wayne's World*?

10 How many brothers were in the original line-up of the Beach Boys?

Medium

11 By which first name is the singer with the other given names Laurie Blue Adkins better known?

12 In 1978, Sir Rod Stewart released a double A-side single of *I Was Only Joking* and which other song?

13 The singer Rihanna was born on which island?

14 What colour eyes provided Sir Elton John with a UK top ten hit in 1982?

15 *Hard Habit to Break* and *Hard to Say I'm Sorry* were 1980s singles by which US rock band?

16 In which decade did All Saints have their first UK no.1?

17 What was the title of George Michael's first UK top ten hit of the 1990s?

18 Jim Lea (b.1949) was a member of which glam rock band?

19 *Doo-Wops and Hooligans* was a 2010 album by which singer?

20 Who topped the UK singles charts with the 2014 song *All About That Bass*?

Hard

Answers to QUIZ 14 – Birds

1 Puffin

2 Avocet

3 Ostrich

4 Wren

5 Magpie

6 Peacock

7 Toucan

8 Pheasant

9 Pelican

1. What word has meanings including a cul-de-sac, a narrow passageway and the grounds around a cathedral?

2. What nickname is given to a police picture of a villain's face?

3. Which saint and apostle is also known as Saul of Tarsus?

4. "I didn't know what day it was when you walked into the room" are the opening lyrics to which song?

5. Egypt lies on which continent?

6. *Das Lied der Deutschen* is the national anthem of which country?

7. What form of vehicle is the Boeing Apache?

8. Which term for a celebrity photographer comes from the name of a character in the Federico Fellini film *La Dolce Vita*?

9. Which letter is on the bottom left of the three rows of alphabetical buttons on a keyboard?

10. What is the main vegetable used layered in a traditional moussaka?

11. The National Academy of Recording Arts and Sciences of the United States presents which prestigious awards?

12. Which animal shares its six-letter name with a verb meaning "to search for something"?

13. Austral refers to which point of the compass?

14. Which duo hosted the 2020 revival of *Crackerjack*?

15. Which sport originally used peach baskets nailed to walls as goals?

16. What colour ball is used in Test cricket?

17. In which decade was Kim Kardashian born?

18. Which meteorological term is used to describe the provision of computer applications over the internet?

19. What was the first name of the presenter of *Whicker's World*?

20. The firmness of which item is measured on a scale from 9B to 9H?

Answers to QUIZ 15 – Pot Luck

1	The thyroid gland	11	Three (Gillard, Rudd, Abbott)
2	St Stephen	12	The common cold
3	Wood	13	Victoria Derby (1855) (Melbourne Cup (1861))
4	M (1000)	14	Empty
5	A bird	15	Tennis
6	*Gone Girl*	16	Cain
7	Uranium	17	The high jump
8	Win	18	Tessie O'Shea
9	Parsley	19	An apple
10	An obelisk	20	Bubble gum

Easy

1   In 1992, in which winter sport did mogul become an official Olympic medal category?

2   Until 1987 the British Formula 1 Grand Prix alternated between Silverstone and which other racetrack?

3   Who won the men's singles title at the 2020 Australian Open tennis championships?

4   Which football club is nicknamed "Pompey"?

5   At which venue did the 2020 Masters Snooker Championship take place?

6   What is the main material used inside a cricket ball?

7   Ruud Gullit managed which Premier League team from 1998 to 1999?

8   In karate, which of these belts is the highest: blue, green or white?

9   Donald Budge was the first player to win all the Grand Slams in a single year (1938) in which sport?

10 In which sport might an armstand back double somersault tuck be performed?

11 As at 2020, which are the only two Australian cities in which the summer Olympic Games have been held?

12 Which boxer did Tyson Fury beat to win the WBC World Heavyweight title in February 2020?

Medium

13 Short dances and free dances are part of which Winter Olympics sport?

14 What is the nickname of the Great Britain national rugby league team?

15 Which major golfing championship took place at Royal Portrush in 2019?

16 In which country of the UK is Kelso Racecourse?

17 Sculling is a form of which sport?

18 Wayne Gretzky is a former professional in which winter sport?

19 Which South African former rugby player became the interim head of Italy's national rugby team in November 2019?

20 What word can mean a continuous series of shots in badminton and a car race?

Hard

Answers to QUIZ 16 – Pop Music

1	Stormzy	11	Adele
2	*Sgt. Pepper's Lonely Hearts Club Band*	12	*Hot Legs*
3	The Pet Shop Boys	13	Barbados
4	Simon and Garfunkel	14	*Blue Eyes*
5	*You Can't Hurry Love*	15	Chicago
6	The Weeknd	16	1990s (*Never Ever*, 1997)
7	*Rasputin* (Boney M)	17	*Praying for Time*
8	Canada	18	Slade
9	*Bohemian Rhapsody*	19	Bruno Mars
10	Three (Brian, Dennis, and Carl Wilson)	20	Meghan Trainor

1. In the song *The Twelve Days of Christmas*, how many lords were a-leaping?
2. Which board game derived from The Landlord's Game, patented in 1904?
3. What type of transport is a Tiger Moth?
4. Utrecht is the fourth-largest city in which country?
5. Who had a hit with *Just the Way You Are* in 1977?
6. Neville Longbottom belonged to which Hogwarts house?
7. The 2020 series of *Race Across the World* took place on which continent?
8. Which chemical element has the symbol Pu?
9. How are father and son Demetrios and Lagi Andreas better known?
10. Which Native American princess became a celebrity after travelling to England in the early 17th century?
11. What is the main colour of the cars in the Ferrari Formula 1 team?
12. What does a person with coeliac disease need to avoid in their diet?
13. In *Breaking Bad*, what subject did Walter White teach before turning to crime?
14. Which iconic car is associated with the character of Mr Bean?
15. Which European capital is described as a "Fair City" in a popular song?
16. Tarzan actor Johnny Weissmuller won Olympic golds in which sport?
17. What type of product might be labelled cuvée?
18. What name is given to the western part of the Serpentine lake?
19. Dawson City, a town in the Canadian territory of Yukon, was the centre of what activity in the late 19th century?
20. What was an arquebus?

Answers to QUIZ 17 – Pot Luck

1	Close	11	Grammys
2	Mugshot	12	Ferret
3	St Paul	13	South
4	*You're in My Heart* (Sir Rod Stewart)	14	Sam (Nixon) and Mark (Rhodes)
5	Africa	15	Basketball
6	Germany	16	Red
7	Helicopter	17	1980s (1980)
8	Paparazzo	18	Cloud
9	Z	19	Alan
10	Aubergine	20	Pencil leads

ANSWERS ON PAGE 22

Easy

1. Who won Best Director at the 2020 BAFTA Film awards?
2. The 1985 film *A Room with a View* was set in England and which other country?
3. What supernatural creature completes the title of the 1994 film starring Brad Pitt and Tom Cruise, *Interview with the ___*?
4. What was the subtitle of the 2016 film based on the *Warcraft* video game series?
5. In the 2015 film *The Martian*, what vegetable does Matt Damon's character begin growing?
6. Who won the Best Actress Oscar at the 2020 award ceremony for her role in the film *Judy*?
7. In the Maleficent films, who plays Aurora?
8. Which series of animated films featured the kingdom of Far Far Away?
9. Which actress co-starred with Robert Redford in the 1967 film *Barefoot in the Park*?
10. Anne Hathaway and Robert De Niro co-starred in which work-based 2015 comedy film?

Medium

11. Young actor Harvey Spencer Stephens played Damien Thorn in which classic 1976 horror film?
12. Which actor said "Call off Christmas" in the 1991 film *Robin Hood: Prince of Thieves*?
13. Which James Bond villain has been played by Max von Sydow and Telly Savalas, amongst others?
14. According to a song from *Bedknobs and Broomsticks*, which street is "where the riches of ages are stowed"?
15. Which leading actor appeared in *American Hustle*, *Silver Linings Playbook*, and *The Hangover* films?
16. Who won three Best Director Oscars for *It Happened One Night* (1934), *Mr Deeds Goes to Town* (1936) and *You Can't Take it With You* (1938)?
17. How many of the dwarfs in *Snow White and the Seven Dwarfs* have a name that begins with the letter D?
18. Which film won two Oscars in 2014, for the best animated film and the best original song?
19. What was the title of the 1978 sequel to the film *The Guns of Navarone*?
20. What is the hair colour of the *Who Framed Roger Rabbit?* character Jessica Rabbit?

Hard

Answers to QUIZ 18 – Sport

1	Skiing	11	Melbourne and Sydney
2	Brands Hatch	12	Deontay Wilder
3	Novak Djokovic	13	Figure skating
4	Portsmouth FC	14	The Lions
5	Alexandra Palace	15	The Open
6	Cork	16	Scotland
7	Newcastle United	17	Rowing
8	Blue	18	Ice hockey
9	Tennis	19	Franco Smith
10	Diving	20	Rally

1 Which real-life couple starred in the 1967 film adaptation of *The Taming of the Shrew*?

2 Who wrote the 2018 horror novel *The Outsider*?

3 In which country is the TV series *The Good Karma Hospital* set?

4 The preparation method of cutting a prawn in half lengthways and flattening it out is named after which insect?

5 What word can mean both a group of eggs and to hold tightly?

6 Petroc Trelawny joined which radio station in 1998?

7 Is blood pressure lower in the arteries or in the veins?

8 Who was the male top ranking tennis player from 1993 to 1998?

9 First made in 1946, what was a Silver Wraith?

10 Which lizard's name is derived from the Greek for "lion on the ground"?

11 The initials BSc after someone's name signify what type of qualification?

12 Ha is the abbreviation for which unit of measurement?

13 As at the end of 2019, who was the youngest person to have been elected as US president?

14 Which pop star recorded at his own Paisley Park Studios?

15 The area known as the Painted Desert lies in which US state?

16 What are the three fire signs of the zodiac?

17 Which Olympic sport uses the lightest ball?

18 How many grooves are there on one side of a vinyl record?

19 By what name was the Chinese leader Mao Zedong better known?

20 What can somebody suffering narcolepsy do at any time without warning?

Answers to QUIZ 19 – Pot Luck

1	Ten	11	Red
2	Monopoly™	12	Gluten
3	Aeroplane (biplane)	13	Chemistry
4	The Netherlands	14	The Mini
5	Billy Joel	15	Dublin (*Molly Malone*)
6	Gryffindor	16	Swimming
7	South America	17	Wine
8	Plutonium	18	The Long Water
9	Stavros Flatley	19	Gold prospecting
10	Pocahontas	20	A gun

ANSWERS ON PAGE 24

Easy

1   In cricket, for what do the letters NB stand?

2   The letter V is in which position in the alphabet?

3   Which London-based musical company is usually known by its initials ENO?

4   In terms of the medical treatment what do the letters HRT stand for?

5   Which letter on a computer keyboard is used for the cut command?

6   For what do the initials CAD stand in relation to technology?

7   Which two colours are used for the "o"s in the Google logo?

8   A stylised winged M is the logo of which car company?

9   What do the initials PTSD stand for?

10   In musical notation which letter is used to denote the need to play loudly?

11   For what do the letters ADHD stand?

Medium

12   Of the three rows of letter keys on a standard keyboard, which has no vowels?

13   In the name of the TV station, for what does CNN stand?

14   For what do the initials OCD stand?

15   In terms of a job, for what do the letters PA stand?

16   HTML is used to create which everyday media?

17   In the phonetic alphabet, the word for which vowel is the name of a Greek nymph?

18   How many points is the letter C worth in a game of Scrabble®?

19   In relation to technology, what is MS-DOS?

20   In terms of economics, for what do the letters GDP stand?

Hard

Answers to QUIZ 20 – Film

1	Sir Sam Mendes	11	*The Omen*
2	Italy	12	Alan Rickman
3	Vampire	13	(Ernst) Blofeld
4	*The Beginning*	14	*Portobello Road*
5	Potatoes	15	Bradley Cooper
6	Renée Zellweger	16	Frank Capra
7	Elle Fanning	17	Two (Doc and Dopey)
8	Shrek	18	*Frozen*
9	Jane Fonda	19	*Force 10 from Navarone*
10	*The Intern*	20	Red

1 How long are the tracks in Olympic velodromes?

2 Mr Slate is the boss of which cartoon character?

3 Which 1980s supermodel was once engaged to magician David Copperfield?

4 How many men were on Noah's Ark?

5 What colour is the Italian liqueur Limoncello?

6 Which dish takes its name from the Hungarian for "herdsman" or "cowboy"?

7 Joséphine de Beauharnais was the wife of which historical European figure?

8 Which film giant launched a subscription service in the UK in March 2020?

9 Which London hotel opened its American Bar in the late 19th century?

10 A Lutheran belongs to which branch of the Christian church?

11 Which group had a hit in 1960 with *Save the Last Dance for Me*?

12 Which TV drama series, first aired in 1997, featured the characters of district nurses and sisters Peggy Snow and Ruth Goddard?

13 From 1977 to 1978, which British boxer held the WBC light heavyweight title?

14 Which ship, now a floating hotel, launched from Clydebank in 1967?

15 Of the seven Oscars that Richard Burton was nominated for, how many did he win?

16 What form of fishing involves using a silk or nylon replica of an insect as bait?

17 What is the Speedo® logo?

18 Which control on movement after nightfall has a name from the old French for "cover-fire"?

19 In the New Testament, which of the apostles was alphabetically first?

20 Which form of entertainment takes its name from the Latin for "ring" or "circle"?

Answers to QUIZ 21 – Pot Luck

1	Richard Burton and Dame Elizabeth Taylor	11	Bachelor of Science
2	Stephen King	12	Hectare
3	India	13	John F Kennedy
4	Butterfly(ing)	14	Prince
5	Clutch	15	Arizona
6	Radio 3	16	Aries, Leo and Sagittarius
7	The veins	17	Table tennis
8	Pete Sampras	18	One
9	A Rolls-Royce	19	Chairman Mao
10	Chameleon	20	Fall asleep

Easy

1   What is the subtitle of the second novel in the Harry Potter series?

2   Which child's play structure takes its name from the play *Peter Pan*?

3   What type of food is pottage?

4   Pancetta is what type of meat?

5   What is a potentilla?

6   Which father and son both presented the BBC series *Panorama*?

7   What is the chemical symbol for potassium?

8   The pancreas is part of which system of the body?

9   In which three indoor sports would you pot a ball?

10   Whose daemon is Pantalaimon in the *His Dark Materials* trilogy?

Medium

11   What is meant by the word "potency" in relation to a chemical?

12   What is kept in a pantry?

13   The Potteries is the name of an area in which English county?

14   What is a pantechnicon?

15   Poteen is the name given to an illicit spirit in which country?

16   What type of clothing are pantaloons?

17   What colour is a pot marigold?

18   On what does a panel beater work?

19   Who wrote and starred in the 1970s *Potty Time* children's series?

20   The dessert panna cotta originated in which country?

Hard

Answers to QUIZ 22 – Letters

1	No ball	11	Attention-deficit hyperactivity disorder
2	22nd	12	The bottom row
3	English National Opera	13	Cable News Network
4	Hormone replacement therapy	14	Obsessive-compulsive disorder
5	X	15	Personal assistant
6	Computer-aided design	16	Websites
7	Red and yellow	17	Echo
8	Mazda	18	Three points
9	Post-traumatic stress disorder	19	A (Microsoft®) operating system
10	F	20	Gross Domestic Product

ANSWERS ON PAGE 27

1   Who played the title role in the 2014 film *Jack Ryan: Shadow Recruit*?

2   The Fire TV range was launched by which retailer?

3   Which Beatles song starts with the introduction to *La Marseillaise*?

4   What type of creature is a boomslang?

5   Which member of JLS became a farmer after the group originally split up?

6   The drink Southern Comfort® originated in which US city?

7   What word can mean both large pieces of wood and "to move clumsily"?

8   Which iconic villain did Sacha Dhawan play in the 2020 series of *Doctor Who*?

9   What is a ship's toilet called?

10 Wayne Pivac, who became head coach of the Welsh national rugby team in 2019, was born in which country?

11 The Chrysler Building in New York is an example of what style of design?

12 Which Asian food is made by coagulating soy milk?

13 In which county is the town of Morpeth?

14 Who is Cosette's mother in *Les Misérables*?

15 Which common font has a name that means "Swiss" in Latin?

16 Which liqueur is used to make a Brown Cow cocktail?

17 Who was the first person to hold the title Lord Protector of the Commonwealth?

18 In economics, what pairs with supply to define a market?

19 Was the triceratops dinosaur a carnivore or a herbivore?

20 What is the plural of "crisis"?

Easy

Medium

Hard

Answers to QUIZ 23 – Pot Luck

1	250m	11	The Drifters
2	Fred Flintstone	12	*Where the Heart is*
3	Claudia Schiffer	13	John Conteh
4	Four (Noah and his three sons)	14	QE2
5	Yellow	15	None
6	Goulash	16	Fly fishing
7	Napoleon Bonaparte	17	A red boomerang
8	Disney (Disney⁺)	18	Curfew
9	Savoy Hotel	19	Andrew
10	Protestantism	20	Circus

ANSWERS ON PAGE 28

1   What name is given to zero in a tennis score?

2   What number is reached by adding the digits of the UK emergency telephone number together?

3   If an item is on sale with 20% off and costs £60, what did it originally cost?

4   Which of these numbers is not a prime number: 11, 13 or 15?

5   Which shape has the most sides, a heptagon, hexagon or pentagon?

6   How many centimetres are there in five kilometres?

7   What number does the prefix "tetra" indicate?

8   Which term is given to a whole number as distinguished from a fraction?

9   How many degrees are there in a square?

10 What is the only even prime number?

11 In probability theory, what shape is used to describe a normal distribution?

12 What is the highest number on a roulette wheel?

13 How many years are there in three and a half decades?

14 What is one cubed + two cubed?

15 How many times does the digit 9 appear in the numbers 1 to 100?

16 Which number can also be referred to as heptad?

17 What is the first three-digit prime number?

18 What is the value of Pi to two decimal places?

19 "Grand" is slang for which number?

20 How many hours are there in two days?

Answers to QUIZ 24 – Pots and Pans

1	*The Chamber of Secrets*	11	Its strength
2	Wendy house (Wendy Darling)	12	Food
3	A (thick) soup	13	Staffordshire
4	Pork (belly)	14	A large (usually furniture) van
5	A shrub	15	Ireland
6	Richard and David Dimbleby	16	Trousers
7	K	17	Orange-yellow
8	The digestive system	18	A vehicle (bodywork)
9	Billiards, pool and snooker	19	Michael Bentine
10	Lyra (Belacqua)	20	Italy

1   Who hosted the 2020 game show *First and Last*?

2   Who joined the judging panel of *Strictly Come Dancing* in 2019?

3   What is Natasha Romanoff's superhero name in the Marvel films?

4   The district and city of Bodrum lies in which country?

5   Which came first, the Iron Age or the Bronze Age?

6   What shape is a yurt?

7   Which enduring toy features a drawing screen coated with aluminum powder?

8   What alternative therapy is concerned with massaging the soles of the feet?

9   Jesuits belong to a branch of which religion?

10 The Bundestag is part of the parliament of which country?

11 Which two words that sound the same but are spelt differently mean a type of singer and a cover?

12 Which is the highest order of mammals?

13 What word can mean both a brass instrument and an elephant's call?

14 Jimmy Somerville and Richard Coles formed which 1980s pop duo?

15 Which order of monks is famed for its beer?

16 *Combine Harvester* was a 1976 novelty hit for which group?

17 In which sport are a highboard and springboard used?

18 What is the general term given to an event where one astronomical body passes in front of another?

19 How many goals did Gary Lineker score in the 1986 FIFA World Cup?

20 Which of these films featuring Meg Ryan was released first: *Courage Under Fire*, *Top Gun* or *You've Got Mail*?

Easy

Medium

Hard

1   Sefton Park is an area of which English city?

2   The clifftop at Dinas Oleu in Gwynedd was the first land to be donated to which conservation organisation?

3   How many years were there between the bombing of the House of Commons debating chamber in 1941 and its re-opening?

4   The Big Feastival event has been held since 2012 on a farm belonging to which member of Blur?

5   Who was appointed UK Foreign Secretary in July 2019?

6   The Belfast Giants play which sport?

7   In which decade did Crufts move from Earl's Court to the NEC in Birmingham?

8   In which English city does an annual Jane Austen Festival take place?

9   The Wellington Arch lies at the edge of which London park?

10 The A7 connects Edinburgh with which other city?

11 St Johnstone FC is based in which Scottish city?

12 The name of which English town is an anagram of "dominates"?

13 The headland Mumbles lies on which coast of Wales?

14 What is the name of the devolved Parliament of Wales?

15 The Royal Oak in Boscobel in Shropshire got its name after which future king hid in it to escape, following a battle?

16 The Campbell clan is associated with which historical region of Scotland?

17 Alum Bay, noted for its coloured sand, is on which island of the UK?

18 Which two English counties with five-letter names have consecutive initial letters?

19 Does County Fermanagh have a coastline?

20 The Kent town of Rochester lies on which river?

Answers to QUIZ 26 – Numbers

1	Love	11	Bell (bell curve)
2	27	12	36
3	£75	13	35
4	15	14	Nine (one + eight)
5	A heptagon (seven)	15	20
6	500,000 centimetres	16	Seven
7	Four	17	101
8	Integer	18	3.14
9	360	19	1000
10	Two	20	48

1 Who hosted the 2018 game show *Hardball*?

2 Who directed the 1938 film *The Lady Vanishes*?

3 The abbreviation for which army rank is the same as the name for a mountain pass?

4 The majority of Bollywood movies are in which language?

5 Saint Germain is the patron saint of which European capital city?

6 Which snack's name is derived from the words "twin biscuit sticks"?

7 How are the two rectus abdominis muscles referred to colloquially?

8 What was a Hawker Hurricane?

9 What was the first name of the title character of the TV series *Dixon of Dock Green*?

10 Which two words that differ only by their first letter mean "idea" and "liquid balm"?

11 In which decade was the 20th Century Fox film studio formed?

12 What is the official language of Cuba?

13 What would you do with spirulina?

14 Keke Rosberg was the first Formula 1 World Champion from which country?

15 Which term was coined by Oscar Wilde to describe the dance performed by Salome before Herod Antipas?

16 What is a *billet-doux*?

17 XC skiing is another name for which winter sport?

18 Who is the frontman of the group Tenpole Tudor?

19 Apart from bread, what is the main ingredient in French toast?

20 What name is given to a baby pig?

Answers to QUIZ 27 – Pot Luck

1	Jason Manford	11	Rapper and wrapper
2	Motsi Mabuse	12	Primates
3	Black Widow	13	Trumpet
4	Turkey	14	The Communards
5	The Bronze Age	15	Trappists
6	Circular	16	The Wurzels
7	Etch-A-Sketch	17	Diving
8	Reflexology	18	Eclipse
9	Roman Catholicism	19	Six
10	Germany	20	*Top Gun* (1986)

What are the names of these musical instruments?

Easy

1

2

3

Medium

4

5

6

7

8

9

Hard

Answers to QUIZ 28 – The UK

1	Liverpool	11	Perth
2	The National Trust	12	Maidstone
3	Nine years (and 4 months)	13	South coast
4	Alex James	14	The National Assembly for Wales
5	Dominic Raab	15	Charles II
6	Ice hockey	16	Argyle
7	1990s (1991)	17	Isle of Wight
8	Bath	18	Devon and Essex
9	Hyde Park	19	No, it is landlocked
10	Carlisle	20	River Medway

1   What word can refer to both a type of foodstuff and a laundry aid?

2   Which monument was completed first: the Eiffel Tower or the Statue of Liberty?

3   The city of Peterborough lies in which English county?

4   Which member of the royal family served in the RAF's Search and Rescue force from 2009 to 2013?

5   What was the title of the last studio album released by The Beatles?

6   The juice of which fruit is used in a Mai Tai cocktail?

7   Who wrote the poem *Address to a Haggis*?

8   Which of Snow White's Seven Dwarfs doesn't speak?

9   What word can mean both a male deer and a slang term for a dollar?

10 By which name are black leopards known?

11 The TV series *Giri/Haji* took place in which two countries?

12 The brain uses approximately what fraction of the oxygen used by the human body?

13 In which winter sport do classical pieces of music often accompany competitors?

14 Which is longer, a nautical mile or a mile measured on land?

15 What is 12 in Roman numerals?

16 Which company became sponsors of the Rugby Super League in 2017?

17 To the nearest ten years, how old was John Wayne when he won his only Best Actor Oscar?

18 What is three squared?

19 Which large creature in a room might you not want to talk about?

20 Which anticoagulant was originally used to kill rodents?

Answers to QUIZ 29 – Pot Luck

1	Ore Oduba	11	1930s (1935)
2	Sir Alfred Hitchcock	12	Spanish
3	Col (colonel)	13	Eat it (food supplement)
4	Hindi	14	Finland
5	Paris	15	Dance of the Seven Veils
6	Twix®	16	A love letter
7	Abs	17	Cross-country skiing
8	A fighter plane	18	Edward Tudor-Pole
9	George	19	Eggs
10	Notion and lotion	20	Piglet

Easy

Medium

Hard

Easy

1   The egg cases of sharks are sometimes nicknamed "purses" belonging to which mythical creature?

2   In which European city was the werewolf in the title of a 1997 film sequel?

3   The Atlantic Ocean is named after which figure of Greek myth?

4   Guy of Gisborne is associated with which legendary character?

5   In Greek mythology, who used a ball of string to escape the Minotaur's labyrinth?

6   Which large mythical bird is associated with the character Sinbad?

7   Which character from Arthurian legend was played by Colin Morgan in a TV series first broadcast in 2008?

8   Which name is shared by the Roman god of war and a chocolate bar?

9   In Greek mythology Helios is the god of which astronomical body?

10   What word for an alluring woman is a shortened version of the name of a mythical creature?

11   Fortuna was the goddess of good luck in which branch of mythology?

12   The 2007 film *The Water Horse: Legend of the Deep* was set in which country?

13   Who starred in the title role of the 2004 film *Anchorman: The Legend of Ron Burgundy*?

14   The Sphinx has the body of which animal?

15   Who directed the 1985 fantasy film *Legend*?

16   From what was the "horse" made in the legend of Troy?

17   Which Walt Disney princess shares her name with the Roman goddess of the dawn?

18   In Greek mythology, the god Pan has the legs of which creature?

19   The TV series *Legends of Tomorrow* features characters from which comic book publishers?

20   Which poet wrote the 1819 poem *Ode to Psyche*?

Answers to QUIZ 30 – Musical Instruments

1   Clarinet
2   Harp
3   Accordion
4   Tuba
5   Saxophone
6   Double bass
7   Flute
8   Bassoon
9   Grand piano

QUIZ 33 – Pot Luck

ANSWERS ON PAGE 35

1 Which was the third official James Bond film, released in 1964?

2 Which word associated with weddings derives from the Italian for "little sweets"?

3 Which singer featured on the 1987 single *What Have I Done to Deserve This* by the Pet Shop Boys?

4 In the French game of pétanque, are the balls rolled towards the jack or thrown towards the jack?

5 Which former empire describes a system that is perceived to be overly complicated?

6 Aztec and Industrial are zones in which game show?

7 Weber is a brand associated with which outdoor activity?

8 Retinol is a type of which vitamin?

9 How many points are there on a Maltese cross?

10 In *Home Alone 2*, what did the thieves Marv and Harry plan to burgle?

11 What anniversary did *The Simpsons* TV series reach in 2019?

12 What are the names of Barack Obama's two daughters?

13 *Aurum* is the Latin name of which precious metal?

14 Which composer was born first, Mozart or Beethoven?

15 Which compound in mint gives the herb its distinctive cool taste?

16 What material is traditionally associated with a third wedding anniversary?

17 Ailments of which organ of the body might be treated with digitalis?

18 As at 2020, Estadio Azteca is the largest sporting stadium in which country?

19 What word can go before "faced", "step" and "timing" to form three phrases?

20 What type of drink is the brand Cinzano®?

Easy

Medium

Hard

Answers to QUIZ 31 – Pot Luck

1	Starch	11	England and Japan
2	The Statue of Liberty (1886)	12	1/5th
3	Cambridgeshire	13	Figure skating (or Ice dance)
4	Prince William	14	A nautical mile
5	*Let it Be*	15	XII
6	Lime	16	BetFred
7	Robert Burns	17	60 (62, for *True Grit*)
8	Dopey	18	Nine
9	Buck	19	The elephant
10	Panthers	20	Warfarin

1   What type of dog is Dug in the 2009 animated film *Up*?

2   What was the title of the 2020 reboot of the TV series *ThunderCats*?

3   In the children's TV series, what is the name of Peppa Pig's brother?

4   Who wrote the 2011 children's book *The Highway Rat*?

5   What breed of dog is Toto in *The Wizard of Oz*?

6   In *The Wind in the Willows*, which two types of creature take over Toad Hall in Mr Toad's absence?

7   Which instrument does Kermit the Frog play?

8   Which fictional animal lives at 32 Windsor Gardens, London?

9   Which animals are featured in the 1972 novel *Watership Down*?

10 Porky Pig is depicted wearing which two items of clothing?

11 What type of animal is the fictional Hairy Maclary?

12 What is the name of Garfield's female feline friend?

13 In the Rudyard Kipling story, what type of snake did Rikki-Tikki-Tavi fight?

14 What was the title of the 2019 film sequel to *A Dog's Purpose*?

15 The Iron Chicken is a character in which children's TV series?

16 Which famous fictional character was originally called Edward Bear?

17 Bernard and Miss Bianca are what type of creatures in the 1977 film *The Rescuers*?

18 What type of owl is Harry Potter's Hedwig?

19 What colour is the face of the Very Hungry Caterpillar?

20 In the theme song, which TV title character was described as "The indisputable leader of the gang"?

Answers to QUIZ 32 – Myth and Legend

1	Mermaid	11	Roman mythology
2	Paris (*An American Werewolf in Paris*)	12	Scotland
3	Atlas	13	Will Ferrell
4	Robin Hood	14	Lion
5	Theseus	15	Sir Ridley Scott
6	Roc	16	Wood
7	Merlin	17	Aurora (*Sleeping Beauty*)
8	Mars	18	A goat
9	The Sun	19	DC Comics
10	Vamp (vampire)	20	John Keats

Easy

Medium

Hard

1   "And I will have my vengeance in this life or the next" is a line from which 2000 film?

2   What is a curmudgeon?

3   Who is the Primate of Italy?

4   In 1994, who became the first solo female host of the Oscars?

5   What colour are Heineken® bottles?

6   Yeast is classified as what type of organism?

7   In Western countries, in which two months can Easter Monday occur?

8   What was the name of Suranne Jones' *Coronation Street* character?

9   Who beat Steve Davis to win the 1985 World Snooker Championship?

10 What type of creature is a cassowary?

11 The slogan "Buy it, Sell it, Love it" is associated with which organisation?

12 Which form of holiday takes its name from the Swahili word for "journey"?

13 What does a saccharometer measure?

14 The tail of a comet always points away from which celestial object?

15 Which cheese has a name that means "slice" in modern Greek?

16 Which of these art movements occurred first: Fauvism, Futurism, or Minimalism?

17 Which Canadian National Park shares its name with a variety of quartz?

18 As at 2020, which two actors have played Sergeant Bilko?

19 Which English sports stadium is nicknamed "The Cabbage Patch" as it was built on the site of a former market garden?

20 Slovenia was part of which country until 1991?

Easy

Medium

Hard

Answers to QUIZ 33 – Pot Luck

1	*Goldfinger*	11	30th anniversary
2	Confetti	12	Malia and Sasha
3	Dusty Springfield	13	Gold
4	Thrown	14	Mozart (1756)
5	Byzantine	15	Menthol
6	*The Crystal Maze*	16	Leather
7	Barbecuing	17	The heart
8	Vitamin A	18	Mexico
9	Eight	19	Two
10	A toy store	20	Vermouth

Easy

1   How many innings are there in a game of baseball?

2   What is the longest running event in a women's heptathlon?

3   In Test cricket, how many overs must be played before the introduction of a new ball?

4   How many referees adjudicate a netball game?

5   Which sport would you be pursuing if you were wearing a hacking jacket?

6   What is the name of Peter Schmeichel's son, who signed for Leicester City FC in 2011?

7   Nordic and Telemark are types of which sport?

8   Which team won the FA Women's League Cup in 2020?

9   The sport of orienteering originated in which country?

10 Which song is traditionally sung before the Rugby League Challenge Cup final?

11 In which decade did Ayrton Senna win his first Formula 1 World Championship?

12 At which event does the Diamond Challenge Sculls take place?

13 After extra time, what was the final score at the 1966 FIFA World Cup Final?

Medium

14 In which US state was the first professional beach volleyball tournament held, in 1976?

15 Which water sport has three elements: slalom, jump and trick?

16 Which Indian cricketer is nicknamed "The Little Master"?

17 American William Shoemaker (d.2003) was a well-known name in which sport?

18 Who is the only member of a hockey team allowed to touch the ball with their body?

19 Who won the 2019 Wimbledon ladies' singles title?

20 In which position did Geraint Thomas finish in the 2019 Tour de France?

Hard

Answers to QUIZ 34 – Fictional Animals

1	A golden retriever	11	A dog
2	*ThunderCats Roar*	12	Arlene
3	George	13	A cobra
4	Julia Donaldson	14	*A Dog's Journey*
5	Cairn terrier	15	*The Clangers*
6	Stoats and weasels	16	Winnie-the-Pooh
7	Banjo	17	Mice
8	Paddington Bear	18	A snowy owl
9	Rabbits	19	Red
10	A jacket and (bow) tie	20	*Top Cat*

1 "Why did it take me so long just to find, The friend that was there all along" is a lyric from which 1998 song?

2 Marcus Tandy, played by Jesse Birdsall, was a leading character in which short-lived series?

3 The Davy lamp was invented to work in which environment?

4 What is burned in a censer?

5 What was John Lennon's middle name?

6 In which month does the Formula 1 season usually start?

7 Anthony Fokker was a pioneer in which field?

8 What word can mean both a lane at traffic lights and a device to remove small particles?

9 What is the international car registration code for Australia?

10 What single word can precede "call", "harmony" and "shave" to make three phrases?

11 The actor Viggo Mortensen was born in which country?

12 Who stepped down as the head coach of the Northern Ireland football team in April 2020?

13 Which anniversary did the Radio 4 programme *Start the Week* celebrate in 2020?

14 What colour is *Sesame Street*'s Cookie Monster?

15 "Silicon Glen" is the nickname for the technology sector of which country?

16 Ingmar Stenmark competed for Sweden in which sport?

17 Who played villain Phoenix Buchanan in the film *Paddington 2*?

18 Which English beer brand has a red triangle as its logo?

19 Colorado and deathwatch are types of which insect?

20 In which decade was the first laser built?

Answers to QUIZ 35 – Pot Luck

1	*Gladiator*	11	eBay
2	A bad-tempered person	12	Safari
3	The Pope	13	Sugar level
4	Whoopi Goldberg	14	The Sun
5	Green	15	Feta
6	A fungus	16	Fauvism (1904)
7	March or April	17	Jasper
8	Karen McDonald	18	Phil Silvers and Steve Martin
9	Dennis Taylor	19	Twickenham
10	A (flightless) bird	20	Yugoslavia

1   What is the title of Hilary Mantel's third novel about Thomas Cromwell, published in 2020?

2   *The Ballad of Songbirds and Snakes* (2020) is a novel in which series for young adults?

3   Which year forms the title of a George Orwell novel?

4   What is Victorian author Richard Doddridge Blackmore's most famous work?

5   Which unfinished Jane Austen novel was adapted for television in 2019?

6   In Longfellow's epic poem *The Song of Hiawatha*, who is Hiawatha's lover?

7   Which gemstone appears in the titles of two Ian Fleming books?

8   The subheading to which famous Evelyn Waugh novel is *The Sacred & Profane Memories of Captain Charles Ryder*?

9   Which novel follows the adventures of Alonso Quixano?

10 Which Dickens novel has a number in its title?

11 In the novel of the same name, what is Wuthering Heights?

12 Which work is considered the sequel to Homer's *The Iliad*?

13 Which US author was awarded the Nobel Prize in Literature in 1962?

14 St John Rivers is a character in which 1847 novel?

15 The name of which unit of measurement is also used to describe the rhythm of poetry?

16 In the George Eliot novel *The Mill on the Floss*, what is the name of Maggie Tulliver's brother?

17 Who rules the land of Mordor in *The Lord of the Rings*?

18 What word completes the title of the trilogy of novels by Flora Thompson, *Lark Rise to ___*?

19 *The Last Battle* (1956) is the seventh and final novel in which children's series?

20 In which century did Anthony Trollope write *Barchester Towers*?

Answers to QUIZ 36 – Outdoor Sports

1	Nine	11	1980s (1988)
2	800m	12	Henley Regatta
3	80	13	4-2
4	Two	14	California
5	Horse-riding	15	Water-skiing
6	Kasper (Schmeichel)	16	Sachin Tendulkar
7	Skiing	17	Horse-racing (jockey)
8	Chelsea	18	Goalkeeper
9	Sweden	19	Simona Halep
10	*Abide with Me*	20	Second

1   Amber Gill and Greg O'Shea won which TV series in July 2019?

2   In the Bible, which woman was present both at Jesus's crucifixion and his resurrection?

3   Which football ground has hosted the majority of Scottish FA Cup Finals?

4   Who created the character of Vicky Pollard?

5   The infection scabies, caused by a mite, affects which part of the human body?

6   Which iconic boxer was born Rocco Francis Marchegiano?

7   What type of food is Taleggio?

8   How many James Bond films did Pierce Brosnan star in?

9   What was the name of Victoria Principal's character in the TV series *Dallas*?

10   What word can go before "drop", "rain" and "test" to form three phrases?

11   In which decade did Persia officially become known as Iran?

12   Which type of monkey shares its name with a blood group?

13   In which sport might a fielder stand at silly point?

14   The duo Lily and Joseph were finalists in which 2020 TV competition?

15   The popular name for a dog, Fido, derives from the Latin for what word?

16   In which decade was Starbucks® first opened in the USA?

17   Madeleine Albright became the first female US Secretary of State during the term of which president?

18   What is a male walrus called?

19   What is the English translation of the French phrase *bon viveur*?

20   The compilation album *25 Years – The Chain* features music by which band?

Answers to QUIZ 37 – Pot Luck

1	*Picture of You* (Boyzone)	11	USA
2	*Eldorado*	12	Michael O'Neill
3	A mine	13	50th anniversary
4	Incense	14	Blue
5	Winston	15	Scotland
6	March	16	Alpine skiing
7	Aviation	17	Hugh Grant
8	Filter	18	Bass
9	AUS	19	Beetle
10	Close	20	1960s (1960)

1   What type of drink is Archers®?

2   What colour is Sebastian the crab in the 1989 film *The Little Mermaid*?

3   Leo (b.2000) is the fourth child of which former UK prime minister?

4   Which planet completes this line in the song *The Age of Aquarius*: "And Jupiter aligns with ___"?

5   Who starred as Mathayus, the title character in *The Scorpion King* (2002)?

6   Which sign of the zodiac has the longest name?

7   The constellation Gemini is associated with Castor and Pollux in which branch of mythology?

8   What name is given to a female goat?

9   Which of the Bee Gees were twins?

10   The sign of Aries covers which two months of the year?

11   Who released the single *Little White Bull* in 1959?

12   Which is north of the equator: the Tropic of Cancer or the Tropic of Capricorn?

13   In the radio series *The Archers*, what is the name of Felicity Finch's character?

14   Which of these zodiac signs is earliest in the year: Leo, Pisces or Taurus?

15   Where in London would you see the Scales of Justice?

16   The Capricorn coast lies in which state of Australia?

17   The lion Aslan first appeared in which Narnia novel?

18   How many fish appear on the sign for Pisces?

19   A scorpion is what type of creature?

20   What was the name of Prunella Scales' character in *Fawlty Towers*?

Answers to QUIZ 38 – Literature

1	*The Mirror & the Light*	11	A farmhouse
2	*The Hunger Games*	12	*The Odyssey*
3	*1984 (Nineteen Eighty-Four)*	13	John Steinbeck
4	*Lorna Doone*	14	*Jane Eyre*
5	*Sanditon*	15	Metre
6	Minnehaha	16	Tom
7	Diamond (*Diamonds are Forever* and *The Diamond Smugglers*)	17	Sauron
8	*Brideshead Revisited*	18	*Candleford*
9	*Don Quixote*	19	*The Chronicles of Narnia*
10	*A Tale of Two Cities*	20	19th century (1857)

1 What is the word for a compulsory call-up to the armed forces?

2 Which colour lies between blue and violet in a rainbow?

3 The neighbourhood of Capitol Hill lies in which US city?

4 Who hosts the 2020 revival of *Ready Steady Cook*?

5 Which household goods company used the slogan "The Appliance of Science"?

6 Main Avenue and the Great Pavilion are features of which annual English event?

7 What four-letter word that means "a smile" becomes the name of a fish with the addition of one letter?

8 In the 1988 film *Working Girl*, who played Jack Trainer?

9 Which 1960 film, starring Laurence Olivier (Baron Olivier), shares its name with a toy shop founded in 1981?

10 Where would you find a maxillary central incisor?

11 The seaside town of Dawlish is in which county?

12 Which Central American country has a name that means "rich shore"?

13 Which cricketer won the BBC Sports Personality of the Year award in 2019?

14 What type of war machine was a dreadnought?

15 Saxophones are most commonly made of which material?

16 How many days are there in 12 weeks?

17 The mojito cocktail originated in which country?

18 Who co-created the comedy show *The Office* with Ricky Gervais?

19 What is a male seal called?

20 Which occurs first in the year: Bastille Day, the Chinese New Year or Armistice Day?

Easy

Medium

Hard

Answers to QUIZ 39 – Pot Luck

1	*Love Island*	11	1930s (1935)
2	Mary Magdalene	12	Rhesus monkey
3	Hampden Park	13	Cricket
4	Matt Lucas	14	*The Greatest Dancer*
5	The skin	15	Faithful
6	Rocky Marciano	16	1970s (1971)
7	(Italian) cheese	17	Bill Clinton
8	Four (*GoldenEye, Tomorrow Never Dies, The World Is Not Enough, Die Another Day*)	18	A bull
		19	Good living person
9	Pam Ewing	20	Fleetwood Mac
10	Acid		

Easy

1   What relation was Arya Stark to Sansa Stark?

2   Who played Jon Snow?

3   What was the first name of the character nicknamed "The Hound"?

4   To which king was Cersei Lannister married at the start of the series?

5   The character of Brienne, played by Gwendoline Christie, was from which house?

6   What colour were the Walkers?

7   Daenerys Targaryen was played by which actress?

8   What other name was given to the Free Folk, who lived outside The Wall?

9   What is the name of the ancestral home of the House of Stark?

10   What colour hair did the priestess Melisandre have?

Medium

11   How many kingdoms were there at the start of the series?

12   What was the name of the group who patrolled The Wall?

13   What was the name of Peter Dinklage's character?

14   The Greyjoy family ruled which group of islands?

15   What was the name of the nomadic horse-riding people led by chiefs called khals?

16   Jonathan Pryce played which religious leader?

17   Which character was nicknamed "The Kingslayer"?

18   The coat of arms of which house featured a direwolf?

19   What was the first name of Cersei Lannister's oldest son?

20   Who played Theon Greyjoy?

Hard

Answers to QUIZ 40 – The Zodiac

1	(Peach) schnapps	11	Tommy Steele
2	Red	12	Tropic of Cancer
3	Tony Blair	13	Ruth Archer
4	Mars	14	Pisces (February and March)
5	Dwayne Johnson	15	On the Old Bailey statue
6	Sagittarius	16	Queensland
7	Greek mythology	17	The Lion, the Witch and the Wardrobe
8	Nanny	18	Two
9	Maurice and Robin	19	An arachnid
10	March and April	20	Sybil Fawlty

QUIZ 43 – Pot Luck

1 Which car manufacturer makes the Kodiaq and the Scala models?

2 What are the two colours on the home kit of Saracens rugby union team?

3 Cousin Itt is a member of which spooky TV family?

4 What is the name of the adhesive device used to stick a stamp in an album?

5 Which girl's name is spelt out by the chemical symbols for titanium and sodium?

6 In which decade was Matt LeBlanc born?

7 Which fish is one of the ingredients in a Caesar salad?

8 Fanny Price is the heroine of which Jane Austen novel?

9 The name of which Egyptian god is an anagram of "hours"?

10 Is a coconut actually a nut?

11 The ceramic willow pattern design uses which two colours?

12 What are held in place by periodontal fibres?

13 What is the main religion of India?

14 How does the Met Office describe a forecast from three to ten days ahead?

15 The scandal nicknamed "Irangate" occurred during the term of which US president?

16 What is the maximum goal handicap in the game of polo?

17 Who played the main baddie, Raoul Silva, in the James Bond film *Skyfall*?

18 Which snack food shares its name with a type of circular toy?

19 The Seven Mile Bridge lies in which East Coast US state?

20 In the traditional bingo call, what number is "Triple dozen"?

Easy
Medium
Hard

Answers to QUIZ 41 – Pot Luck

1	Conscription	11	Devon
2	Indigo	12	Costa Rica
3	Washington DC	13	Ben Stokes
4	Rylan Clark-Neal	14	Battleship
5	Zanussi	15	Brass
6	RHS Chelsea Flower Show	16	84
7	Beam (Bream)	17	Cuba
8	Harrison Ford	18	Stephen Merchant
9	*The Entertainer*	19	A bull
10	Human mouth (a front, top tooth)	20	The Chinese New Year (January or February)

What are the names of these London landmarks?

Easy

1

2

3

4

Medium

5

6

7

8

Hard

Answers to QUIZ 42 – Game of Thrones

1	Sister	11	Seven
2	Kit Harington	12	The Night's Watch
3	Sandor	13	Tyrion Lannister
4	Robert Baratheon	14	The Iron Islands
5	Tarth	15	The Dothraki
6	White	16	The High Sparrow
7	Emilia Clarke	17	Jaime Lannister
8	The Wildlings	18	House of Stark
9	Winterfell	19	Joffrey
10	Red	20	Alfie Allen

1   Who won the 2020 UK series of *The Masked Singer*?

2   The Ospreys rugby union team is based in which country?

3   "I got my first real six string" is the opening lyric from which song?

4   Which star of silent films was nicknamed "The Great Stone Face"?

5   Which part of a chicken is served Buffalo-style?

6   Hannibal Heyes and "Kid" Curry were the title characters in which 1970s TV series?

7   What word can mean both a bullet cartridge and a periodical?

8   Which superhero shares his name with a word for an abandoned ship?

9   How many different husbands did Dame Elizabeth Taylor have?

10   Which sword is used to describe a cutting wit?

11   Which character in *A Christmas Carol* says "God bless us, every one"?

12   In the New Testament, by whom was the Annunciation delivered?

13   Which car manufacturer made the Avenger and the Imp?

14   Which of these Beatles albums was released first: *A Hard Day's Night, Help!* or *The White Album*?

15   Traditionally, the four herbs included in French fines herbs are chives, chervil, tarragon and which other?

16   Which creatures spread Lyme disease?

17   How many US states begin with the word "New"?

18   Who was appointed the UK's Chief Scientific Officer in March 2018?

19   Tynecastle Park is the home of which Scottish football club?

20   The National People's Congress is the highest level of government in which country?

Easy

Medium

Hard

Answers to QUIZ 43 – Pot Luck

1	Škoda	11	Blue and white
2	Black and red	12	Teeth
3	The Addams family	13	Hinduism
4	Hinge	14	Medium range
5	Tina	15	Ronald Reagan
6	1960s (1967)	16	Ten goals
7	Anchovy	17	Javier Bardem
8	*Mansfield Park*	18	Hula Hoops
9	Horus	19	Florida
10	No, it is a drupe	20	36

Easy

1 Which author created the clown Pennywise in the 1986 novel *It*?

2 Who won the Best Actor Oscar at the 2020 award ceremony for his role in the film *Joker*?

3 Which comedian was *At Large* in the title of a 1970s TV series?

4 *Send in the Clowns* is a song from which 1973 musical?

5 Which comedian hosted the TV series *The Family Brain Games*?

6 What nickname are clowns often known by, originating from the actor Joseph Grimaldi?

7 Which band released the 1973 album *The Joker*?

8 In the Smokey Robinson song *Tears of a Clown*, what line follows "If there's a smile on my face"?

9 Who played the Joker in the 1989 film *Batman*?

10 Which comedian is Elis James' regular co-presenter on a Radio 5 lunchtime show?

Medium

11 Which famous mime artist created Bip the Clown?

12 What is the name of the clown in *The Simpsons*?

13 What colour hair does Ronald McDonald have?

14 In which country was comedian Stanley Baxter born?

15 The jester Feste appears in which play by Shakespeare?

16 How many jokers are there in a standard pack of cards?

17 In which 1983 film does James Bond disguise himself as a clown?

18 Which comedian had the catchphrase "Just like that"?

19 What was the name of the deceased jester in Shakepeare's *Hamlet*?

20 "Clowns to the left of me, jokers to the right" is a lyric from which song?

Hard

Answers to QUIZ 44 – London Landmarks

1 Natural History Museum
2 The Barbican
3 Westminster Abbey
4 Marble Arch
5 The National Theatre
6 The Lloyd's Building
7 HMS Belfast
8 St Pancras Station

ANSWERS ON PAGE 49

1   Which letter lies between A and D on a standard keyboard?

2   Which is higher in a standing human: the patella, the tarsals or the scapula?

3   In which decade did Dame Ellen MacArthur break the world record for the fastest circumnavigation of the globe?

4   Which group had a hit in 1962 with *Sherry*?

5   Who managed the England football team from 1974 to 1977?

6   Which hurricane caused the flooding of New Orleans in 2005?

7   Mila Kunis and Ashton Kutcher first worked together on which series first broadcast in 1998?

8   What would you do with a galette?

9   The Australian city of Fremantle lies on which ocean?

10   What word for a computer systems failure can also describe a form of diet?

11   What number do the Roman numerals XV represent?

12   In 1979, who set three world records in the space of six weeks, in the 800m, 1500m and the mile?

13   Facebook™ was originally founded for students at which university?

14   In the 2016 film *A Monster Calls*, who voiced the monster?

15   Which DJ played the first record on Radio 1?

16   The 1998 film *Sliding Doors* was set in which city?

17   The jackrabbit is not a rabbit. What type of creature is it?

18   What colour is the Barclays Bank logo?

19   Which of the Muppets shares his name with a mode of transport?

20   Which ailment was historically called consumption?

Answers to QUIZ 45 – Pot Luck

1	Nicola Roberts	11	Tiny Tim
2	Wales (Swansea)	12	The Angel Gabriel (to Mary)
3	*Summer of '69* (Bryan Adams)	13	Hillman
4	Buster Keaton	14	*A Hard Day's Night* (1964)
5	Wings	15	Parsley
6	*Alias Smith and Jones*	16	Ticks
7	Magazine	17	Four (Hampshire, Jersey, Mexico and York)
8	Hulk	18	Sir Patrick Vallance
9	Seven	19	Heart of Midlothian (Hearts)
10	Rapier	20	China

Easy

Medium

Hard

Easy

1 In which decade was DEFRA formed by merging two government departments?

2 With which UK political party is the Fabian Society affiliated?

3 What two words were added to the title of Secretary of State for Foreign Affairs in 1968?

4 Who became Chancellor of the Exchequer in February 2020?

5 The role of prime minister of Great Britain was created during the reign of which king?

6 On what date did the UK exit the European Union?

7 Which term, much in use in 2019, means to discontinue the meetings of Parliament without dissolving it?

8 UK MPs first received an annual salary in 1911. Was this £200, £300 or £400?

9 Who was elected as the leader of the Labour Party in April 2020?

10 How many times did the Duke of Wellington serve as prime minister in the 19th century?

11 William Beveridge (First Baron Beveridge), belonged to which political party?

12 What relation was Home Secretary Herbert Gladstone (First Viscount Gladstone) to William Gladstone?

13 Clement Attlee (First Earl Attlee) was the leader of which political party?

Medium

14 What is the name of the device used by the BBC at elections to predict the change of seats as a result of the vote?

15 Which politician was first featured on the Bank of England £5 note in 2016?

16 Which post did Sir John Major hold first: Chancellor of the Exchequer or Foreign Secretary?

17 Who succeeded Jack Straw as UK Foreign Secretary?

18 Baroness Shirley Williams was the president of which political party from 1982 to 1987?

19 In which month did the general election take place in 2019?

20 Who was voted leader of the Liberal Democrat Party in July 2019, stepping down the day after the next General Election?

Hard

Answers to QUIZ 46 – Clowns and Jokers

1	Stephen King	11	Marcel Marceau
2	Joaquin Phoenix	12	Krusty
3	Dave Allen	13	Red
4	*A Little Night Music*	14	Scotland
5	Dara Ó Briain	15	*Twelfth Night*
6	Joey	16	Two
7	The Steve Miller Band	17	*Octopussy*
8	"It's only there to fool the public"	18	Tommy Cooper
9	Jack Nicholson	19	Yorick
10	John Robins	20	*Stuck in the Middle with You* (Stealers Wheel)

QUIZ 49 – Pot Luck

ANSWERS ON PAGE 51

1 The Epsom Derby was first run in which century?

2 The comedy series *Seinfeld* was first screened in which decade?

3 Which period came first: the Renaissance or the Baroque?

4 Scone Palace is situated near which Scottish city?

5 Who played the title role in the 2001 film *Shallow Hal*?

6 What kind of animal is a burbot?

7 Which of these Batman films was released the earliest: *Batman and Robin*, *Batman Begins*, or *Batman Returns*?

8 In which century was the mechanical hare introduced into greyhound racing?

9 Popular in the 18th century, what was a pompadour?

10 Who won the International Female Solo Artist Brit award in 2020?

11 What was the title of the previously unheard demo song by Oasis that was released in April 2020?

12 Who played Dan Conner in the TV series *Roseanne*?

13 The company Compaq manufactured what type of product?

14 The US state of Alaska has a border with British Columbia and which other Canadian territory?

15 What word can mean both "an argument" and "a gaiter"?

16 What term is given to the imaginary line between two signs of the zodiac?

17 Portchester Castle is in which English county?

18 How many feet are there in twelve fathoms?

19 Which alcoholic drink has a label with the words "Old No.7 Brand"?

20 What was the name of the horse in the novel and film *War Horse*?

Easy / Medium / Hard

Answers to QUIZ 47 – Pot Luck

1 S
2 The scapula (shoulder blade)
3 2000s (2005)
4 The Four Seasons
5 Don Revie
6 Hurricane Katrina
7 *That '70s Show*
8 Eat it (a flat cake or pancake)
9 Indian Ocean
10 Crash
11 15
12 Sebastian Coe (Lord Coe)
13 Harvard
14 Liam Neeson
15 Tony Blackburn
16 London
17 A hare
18 Blue
19 Scooter
20 Tuberculosis

1   Which rock band released the 2020 single *Living in a Ghost Town*?

2   *Circus* was a 2008 single and album by which female singer?

3   Carrie Underwood is a well-known singer in which genre?

4   *Dangerously in Love* was a 2003 album released by which singer?

5   Which rapper had a 2007 hit with *Stronger*?

6   In which decade was Adele born?

7   *Girlfriend* was a chart-topping single in 2007 for which female singer?

8   Which female popstar had a 2001 hit with *Play*?

9   Who featured on Rihanna's smash hit *Umbrella*?

10 What kind of weapon did Bruno Mars sing about in 2011?

11 Gnarls Barkley topped the UK charts in 2006 with which song?

12 Which city featured in the title of a 2006 Fergie song?

13 Who featured on Justin Timberlake's 2006 song *SexyBack*?

14 *Believe*, released in 2012, was the third album by which singer?

15 In which year did One Direction release their debut single *What Makes You Beautiful*?

16 Which chemical element was the title of a 2012 hit for David Guetta?

17 Jay McGuiness is a member of which boy band?

18 Which is the main city mentioned in the chorus of the hit *Empire State of Mind*?

19 "I want your love, and I want your revenge" is a lyric from which 2009 song?

20 Who had hits in 2019 with *Circles* and *Wow*?

Answers to QUIZ 48 – UK Politics

1	2000s (2001)	11	The Liberal Party
2	The Labour Party	12	Son
3	"And Commonwealth" (before Affairs)	13	The Labour Party
4	Rishi Sunak	14	Swingometer
5	George I (1721)	15	Sir Winston Churchill
6	January 31, 2020	16	Foreign Secretary (July 1989)
7	Prorogue	17	Dame Margaret Beckett
8	£400	18	The Social Democratic Party
9	Sir Keir Starmer	19	December
10	Twice (1828-30 and 1834)	20	Jo Swinson

1 What is the first name of AJ Pritchard's brother and fellow dancer?

2 What is the main pain-killing ingredient in the Nurofen™ brand of medication?

3 How many ounces are there in two pounds?

4 Whom did Warren Beatty marry in 1992?

5 In 1993, which English driver became the first person to both take pole position and win in his first IndyCar race?

6 Hywel Bennett played the title character in which sitcom, first broadcast in 1979?

7 Which brand of tea has been advertised by the Tea Folk?

8 Which 1990 film set in Brooklyn featured Ray Liotta as Henry Hill?

9 *Power of a Woman* and *Stay* were 1990s hits for which girl group?

10 What sport is played by the Paris-based team Stade Français?

11 What is a female alligator called?

12 Which browser shares its name with a 1982 film starring Clint Eastwood?

13 In which decade was *The Godfather Part III* released in cinemas?

14 *Rive Gauche* is a perfume from which fashion house?

15 To the nearest ten, how many full-length novels did Dame Agatha Christie write?

16 In which city is the oldest church building in England that is still in use?

17 Who was the mother of David Linley (b.1961), Second Earl of Snowdon?

18 Castanets are associated with which country?

19 Which was invented first, the paper clip or the safety pin?

20 Who was the director-general of the BBC from 2000 to 2004?

Answers to QUIZ 49 – Pot Luck

1	18th century (1780)	11	*Don't Stop*
2	1980s (1989)	12	John Goodman
3	Renaissance	13	Computers
4	Perth	14	Yukon
5	Jack Black	15	Spat
6	Fish (freshwater cod)	16	The cusp
7	*Batman Returns* (1992)	17	Hampshire (near Portsmouth)
8	20th century (1912)	18	72
9	A hairstyle	19	Jack Daniel's
10	Billie Eilish	20	Joey

1   Which character from *Alice's Adventures in Wonderland* is named after a soup?

2   What colour are Mickey Mouse's shoes?

3   Which Peanuts character carries a blue security blanket?

4   What is Desperate Dan's favourite food?

5   Which cartoon character married Wilma Slaghoople?

6   As a child, actor Henry Thomas played a character called Elliott in which classic film?

7   Bingo and Drooper appeared on which children's television show, first broadcast in the late 1960s?

8   What does Paddington Bear keep under his hat?

9   Which character in *Treasure Island* had a craving for cheese?

10   Which was the oldest and largest of the Teletubbies?

11   In which decade was *The Clangers* first broadcast on television?

12   Which animated character's name means "to transform"?

13   Which children's author created the character of Benjamin Bunny?

14   The catchphrase "Izzy, wizzy, let's get busy" is associated with which puppet?

15   What is the subtitle of the sixth novel in the Harry Potter series?

16   What word completes the title of the nursery rhyme *Peter, Peter, ___ Eater*?

17   Hetty Feather was created by which author?

18   Darrell and Felicity Rivers are characters in which series of children's novels?

19   Rory, Ginger and Merrylegs appear in which novel of 1877?

20   Which animated character is associated with the phrase "cracking cheese"?

Answers to QUIZ 50 – 21st-Century Music

1	The Rolling Stones	11	*Crazy*
2	Britney Spears	12	London (*London Bridge*)
3	Country music	13	Timbaland
4	Beyoncé	14	Justin Bieber
5	Kanye West	15	2011
6	1980s (1988)	16	Titanium
7	Avril Lavigne	17	The Wanted
8	Jennifer Lopez	18	New York
9	Jay-Z	19	*Bad Romance* (Lady Gaga)
10	*Grenade*	20	Post Malone

1   What is Australia's largest inland city?

2   Which city lies furthest north: Dundee, Glasgow or Stirling?

3   Stableford is a scoring system in which sport?

4   What word completes the title of the Rodgers and Hart song, *Bewitched, ___ and Bewildered*?

5   What was the title of the 1991 sequel to *Bill & Ted's Excellent Adventure*?

6   What type of creature is a black widow?

7   Which form of transport featured in the 1953 film *The Titfield Thunderbolt*?

8   The 2019 series *Gold Digger* was set in London and which county?

9   Which branch of mathematics takes its name from the Latin for "the reunion of broken parts"?

10 Which 1977 song by Chic had *Yowsah, Yowsah, Yowsah* in brackets after its main title?

11 Bob Willis (d.2019) played which role in the England cricket team?

12 Which fictional detective has been portrayed on television by Martin Shaw and Roy Marsden?

13 Who said; "I have had a perfectly wonderful evening, but this wasn't it"?

14 In wiring, which two colours are on the earth wire?

15 What type of animal is the fictional Oozlum?

16 In which decade was smoking banned in the workplace in the UK?

17 What type of food is a churro?

18 In the traditional bingo call, what number is "39 More Steps"?

19 What does a strobe produce?

20 For how many years was Bill Clinton president of the USA?

Answers to QUIZ 51 – Pot Luck

1	Curtis	11	A cow
2	Ibuprofen	12	Firefox
3	32	13	1990s (1990)
4	Annette Bening	14	Yves Saint Laurent
5	Nigel Mansell	15	70 (66)
6	*Shelley*	16	Canterbury (St Martin's Church)
7	Tetley	17	Princess Margaret
8	*Goodfellas*	18	Spain
9	Eternal	19	The safety pin (1849)
10	Rugby union	20	Greg Dyke

1 The cascade of Cauldron Snout on the River Tees lies on the borders of which two counties?

2 Leander Rowing Club is situated next to which river?

3 The Gulf of Taranto lies off the coast of which European country?

4 Which river, Europe's second longest, originates in the Black Forest?

5 The village of Symonds Yat lies on the banks of which river?

6 The Transporter Bridge at Middlesbrough spans which river?

7 How is the Istanbul Strait more commonly known?

8 Eads Bridge connects St Louis with East St Louis over which river?

9 The Jordan River flows through the Sea of Galilee into which expanse of water?

10 What is the collective name for the Horseshoe Falls, the American Falls and the Bridal Veil Falls?

11 Which gulf of the Pacific Ocean is also known as the Sea of Cortés or the Vermilion Sea?

12 The narwhal is found in which ocean?

13 Which Russian city lies on the river Neva at the head of the Gulf of Finland?

14 Seaforth Dock lies on which North of England river?

15 Which explorer gave the Victoria Falls its English name?

16 In the Bible, which sea did Moses part?

17 The name of which African river is an anagram of a word meaning "queue"?

18 What word for a major event that marks a change is taken from an area of high ground that divides two river systems?

19 Hadrian's Wall ran from the Solway Firth to which river?

20 The Dardanelles is a strait in which country?

Answers to QUIZ 52 – Children's Characters

1	The Mock Turtle	11	1960s (1969)
2	Yellow	12	Morph
3	Linus	13	Beatrix Potter
4	Cow pie	14	Sooty
5	Fred Flintstone	15	*The Half-Blood Prince*
6	*E.T. the Extra-Terrestrial*	16	*Pumpkin*
7	*The Banana Splits*	17	Dame Jacqueline Wilson
8	A marmalade sandwich	18	*Malory Towers* (Enid Blyton)
9	Ben Gunn	19	*Black Beauty*
10	Tinky Winky	20	Wallace

1. Which two words that sound the same but are spelt differently mean a "polite remark" and "to go well with"?

2. Which mythical creature appears on the front of a British passport?

3. Which US president was nicknamed "Honest"?

4. Who played Amy in the 2019 film *Little Women*?

5. "Louis, I think this is the beginning of a beautiful friendship" is the last line from which film?

6. Which sport is played on an area 78ft (23.78m) by either 36 feet (10.97m) or 27ft (8.23m)?

7. What type of creature is a crown-of-thorns?

8. Ben Gurion airport is the main international airport of which country?

9. Which group had a 1985 hit with *Something About You*?

10. What type of pastry is used to make a traditional Cornish pasty?

11. Which leafy vegetable has ruby and Swiss varieties?

12. Do peanuts grow underground or above ground?

13. Which of the main characters in the TV series *Friends* was a twin?

14. Which saint was the first Christian martyr?

15. Mombasa is the second-largest city in which country?

16. What nationality was the actress Ingrid Bergman?

17. What colour are the flowers on the plant ragwort?

18. How many years are there in two centuries?

19. Which Dorset football team is nicknamed "The Cherries"?

20. What type of creature is a guinea pig?

Easy

Medium

Hard

Answers to QUIZ 53 – Pot Luck

1	Canberra	11	Bowler
2	Dundee	12	Adam Dalgliesh
3	Golf	13	Groucho Marx
4	*Bothered*	14	Green and yellow
5	*Bill & Ted's Bogus Journey*	15	Bird
6	A spider	16	2000s (2007)
7	Train	17	A strip or ring of fried dough
8	Devon	18	78
9	Algebra	19	Flashing light
10	*Dance, Dance, Dance*	20	Eight (1993-2001)

1   Which wild flower takes its name from the French for "tooth of a lion"?

2   Which UK medical charity has a daffodil as its emblem?

3   The daisy and the sweet pea are traditionally associated with which month?

4   "I hope he buys you flowers, I hope he holds your hand" is a lyric from which 2013 song?

5   What is the alternative name for the echinacea plant?

6   Sunflowers are most commonly what colour?

7   Which film and musical features a man-eating plant called Audrey II?

8   Gladiolus is part of which family of flowers?

9   In gardening, what five-letter name is given to a layer of matter put round plants to protect and help them grow?

10 What type of soil is not tolerated by an ericaceous plant?

11 What is the national flower of France, represented by the fleur-de-lys?

12 The shrub *ceanothus* has a common name that includes which colour?

13 The Asian lotus plant grows in what environment?

14 What name is given to the male reproductive organ of a flowering plant?

15 What colour are the flowers of love-lies-bleeding?

16 Which daisy-like plant has a name that goes with lawn and tea?

17 In the musical *My Fair Lady*, what is the name of the flower girl?

18 What type of flower is a cymbidium?

19 What colour is lavender in the title of a nursery rhyme?

20 Wisteria Lane was the main location for which TV series?

Easy

Medium

Hard

---

1   Cliveden House is situated on the banks of which river?

2   Who played Dr Richard Kimble in the 1993 film *The Fugitive*?

3   In which decade did John Parrott win the World Snooker Championship?

4   What word can mean both "artillery unit" and "a container for electric cells"?

5   Microsoft® has its headquarters in which US state?

6   Which spice is used to season goulash?

7   Bardsey Lighthouse is situated in which country of the UK?

8   Which former *Doctor Who* star narrated *Little Britain*?

9   The phrase "Come on down!" was associated with which game show?

10   The names of which city in the north west of England can follow "Man" and "Win" to make the name of two other cities?

11   What are the surnames of Ant and Dec?

12   Which video-conferencing app shares its name with a type of camera lens for close-up shots?

13   What name is given to a baby hyena?

14   At what age can someone legally ride a moped in the UK?

15   Which magical being shares its name with the German word for 11?

16   The 2020 series of *Homeland* was set in which country?

17   What is the alternative name for the junior lightweight category of boxing?

18   Which of these Stephen King novels was published first: *Bag of Bones*, *Cujo* or *'Salem's Lot*?

19   How many Jonas Brothers are there in the US band?

20   Which king is reputed to have said, "Will no-one rid me of this turbulent priest"?

Answers to QUIZ 55 – Pot Luck

1	Compliment and complement	11	Chard
2	Unicorn	12	Underground
3	Abraham Lincoln (Honest Abe)	13	Phoebe
4	Florence Pugh	14	St Stephen
5	*Casablanca*	15	Kenya
6	Tennis	16	Swedish
7	A starfish	17	Yellow
8	Israel	18	200
9	Level 42	19	AFC Bournemouth
10	Shortcrust pastry	20	A rodent

1 The character of Mrs Betty Slocombe was first seen on television in which sitcom?

2 Ted Bovis was a leading character in which sitcom?

3 Nicholas Lyndhurst played Adam in which series, first broadcast in 1978?

4 Onslow, played by Geoffrey Hughes, was the brother-in-law of the main character in which sitcom?

5 Richard Richard was a character in which sitcom?

6 *Sykes* first aired in which decade?

7 Nick, Janey, Michael and Abi were main characters in which sitcom, first broadcast in 2000?

8 *The Nag's Head* pub featured in which UK sitcom?

9 Sid and Jean Abbott were the main couple in which 1970s sitcom?

10 What was the surname of the family in *2.4 Children*?

11 Neil Morrissey played Tony Smart in which sitcom?

12 What was the name of the Director of Communications in *The Thick of It*?

13 *Dad's Army* was set during which conflict?

14 What was the surname of the title characters in the sitcom *George and Mildred*?

15 Peter Sallis played Norman Clegg in which sitcom?

16 *The Thin Blue Line* was set in what type of building?

17 Sheridan was the unseen son in which 1990s sitcom?

18 Saffron was the name of the main character's daughter in which sitcom?

19 Dame Penelope Wilton played Ann Bryce in which sitcom?

20 René Artois was the leading character in which sitcom?

Answers to QUIZ 56 – Flowers and Plants

1	Dandelion	11	The iris
2	Marie Curie	12	Lilac (Californian lilac)
3	April	13	Water
4	*When I Was Your Man* (Bruno Mars)	14	Stamen
5	Coneflower	15	Red
6	Yellow	16	Chamomile (or camomile)
7	*The Little Shop of Horrors*	17	Eliza Doolittle
8	Iris	18	An orchid
9	Mulch	19	Blue
10	Chalk (or lime)	20	*Desperate Housewives*

1 The island of Raasay lies off which coast of Scotland?

2 Which is the only word in the radio phonetic alphabet that contains a hyphen?

3 What is the name of Kirsty Mitchell's current *Casualty* character?

4 *The Next Day* was a 2013 album by which musician?

5 What word can go after "country", "housing" and "real" to form three phrases?

6 What is 19 in Roman numerals?

7 Retired footballer Brad Friedel (b.1971) played in which position?

8 Which fielding position in cricket shares its name with a short name for a petticoat?

9 The fictional Inspector Lestrade is associated with which sleuth?

10 Which music app shares its name with a 2019 superhero film?

11 How often does a septennial event happen?

12 Where was the genie trapped in the story of Aladdin?

13 What is the name of the religious order founded by St Francis of Assisi?

14 The UK scientific group that advises on emergencies has an acronym corresponding to which herb?

15 Which of these Dan Brown novels was published first: *Deception Point*, *Origin* or *The Lost Symbol*?

16 Which novel begins with the words "The great fish moved silently through the night water"?

17 The cartoon character Bazooka Joe was associated with what type of sweet?

18 Who was reputed to have said: "Let them eat cake"?

19 In which decade was the *Radio Times* first published?

20 Which singer/songwriter released the 1975 album *Captain Fantastic and the Brown Dirt Cowboy*?

Answers to QUIZ 57 – Pot Luck

1	River Thames	11	McPartlin and Donnelly
2	Harrison Ford	12	Zoom
3	1990s (1991)	13	Cub
4	Battery	14	16
5	Washington (Redmond)	15	Elf
6	Paprika	16	Afghanistan
7	Wales	17	Super featherweight
8	Tom Baker	18	'Salem's Lot (1975)
9	*The Price is Right*	19	Three
10	Chester	20	Henry II (of Thomas à Becket)

1 Dave Brubeck (d.2012) was associated with which style of music?

2 In which decade did the first Coachella music and arts festival take place?

3 The soundtrack to which film musical includes the songs *I Have Confidence* and *Something Good*?

4 To which section of an orchestra does the triangle belong?

5 Which album by the Beatles was re-released in September 2019 to mark its 50th anniversary?

6 In which music genre is Reba McEntire is a well-known name?

7 "Those cats were fast as lightning" is a lyric from which song?

8 How many valves are there on a trumpet?

9 Brian May is famous for playing what instrument?

10 What word completes the title of a Green Day song, *Boulevard of Broken ____*?

11 Which note is equal to four beats in 4-4 time?

12 Vivaldi's *The Four Seasons* are concertos for which instrument?

13 Which Bee Gees song has a title that is an American state?

14 *Annie I'm Not Your Daddy* and *Stool Pigeon* were 1982 UK hits for which singer?

15 Which is the largest section of an orchestra?

16 Which influential German electronic band was formed by Ralf Hütter and Florian Schneider in 1970?

17 *Cold as Ice* was a 1977 hit for which band?

18 The bars on a glockenspiel are made of what material?

19 Blur and Oasis were part of which musical genre?

20 Which hard wood is traditionally used to make black piano keys?

Answers to QUIZ 58 – British Sitcoms

1	*Are You Being Served?*	11	*Men Behaving Badly*
2	*Hi-De-Hi!*	12	Malcolm Tucker
3	*Butterflies*	13	WWII
4	*Keeping Up Appearances*	14	Roper
5	*Bottom*	15	*Last of the Summer Wine*
6	1970s (1972)	16	A police station
7	*My Family*	17	*Keeping Up Appearances*
8	*Only Fools and Horses*	18	*Absolutely Fabulous*
9	*Bless This House*	19	*Ever Decreasing Circles*
10	Porter	20	*'Allo 'Allo!*

1 What force keeps the solar system in orbit around the Sun?

2 To the nearest 100 miles, how long is the coastline of California?

3 Which former MP took part in the 2020 BBC series of *Pilgrimage*?

4 Which ancient form of communication derives its name from the Greek for "sacred carving"?

5 Hickory, Hunk and Zeke are characters in which 1939 film?

6 Who presents the Channel 5 series *Secret Scotland*?

7 In which decade did the Sydney Harbour Bridge open?

8 Which Shakespearean character delivers the line: "Out, damned spot!"?

9 Which retired boxer was nicknamed "The Clones Cyclone"?

10 In which Bond film did Jill St John play Tiffany Case?

11 The month associated with which of these birthstones occurs earliest in the calendar year: amethyst, emerald or ruby?

12 What does "cc" indicate when it appears on a letter or email before the name of another recipient?

13 The building of which London hotel was financed by Gilbert and Sullivan operas?

14 In the Stevie Wonder song Sir Duke, which Duke is being referred to?

15 Which children's TV series includes the character Count von Count?

16 What is the English equivalent of the Spanish name Juan?

17 What does the letter "P" stand for on an automatic gearbox?

18 Risers and treads are components of which part of a building?

19 Which Australian state is alphabetically last?

20 Robbie Grabarz won the bronze medal in which field event at the 2012 Olympic Games?

Easy

Medium

Hard

Answers to QUIZ 59 – Pot Luck

1 The west coast (off the Isle of Skye)
2 X-ray
3 Faith Cadogan
4 David Bowie
5 Estate
6 XIX
7 Goalkeeper
8 Slip
9 Sherlock Holmes
10 Shazam
11 Every seven years
12 In a lamp
13 Franciscans
14 Sage (Scientific Advisory Group for Emergencies)
15 *Deception Point* (2001)
16 *Jaws*
17 Bubble gum
18 Marie Antoinette
19 1920s (1923)
20 Sir Elton John

What are the names of these pasta shapes?

Easy

1

2

3

4

Medium

5

6

7

8

Hard

Answers to QUIZ 60 – Music

1	Jazz	**11**	Semibreve
2	1990s (1999)	**12**	The violin
3	*The Sound of Music*	**13**	*Massachusetts*
4	Percussion	**14**	Kid Creole and the Coconuts
5	*Abbey Road*	**15**	Strings
6	Country music	**16**	Kraftwerk
7	*Kung Fu Fighting* (Carl Douglas)	**17**	Foreigner
8	Three	**18**	Metal
9	Guitar	**19**	Britpop
10	*Dreams*	**20**	Ebony

ANSWERS ON PAGE 65

1   Which band did Sir Paul McCartney form after The Beatles?

2   What two flavours are in the soft drink Sprite®?

3   The fashion house Max Mara was founded in which country?

4   How many sisters does Bart Simpson have?

5   Who won the Best Actor Oscar in both 1994 and 1995?

6   Which religion is followed by the majority of the population in Iran?

7   What two colours are used for the poles in slalom skiing?

8   Which two words that differ only by their first letter mean "look at closely" and "turn suddenly"?

9   BG is the international car registration for which European country?

10 What name is given to a baby koala?

11 Which of these artists was born first: Cézanne, Gauguin or Seurat?

12 In TH White's novel *The Sword in the Stone*, who does the young character Wart become?

13 Which UK prime minister said "Democracy is the worst form of Government, except for all those other forms that have been tried from time to time"?

14 Which Swiss hero was required to shoot an apple from his son's head with a crossbow?

15 Julian Kirrin is the oldest member of which group in a series of children's novels?

16 In which TV crime series did Philip Michael Thomas play Rico Tubbs?

17 Which rugby union team is nicknamed the "Baa Baas"?

18 On which day of the year did the first two Die Hard films take place?

19 What name is given to the study of general questions of existence?

20 What number is obtained by subtracting the number of hours in five days from the number of seconds in five minutes?

Easy
Medium
Hard

Answers to QUIZ 61 – Pot Luck

1	Gravity	11	Amethyst (February)
2	800 miles (840 miles)	12	Carbon copy
3	Edwina Currie	13	The Savoy Hotel
4	Hieroglyphics	14	Duke Ellington
5	*The Wizard of Oz*	15	*Sesame Street*
6	Susan Calman	16	John
7	1930s (1932)	17	Parking
8	Lady Macbeth	18	A staircase
9	Barry McGuigan	19	Western Australia
10	*Diamonds are Forever*	20	High jump

Easy

1 Who succeeded Joe Schmidt as the head coach of Ireland's rugby union team?

2 Manchester City FC and which Midlands football club are nicknamed "the Sky Blues"?

3 What do the letters "GD" stand for in the netball position?

4 In which athletics team event do competitors pass on a baton?

5 What colour is the number 1 in the current Formula 1 logo?

6 St Mirren FC is based in which Scottish town?

7 What two colours are the stripes on the shirts of American football referees?

8 Which of these sports was invented first: baseball, basketball or volleyball?

9 The final of the 2020 Women's T20 Cricket World Cup was held in which city?

10 Which sport would you be watching if you were at a Chicago Bulls game?

11 Who captained England during the 2019 Ashes series?

Medium

12 How many disciplines comprise the men's all-round team gymnastics competition at the Olympic Games?

13 Which team cycling event takes its name from the New York venue at which it was first held?

14 Bowls players must stand on what to deliver a bowl on a green?

15 Which ice hockey manoeuvre is not permitted in the women's game?

16 What is the maximum number of rowers in a sculling team in an Olympic event?

17 Indoor hockey balls are usually what colour?

18 Sevens is a form of which team sport?

19 Which English football club is nicknamed "The Hornets"?

20 Which team was runner-up in the 2019 Super League final?

Hard

Answers to QUIZ 62 – Pasta Shapes

1 Farfalle
2 Radiatore
3 Penne
4 Rigatoni
5 Ravioli
6 Conchiglie
7 Fusilli
8 Cannelloni

1   In the song *The Twelve Days of Christmas*, how many swans were a-swimming?

2   What type of animal is a chinchilla?

3   What was the name of the diner in the TV series *Happy Days*?

4   Which term means to forcefully enlist a person into the army or navy?

5   In which New Testament Gospel is the Sermon on the Mount?

6   What is a punnet?

7   Which writer wrote in a cable, "The reports of my death are greatly exaggerated"?

8   What is the name of the baby associated with Popeye?

9   Which Rodgers and Hammerstein musical is set in the US military during WWII?

10 Is an ectomorph thin or plump?

11 Which Scottish football team was nicknamed "the Lisbon Lions" after its European Cup success in 1967?

12 What was the most popular name for a baby girl in the UK in 2019: Amelia, Olivia or Sophie?

13 Who succeeded Jeremy Hunt as UK Health Secretary?

14 According to the proverb, what is it better to be safe than?

15 What was Strawberry Field, John Lennon's inspiration for the song *Strawberry Fields Forever*?

16 Who played lawyer Frank Galvin in the 1982 film *The Verdict*?

17 Which poetical characters were married by the turkey who lives on the hill?

18 What is Bloomingdale's?

19 In Spanish cuisine, what is *pollo*?

20 The 1908 Olympics were moved to London from Rome following which natural event?

Easy

Medium

Hard

Answers to QUIZ 63 – Pot Luck

1	Wings	11	Cézanne (1839)
2	Lemon and lime	12	King Arthur
3	Italy	13	Sir Winston Churchill
4	Two (Lisa and Maggie)	14	William Tell
5	Tom Hanks (*Philadelphia* and *Forrest Gump*)	15	The Famous Five
6	Islam	16	*Miami Vice*
7	Blue and red	17	The Barbarians
8	Peer and veer	18	Christmas Eve
9	Bulgaria	19	Philosophy
10	A joey	20	180 (300 – 120)

Easy

1   In the title of the 1850s song, what colour hair does Jeanie have?

2   Who co-starred with Andie MacDowell in the 1990 film *Green Card*?

3   What colour is the chemical curcumin, found in turmeric?

4   Before 2004, what colour was used in wiring to indicate the neutral wire?

5   What is the natural colour of unripe coffee beans?

6   What colour is the alcoholic drink Jägermeister?

7   The name of which colour is given to the fat found in newborn babies that helps them make heat?

8   What colour envelope, symbolising luck, is it traditional to send at Chinese New Year?

9   An animal of which colour is often used to represent depression?

10 Who said "Any customer can have a car painted any colour that he wants so long as it is black"?

11 Fire exit signs in the UK are usually what colour?

12 A football referee uses cards of which two colours to discipline players?

13 What colour is the "e" in the Google logo?

14 What colour is the writing on the British Airways logo?

15 Which colour lies between yellow and blue in a rainbow?

16 Musically, what colour links a song by Coldplay with the Beatles' submarine?

17 What colour are the animated film creatures the Minions?

18 A Rhode Island Red is a breed of which animal?

19 Which three colours are on the Jamaican flag?

20 What colour flag is waved in surrender?

Medium

Hard

Answers to QUIZ 64 – Team Sports

1	Andy Farrell	11	Joe Root
2	Coventry City FC	12	Six
3	Goal defence	13	Madison
4	Relay race	14	A mat
5	Red	15	Body checking
6	Paisley	16	Four
7	Black and white	17	White
8	Baseball (1845)	18	Rugby union
9	Melbourne	19	Watford FC
10	Basketball	20	Salford Red Devils

1. "Once I had a love and it was a gas" is the opening line from which song?
2. What is the name of Joe McGann's *Hollyoaks* character?
3. What single word can precede "city", "sanctum" and "tube" to make three phrases?
4. In *The Wind in the Willows*, what disguise did Mr Toad adopt to escape from prison after being convicted of car theft?
5. Which historical character was Kenneth Williams playing when he delivered the line "Infamy! Infamy, they've all got it in for me!"?
6. Which of these elements has the highest atomic number: calcium, lithium or gold?
7. Conga music originated in which country?
8. Who released the 2011 single *Born This Way*?
9. For what is the company Cammell Laird known?
10. Which Welsh boxer retired in 2009 with an undefeated record in 46 bouts?
11. Who wrote the music and lyrics to the 1970 musical *Company*?
12. What vehicle acted as a den for the gang in the children's TV series *Here Come the Double Deckers*?
13. If someone is described as ebullient, are they lively or subdued?
14. Which 2001 starred Reese Witherspoon as Elle Woods?
15. The character of Freddy Eynsford-Hill appears in which musical?
16. Was the tyrannosaurus a carnivore or a herbivore?
17. The Dome of the Rock is a shrine in which religion?
18. By what means did barges originally move?
19. In which English city is the National Football Museum?
20. What does a stale egg do when dropped into water?

Easy

Medium

Hard

Answers to QUIZ 65 – Pot Luck

1	Seven	11	Celtic FC
2	Rodent	12	Olivia
3	Arnold's	13	Matt Hancock
4	Press-gang	14	Sorry
5	Gospel of Matthew	15	A (Salvation Army) children's home
6	A small basket or box (for fruit)	16	Paul Newman
7	Mark Twain	17	The Owl and the Pussycat
8	Swee' Pea	18	A US department store chain
9	*South Pacific*	19	Chicken
10	Thin	20	The eruption of Mount Vesuvius

Easy

1 How many legs did the Martian fighting machines have in *The War of the Worlds*?

2 What was the title of the final film in the main Star Wars series, released in 2019?

3 Which Netflix series, first shown in 2016, is set in the fictional town of Hawkins, Indiana in the 1980s?

4 Which classic TV show started each episode with the words: "Space: the final frontier"?

5 Who played President James Dale in the 1996 film *Mars Attacks!*?

6 Walter Skinner was a character in which TV sci-fi series?

7 *Pigs in Space* was a sci-fi spoof that appeared as part of which TV show?

8 What was the name of Paul Darrow's character in the TV series *Blake's 7*?

9 Which Star Trek character returned to the small screen in a 2020 Netflix series?

10 The explosion of a particle accelerator at S.T.A.R. Labs forms the basis for which TV series?

Medium

11 What was the first name of Catherine Tate's *Doctor Who* character?

12 Which future Hollywood legend starred in the 1958 film *The Blob*?

13 *Dark of the Moon* was the subtitle of the 2011 film in which sci-fi franchise?

14 What was the title of the 2020 TV miniseries that starred Nick Offerman as the CEO of a tech company?

15 Which country provided Terry Gilliam with the title for a 1985 sci-fi film?

16 Who played Captain Jack Harkness in the series *Torchwood*?

17 Which 1990 sci-fi film, starring Julia Roberts and Kiefer Sutherland, was remade in 2017?

18 Who played Major Roy McBride in the 2019 sci-fi film *Ad Astra*?

19 Oscar Isaac played which Star Wars character?

20 Which sci-fi film featuring Will Smith was the highest-grossing film of 1996?

Hard

Answers to QUIZ 66 – Colours

1	Light brown	11	Green
2	Gérard Depardieu	12	Red and yellow
3	Yellow	13	Red
4	Black	14	Blue
5	Green	15	Green
6	Brown	16	Yellow
7	Brown	17	Yellow
8	Red envelope	18	Chicken
9	Black dog	19	Black, gold and green
10	Henry Ford	20	White flag

1. "In the dock of Tiger Bay and the road to Mandalay" are lyrics from which 1978 single?

2. What word can refer both to a wild horse and a make of Ford car?

3. In life, what is your métier?

4. Which religious exclamation translates as "praise ye the Lord"?

5. Which is the only Shakespeare play to feature the name of an animal in its title?

6. How old was Denis Compton when he became the youngest person to score a Test century?

7. What part of the human body is affected by ophthalmia?

8. Which book of the Bible has the shortest name?

9. In which US state is the Green Bay Packers American football team based?

10. Which duo hosted the 1997 to 1999 chat show *Light Lunch*?

11. In which decade were chairs for players introduced at the Wimbledon tennis championships?

12. In which Carry On film did Roy Castle play Captain Keene of the 3rd Foot and Mouth Regiment?

13. Which 2000s song was no. 1 in the UK first: *Dry Your Eyes*, *Gotta Get Thru This*, or *Leave Right Now*?

14. Wayne Rooney signed for Manchester United FC in 2004 from which other English club?

15. Which is the correct spelling: concensus, conscensus or consensus?

16. Sharwood's specialises in food ingredients from which continent?

17. The Isle of Portland is the southernmost point of which county?

18. In which Dan Brown novel did the character of Professor Robert Langdon first appear?

19. Which US political party, formed in 2006 and disbanded in 2012, was named after a protest that took place in 1773?

20. If a German wine is described as *Rotwein*, what colour is it?

Answers to QUIZ 67 – Pot Luck

1	*Heart of Glass* (Blondie)	11	Stephen Sondheim
2	Edward Hutchinson	12	A (London) bus
3	Inner	13	Lively
4	A washerwoman	14	*Legally Blonde*
5	Julius Caesar	15	*My Fair Lady*
6	Gold (79)	16	A carnivore
7	Cuba	17	Islam
8	Lady Gaga	18	Towed by a horse
9	Shipbuilding	19	Manchester
10	Joe Calzaghe	20	Float

1   After Sicily, what is the second largest island in the Mediterranean?

2   On which of New Zealand's islands is the city of Tauranga?

3   Magna Carta Island lies in which English river?

4   Who bought Necker Island in the late 1970s?

5   After which day of the week was Robinson Crusoe's island companion named?

6   Coney Island is part of which US city?

7   Eriskay and Scalpay are part of which island group?

8   The volcanic island of Krakatoa is situated in which country?

9   El Hierro and La Gomera are part of which island group?

10 Which of these islands has the smallest area: Madagascar, New Guinea or Sumatra?

11 Which group had a hit in 1979 with *Living on an Island*?

12 In which decade was the TV series *Fantasy Island* first broadcast?

13 The capital city of the Seychelles is named after which queen?

14 Which group of islands lie across the Pentland Firth from Caithness?

15 Which television crime series takes place on the fictional island of Saint Marie?

16 Does Cape Verde lie off the east coast or the west coast of Africa?

17 Hokkaido is the second-largest island in which country?

18 What word preceded *(Islands in the Stream)* in the title of the 2009 Comic Relief song?

19 The Cayman Islands lie in which body of water?

20 Which group of islands was named in honour of King Philip II of Spain?

Answers to QUIZ 68 – Science Fiction

1	Three	11	Donna (Noble)
2	*Star Wars: The Rise of Skywalker*	12	Steve McQueen
3	*Stranger Things*	13	Transformers
4	*Star Trek*	14	*Devs*
5	Jack Nicholson	15	Brazil
6	*The X-Files*	16	John Barrowman
7	*The Muppet Show*	17	*Flatliners*
8	(Kerr) Avon	18	Brad Pitt
9	Jean-Luc Picard (*Star Trek: Picard*)	19	Poe (Dameron)
10	*The Flash*	20	*Independence Day*

1 What is the name of Alan Halsall's *Coronation Street* character?

2 Which material is an anagram of "olive"?

3 As at 2020, Camp Nou is the largest stadium in which country?

4 Which of these playwrights was born first: Henrik Ibsen, Sir Terence Rattigan or TS Eliot?

5 The spirit ouzo originated in which country?

6 How many entrants are invited to take part in the 75th Hunger Games?

7 Which anniversary of VE Day was commemorated in 2020?

8 Proverbially, what can beggars not be?

9 What are the surnames of Richard and Judy?

10 Strax the Sontaran first appeared in which TV series?

11 In 1964, whom did Leonid Brezhnev succeed as leader of the Soviet Union?

12 The *Rutshire Chronicles,* the most recent of which was entitled *Mount!* (2016), is a series of novels by which author?

13 Sir Christopher Wren is buried in the crypt of which building?

14 In a game of American football, how many points are awarded for a field goal?

15 In which decade was the postal service split into first and second class in the UK?

16 Which relative was Red Riding Hood going to visit?

17 The term "seismic event" refers to what natural occurrence?

18 What type of building is the Colosseum in Rome?

19 Who was the sister of Laertes in Shakespeare's *Hamlet*?

20 *Food, Glorious Food* is a song from which musical?

Easy

Medium

Hard

Answers to QUIZ 69 – Pot Luck

1	*Hit Me with Your Rhythm Stick* (Ian Dury and the Blockheads)	11	1970s (1975)
2	Mustang	12	*Carry On Up the Khyber*
3	Your profession or talent	13	*Gotta Get Thru This* (Daniel Bedingfield, 2001)
4	Hallelujah	14	Everton FC
5	*The Taming of the Shrew*	15	Consensus
6	20 years old	16	Asia
7	The eye	17	Dorset
8	Job	18	*Angels & Demons* (2000)
9	Wisconsin	19	The Boston Tea Party
10	Mel Giedroyc and Sue Perkins	20	Red

ANSWERS ON PAGE 74

Easy

1   What type of juice is used to make a Piña colada cocktail?

2   How many children win golden tickets in *Charlie and the Chocolate Factory*?

3   Fruit Gums, Fruit Pastilles and Jelly Tots are sold under which brand name in the UK?

4   Ben Cohen and Jerry Greenfield founded a company producing which foodstuff?

5   Which Swiss chocolate has a distinctive triangular shape?

6   ANZAC biscuits are mainly eaten in which two countries?

7   What is the main component in the Neapolitan dessert cassata?

8   Created in 2013, a Cronut is a combination of which two food items?

9   Sponge fingers are also known by the name of which French room?

10   The Battenberg cake is named after a town in which country?

11   What do Americans call a toffee apple?

12   What is the English meaning of the name of the Italian dessert *panforte*?

Medium

13   The slogan "Made for sharing" has been used to advertise which brand of confectionery?

14   Which chocolate bar was advertised as having "A hazelnut in every bite"?

15   What were Starburst® sweets originally called?

16   Which company makes the Milk Tray selection of chocolates?

17   Pontefract, after which the liquorice cakes are named, is in which English county?

18   Which Scottish company is famous for its caramel wafer and teacake?

19   Which type of cake shares its name with a gauzy fabric?

20   What is added to chocolate to make a ganache?

Hard

Answers to QUIZ 70 – Islands

1	Sardinia	11	Status Quo
2	North Island	12	1970s (1977)
3	River Thames	13	Victoria
4	Sir Richard Branson	14	The Orkney Islands
5	Friday (Man Friday)	15	*Death in Paradise*
6	New York	16	The west coast
7	The Outer Hebrides	17	Japan
8	Indonesia	18	*Barry*
9	The Canary Islands	19	The Caribbean Sea
10	Sumatra (182,000 sq miles)	20	The Philippines

QUIZ 73 – Pot Luck

ANSWERS ON PAGE 75

1   What word for water vapour is an anagram of a word meaning "friends"?

2   According to the nursery rhyme, Old Mother Hubbard has what kind of pet?

3   In which type of building would the workers wear scrubs?

4   What is 11 squared?

5   Ricky Tomlinson played which character in *Brookside*?

6   What type of substance is affected by dry rot?

7   Who played the title character in the early series of *Taggart*?

8   What word can describe both something that is lit up and a decorated manuscript?

9   Olympic 1500m champion Sir John Walker represented which country?

10 Which album was released first: *Beatles for Sale*, *Please Please Me*, or *With the Beatles*?

11 In the name of the sporting body, for what does the "G" stand in PGA?

12 Jade Thirwell is a member of which girl group?

13 In Prokofiev's *Peter and the Wolf*, which instrument represents the cat?

14 The "Mexican wave" first became popular in 1986 at which sporting event?

15 How many land borders does Sweden have?

16 Which town is the administrative centre of Powys?

17 What relative to you is your father's brother's son?

18 Which is the longest river in Asia?

19 What colour is pak choi?

20 Chuck Noland, played by Tom Hanks, was the central character in which 2000 film?

Easy

Medium

Hard

Answers to QUIZ 71 – Pot Luck

1	Tyrone Dobbs	11	Nikita Khrushchev
2	Voile	12	Jilly Cooper
3	Spain	13	St Paul's Cathedral
4	Henrik Ibsen (1828)	14	Three
5	Greece	15	1960s (1968)
6	24	16	Her grandmother
7	75th anniversary	17	An earthquake
8	Choosers	18	An amphitheatre
9	Madeley and Finnigan	19	Ophelia
10	*Doctor Who*	20	*Oliver!*

Easy

1. In poker, what name is given to a hand containing three cards of one rank and two of another rank?

2. Which square is diagonally opposite Go on a traditional Monopoly™ board?

3. "Cavity Sam" is a character central to which children's electronic game?

4. What is the highest number card in a standard pack of playing cards?

5. Which chess piece starts the game in the square A1?

6. How many wedges are there on a Trivial Pursuit™ playing piece?

7. What number is obtained by adding 20 to the numbers either side of it on a dartboard?

8. Where was the hula hoop invented?

9. What is the title of the BBC2 series in which celebrities play games during dinner to decide who foots the bill?

Medium

10. How many points is the letter L worth in a game of Scrabble®?

11. What was the subtitle of the 2019 film in the Jumanji series?

12. In the traditional bingo call, what number is "Lucky"?

13. What game was the girl playing on the famous BBC Test Card first broadcast in 1967?

14. Which Cluedo® character was replaced by Dr Orchid in 2016?

15. Which card game takes its name from the Italian and Spanish for "one"?

16. In which decade was the game of Twister® invented?

17. How many dice are there in a set of poker dice?

18. If the person miming in a game of charades touches their earlobe, what does that indicate?

19. Which sewing aid is searched for in a traditional party game?

20. *Jelly Saga* and *Soda Saga* are versions of which video game?

Hard

Answers to QUIZ 72 – Sweet Things

1	Pineapple juice	11	Candy apple
2	Five	12	Strong bread
3	Rowntree's	13	Quality Street®
4	Ice cream	14	Topic
5	Toblerone®	15	Opal Fruits
6	Australia and New Zealand	16	Cadbury
7	Ice cream	17	West Yorkshire
8	A croissant and a doughnut	18	Tunnock's
9	Boudoir biscuits	19	Chiffon cake
10	Germany	20	Cream

1   The 2000 musical *Seussical* is based on the characters of which children's author?

2   In which county is the city of Ely?

3   What number do the Roman numerals XLIV represent?

4   The market town of Oswestry lies in which English county?

5   The 1980s TV series *The Colbys* was a spin-off from which US series?

6   Which fictional boxer had the nickname "The Italian Stallion"?

7   As at the end of 2019, how many times had Tiger Woods won The Masters golf championship?

8   *The Groovy Greeks* is part of which series of children's books?

9   Which football club plays in the derby known as *El Clásico* against FC Barcelona?

10 Who was the UK Leader of the Opposition from 2015 to 2020?

11 Which was the last Android operating system to be named after a sweet object?

12 Which fictional village takes its name from the two Welsh towns of Pontypridd and Tonypandy?

13 The East China Sea is part of which ocean?

14 What name for the American Mafia translates as "This thing of ours"?

15 In musical notation with treble clef, which note is written on the bottom line of a stave?

16 Who camped under the shade of a billabong tree in the song *Waltzing Matilda*?

17 What was the title of the 2011 film in the *Johnny English* series?

18 What type of drink would you expect to have a crema on top?

19 *Rumour Has It* was taken from which album by Adele?

20 Other than "chick", what name is given to the young of an eagle?

Easy

Medium

Hard

Answers to QUIZ 73 – Pot Luck

1	Steam (mates)	11	Golf
2	A dog	12	Little Mix
3	A hospital (operating theatre)	13	Clarinet
4	121	14	FIFA World Cup
5	Bobby (Grant)	15	Two (Finland and Norway)
6	Wood	16	Llandrindod Wells
7	Mark McManus	17	Cousin
8	Illuminated	18	The Yangtze River (3915 miles)
9	New Zealand	19	Green
10	*Please Please Me* (March 1963)	20	*Cast Away*

What are the names of these Scottish actors?

1

2

3

4

5

6

7

8

9

Answers to QUIZ 74 – Fun and Games

1	Full house	11	*Jumanji: the Next Level*
2	Free Parking	12	Seven
3	Operation	13	Noughts and crosses
4	Ten	14	Mrs White
5	Rook (or castle)	15	Uno
6	Six	16	1960s (1966)
7	26 (1 and 5)	17	Five
8	Hawaii	18	Sounds like
9	*I'll Get This*	19	A thimble (Hunt the thimble)
10	One point	20	*Candy Crush*

1 What would you be looking at if you were taking a Rorschach test?

2 Who played former naval captain Jonas Taylor in the 2018 film *The Meg*?

3 Who said "Ask not what your country can do for you, but what you can do for your country"?

4 Which of these Elvis albums was released first: *Blue Hawaii, GI Blues* or *Pot Luck*?

5 On which part of the body would a crampon be worn?

6 "Connecting People" is the slogan of which communications company?

7 In which 2019 film did Stephen Merchant play Deertz, a Gestapo agent?

8 What type of meat is used to make lardons?

9 Which famous cartoon character was born Marjorie Jacqueline Bouvier?

10 In which month is the Tour de France usually held?

11 What is the official language of Senegal?

12 In which decade was the tie-break first introduced at the Wimbledon tennis championships?

13 Which Shakespeare play includes the line: "The dogs of war"?

14 Ocular refers to which part of the body?

15 Which is the largest hot desert in the world?

16 The town of Frinton-on-sea is in which English county?

17 Jamie Oliver first appeared on television in a documentary about which London restaurant?

18 Which leader takes an oath to "preserve, protect and defend the Constitution" of their country?

19 What religion is followed by the majority of the population in Iceland?

20 What colour is the laughing cavalier's hat in the 1624 portrait by Frans Hals?

Easy

Medium

Hard

Answers to QUIZ 75 – Pot Luck

1	Dr Seuss	11	Pie
2	Cambridgeshire	12	Pontypandy (*Fireman Sam*)
3	44	13	The Pacific Ocean
4	Shropshire	14	Cosa Nostra
5	*Dynasty*	15	E
6	Rocky Balboa	16	A jolly swagman
7	Five (1997, 2001, 2002, 2005, 2019)	17	*Johnny English Reborn*
8	Horrible Histories	18	(Espresso) coffee
9	Real Madrid CF	19	21
10	Jeremy Corbyn	20	Eaglet

1. Introduced in 2017, what is a LISA in relation to finance?

2. In which decade was the 20p coin introduced in the UK?

3. How many sides are there on the pound coin introduced in 2017?

4. Which common type of loan has a name that comes from the French for "dead pledge"?

5. The catchphrase "It's fast and furious in the Ready Money round" was associated with which game show?

6. In which city does American Express have its headquarters?

7. In economics, what three-word term is given to the reduction in costs associated with producing more output?

8. According to the Beatles song, what can't money buy?

9. Doubloons were minted in which metal?

10. What is the minimum number of British coins needed to make up £3.68?

11. The price of oil is recorded in which currency?

12. What name is given to very severe inflation?

13. In which decade did sixpences cease to be legal tender in the UK?

14. On which English banknote did George Stephenson replace the Duke of Wellington in 1990?

15. Which tax briefly replaced rates in England and Wales in 1990?

16. What unit of currency is used by Libya, Jordan and Kuwait, amongst others?

17. In which city was the 2013 film *The Wolf of Wall Street* set?

18. The former bank Abbey National became part of which larger bank in 2004?

19. "So I went to the bank to see what they could do" is a lyric from which Simply Red song?

20. Which indoor sport featured in the 1986 film *The Color of Money*?

Answers to QUIZ 76 – Scottish Actors

1. David Tennant
2. Karen Gillan
3. James McAvoy
4. Sir Sean Connery
5. Gerard Butler
6. Ashley Jensen
7. Peter Capaldi
8. Kelly Macdonald
9. Iain Glen

1 "They call it a Royale with cheese" is a line from which 1994 film?

2 "Neddy" is a slang term for what type of animal?

3 In the USA, which frozen dessert is similar to sorbet?

4 What is the name of David and Victoria Beckham's daughter, born in 2011?

5 In which decade was the Intel® Corporation founded?

6 Which London rugby club has a shirt that is divided into four different-coloured quarters?

7 In 2019, Egan Bernal became the first Latin American winner of the Tour de France. Which country did he represent?

8 The most southerly point of which country lies in the province of Western Cape?

9 Which real-life brothers starred in the title roles in the 1989 film *The Fabulous Baker Boys*?

10 What word completes the phrase: "There are lies, damned lies and ___"?

11 How are eggs served in the dish Eggs Benedict?

12 Which former UK prime minister wrote the 2019 political memoir *For the Record*?

13 The name of which extinct creature means "fearful lizard"?

14 What nationality was the poet Robert Browning?

15 In the famous speech by Sir Winston Churchill, "The Few" belonged to which branch of the services?

16 Along with "Black's", which other colour appears in the name of a confectionery brand?

17 Who wrote the 2003 novel *Private Peaceful*?

18 What is the name of AFC Ajax's home stadium?

19 Kelvinside and Scotstoun are areas of which Scottish city?

20 In May 2020, who announced that she was stepping down as a team captain on the TV series *Celebrity Juice*?

Easy

Medium

Hard

Answers to QUIZ 77 – Pot Luck

1	Ink blots	11	French
2	Jason Statham	12	1970s (1971)
3	John F Kennedy	13	Julius Caesar
4	*GI Blues* (1960)	14	The eye
5	On the foot	15	The Sahara Desert
6	Nokia	16	Essex
7	*Jojo Rabbit*	17	The River Café
8	Bacon (or pork)	18	The US president
9	Marge Simpson	19	Christianity
10	July	20	Black

1   From which English port did the *Mayflower* sail to America?

2   Which half-sister of Edward VI became queen of England in 1553?

3   What word completes the name of the WWII campaign: ___ for Victory?

4   Florence Nightingale became famous for her nursing work during which war?

5   On which country did Japan declare war in 1914 on entering WWI?

6   Which battle is the centrepiece of Shakespeare's play *Henry V*?

7   Who founded the city of St Petersburg, in 1703?

8   The Volstead Act controlled the sale of which commodity during the 1920s in the USA?

9   In which century did Oliver Cromwell die?

10 In 1876, Alfred Johnson made the first recorded single-handed crossing of which expanse of water?

11 Which WWII naval battle occurred first: the Battle of Midway or the Battle of the Coral Sea?

12 Tenochtitlan was the capital city of which ancient empire?

13 Which two countries did the *Titanic* visit before it sank?

14 Which African republic was formed by freed American slaves?

15 Which spy held the position of Surveyor of the Queen's Pictures from 1945 to 1972?

16 In some cultures, the Copper Age came between the Stone Age and which other?

17 What was the name of Henry I's daughter, who fought her cousin Stephen for the throne of England?

18 Which ancient unit of measurement was based on the length of the forearm?

19 In which century was the original Geneva Convention signed, setting standards for humanitarian treatment during war?

20 Which former US president survived an assassination attempt in 1912 after a bullet passed through his glasses case and a thick wad of paper?

Answers to QUIZ 78 – Money

1	Lifetime ISA	11	US dollars
2	1980s (1982)	12	Hyperinflation
3	12	13	1980s (1980)
4	Mortgage	14	The £5 note
5	*Catchphrase* (Roy Walker)	15	The community charge ("poll tax")
6	New York	16	The dinar
7	Economies of scale	17	New York
8	Love	18	Santander
9	Gold	19	*Money's Too Tight (To Mention)*
10	Seven (£2, £1, 50p, 10p, 5p, 2p, 1p)	20	Pool

1   On which US series did *The Simpsons* begin, as a series of short films?

2   "Forget that boy I'm over it" is a lyric from which 2016 song?

3   Who composed the music to the 1930 song *I Got Rhythm*?

4   Chablis wine is made from which grape?

5   Which Central American country has a name that means "the saviour"?

6   In which film did Al Pacino play a character called Tony Montana?

7   What is a male dolphin called?

8   What is the main flavour of Mississippi mud pie?

9   Which Olympic tradition was reintroduced to the modern Summer Games in Amsterdam in 1928?

10 How old was Paralympic swimmer Ellie Simmonds when she was awarded the MBE, the youngest person to have been given this honour?

11 Which language was given equal status with English in Canada in the late 1960s?

12 What is a sepulchre?

13 What word can mean both "marriage" and "workers' guild"?

14 In which decade did the Indian city of Madras become officially known as Chennai?

15 The Battle of Mons took place during which conflict?

16 Which of these classic novels was published first: *For Whom the Bell Tolls*, *Oliver Twist* or *The Great Gatsby*?

17 What is the name of the city of Rome in Italian?

18 What, in mathematics, is defined as length without breadth?

19 In which decade did the World Wrestling Federation change its name to World Wrestling Entertainment?

20 In the New Testament, what was the name of the mother of John the Baptist?

Answers to QUIZ 79 – Pot Luck

1	*Pulp Fiction*	11	Poached
2	A donkey	12	David Cameron
3	Sherbet	13	Dinosaur
4	Harper Seven	14	English
5	1960s (1968)	15	The RAF
6	Harlequins	16	Green (Green & Blacks)
7	Colombia	17	Michael Morpurgo
8	South Africa	18	Johan Cruyff Arena (since 2019)
9	Beau and Jeff Bridges	19	Glasgow
10	Statistics	20	Holly Willoughby

ANSWERS ON PAGE 84

1 What are the three *Wyrd Sisters* in the title of the 1988 Discworld novel?

2 Which country was the inspiration for the continent of Xxxx?

3 In which decade was the first Discworld novel, *The Colour of Magic*, published?

4 Which character was introduced in *Guards! Guards!* as the captain of the City Watch?

5 The pale horse Binky belonged to which character?

6 What was the name of the barbarian leader in the 2001 novel *The Last Hero*?

7 Which character was noted for her use of headology?

8 What type of creature is Great A'Tuin?

9 The Ramtops are what type of geographical feature?

10 The Hogfather is the Discworld equivalent of which seasonal figure?

11 What is taught at the Unseen University?

12 What is the name of the most powerful book of magic on the Discworld?

13 Which 1990 novel is set on a hill called Holy Wood?

14 The Patrician presides over which fictional city?

15 The plot of the 1992 novel *Lords and Ladies* references events in which Shakespeare play?

16 Which worker at the Unseen University was transformed by magic into an orang-utan?

17 What type of animals are Berilia, Tubul, Great T'Phon, and Jerakeen, who carry the Discworld on their shoulders?

18 Jason, Neville, Shane and Shawn are amongst the children of which character?

19 Who is the title character of the fourth novel in the series, who becomes Death's apprentice?

20 What is the name of the inept wizard who features prominently in *The Colour of Magic* and appears in several other novels?

Answers to QUIZ 80 – History

1	Plymouth	11	The Battle of the Coral Sea (May 1942)
2	Mary I (Mary Tudor)	12	Aztec Empire
3	Dig	13	France and Ireland
4	The Crimean War	14	Liberia
5	Germany	15	Anthony Blunt
6	The Battle of Agincourt	16	The Bronze Age
7	Peter the Great	17	Matilda
8	Alcohol	18	Cubit
9	17th century (1658)	19	19th century (1864)
10	Atlantic Ocean	20	Theodore Roosevelt

1 To which food group does meat belong?

2 Which of these was made a city most recently: Leeds, Salisbury or Wells?

3 *Eternal Flame* was a 1989 hit for which group?

4 What word can mean both "to avoid eating" and "speedy"?

5 Fabien Galthié became the head coach of the national rugby union team of which country in 2020?

6 Where is a hock joint on a horse?

7 Which government meeting takes its name from the Cabinet Office Briefing Rooms?

8 How many golf majors are played in America?

9 The character of Phil Mitchell first appeared in *EastEnders* in which decade?

10 What was the first name of John Lennon's first wife?

11 Who played the lead role in the 1938 film *Angels with Dirty Faces*?

12 How many stripes are there on a tricolore flag?

13 Which character in *Charlie and the Chocolate Factory* is blown up to resemble a giant blueberry?

14 What is the name of the primary residence of the Emperor of Japan?

15 On a knitting pattern, for what does the letter p stand?

16 What is the second-longest river in Scotland?

17 The song *Never Smile at a Crocodile* is from which 1953 Disney film?

18 Which annual garden show has featured the Artisan Gardens since 2011?

19 Which country won the 2019 Eurovision Song Contest?

20 How many series of *Pop Idol* were made?

Easy

Medium

Hard

Answers to QUIZ 81 – Pot Luck

1	*The Tracey Ullman Show*	11	French
2	*Shout Out to My Ex* (Little Mix)	12	A tomb
3	George Gershwin	13	Union
4	Chardonnay	14	1990s (1996)
5	El Salvador	15	WWI
6	*Scarface* (1983)	16	*Oliver Twist* (1839)
7	A bull	17	Roma
8	Chocolate	18	A line
9	The Olympic Flame	19	2000s (2002)
10	14 years old	20	Elizabeth

1. What name is given to a young dolphin?

2. Which creature's name translates as "pig with spines"?

3. Belted Galloway is a breed of which types of creature?

4. Which small crustacean is noted for attaching itself to rocks and the bottom of boats?

5. A research and breeding centre for which animal is based in Chengdu in China?

6. To which class of creatures do salamanders belong?

7. How many wings does a dragonfly have?

8. A bantam is a small animal of what type?

9. Which insects can be army, carpenter or fire?

10. Which animal is used to describe a fall in the stock market?

11. Which type of fox has fur on the bottom of its paws?

12. How many legs does an adult tick have?

13. Which animal has the Latin name *Rattus norvegicus*?

14. What name is given to a creature that can live both on land and in water?

15. Which is the largest creature to live on land?

16. Does a crayfish live in fresh water or salt water?

17. To the nearest five, how many adult teeth does a rabbit usually have?

18. What is the more common three-word term for a raptor?

19. A bird's bill is known by what other name, beginning with the same letter?

20. What is the highest part of a horse called?

Easy

Medium

Hard

1 In which English county is there is a town with a French-derived name that means "chapel in the forest"?

2 Which is the only major motorway in Wales?

3 On the foot, what is a hallux valgus deformity more commonly called?

4 "Camelot" is often used to describe the presidency of which US politician?

5 Which drink was advertised as being "made in Scotland from girders"?

6 In the New Testament, the parable of the Prodigal Son appears in which gospel?

7 What word can go before "column", "committee" and "wheel" to form three phrases?

8 What was the name of the orang-utan in the 1978 film *Every Which Way But Loose*?

9 Who won the Best Group Brit award in 2020?

10 Which song was a UK Christmas no.1 first: *Can We Fix It?*, *Skyscraper* or *That's My Goal*?

11 How many Crocodile Dundee films did Paul Hogan make?

12 In which decade was tennis player Naomi Osaka born?

13 In Germany, "gymnasium" can refer to what type of establishment as well as a place to keep fit?

14 Which type of flatfish includes the name of a coastal town in the south-east of England?

15 Dennis Healey (Baron Healey) belonged to which political party?

16 What colour is the background of the label on a standard can of Heinz soup?

17 What type of transport is a Brompton?

18 In what sport did Sonia O'Sullivan compete?

19 *Little Things* and *Live While We're Young* were 2012 hits for which group?

20 In which century was the Trooping the Colour ceremony first performed?

Answers to QUIZ 83 – Pot Luck

1	Proteins	11	James Cagney
2	Leeds (1893)	12	Three
3	The Bangles	13	Violet (Beauregarde)
4	Fast	14	The Imperial Palace
5	France	15	Purl
6	In its leg	16	River Clyde
7	COBRA	17	*Peter Pan*
8	Three (The US Open, The PGA and The Masters)	18	Chelsea Flower Show
9	1990s (1990)	19	The Netherlands
10	Cynthia	20	Two

Easy

1 What was the subtitle of the 2019 *Shaun the Sheep* film?

2 What is the name of Ariel's fish best friend in *The Little Mermaid*?

3 Ray Romano voices Manny, a woolly mammoth, in which series of films?

4 What did Ralph break in the title of a 2018 film?

5 *Ratatouille* (2007) is mostly set in which European city?

6 Which of Snow White's Seven Dwarfs is alphabetically last?

7 What is the name of Marlin's wife in *Finding Nemo*?

8 In *Pinocchio*, the title character is told that he must be brave, truthful and unselfish in order to become what?

9 What is the name of the bloodhound dog featured in *Lady and the Tramp*?

10 *Frozen II* is set how many years after Elsa's coronation?

Medium

11 What is the name of the sultan's daughter in *Aladdin*?

12 The siblings Dash, Jack-Jack and Violet appear in which series of films?

13 What kind of animal is Wheezy, whom Woody meets in *Toy Story 2*?

14 Which African country are the animals shipped to in *Madagascar*?

15 Which 2008 film was set in the Valley of Peace?

16 *Fantastic Mr Fox* (2009) was based on a children's book by which author?

17 What colour is the *Monsters Inc* character Mike Wazowski?

18 The imaginary friend of Bing Bong appeared in which 2015 film?

19 Which Disney film had the tagline: "One Great Big ONEderful Motion Picture"?

20 Which 2016 film was set on the Polynesian island of Motunui?

Hard

Answers to QUIZ 84 – Animal World

1 A calf
2 Porcupine
3 Cattle
4 Barnacle
5 The giant panda
6 Amphibians
7 Four
8 Chicken
9 Ants
10 Bear
11 Arctic fox
12 Eight
13 The brown rat
14 Amphibian
15 (African) elephant
16 Fresh water
17 30 (28)
18 Bird of prey
19 Beak
20 Withers

1   The name of which station worker is an anagram of a type of written document?

2   Which two four-letter words that differ only by their first letter mean "a period of time" and "an ursine animal"?

3   What are the blue lines that occur in some cheese called?

4   Tumbling is part of which gymnastics event?

5   Which branch of psychology deals with thinking and perception?

6   Which group released their debut album first: The Beach Boys, The Rolling Stones or The Who?

7   In the James Bond books and films, the oo designation gives operatives a licence to do what?

8   Which sketch show featured the comedy serial *The Phantom Raspberry Blower of Old London Town*?

9   What colour flag is waved during a horse race to indicate that a serious incident has taken place?

10 What term is given to the practice of not assigning staff permanent desks in an office?

11 In the TV series *Dad's Army*, who played ARP warden William Hodges?

12 What is a brig on a ship used for?

13 The Fortnum & Mason department store is on which London thoroughfare?

14 Which letter on a computer keyboard is used for the copy command?

15 A hawfinch is what type of creature?

16 What colour are petit pois?

17 To what did the bingo call for the number ten change in July 2019?

18 In 1975, which was the first David Bowie single to reach no.1 in the UK charts?

19 The Mackenzie River flows through which country?

20 What word completes the title of the 2005 Black Eyed Peas hit: *Don't___*?

Answers to QUIZ 85 – Pot Luck

1	Derbyshire (Chapel-en-le-Frith)	11	Three
2	The M4	12	1990s (1997)
3	Bunion	13	(Secondary) school
4	John F Kennedy	14	Dover sole
5	Irn-Bru®	15	The Labour Party
6	Gospel of Luke	16	Red
7	Steering	17	A (folding) bicycle
8	Clyde	18	Athletics
9	Foals	19	One Direction
10	*Can We Fix It?* (Bob the Builder, 2000)	20	18th century (1748)

1   Townsville Airport is located in which country?

2   Which major US airline takes its name from a Greek letter?

3   In which decade was Ryanair founded?

4   What is the name of Italy's flag-carrying airline?

5   As at the end of 2019, which was London's least busy airport in terms of passenger numbers?

6   What name is given to someone who drives a dog sled?

7   Blackfriars London Underground station lies on the Circle Line and which other line?

8   In which century was the bicycle invented?

9   "I'm on my way, Driving at ninety down those country lanes" is a lyric from which 2017 song?

10   What is the national airline of Dubai?

11   RJ Mitchell (d.1937) designed which iconic WWII fighter plane?

12   Which two colours feature on the Ford car manufacturer's logo?

13   Between 1865 and 1896 in the UK, a motorcar was required to be preceded by a pedestrian waving what?

14   Is a poop deck at the fore or the stern of a ship?

15   Which form of transport has a name that derives from the Japanese for "human powered vehicle"?

16   The Tupolev Tu-144, which was first flown in 1968, was the Soviet Union's version of which plane?

17   In which decade was the Forth Road Bridge opened?

18   Who launched the Skytrain service between London and New York in 1977?

19   How many masts are there on a ketch?

20   What name is given to the part of a plane where the pilot sits?

Easy

Medium

Hard

Answers to QUIZ 86 – Animated Films

1	*Farmageddon*	11	Jasmine
2	Flounder	12	The Incredibles
3	Ice Age	13	Penguin
4	The Internet *(Ralph Breaks the Internet)*	14	Kenya
5	Paris	15	*Kung Fu Panda*
6	Sneezy	16	Roald Dahl
7	Coral	17	Green
8	A real boy	18	*Inside Out*
9	Trusty	19	*One Hundred and One Dalmatians*
10	Three	20	*Moana*

ANSWERS ON PAGE 91

1 Who was the last member to join the Beatles?

2 "Wax on, wax off" is a line from which 1984 film?

3 What are the three water signs of the zodiac?

4 The motor companies Kia and Hyundai are based in which country?

5 What type of instrument is a dulcimer?

6 Which of these Renée Zellweger films was released first: *Chicago*, *Cold Mountain* or *Jerry Maguire*?

7 What is the national flower of Wales?

8 In relation to events, "Expo" is short for which word?

9 Which European country is bordered only by Spain?

10 Which two four-letter words that differ only by their last letter mean "a young sheep" and "a light"?

11 Which country won the 2015 Rugby World Cup?

12 In which part of the British Isles do internet domain names end in .gg?

13 Which food writer hosts the Radio 4 panel show *Kitchen Cabinet*?

14 Who sang the wartime song (*There'll Be Bluebirds Over*) *the White Cliffs of Dover*?

15 What were the first names of the characters Bodie and Doyle in the TV series *The Professionals*?

16 The name of which philosopher is an anagram of "coasters"?

17 What name is used in America for the wing of a car?

18 In which sport do participants reach a faster speed, luge or skeleton?

19 *Songs of Experience* was a 2017 album by which band?

20 What were the names of the two main characters in the TV series *Peep Show*?

Answers to QUIZ 87 – Pot Luck

1	Porter (report)	11	Bill Pertwee
2	Year and bear	12	Holding prisoners
3	Veins	13	Piccadilly
4	Floor exercise	14	C
5	Cognitive psychology	15	A bird
6	The Beach Boys (1962)	16	Green (peas)
7	Kill	17	Boris's Den
8	*The Two Ronnies*	18	*Space Oddity*
9	Yellow	19	Canada
10	Hot-desking	20	*Lie*

What are the names of these sea creatures?

Easy

Medium

Hard

1

2

3

4

5

6

7

8

Answers to QUIZ 88 – Travel and Transport

1	Australia (Queensland)	11	Spitfire
2	Delta Airlines	12	Blue and white
3	1980s (1984)	13	A red flag
4	Alitalia	14	Stern
5	London City Airport	15	Rickshaw
6	Musher	16	Concorde
7	The District Line	17	1960s (1964)
8	19th century (1830s)	18	Sir Freddie Laker
9	*Castle on the Hill* (Ed Sheeran)	19	Two
10	Emirates	20	Cockpit

1 What is the first name of Robert Bathurst's *Cold Feet* character?

2 What word completes the title of Adele's 2012 single: *Set Fire to the ___*?

3 The letter J is in which position in the alphabet?

4 Which part of the body might be described as "forked" in someone who is deceitful?

5 Actor Sir Anthony Hopkins was born in which country of the UK?

6 Which crunchy vegetable is often served as a garnish with a Bloody Mary cocktail?

7 Hock wine is from which country?

8 Which two words that differ only by their first letter mean "airline journey" and "to ignore"?

9 Which of the following did not judge the first series of *The X Factor*: Gary Barlow, Louis Walsh or Sharon Osbourne?

10 In which 1967 film did Warren Beatty say "We rob banks"?

11 The Canary Islands lie in which expanse of water?

12 The story of Lot is told in which book of the Bible?

13 Do navel oranges usually have seeds?

14 What is the score in a game of tennis when the server has won the first three points of the game?

15 In the cartoon series *Tom and Jerry*, what colour was Jerry?

16 Manchego cheese is from which country?

17 What is a hawser?

18 What was the stage name of the lead singer of the Sex Pistols?

19 In 1962, which Sunday paper became the first to publish a colour supplement?

20 What is the official language of Honduras?

Answers to QUIZ 89 – Pot Luck

1	Sir Ringo Starr	11	New Zealand
2	*The Karate Kid*	12	Guernsey
3	Cancer, Scorpio and Pisces	13	Jay Rayner
4	South Korea	14	Dame Vera Lynn
5	A stringed instrument	15	Ray and William
6	*Jerry Maguire* (1996)	16	Socrates
7	The daffodil	17	Fender
8	Exposition	18	Luge
9	Portugal	19	U2
10	Lamb and lamp	20	Mark and Jeremy

Easy

Medium

Hard

1   Which Scottish island has a name meaning "shout"?

2   What word for a news article also means a loud noise, such as when a gun is fired?

3   *Sound of the Underground* was the 2003 debut album of which group?

4   For which astronomical object are you said to cry, if you want the impossible?

5   In which decade was a film version of Michael Frayn's play *Noises Off* released?

6   What type of vessels are said to make most noise?

7   The 2018 TV series *The Cry* was set in which country?

8   Who released the 2012 single *Call My Name*?

9   What number is called as "clickety-click" in traditional bingo?

10   "Me? I guess I was a shoulder to cry on" is a lyric from which 1984 song?

11   What colour murder is someone said to scream, if they are making a great fuss?

12   *Big Girls Don't Cry* was a 1962 hit for which group?

13   In which century did Edvard Munch paint *The Scream*?

14   Who released the 1983 single *Rebel Yell*?

15   In which decade was the pop group The Art of Noise founded?

16   What word for noise can also refer to an illegal money-making scheme?

17   What is the first name of Dame Julie Andrews' character in the film *The Sound of Music*?

18   Which two words that differ only by their last letter mean "head covering" and "owl noise"?

19   Who directed the first four films in the Scream franchise?

20   The Sound of Sleat lies off which coast of Scotland?

Easy

Medium

Hard

Answers to QUIZ 90 – Sea Life

1   Seahorse

2   Scallop

3   Octopus

4   Manta ray

5   Hammerhead shark

6   Walrus

7   Sea anemone

8   Bottlenose dolphin

1 Which gems are made of calcium carbonate?

2 What is 23 in Roman numerals?

3 The perfume Poison is made by which fashion house?

4 Which word for a grand residence originates from the name of a hill in Rome?

5 Which Stylistics song was a 1974 hit for Diana Ross and Marvin Gaye?

6 The Berlingo car model is manufactured by which company?

7 What did Jack break in the nursery rhyme *Jack and Jill*?

8 Which two letters link a luxury goods company and a UK insurance company?

9 Which 1980 comedy film followed an eventful journey from Los Angeles to Chicago?

10 *Open* (2009) was the autobiography of which tennis star?

11 The name of which angel is often applied to an innocent child?

12 Who co-starred with Eddie Murphy in the 1983 film *Trading Places*?

13 Nicolas Anelka first played in the Premier League for which football club?

14 Which of these John Grisham novels was published first: *The Appeal*, *The Firm* or *The Last Juror*?

15 How were Bree, Gaby, Lynette and Susan described in the title of a series first broadcast in 2004?

16 What term, much used in 2020, means the staying away from work for a period of time?

17 Kaley Cuoco played the character Penny in which sitcom?

18 With which meat is horseradish sauce traditionally served?

19 Which branch of geology deals with the study of fossils?

20 What is the nickname for the US state of Utah, which shares its name with a type of hairstyle?

Easy

Medium

Hard

Answers to QUIZ 91 – Pot Luck

1	David	11	Atlantic Ocean
2	*Rain*	12	Genesis
3	Tenth	13	No
4	The tongue	14	Forty-love
5	Wales	15	Brown
6	Celery stalk	16	Spain
7	Germany	17	A heavy rope (for mooring or towing a ship)
8	Flight and slight	18	Johnny Rotten
9	Gary Barlow	19	*The Sunday Times*
10	*Bonnie and Clyde*	20	Spanish

Easy

1 Which French art gallery has a large glass pyramid as its main entrance?

2 Which artist (d.1564) was known as "Il Divino"?

3 If a painting is trichromatic how many colours does it feature?

4 Which artist is associated with the New York studio known as The Factory?

5 What name is given to the craft of rolling paper, using a thin tool, to create decorative shapes?

6 In which UK city did the School of Art suffer a devastating fire in 2018?

7 What word can refer both to an artist's collection of work and a Government minister's area of responsibility?

8 In the art style "op art", for what word is "op" short?

9 What nationality was the artist William Holman Hunt (d.1910)?

10 The decorative washi tape originated in which country?

11 Which UK artist is famous for his works involving animals preserved in formaldehyde?

Medium

12 Gouache is a form of what type of paint?

13 By which name is the 18th-century Italian artist Giovanni Antonio Canal better known?

14 In which museum is the Venus de Milo displayed?

15 What type of oil is most commonly used in oil paint?

16 In which museum are the Raphael Rooms?

17 What name is given to a template that has a design cut from it, through which colour is applied to a surface?

18 How often does a Biennale art exhibition take place?

19 The art installation *Sunflower Seeds* was exhibited at which London gallery from 2010 to 2011?

20 The basis for which drawing medium is obtained by burning wood?

Hard

Answers to QUIZ 92 – Make Some Noise

1	Yell	11	Blue
2	Report	12	The Four Seasons
3	Girls Aloud	13	19th century (1893)
4	The Moon	14	Billy Idol
5	1990s (1992)	15	1980s (1983)
6	Empty vessels	16	Racket
7	Australia	17	Maria
8	Cheryl	18	Hood and hoot
9	66	19	Wes Craven
10	*Last Christmas* (Wham!)	20	The west coast

1 Who portrayed Detective Superintendent Stephen Fulcher in the 2019 TV series *A Confession*?

2 The character of JR Hartley, author of a book on fly fishing, appeared in an advertisement for which company?

3 CY is the international car registration for which country?

4 *The Lumberjack Song* is associated with which comedy group?

5 Which WWII veteran celebrated his 100th birthday in April 2020 having raised nearly £33 million for the NHS in the preceding weeks?

6 Which of these Russell Crowe films was released first: *A Beautiful Mind*, *Cinderella Man* or *Gladiator*?

7 What name is given to the young of a hedgehog?

8 *Stop the Cavalry* was a 1980 single by which singer?

9 To the nearest 25 miles, how long is the Grand Canyon?

10 The 1975 single *The Trail of the Lonesome Pine* was sung by which comedy duo?

11 What was the name of the girl in the TV series *Bagpuss*?

12 Which device that consists of a series of swinging spheres is named after the scientist who formulated the law of gravity?

13 The Body Shop was founded in which South Coast resort?

14 According to the proverb, what should you do before you leap?

15 What is the name of the theme park partly owned by Dolly Parton?

16 Which of the Great Lakes is alphabetically first?

17 Which French existentialist philosopher died in 1980?

18 In what type of building would you find a mihrab and a minbar?

19 Which explorer was *Walking with Elephants* in a 2020 Channel 4 series?

20 Which model of Ford car was named after an island in the Bay of Naples?

---

1   The Campaign for Nuclear Disarmament was founded in which decade?

2   Which UK record label shares its name with a stage in the development of a butterfly or moth?

3   The Wellcome Trust funds research in what area?

4   Who was the deputy leader of the Labour party from 2007 to 2015?

5   Somerville College was one of the first women-only colleges at which university?

6   Javier Pérez de Cuéllar (d.2020) was the Secretary-General of which organisation from 1981 to 1992?

7   In which century was the Met Office founded?

8   To which organisation did the members of *Dad's Army* belong?

9   What animal is featured on the logo of Lloyds Bank?

10 The International Court of Justice is situated in which European city?

11 In which decade did the London Stock Exchange allow women to be admitted to the floor?

12 The name of which fairy-tale character is used to describe an organisation that deserves to receive more attention?

13 Which organisation was associated with the former Bob-a-Job Week?

14 How many stripes are on the Adidas® logo?

15 The RHS gardens of Wisley are in which English county?

16 Which car company established its first European manufacturing plant in Sunderland in 1986?

17 The restaurant chain Taco Bell serves what type of food?

18 In which decade was the charity Help for Heroes founded?

19 Cadbury was founded near which city?

20 In relation to sport, for what do the initials ECB stand?

Answers to QUIZ 94 – Art and Crafts

1	The Louvre	11	Damien Hirst
2	Michelangelo	12	Watercolour
3	Three	13	Canaletto
4	Andy Warhol	14	The Louvre
5	Quilling	15	Linseed oil
6	Glasgow	16	The Vatican Museums
7	Portfolio	17	A stencil
8	Optical	18	Every two years
9	English	19	The Tate Modern
10	Japan	20	Charcoal

ANSWERS ON PAGE 99

1   In the song *The Twelve Days of Christmas*, what was given on the eleventh day?

2   Who was the runner-up on the 2020 UK series of *The Masked Singer*?

3   In what country was the philosopher Confucius born?

4   What colour is most wine from the Bordeaux region of France?

5   What is the name of Kim Kardashian's mother?

6   Who directed the 2019 film *The Gentlemen*?

7   In which county does the Glastonbury musical festival take place?

8   Who was the runner-up in the 2019 Wimbledon men's singles championship?

9   Which of these is the shortest mountain range: the Himalayas, the Rocky Mountains, or the Smoky Mountains?

10 A fire at Crossgill Farm occurred in which TV series in 1988?

11 Which ice cream product has been advertised to the tune of *O Sole Mio*?

12 What was missing from the title of *The Daily Mirror* from 1985 to 1987 and 1997 to 2002?

13 In which year was George W Bush first elected President of the USA?

14 What seasonal name is given to hidden messages or features inserted into computer software by developers?

15 The 1962 novel *Life at the Top*, by John Braine, was a sequel to which 1957 novel?

16 What word for part of a ship's hull is also used to mean "nonsense"?

17 *Anything for You* and 1-2-3 were 1988 hits for which singer?

18 In which decade did referees first use cards in English football matches?

19 Kabbalah is a discipline in which religion?

20 Who stabbed Caesar for the final time in the Shakespeare play *Julius Caesar*?

Answers to QUIZ 95 – Pot Luck

1	Martin Freeman	11	Emily
2	Yellow Pages	12	Newton's cradle
3	Cyprus	13	Brighton
4	Monty Python	14	Look
5	Tom Moore	15	Dollywood
6	*Gladiator* (2000)	16	Erie
7	Hoglet	17	Jean-Paul Sartre
8	Jona Lewie	18	A mosque
9	275 miles (277)	19	Levison Wood
10	Laurel and Hardy	20	Ford Capri

Easy

1   Which type of cleaner shares its name with a word for an empty space?

2   Which Christmas decoration derives its name from the French word for "a spark"?

3   What word can mean both a computer screen and "to keep a watch on"?

4   What are you, if you are discombobulated?

5   "Enemy" is an anagram of which country?

6   Which type of street gets its name from the French term for "bottom of a bag"?

7   What is the opposite of posterior?

8   The word "Teutonic" refers to which nationality?

9   What word describes a follower of St Augustine of Hippo?

10 What is meant by the French phrase *cri de coeur*?

11 What is a plethora?

12 A tetragram is a word with how many letters?

13 What name is given to either of the two words with the same meaning, for example: sad and glum?

Medium

14 What is the more common term for a groundnut?

15 If you do something postprandial, when do you do it?

16 Which is the correct spelling for an ecclesiastical rule: canon, cannon or cannonn?

17 What are you, if you are described as gauche?

18 Sororal refers to what type of relationship?

19 What is the word for a tune or jingle that stays in your head?

20 What is the humorous term used for Australian English?

Hard

Answers to QUIZ 96 – Organisations

1	1950s (1957)	11	1970s (1973)
2	Chrysalis	12	Cinderella
3	Health	13	The Scouts
4	Harriet Harman	14	Three
5	Oxford	15	Surrey
6	The United Nations	16	Nissan
7	19th century (1854)	17	Tex-Mex
8	The Home Guard	18	2000s (2007)
9	A (black) horse	19	Birmingham
10	The Hague	20	England and Wales Cricket Board

1 Which word in the radio phonetic alphabet is also a word for a mountain range?

2 What do the letters "WD" stand for in the netball position?

3 In the TV series *Belgravia*, what is the name of Philip Glenister's character?

4 Which food item provided Streetband with a novelty hit in 1978?

5 What is pappardelle?

6 Who played Charles Ingram in the 2020 miniseries *Quiz*?

7 What word can mean both "a game of golf" and "circular"?

8 The 2019 FA Community Shield was won by which team?

9 What is the word for a female alligator?

10 How many days are there in five weeks?

11 Which northern region of Italy lends its name to a type of poplar tree?

12 In which county is the town of King's Lynn?

13 *Have You Ever* was a 2001 UK no.1 hit for which group?

14 Which of the March sisters did Emma Watson play in the 2019 film *Little Women*?

15 What is the French name for a chocolate croissant?

16 In which English city was the first International Garden Festival held, in 1984?

17 Which comedian created the spoof superhero Cooperman?

18 What is the English translation of the title of the 1960 film *La Dolce Vita*?

19 Which of these Rolling Stones albums was released first: *Let It Bleed*, *Some Girls* or *Sticky Fingers*?

20 What was the first name of Baroness Margaret Thatcher's husband?

Easy

Medium

Hard

Answers to QUIZ 97 – Pot Luck

1	Pipers piping	11	Cornetto®
2	Jason Manford	12	The word "*Daily*"
3	China	13	2000
4	Red	14	Easter eggs
5	Kris Jenner	15	*Room at the Top*
6	Guy Ritchie	16	Bilge
7	Somerset	17	Gloria Estefan (with Miami Sound Machine)
8	Roger Federer	18	1970s (1976)
9	The Smoky Mountains (70 miles)	19	Judaism
10	*Emmerdale*	20	Brutus

Easy

1 Which fictional school has the motto "*Draco dormiens nunquam titillandus*" (Never tickle a sleeping dragon)?

2 The name of which fictional horror character is derived from the Latin for "little dragon"?

3 What was the name of the "Mother of Dragons" in the TV series *Game of Thrones*?

4 What is the name of the girl with the dragon tattoo in the novel and film of the same name?

5 What colour is the outside of a dragonfruit?

6 Who joined the *Dragons' Den* panel in 2019?

7 The character of Sybil Vimes (née Ramkin), breeder of swamp dragons, appears in which series of fantasy novels?

8 From which country does the dragon boat originate?

9 Which UK patron saint is reputed to have defeated a dragon?

10 What is a snapdragon?

Medium

11 What colour is the resin called dragon's blood?

12 In which decade was the martial arts film *Enter the Dragon* released?

13 What is the name of the magic dragon in the song by Peter, Paul and Mary?

14 How often does the Year of the Dragon occur in the Chinese zodiac?

15 Tiles featuring dragons are used in which oriental game?

16 A red dragon on a white and green background is the flag of which country?

17 Who provided the voice of the dragon Smaug in The Hobbit series of films?

18 Arthur Pendragon, nicknamed "Artie", appeared in the third film in which animated series?

19 What sport is played by the Catalan Dragons?

20 Which fictional serial killer was introduced in the 1981 novel *Red Dragon*?

Hard

Answers to QUIZ 98 – Words

1	Vacuum	11	A large amount
2	Tinsel (étincelle)	12	Four
3	Monitor	13	Synonym
4	Confused	14	Peanut
5	Yemen	15	After a meal
6	Cul-de-sac	16	Canon
7	Anterior	17	Clumsy, awkward
8	German	18	Sisterly
9	Augustinian	19	Earworm
10	Cry from the heart	20	Strine

1 In the classic video game, what colour is Pac-Man™?

2 Siobhan Fahey was a founding member of which girl group?

3 Elle Macpherson had a recurring role as Janine in which US sitcom?

4 Which meat product is advertised with the slogan "It's a bit of an animal"?

5 How many original members were there in the Beach Boys?

6 In politics, what two-word term is given to an adviser who is skilled in public relations?

7 Which 2020 TV series took its name from the branch of mathematics that deals with calculating angles and side lengths of triangles?

8 What single word can follow "financial", "light" and "new" to make three phrases?

9 Which player in a football team traditionally wears the number one shirt?

10 What type of instrument is a tabor?

11 What name is given to the ropes that support the masts and sails on a boat?

12 In which decade was Cobra Beer first produced?

13 Which 1956 film, starring Burt Lancaster, shares its name with a legal drama of 1997 starring Matt Damon?

14 Which horse won the virtual Grand National in April 2020?

15 In the traditional bingo call, what number is "Tickety-boo"?

16 What type of drink is Maxwell House™?

17 The islands of Trinidad and Tobago lie in which sea?

18 Mr and Mrs Tweedy are the farm owners in which 2000 animated film?

19 *Weihnachten* is the German word for which festive season?

20 In which decade was the telegram service discontinued in the UK?

Answers to QUIZ 99 – Pot Luck

1	Sierra	11	Lombardy
2	Wing defence	12	Norfolk
3	James Trenchard	13	S Club 7
4	*Toast*	14	Meg
5	Pasta	15	*Pain au chocolat*
6	Matthew Macfadyen	16	Liverpool
7	Round	17	Russ Abbot
8	Manchester City FC	18	The Sweet Life
9	Cow	19	*Let It Bleed* (1969)
10	35	20	Denis

1   The James Webb Space Telescope is set to succeed which famous astronomical device?

2   Are sunspots hot regions or cold regions on the Sun?

3   Which planet is named after the Roman goddess of beauty?

4   The Sun predominantly consists of which gas?

5   The Starlink satellite constellation is being constructed by which company?

6   In which decade did Svetlana Savitskaya become the first woman to perform a spacewalk?

7   What was the name of the first space shuttle to be launched, in 1981?

8   Which planet shares its name with a metallic element?

9   In astronomy, what name is given to a small body that orbits a larger one?

10 What is the second brightest object in the night sky after the Moon?

11 Which constellation famously has a belt?

12 The Galactic space tourism company was founded as part of which business group?

13 For what do the initials UFO stand?

14 17th-century astronomer Johannes Kepler published how many laws of planetary motion?

15 What is the literal meaning of the word "asteroid"?

16 On the Moon, what is a crater?

17 As at 2020, which planet of the solar system has 14 known moons?

18 In which year was the first spacewalk carried out, by cosmonaut Alexei Leonov?

19 Which planet lies between Earth and Jupiter?

20 Alphabetically, which is the penultimate planet of the solar system?

Answers to QUIZ 100 – Here Be Dragons

1	Hogwarts	11	Red
2	Dracula	12	1970s (1973)
3	Daenerys Targaryen	13	Puff
4	Lisbeth Salander	14	Every 12 years
5	Pink	15	Mahjong
6	Sara Davies	16	Wales
7	The Discworld	17	Benedict Cumberbatch
8	China	18	Shrek
9	St George	19	Rugby league
10	A flower (of the genus Antirrhinum)	20	Hannibal Lecter

ANSWERS ON PAGE 105

1 Tim Paine became the captain of which international cricket team in 2018?

2 Which celebrity won *Strictly Come Dancing* in 2019?

3 The name of which Germanic tribe is used as a term for people who indulge in wanton destruction?

4 Which duo starred in the 2020 series *Hitmen*?

5 The 1966 FIFA World Cup Final was held at which English stadium?

6 Which poet (d.1965) had the nickname "Old Possum"?

7 Casey Jones was associated with which train?

8 What is the official language of the Ivory Coast?

9 Aunt Hilda and Aunt Zelda appeared in which TV series?

10 How was Josey Wales described in the title of a 1976 film?

11 "Gully" and "slip" are positions in which sport?

12 Who played Samantha Jones in *Sex and the City*?

13 In which country was the Hunger Games author Suzanne Collins born?

14 Which artist had an *Art Club* on Channel 4 in 2020?

15 Which colour ring is horizontally between the blue ring and the red ring on the Olympic flag?

16 2019 marked which anniversary of the fall of the Berlin Wall?

17 What is the lowest number playing card used for the game of bezique?

18 Which Hertfordshire town is named after the first English saint?

19 The surname of which music producer accompanied Aitken and Waterman in the 1980s and 1990s?

20 In which country did the lambada dance originate?

Answers to QUIZ 101 – Pot Luck

1	Yellow	11	Rigging
2	Bananarama	12	1980s (1989)
3	*Friends*	13	*The Rainmaker*
4	Peperami	14	Potter's Corner
5	Five	15	62
6	Spin doctor	16	(Instant) coffee
7	*Trigonometry*	17	Caribbean Sea
8	Year	18	*Chicken Run*
9	The goalkeeper	19	Christmas
10	A (small) drum	20	1980s (1982)

Easy

Medium

Hard

Easy

What are the names of these flowers?

1

2

3

4

Medium

5

6

7

8
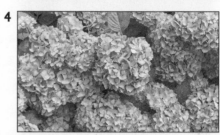

Hard

Answers to QUIZ 102 – Space

1	The Hubble Telescope	11	Orion
2	Cold regions	12	Virgin
3	Venus	13	Unidentified Flying Object
4	Hydrogen (over 70% by mass)	14	Three
5	SpaceX	15	Star-like
6	1980s (1984)	16	A large depression in the surface
7	*Columbia*	17	Neptune
8	Mercury	18	1965
9	Satellite (or moon)	19	Mars
10	Venus	20	Uranus

QUIZ 105 – Pot Luck

ANSWERS ON PAGE 107

1   "Into this house we're born, Into this world we're thrown" is a lyric from which 1970 song?

2   Who played the title role in the 2020 TV series *Batwoman*?

3   Which of these classic novels was published first: *Gulliver's Travels*, *Mary Poppins* or *Peter Pan*?

4   What is the par for a short hole in tournament golf?

5   Which Soviet leader expelled Leon Trotsky from the Communist Party in 1927?

6   How many clubs compete in the rugby Super League?

7   What name is given to the change of a traditionally working-class area as a result of more affluent people taking up residence?

8   What shape is a jib on a boat?

9   Who presented the 2020 series *A Country Life for Half the Price*?

10 What is a loggia?

11 In which decade was the Humber Bridge opened?

12 What song title (with different lyrics) was a hit for both Dolly Parton and Sheena Easton in 1980?

13 For what do the letters CB stand in the communication method of CB radio?

14 Which group released the 1983 single *Many Rivers to Cross*?

15 Coco Hernandez was a character in which 1980s film and TV series?

16 Which animal is used to advertise Duracell® batteries?

17 The remains of the settlement of Old Sarum lie in which English county?

18 What is the background colour of the Australian flag?

19 Which US activity was the origin of the ra-ra skirt?

20 What nationality was the philosopher Niccolò Machiavelli?

Easy

Medium

Hard

Answers to QUIZ 103 – Pot Luck

1	Australia	11	Cricket
2	Kelvin Fletcher	12	Kim Cattrall
3	Vandals	13	USA
4	Mel Giedroyc and Sue Perkins	14	Grayson Perry
5	Wembley	15	Black
6	TS Eliot	16	30th anniversary
7	*The Cannonball Express*	17	Seven
8	French	18	St Albans
9	*Sabrina the Teenage Witch*	19	Stock
10	*Outlaw (The Outlaw Josey Wales)*	20	Brazil

Easy

1   The musical *Six*, first performed in 2017, features the wives of which monarch?

2   The Duke of Albany is married to Goneril in which Shakespeare play?

3   What does the French term "encore", sometimes shouted at the end of a performance, translate to in English?

4   Which cupboard lends its name to the collection of costumes required for a performance?

5   Which *Strictly Come Dancing* judge has played Miss Hannigan in tours of the musical *Annie*?

6   What name is given to a piece of music that is played between acts or scenes of an opera or play?

7   Act 1 of *The Nutcracker* opens on which seasonal date?

8   Which part of a theatre shares its name with the name of a band formed in 1971?

9   Which of these musicals was performed first: *Cats*, *Jesus Christ Superstar* or *The Phantom of the Opera*?

10   Which former politician wrote the 1987 play *Beyond Reasonable Doubt*?

Medium

11   What nationality was the playwright Neil Simon?

12   Who starred in the lead role in the original London production of *Barnum*?

13   What does one actor do to mask another?

14   *Revolting Children* is a song from which musical?

15   What name is given to the illumination cast on someone performing a solo?

16   Which Asian city links the musicals *Chess* and *The King and I*?

17   The dance competition the Prix de Lausanne takes its name from a town in which country?

18   In a theatre company, what name is given to a person who prepares to act a main part if necessary?

19   *Close Every Door* is sung by the title character in which musical?

20   What name is given to the full text of a play?

Hard

Answers to QUIZ 104 – Flowers

1   Foxglove
2   Tulip
3   Fuchsia
4   Hydrangea
5   Lily
6   Lupin
7   Rose
8   Crocus

1   At what age does someone become an octogenarian?

2   The character Ian Beale first appeared in *EastEnders* in which year?

3   Semaphore using flags was first adopted in which century?

4   What is the occupation of David Bowie's Major Tom?

5   The company Ray-Ban™ is best known for what accessory?

6   Roy Batty, played by Rutger Hauer, was a character in which classic 1982 sci-fi film?

7   Which 1976 single was ABBA's only US chart-topper?

8   How many hours are there in three days?

9   Harold Macmillan (First Earl of Stockton) died in which decade?

10 On what are you said to sit if you are undecided about something?

11 Commentator Harry Carpenter (d.2010) was particularly associated with which sport?

12 Who wrote and starred in the 2020 TV series *I May Destroy You*?

13 Which TV series featured a private detective who had a radio show on Radio West?

14 Malcolm McDowell played Alex DeLarge in which 1970s film?

15 *So What* was a hit for which female singer in 2008?

16 Bayeux, famous for its tapestry, is in which country?

17 Which country won the men's 4 x 100m and the 4 x 400m relay finals at the 2019 World Athletics Championship?

18 The River Medway opens into which estuary?

19 Osborne House on the Isle of Wight was built for which monarch?

20 To what does the word "nautical" relate?

Easy

Medium

Hard

Answers to QUIZ 105 – Pot Luck

1	*Riders on the Storm* (The Doors)	11	1980s (1981)
2	Ruby Rose	12	9 to 5
3	*Gulliver's Travels* (1726)	13	Citizens' Band
4	Three	14	UB40
5	Joseph Stalin	15	*Fame*
6	12	16	A rabbit
7	Gentrification	17	Wiltshire
8	Triangular (a sail)	18	Blue
9	Kate Humble	19	Cheerleading
10	A covered area on the side of a building	20	Italian

1   In which decade was the card game Top Trumps launched?

2   What is a top-knot?

3   The name of which vehicle precedes "top" to make the name of a knitted garment?

4   In musical notation with the treble clef, which note is written on the top line of a stave?

5   Which animated pair ran the business Top Bun in the film *A Matter of Loaf and Death*?

6   What approach is the opposite of top-down?

7   "Such a feeling's coming over me" is the opening line to which 1972 single?

8   Which 1986 film was set at the Naval Air Station Miramar?

9   The singing group The Four Tops was formed in which city?

10 Elizabeth Moss played detective Robin Griffin in which TV series?

11 Topeka is the capital of which US state?

12 *Shout to the Top!* was a 1984 hit for which group?

13 Which kitchen appliance might be known as a top-loader?

14 The name of which alloy follows "top" to make a familiar name for military leaders?

15 In which decade was the TV series *Top Gear* originally broadcast?

16 Topman is part of which retail group?

17 In which capital city is the Topkapi Palace?

18 The greeting "the top of the morning" is associated with people from which island?

19 Topside is a cut of which meat?

20 In which decade was *Top of the Pops* first broadcast?

Answers to QUIZ 106 – On Stage

1	Henry VIII	11	American
2	*King Lear*	12	Michael Crawford
3	Again	13	Move to stand between the other actor and the audience
4	Wardrobe		
5	Craig Revel Horwood	14	*Matilda*
6	Intermezzo (or entr'acte)	15	Spotlight
7	Christmas Eve	16	Bangkok
8	Wings	17	Switzerland
9	*Jesus Christ Superstar* (1971)	18	Understudy
10	Jeffrey Archer	19	*Joseph and the Amazing Technicolor Dreamcoat*
		20	Script

1   What is the first name of Stephen Mangan's character in the TV series *The Split*?

2   Björn Again is a tribute act to which group?

3   What number do the Roman numerals LXVIII represent?

4   In which decade was the electronic camera flash invented?

5   How many own goals were scored at the 2018 FIFA World Cup, surpassing the previous record of six?

6   *Always and Forever* was a 1976 hit for which group?

7   The Rollright Stones cross the borders of which two counties?

8   Which of these films was released first: *Dante's Peak*, *The Day After Tomorrow* or *The Poseidon Adventure*?

9   In which sport are matches divided into chukkas?

10 Which people invaded England in 1066?

11 Carl, Ian and Lip were amongst the children of which *Shameless* character?

12 Michael Jordan (b.1963) is associated with what sport?

13 What relation was Elizabeth I to Henry VIII?

14 Which comedian created the character of DJ Delbert Wilkins?

15 In which decade was the New Labour branding first used?

16 Which whistleblower copied classified information from the US National Security Agency in 2013?

17 In which Australian state is the headquarters of Qantas Airways?

18 What colour were the Meanies in the Beatles film *Yellow Submarine*?

19 What name is given to the Moon when it is closest to the Earth and appears larger than usual?

20 How many of the Isles of Scilly are inhabited?

Easy

Medium

Hard

Answers to QUIZ 107 – Pot Luck

1	80	11	Boxing
2	1985	12	Michaela Coel
3	19th century (1866)	13	*Shoestring*
4	Astronaut	14	*A Clockwork Orange*
5	Sunglasses	15	Pink
6	*Blade Runner*	16	France
7	*Dancing Queen*	17	The USA
8	72	18	The Thames Estuary
9	1980s (1986)	19	Queen Victoria
10	The fence	20	Ships and sailing

Easy

1 Which word describes bread made without yeast?

2 Butterfly is a technique in which sport?

3 Which Greek bread is pocket-shaped?

4 Which brand of bread was advertised by a man pushing a bicycle up a very steep hill?

5 Who was the sister of Adrian, Billy, Jack and Joey in the sitcom *Bread*?

6 "Just to let me down (let me down) and mess me around" is a lyric from which song?

7 Bread sauce is traditionally served at which festive meal?

8 The name of which snack provided Hot Butter with a hit in 1972?

9 The restaurant Breadstix featured in which US TV series?

10 Buttermere is a lake in which English county?

11 In which country is the opera *Madame Butterfly* set?

12 Butterscotch is a variety of what type of sweet?

Medium

13 Bread and which other item are taken at Holy Communion in the Christian church?

14 Which spice is traditionally added to bread and butter pudding?

15 What part of an animal is the sweetbread?

16 The song *I'm Called Little Buttercup* appears in which Gilbert and Sullivan operetta?

17 What is the French term for butter sauce?

18 What colour is a butter bean?

19 What word completes the phrase: "Bread is the staff of ___"?

20 The band Bread was formed in which decade?

Answers to QUIZ 108 – At the Top

1	1970s (1978)	11	Kansas
2	A hairstyle	12	The Style Council
3	Tank	13	Washing machine
4	F	14	Brass
5	Wallace and Gromit	15	1970s (1977)
6	Bottom-up	16	Arcadia
7	*Top of the World* (The Carpenters)	17	Istanbul
8	*Top Gun*	18	Ireland
9	Detroit	19	Beef
10	*Top of the Lake*	20	1960s (1964)

1 Sócrates (d.2011) was a star in which sport?

2 To which class of creatures do tortoises belong?

3 Which sign of the zodiac is an anagram of "raise"?

4 How much longer is a football match than a rugby union match?

5 Kurt Waldheim was the president of which European country from 1986 to 1992?

6 A film of which period drama TV series, last aired in 2015, was released in 2019?

7 In which winter sport are tee lines and hog lines marked on the playing surface?

8 Voiced by Dominic West and Idris Elba, what type of creatures are Flook and Rudder in *Finding Dory*?

9 In the English version of Scrabble®, how many "W" tiles are there?

10 Which TV presenter hosts the podcast *Happy Place*?

11 During the English Civil War, a Royalist was a supporter of which king?

12 What is the name of Jaye Jacobs' *Holby City* character?

13 Which Madness single was the group's only no.1 hit in the UK?

14 The French abbreviation *Mme* is short for which form of address?

15 For what was Charles Blondin (d.1897) famous?

16 Who released the 2019 album *Heavy is the Head*?

17 What is the name of a shape in which all four sides are the same length with no right angles?

18 Which Scandinavian country calls itself "the country of a thousand lakes"?

19 How many spots are there on two dice?

20 What is the name of the newsagent's in *Coronation Street*?

Easy

Medium

Hard

Answers to QUIZ 109 – Pot Luck

1	Nathan (Stern)	11	Frank Gallagher
2	ABBA	12	Basketball
3	68	13	Daughter
4	1930s (1931)	14	Sir Lenny Henry
5	12	15	1997
6	Heatwave	16	Edward Snowden
7	Oxfordshire and Warwickshire	17	New South Wales (just south of Sydney)
8	*The Poseidon Adventure* (1972)	18	Blue
9	Polo	19	A supermoon
10	The Normans	20	Five

1   Coined in the 1980s, for what does the acronym DINKY stand?

2   What was the title of the first James Bond film of the 1980s?

3   Did Sharon Gless play Cagney or Lacey on the TV show?

4   Which Hollywood actress released her first fitness video in 1982?

5   Which English golfer won the US Women's Open in 1987?

6   Which group released the 1985 album *Brothers in Arms*?

7   How many times did Cambridge win the men's Boat Race in the 1980s?

8   In 1983, which US president signed the bill to establish a national holiday to honour Martin Luther King Jr?

9   Who was awarded the Olympic 100m gold medal in 1988 following Ben Johnson's disqualification?

10 Which group released the 1980 single *De Do Do Do, De Da Da Da*?

11 First broadcast in 1988, in which country was the sitcom *Rab C Nesbitt* set?

12 For which 1989 film, his directorial debut, was Sir Kenneth Branagh nominated for the Best Director Oscar?

13 Which U2 album was the first CD album to sell a million copies in the US?

14 Which boxer fought his penultimate bout in 1980, against Larry Holmes?

15 The name of which actor gave Madness a hit single in 1984?

16 What was the title of the 1987 memoir by former MI5 officer Peter Wright, that was originally banned in England?

17 Which dance, popular in the 1980s, has a name that means "crack of the whip" or strong slap?

18 In which year of the 1980s did the England cricket team have four different captains, including Graham Gooch and Mike Gatting?

19 Who wrote and originally recorded Chaka Khan's 1984 hit *I Feel for You*?

20 Which short-lived individual form of transport, introduced in 1985, had a maximum speed of 15 miles per hour?

Answers to QUIZ 110 – Bread and Butter

1	Unleavened	11	Japan
2	Swimming	12	Toffee
3	Pitta	13	Wine
4	Hovis®	14	Nutmeg
5	Aveline	15	The pancreas
6	*Build Me Up Buttercup* (The Foundations)	16	*HMS Pinafore*
7	Christmas lunch	17	*Beurre blanc*
8	Popcorn	18	White
9	*Glee*	19	Life
10	Cumbria	20	1960s (1968)

1. Who played Mr Woodhouse in the 2020 film version of *Emma*?

2. Which city lies furthest west: Aberdeen, Belfast or Swansea?

3. "I should have changed that stupid lock" is a lyric from which classic song?

4. How many points is the letter O worth in a game of Scrabble®?

5. What is the name of Danielle Harold's character in *EastEnders*?

6. On a ship, what name is given to the rotating cylinder around which cables are wound?

7. Which Scottish rock band takes its name from an assassinated archduke?

8. Which two words that differ only by their last letter, mean "dried grass" and "pig meat"?

9. The characters of Terry Collier and Bob Ferris first appeared in which sitcom?

10. In which place did the England team finish at the 2018 FIFA World Cup?

11. "Think of all the animals you've ever heard about, Like rhinoceroses and tigers, cats and mink" were the opening lines to the theme of which TV series?

12. In which mockumentary film of 1984 was there an amplifier that turned up to 11?

13. Which group had a hit with *Another Brick in the Wall Part 2* (1979)?

14. What name is given to the act of leaving a political group or country to join an opposing body?

15. Cockney gangster Charlie Croker is the main character in which film?

16. Eddie Waring (d.1986) commented on which sport?

17. For what do the letters WTO stand in relation to economics?

18. What colour is the word "Wispa" on the chocolate bar?

19. Who was the UK's Leader of the Opposition from 2005 to 2010?

20. "Yo! Adrian" is a line from which 1979 film?

Answers to QUIZ 111 – Pot Luck

1	Football (Brazilian)	11	Charles I
2	Reptiles	12	Donna (Jackson)
3	Aries	13	*House of Fun* (1982)
4	10 minutes (90 mins/80 mins)	14	Madame
5	Austria	15	Tightrope walking
6	*Downton Abbey*	16	Stormzy
7	Curling	17	Rhombus (or diamond)
8	(Californian) sea lions	18	Finland
9	Two	19	42
10	Fearne Cotton	20	The Kabin

Easy

1   What word can mean both "a work of fiction" and "new"?

2   A Ford car model manufactured from 1983 to 1993 was named after which constellation?

3   What word can mean both "fracture" and "pause"?

4   An error in a computer program and a general term for an insect share what name?

5   What word can mean both "an injection" and "a short drink"?

6   Which part of a set of in-ear headphones shares its name with part of a plant that develops into a flower or leaf?

7   What word can mean both "an electoral division" and "a hospital room"?

8   A Scottish sweet and a type of portable computer share what name?

9   What word can mean both "determination" and "to find a solution"?

10 Which Dorset town shares its name with a large city on New Zealand's South Island?

11 What word can mean both "admission" and "item in a diary"?

12 A game that involves guessing the sequence of coloured pegs shares its name with which quiz show?

Medium

13 What word can mean both a person who carries things and a dark ale?

14 Which part of a castle has a name that also means "retain"?

15 What word can mean both "a place of learning" and "a group of fish"?

16 One of the seven deadly sins shares its name with which animal?

17 What word for an animal's mother is also used to refer to a structure that blocks the flow of a river?

18 The airport in which Italian city shares its three-letter code with the name of an Indian state?

19 Which food item means to rapidly increase?

20 What word for a publication can also refer to part of an automatic gun?

Hard

Answers to QUIZ 112 – The 1980s

1	Double income, no kids yet	11	Scotland (Glasgow)
2	*For Your Eyes Only* (1981)	12	*Henry V*
3	Cagney	13	*The Joshua Tree*
4	Jane Fonda	14	Muhammad Ali
5	Dame Laura Davies	15	(Sir) *Michael Caine*
6	Dire Straits	16	*Spycatcher*
7	Once (1986)	17	The lambada
8	Ronald Reagan	18	1988
9	Carl Lewis	19	Prince
10	The Police	20	The Sinclair C5

1. In the Disney film *Mickey's Christmas Carol*, which character was portrayed by Mickey Mouse?

2. Which of these singers was born first: Annie Lennox, Enya or Sinead O'Connor?

3. Which company produced the Metro car when it was launched in 1980?

4. In which city was the English Greyhound Derby run for the first time in 2019?

5. Which two words that differ only by their last letter mean "cosy" and "ignore"?

6. Buffalo is the second-largest city in which US state?

7. Which spin-off from *Mrs Brown's Boys* was first broadcast in 2017?

8. Which former bank advertised itself as "the listening bank"?

9. What number do you get if you add the number of minutes in an hour to the number of seconds in two minutes?

10. In golf, with what is a bunker usually filled?

11. Penguins called Skipper, Rico and Private appear in which animated film?

12. As at the beginning of 2020, what was the standard charge for a UK prescription?

13. What colour was the children's character Orville the Duck?

14. What are you doing if you are yomping?

15. Dennis Bergkamp began his football career with which Dutch side?

16. What decorative term is used for the picture background on a computer?

17. The pot-bellied pig is associated with which Asian country?

18. Who was the gardener in the children's TV series *The Herbs*?

19. The Congo River twice crosses which major line of latitude?

20. Which band topped the UK charts in 1981 with the double-sided hit *Computer Love* and *The Model*?

Answers to QUIZ 113 – Pot Luck

1	Bill Nighy	11	*The Pink Panther Show*
2	Belfast	12	*This is Spinal Tap*
3	*I Will Survive* (Gloria Gaynor)	13	Pink Floyd
4	One point	14	Defection
5	Lola Pearce	15	*The Italian Job*
6	Capstan	16	Rugby league
7	Franz Ferdinand	17	World Trade Organisation
8	Hay and ham	18	Red
9	*The Likely Lads*	19	David Cameron
10	Fourth place	20	*Rocky II*

Easy

1   Who sang the theme to the 2020 Bond film, *No Time to Die*?

2   *The Bare Necessities* is a song from which famous animated film?

3   Who sang the title song for the 1963 film *Move Over, Darling*?

4   *The Jellicle Ball* is a song from which 2019 film?

5   In which musical is there "a bright golden haze on the meadow"?

6   Which character in *Grease* sings *Hopelessly Devoted to You*?

7   *Trip a Little Light Fantastic* is a song from which 2018 film?

8   Which songwriting duo won the Best Original Song Oscar at the 2020 award ceremony for *(I'm Gonna) Love Me Again* from *Rocketman*?

9   Which actress sang *Mein Herr* in the 1972 film *Cabaret*?

10   Bryan Adams' *Everything I Do (I Do It For You)* was from which 1991 film?

11   Which song from *The Greatest Showman* (2017) opens with the line "I am not a stranger to the dark"?

Medium

12   Which actor sang *Empty Chairs at Empty Tables* in the 2012 film *Les Misérables*?

13   Who sang the *Dirty Dancing* song *I've Had the Time of My Life*?

14   The song *The Candy Man* first appeared in which 1971 children's film?

15   *Anything You Can Do (I Can Do Better)* is a song from which 1946 musical?

16   Which singer performed *Fernando* in *Mamma Mia! Here We Go Again*?

17   What are the first four words sung in the film *The Sound of Music*?

18   In which film does the character of Anita sing "Everything free in America"?

19   *Another Day of Sun* is the opening number in which 2016 musical film?

20   In which animated film did the song *Little April Shower* feature?

Hard

Answers to QUIZ 114 – Double Meaning

1	Novel	11	Entry
2	Orion	12	*Mastermind* (or *Master Mind*)
3	Break	13	Porter
4	Bug	14	The keep
5	Shot	15	School
6	Bud	16	The sloth
7	Ward	17	Dam
8	Tablet	18	Genoa (GOA)
9	Resolve	19	Mushroom
10	Christchurch	20	Magazine

1   What relative to you is your mother's father's brother?

2   *Roll Away the Stone* was a 1973 hit for which group?

3   Elliot and Nancy Weston were characters in which US TV series, for which a pilot sequel was announced in 2020?

4   Is the Dáil Érieann the lower house or the upper house of the Irish government?

5   Which medical organisation was originally known as the British United Provident Association?

6   In which decade was the dog licence abolished in England, Wales and Scotland?

7   As at 2020, which band had won the British Album of the Year Brit Award three times, in 2001, 2003 and 2006?

8   Greg Chappell (b.1948) played international cricket for which country?

9   Yarmouth Castle lies on which island of the UK?

10 Which of the following actors starred in *Doctor Who* first: Jon Pertwee, Sylvester McCoy or Tom Baker?

11 Which hairspray was advertised with the slogan "Is she or isn't she"?

12 In 1987, which country won the first Rugby World Cup?

13 The TV series *The Beechgrove Garden* is broadcast from which country?

14 What is described in a poem by Robert Burns as "great chieftain o' the pudding-race"?

15 The period described as "the Phoney War" took place during which conflict?

16 Gizmo is a character in which 1984 film?

17 A sward is an area covered in what?

18 Which English football club is nicknamed "the Red Devils"?

19 The West Point military academy lies in which US state?

20 Who stepped onto the Moon in 1969 and described it as "one giant leap for mankind"?

Easy

Medium

Hard

Answers to QUIZ 115 – Pot Luck

1	Bob Cratchit	11	*Madagascar*
2	Annie Lennox (1954)	12	£9.15
3	British Leyland	13	Green
4	Nottingham	14	Walking over difficult terrain
5	Snug and snub	15	AFC Ajax
6	New York	16	Wallpaper
7	*All Round to Mrs Brown's*	17	Vietnam (Vietnamese)
8	The Midland Bank	18	Bayleaf
9	180 (60 + 120)	19	The Equator
10	Sand	20	Kraftwerk

ANSWERS ON PAGE 120

1   According to its advertising slogan, which drink "gives you wings"?

2   What colour is the drink Aperol?

3   Which bottled water brand began sponsoring a comedy award at the Edinburgh Festival Fringe in 1981?

4   What type of drink is Madeira?

5   Which beer has been advertised with the slogan "Refreshes the parts that other beers cannot reach"?

6   What two colours are the flowers of the camomile plant, used to make a herbal tea?

7   Bollinger is a brand of what type of drink?

8   Which lager was advertised by Paul Hogan in the 1980s?

9   In which English city are the distillers Sipsmith located?

10 What type of drink is Red Mountain?

11 John Smith's is what variety of beer?

12 Volvic mineral water is from which country?

13 Harveys Bristol Cream sherry is sold in what colour bottles?

14 Which lager was advertised with the slogan "Follow the bear"?

15 What shape of tea bag was introduced in 1997?

16 Which company launched Dasani bottled water in the UK in 2004, only to withdraw it a few weeks later?

17 Jose Cuervo is a brand of which drink?

18 Darjeeling tea comes from which country?

19 Which soft drink was originally sold under the name Vim Tonic?

20 What was the original flavour of Ribena?

Answers to QUIZ 116 – Film Music

1	Billie Eilish	11	*This is Me*
2	*The Jungle Book*	12	Eddie Redmayne
3	Doris Day	13	Bill Medley and Jennifer Warnes
4	*Cats*	14	*Willy Wonka & the Chocolate Factory*
5	*Oklahoma!*	15	*Annie Get Your Gun*
6	Sandy	16	Cher
7	*Mary Poppins Returns*	17	"The hills are alive"
8	Sir Elton John and Bernie Taupin	18	*West Side Story*
9	Liza Minnelli	19	*La La Land*
10	*Robin Hood: Prince of Thieves*	20	*Bambi*

1   On which night of the week is the final of the Eurovision Song Contest usually held?

2   Which game show might include rounds titled "Distinctly Average" and "The Answer's in the Question"?

3   Which darts player (d.2018) was nicknamed "The Crafty Cockney"?

4   *The Liver Birds* was first shown on TV in which decade?

5   Which member of the Beatles was the first to have a solo UK no.1?

6   How many fluid ounces are there in two pints?

7   Who established The Silver Line helpline for older people?

8   The character of Bilbo Baggins first appeared in which children's novel?

9   Which 1971 song refers to "the day the music died"?

10   Henrik Larsen (b.1966) represented which country in international football?

11   In relation to qualifications, for what do the letters MBA stand?

12   What name is given to a piece of armour that protects the chest?

13   What part of a meal is an *amuse-bouche?*

14   In the film *The Inbetweeners 2*, which character had emigrated to Australia?

15   Which two letters preceded "Spectrum" in the name of the 1982 personal computer?

16   The island of Murano, famous for glass-making, lies close to which Italian city?

17   What adjective relates to the reign of James I?

18   What form of clothing can be "polo" or "sweat"?

19   *(Si Si) Je Suis un Rock Star* was a 1981 hit for which member of the Rolling Stones?

20   The name of which prophetess in Greek mythology is given to someone who predicts gloomy outcomes but is not believed?

Easy

Medium

Hard

Answers to QUIZ 117 – Pot Luck

1	Great-uncle	11	Harmony
2	Mott the Hoople	12	New Zealand
3	*Thirtysomething*	13	Scotland
4	Lower house	14	Haggis
5	Bupa	15	WWII (1939-40)
6	1980s (1987)	16	*Gremlins*
7	Coldplay	17	Grass
8	Australia	18	Manchester United FC
9	The Isle of Wight	19	New York
10	Jon Pertwee	20	Neil Armstrong

Easy

Medium

Hard

What are the names of these authors?

1
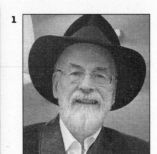

2

3

4

5

6

7

8

9

Answers to QUIZ 118 – Drink Up!

1   Red Bull®
2   Orange
3   Perrier®
4   A fortified wine
5   Heineken®
6   White (and yellow)
7   Champagne
8   Foster's
9   London
10 (Instant) coffee

11 Bitter
12 France
13 Blue
14 Hofmeister®
15 Pyramid (Brooke Bond)
16 The Coca-Cola Company
17 Tequila
18 India
19 Vimto®
20 Blackcurrant

1 In the traditional bingo call, what number is "Rise and Shine"?

2 Which *Line of Duty* actor starred in the 2020 TV series *The Nest*?

3 The ballroom, billiard room and study appear on the board of which classic game?

4 In which country did the first final of the European Cup football tournament take place, in 1956?

5 Uffington in Oxfordshire is the site of the oldest UK chalk drawing of which animal?

6 Who starred as prosecutor Rozat Sabich in the 1990 film *Presumed Innocent*?

7 "Saw the ghost of Elvis On Union Avenue" is a lyric from which song?

8 Which author wrote the collection of children's poems *When We Were Very Young* (1924)?

9 Which actor has been married to both Madonna and Robin Wright?

10 Which 2020 film had the subtitle *(and the Fantabulous Emancipation of One Harley Quinn)*?

11 In which decade was the reservoir Kielder Water completed?

12 The estuary of the River Foyle is on which coast of the island of Ireland?

13 As at the end of 2019, who held the British record for the highest number of points in the decathlon?

14 The line "The lady doth protest too much, methinks" is from which Shakespeare play?

15 On which of the Channel Islands is a "Royal" potato cultivated?

16 The 2002 hit *Dilemma* was a duet between Kelly Rowland and which other pop star?

17 Sir Richard Hadlee represented which country at cricket?

18 What are victuals?

19 What colour coats did the entertainers wear in the sitcom *Hi-de-Hi!*?

20 What word accompanies "top hat" to describe a formal suit worn at a wedding?

Easy / Medium / Hard

Answers to QUIZ 119 – Pot Luck

1 Saturday
2 *Richard Osman's House of Games*
3 Eric Bristow
4 1960s (1969)
5 George Harrison (*My Sweet Lord* (1971))
6 40 fluid ounces
7 Dame Esther Rantzen
8 *The Hobbit* (JRR Tolkien)
9 *American Pie* (Don McLean)
10 Denmark
11 Master of Business Administration
12 Breastplate
13 An appetiser (hors d'oeuvre)
14 Jay
15 ZX (Sinclair)
16 Venice
17 Jacobean
18 Shirt
19 Bill Wyman
20 Cassandra

Easy

1   Michael and Jowita were the winners of which 2020 TV talent competition?

2   Christopher Parker came runner-up to which fellow competitor on the first series of *Strictly Come Dancing*?

3   How many series of *Fame Academy* were made, excluding celebrity versions?

4   *Beyond the Boardroom* is a companion to which reality show?

5   Emon and Jamiul won which 2020 TV competition by less than half a minute?

6   In March 2020 it was announced that which comedian would be replacing Sandi Toksvig on *The Great British Bake Off*?

7   Which celebrity won the 2020 series of *Dancing on Ice*?

8   Jennifer Lopez, Nicki Minaj and Paula Abdul have been judges on which singing competition?

9   Which act was the earliest to win the Eurovision Song Contest: Brotherhood of Man, Bucks Fizz, or Johnny Logan?

10   Michelle Visage was a judge on which show, first broadcast in 2019?

Medium

11   What was the theme of the 2020 series of *Great British Menu*?

12   Jessie J was a judge on which TV show from 2012 to 2013?

13   Which *Strictly Come Dancing* professional was also a dance captain on *The Greatest Dancer*?

14   Which 2020 culinary competition was won by Thomas Frake?

15   In which decade did the first series of *Celebrity Big Brother* air in the UK?

16   Which shape lends its name to the title of the Channel 4 reality show based on social media?

17   Who is head chef in the series *Hell's Kitchen USA*?

18   In the series *Million Pound Menu*, in which city do competitors open a trial restaurant?

19   In which year was *Popstars: The Rivals* launched?

20   The Dingo Dollar Challenges occur on which show?

Hard

Answers to QUIZ 120 – Authors

1   Sir Terry Pratchett
2   JK Rowling
3   David Walliams
4   Jeffrey Archer
5   Leo Tolstoy
6   Neil Gaiman
7   George RR Martin
8   Fern Britton
9   Stephen King

1   What source of water might be described as "artesian"?

2   MA is the abbreviation for which US state?

3   Which BBC sitcom returned for a Christmas special in 2019, having previously finished broadcasting in 2009?

4   Who first became president of Russia in 2000?

5   The TGWU and Amicus merged in 2007 to form which union?

6   At what age does a golfer become eligible to take part in the PGA Tour Champions?

7   Which 2008 single by the Killers shares its title with a 2016 song by Rag'n'Bone Man?

8   Which country did Paul Hollywood *Eat* in the title of a 2020 documentary series?

9   99% of the calcium found in the human body is in the bones and which other part?

10 What colour is matcha powder?

11 Is the Campania region in the north or the south of Italy?

12 Clive Tyldesley is particularly noted for commenting on which sport?

13 Who writes the blog *Cooking on a Bootstrap*, originally entitled *A Girl Called Jack*?

14 The llama is native to which continent?

15 Which Australian landmark did it become illegal to climb in October 2019?

16 What is the first name of chef and food broadcaster Mr Ottolenghi?

17 Which 1989 film covered the same events as the TV series *The Trial of Christine Keeler*?

18 Released in 1998, what was Robbie Williams' first solo no.1?

19 What is the name of the gamekeeper in DH Lawrence's *Lady Chatterley's Lover*?

20 Which constituency did Tony Blair represent when he became UK prime minister?

Answers to QUIZ 121 – Pot Luck

1	29	11	1980s (1981)
2	Martin Compston	12	The north coast
3	Cluedo®	13	Daley Thompson (from 1984)
4	France	14	*Hamlet*
5	(White) horse	15	Jersey
6	Harrison Ford	16	Nelly
7	*Walking in Memphis* (Marc Cohn)	17	New Zealand
8	AA Milne	18	Food or provisions
9	Sean Penn	19	Yellow
10	*Birds of Prey*	20	Tails

Medium

Hard

Easy

1 In which country were the Michelin guides first published?

2 Tempelhof Airport was located in which capital city?

3 *Österreich* is the name of which European country in its own language?

4 Which large animal features on the coat of arms of Madrid?

5 The island of Santorini lies in which sea?

6 What colour is the cross on the Swedish flag?

7 Andorra lies within which mountain range?

8 What name was given to the clandestine organisation that fought for French liberty during WWII?

9 What type of food is Jamón Ibérico, produced in Portugal and Spain?

10 The main square in Vatican City is named after which saint?

Medium

11 Which year of the 20th century saw the reunification of Germany?

12 Luxembourg has borders with how many countries?

13 What is the international car registration code for Finland?

14 French, Italian and Spanish are part of which group of languages?

15 Which province in the Netherlands has a name meaning "Sealand"?

16 What is the official language of Liechtenstein?

17 The River Danube flows through Belgrade, Bratislava and which other two European capital cities?

18 Italy has three active volcanoes, Mount Etna, Mount Vesuvius and which other?

19 Which historical region of central Europe gives its name to a word describing unconventional arty people?

20 Which mountain in the Alps has a name that means "White Mountain"?

Hard

Answers to QUIZ 122 – TV Competitions

1	*The Greatest Dancer*	11	Children's literature
2	Natasha Kaplinksy	12	*The Voice UK*
3	Two	13	Oti Mabuse
4	*The Apprentice*	14	*MasterChef*
5	*Race Across the World*	15	2000s (2001)
6	Matt Lucas	16	Circle *(The Circle)*
7	Joe Swash	17	Gordon Ramsay
8	*American Idol*	18	Manchester
9	Brotherhood of Man (1976)	19	2002
10	*RuPaul's Drag Race*	20	*I'm a Celebrity…Get Me Out of Here!*

QUIZ 125 – Pot Luck

ANSWERS ON PAGE 127

1   Which Irish racecourse hosts all five classic Irish flat races?

2   Which wife did Henry VIII marry first: Anne Boleyn, Anne of Cleves or Jane Seymour?

3   Which rock band had a 2005 hit with *Best of You*?

4   Roger Sterling, played by John Slattery, was a main character in which US TV series, first shown in 2007?

5   Which former boxer made a cameo appearance in the 2009 film *The Hangover*?

6   What is the usual abbreviation for the county of Lancashire?

7   As at the end of 2019, who was the only woman to have been prime minister of Israel?

8   The castles of Pendennis and St Mawes lie at the mouth of which Cornish river?

9   At which circuit is the Italian Formula 1 Grand Prix usually held?

10 *Uptight (Everything's Alright)* was a 1965 single by which Motown star?

11 What is the provenance of an object?

12 Which English football club's home ground is St James' Park?

13 What are the initials of the body responsible for approving films in the UK?

14 Which poet wrote "She walks in beauty, like the night"?

15 A Brahman is a priest in which religion?

16 Which company manufactures the Cayman sports car?

17 Who directed the 1963 film *The Birds*?

18 Who composed and sang the theme tune to *One Foot in the Grave*?

19 Piers Gaveston was a favourite of which English king?

20 Mrs Wilberforce is the name of the landlady in which classic 1955 Ealing comedy, remade in 2004?

Easy

Medium

Hard

Answers to QUIZ 123 – Pot Luck

1	A well	11	The south
2	Massachusetts	12	Football
3	*Gavin & Stacey*	13	Jack Monroe
4	Vladimir Putin	14	South America
5	Unite	15	Uluru (Ayers Rock)
6	50 years	16	Yotam
7	*Human*	17	*Scandal*
8	Japan *(Paul Hollywood Eats Japan)*	18	*Millennium*
9	The teeth	19	(Oliver) Mellors
10	Green	20	Sedgefield

Easy

1   Which TV couple are voiced by Dan Castellaneta and Julie Kavner?

2   Satine and Christian are the main characters in which 2001 film?

3   Which acting duo released *You'll Never Walk Alone* as part of a triple-A sided single in 1996?

4   Which 2020 TV series starred Daisy Edgar-Jones and Paul Mescal?

5   Who accompanies *Rick* in the title of an animated sci-fi series?

6   Which comedy duo introduced their show with the words "In a packed programme tonight…"?

7   *For All We Know* was a hit for which duo in 1971?

8   What was the relationship between the title characters of the TV series *Hart to Hart*?

9   Which duo released the 1965 song *I Am A Rock*?

10   Which comedian referred to his partner as "Little Ern"?

11   What was the surname of aviation pioneers Orville and Wilbur?

Medium

12   Atomic Kitten, a duo since 2017, topped the charts in 2002 with a cover version of which Blondie song?

13   Which comedy duo featured in the 1937 film *Way Out West*?

14   In which year did Holly Willoughby join Phillip Schofield on the *This Morning* sofa?

15   For which fund-raising cause did Sir Mick Jagger and David Bowie record *Dancing in the Street* in 1985?

16   Which brothers directed the 2000 film *O Brother, Where Art Thou*?

17   Monsoon and Stone were the surnames of the leading characters in which sitcom?

18   What term is used to describe the crime-fighting duo of Batman and Robin?

19   Who appeared with James Corden in a 2009 sketch show?

20   Which brotherly duo released the 1987 single *Letter from America*?

Hard

Answers to QUIZ 124 – Europe

1	France	11	1990
2	Berlin	12	Three (Belgium, France and Germany)
3	Austria	13	FIN
4	A bear	14	The Romance languages
5	The Aegean Sea	15	Zeeland
6	Yellow	16	German
7	The Pyrenees	17	Budapest and Vienna
8	The (French) Resistance	18	Stromboli
9	(Cured) ham	19	Bohemia (Bohemian)
10	Saint Peter	20	Mont Blanc

QUIZ 127 – Pot Luck

ANSWERS ON PAGE 129

1   Which military honour is abbreviated to VC?

2   What was the name of Ted Danson's character in the TV series *Cheers*?

3   In which country was Mel Gibson born?

4   Jo Durie (b.1960) is a retired competitor in which sport?

5   Which actress co-starred with Bill Murray in the 1993 film *Groundhog Day*?

6   What type of animal is a muntjac?

7   Cajun cuisine is mostly associated with which US state?

8   According to the WWII poster, what did loose lips do?

9   In which decade was the breathalyser introduced in the UK?

10 Which band released the 1979 album *Eat to the Beat*?

11 In the name of the employee benefit, for what do the initials "LV" stand"?

12 For what do the initials MTV stand in the name of the entertainment channel?

13 Which record label has the silhouette of a palm tree as its logo?

14 In which country is the Morgan car built?

15 The town of Kirkcaldy lies on which firth?

16 The Great Barrier Reef lies off the coast of which Australian state?

17 Who recorded the 1985 single *Say You, Say Me*?

18 In 2012, Disneyland lifted a ban on their employees having what facial feature?

19 The TV series *Van der Valk* is set in which European city?

20 What is the international car registration code for New Zealand?

Easy

Medium

Hard

Answers to QUIZ 125 – Pot Luck

1	The Curragh Racecourse	11	Its confirmed history
2	Anne Boleyn (1533)	12	Newcastle FC
3	Foo Fighters	13	BBFC (British Board of Film Censors)
4	*Mad Men*	14	Lord Byron
5	Mike Tyson	15	Hinduism
6	Lancs	16	Porsche
7	Golda Meir	17	Sir Alfred Hitchcock
8	The Fal	18	Eric Idle
9	Monza	19	Edward II
10	Stevie Wonder	20	*The Ladykillers*

Easy

1   In retail terms, who is always right?

2   On what type of item are Public Lending Rights payable?

3   Which game show, originally shown in the 1980s, required contestants to guess "higher" or "lower"?

4   What word follows "Right" in referring to members of the House of Commons?

5   In which decade did the Righteous Brothers have a hit with *You've Lost That Lovin' Feelin'*?

6   If you are healthy, what type of weather would you be as right as?

7   Who was the original host of the UK version of *The Price is Right*?

8   How many degrees does a soldier turn through to execute the command "Right about"?

9   *Right Here, Right Now* was a hit in 1999 for which musician?

10 The viewers' complaints programme *Right to Reply* was broadcast on which TV channel from 1982 to 2001?

11 What three-word term is given to the legal entitlement to cross another person's land, such as via a footpath?

12 *Right Place Right Time* was a 2012 album by which former *The X Factor* contestant?

13 What name is given to a new set of shares offered to an existing shareholder?

14 Which UK prime minister brought in the Right to Buy policy for council tenants?

15 The Right Bank of the Seine forms part of which European capital city?

16 Proverbially, what do not make a right?

17 *Deeply Dippy* was a 1992 single by which group?

18 Who would be addressed as "Right Reverend"?

19 In which decade was the Human Rights Act passed in the UK to incorporate the European Convention on Human Rights?

20 Which group had a hit in 1970 with *All Right Now*?

Medium

Hard

Answers to QUIZ 126 – Couples and Duos

1	Homer and Marge Simpson	11	Wright
2	*Moulin Rouge!*	12	*The Tide is High*
3	Robson and Jerome	13	*Laurel & Hardy*
4	*Normal People*	14	2009
5	*Morty*	15	Live Aid
6	The Two Ronnies	16	Ethan and Joel Coen
7	The Carpenters	17	*Absolutely Fabulous* (Edina and Patsy)
8	Husband and wife	18	The Dynamic Duo
9	Simon and Garfunkel	19	Mathew Horne (*Horne and Corden*)
10	Eric Morecambe	20	The Proclaimers

1   Which of golf's four major tournaments was the only one that Arnold Palmer did not win?

2   What single word can precede "care", "noon" and "shave" to make three phrases?

3   Who starred as Simon Templar in the 1970s TV series *Return of the Saint*?

4   In Edward Lear's *The Owl and the Pussycat*, on what did the characters dine along with mince?

5   Which of the following is the deepest in the internal structure of the Earth: the crust, the mantle, or the upper mantle?

6   Jesy Nelson is a member of which group?

7   Was the stegosaurus a carnivore or a herbivore?

8   DK is the international car registration for which country?

9   Which group released the 1985 single *Nightshift*?

10 As at 2020, who is the only Canadian snooker player to have won the World Championship?

11 Biceps and triceps are part of which human limb?

12 Karachi is the largest city in which country?

13 Who sang *Holding Out for a Hero*, which featured in the 1984 film *Footloose*?

14 What form of radiation is abbreviated to "UV"?

15 In the novel *Little Women*, what is Jo's full name?

16 In which county is the National Trust property of Knole House and Park?

17 What name was given to an old-fashioned pen fashioned from a bird's feather?

18 What type of plant is wisteria?

19 Which Greek letter completes the title of the 2012 film: *Life of ___*?

20 The TV series *The Mandalorian* is a spin-off from which film franchise?

Answers to QUIZ 127 – Pot Luck

1	Victoria Cross	11	Luncheon Vouchers
2	Sam Malone	12	Music Television
3	USA	13	Island Records
4	Tennis	14	England (Worcestershire)
5	Andie MacDowell	15	The Firth of Forth
6	A deer	16	Queensland
7	Louisiana	17	Lionel Richie
8	Sink ships	18	A beard
9	1960s (1967)	19	Amsterdam
10	Blondie	20	NZ

Easy

Medium

Hard

Easy

1   In the King James Bible, what is the first Commandment?

2   Which branch of religion is indicated by the letters RC?

3   In which decade were women first ordained as Church of England priests?

4   In the New Testament, which of the four gospels is alphabetically first?

5   "All creatures great and small" is the second line of which hymn?

6   What name is given to a special council of members of a church that meets to discuss church matters?

7   In the New Testament, what was the original name of the apostle Peter?

8   *We Plough the Fields and Scatter* is traditionally sung at which autumn festival?

9   In which Gospel did the parable of the Good Samaritan appear?

10   What name is given to the bowl filled with water used for baptisms?

11   In the Old Testament, as whom did Jacob disguise himself?

12   What position is also known as the Bishop of Rome?

13   The departure of the Israelites from which country is described in the Book of Exodus?

Medium

14   What is an alb?

15   Potiphar appears in the story of which Old Testament character?

16   Which part of a church sounds like the name of a playing card?

17   In the New Testament, which insects did John the Baptist eat in the wilderness?

18   What is the name given to a church in Scotland?

19   Seth was the third son of which biblical couple?

20   What is the last book of the New Testament?

Hard

Answers to QUIZ 128 – Right On

1	The customer	11	Right of way
2	Books	12	Olly Murs
3	*Play Your Cards Right*	13	Rights issue
4	Honourable	14	Baroness Margaret Thatcher
5	1960s (1964)	15	Paris
6	Rain	16	Two wrongs
7	Leslie Crowther	17	Right Said Fred
8	180 degrees	18	A bishop
9	Fatboy Slim	19	1990s (1998)
10	Channel 4	20	Free

ANSWERS ON PAGE 133

1   What is 37 in Roman numerals?

2   The Tears for Fears song *Everybody Wants to Rule the World* was re-recorded under what title for a 1986 Sport Relief campaign?

3   Which US state lies between California and New Mexico?

4   Vidal Sassoon was a famous name in which profession?

5   Which London borough is alphabetically first?

6   Who wrote the 1970 book *The Female Eunuch*?

7   In which country of the UK are there the most red-haired people in the world, at approximately 13% of the population?

8   "How are you today? I'm in trouble please put me away" are lyrics from which 1977 song?

9   What does the letter "N" stand for on an automatic gearbox?

10   How many times did Lester Piggott win the Derby?

11   Emma Bunton and Victoria Beckham made cameo appearances in which 2001 film that satirised the fashion industry?

12   *Shuffle Off to Buffalo* is a song from which 1933 musical?

13   Which football club released the 1981 single *Ossie's Dream*?

14   In which decade did the puppet Muffin the Mule first appear on television?

15   What German word is used to refer to a child prodigy?

16   For what does the letter "E" stand in the name of the organisation UNESCO?

17   Veuve Clicquot is a famous brand of which type of drink?

18   What sport is played by the Worcester Wolves?

19   The Limpopo River flows across which continent?

20   What type of creature is an oystercatcher?

Easy

Medium

Hard

Answers to QUIZ 129 – Pot Luck

1	US PGA	11	The arm
2	After	12	Pakistan
3	Ian Ogilvy	13	Bonnie Tyler
4	Slices of quince	14	Ultraviolet
5	The mantle	15	Josephine (March)
6	Little Mix	16	Kent
7	A herbivore	17	Quill
8	Denmark	18	A climber
9	Commodores (US group)	19	Pi
10	Cliff Thorburn (1980)	20	Star Wars

QUIZ 132 – The Olympics

ANSWERS ON PAGE 134

1 In which decade did rhythmic gymnastics first become an Olympic sport?

2 Traditionally, the host nation enters in which position in the opening ceremony parade?

3 In which country are the 2026 Winter Games due to be held?

4 As at the end of 2019, which Olympic champions have been the only joint winners of the BBC Sports Personality of the Year Award?

5 In which European city were the Summer Games held when the first torch relay took place?

6 The gold postbox in Sheffield marked the gold medal won by which track and field athlete in 2012?

7 Did the Olympic and world champion athlete Said Aouita win his first gold medal in a sprint, middle-distance or long-distance race?

8 The Winter Olympics were held in Albertville in 1992, in which country?

9 What event replaced the women's pentathlon in 1984?

10 Which European city won the bid to host the 2024 Summer Olympics?

11 Chris Boardman won an Olympic gold medal in which sport?

12 Which country has won the most medals in total at the Winter Games?

13 As at 2020, Alberto Juantorena, was the only man to win both the 400m and 800m Olympic title at the same games. In which decade did he achieve this?

14 Which former defender coached the men's Great Britain football team for the 2012 Summer Games?

15 In which decade did Joaquim Cruz win the Olympic 800m gold medal for Brazil?

16 The butterfly swimming events take place over which two distances?

17 As at the end of 2019, how many times had the modern Olympic Games been cancelled?

18 Which colour ring is horizontally next to green on the Olympic flag?

19 Which country hosted the Winter Games in 1994, marking the first games to be held in a different four-year cycle from the Summer Games?

20 How many disciplines are included in the women's all-round gymnastics competition at the Summer Games?

Easy

Medium

Hard

Answers to QUIZ 130 – Church and the Bible

1 Thou shalt have no other gods before me
2 Roman Catholic
3 1990s (1994)
4 John
5 *All Things Bright and Beautiful*
6 Synod
7 Simon
8 Harvest Festival
9 Luke
10 Font

11 Esau (his brother)
12 The Pope
13 Egypt
14 A vestment worn by a priest
15 Joseph
16 Nave (knave)
17 Locusts
18 Kirk
19 Adam and Eve
20 Revelations

132

QUIZ 133 – Pot Luck

ANSWERS ON PAGE 135

1   Titania and Oberon are featured characters in which Shakespeare play?

2   From 1982 to 1985, former athlete David Moorcroft held the world record at which distance ?

3   According to the proverb, by what should you not judge a book?

4   What number is obtained by adding the number three to the numbers either side of it on a dartboard?

5   Which sci-fi writer presented a *Mysterious World* TV series about unexplained phenomena?

6   Which country did boxer Lennox Lewis represent during his amateur career?

7   Angora is a breed of rabbit and which other creature?

8   Which island country is separated from the mainland continent of Africa by the Mozambique Channel?

9   What is the title of the third novel in the Twilight series?

10 The sitcom *The Golden Girls* was set in which US state?

11 Which singer did Andy Serkis portray in the 2010 film *Sex & Drugs & Rock & Roll*?

12 Which branch of Greek philosophy is associated with being impassive?

13 The 1979 song *Geno* by Dexys Midnight Runners was a tribute to which soul singer?

14 The Caucasus Mountains lie on the border of which two continents?

15 Which airport, no longer in use, was London's main international airport between its opening and the start of WWII?

16 Which fashion house created the *L'Air du Temps* perfume?

17 Taken in 1972, what was the subject of the photograph *The Blue Marble*?

18 Which of these Martin Scorsese films was released first: *Cape Fear*, *Taxi Driver* or *The Departed*?

19 Which county of the Republic of Ireland is alphabetically last?

20 Which F1 team did Sebastian Vettel join in 2015?

Answers to QUIZ 131 – Pot Luck

1	XXXVII	11	*Zoolander*
2	*Everybody Wants to Run the World*	12	*42nd Street*
3	Arizona	13	Tottenham Hotspur FC
4	Hairdressing	14	1940s (1946)
5	Barking and Dagenham	15	*Wunderkind*
6	Germaine Greer	16	Educational
7	Scotland	17	Champagne
8	*Good Morning Judge* (10cc)	18	Basketball
9	Neutral	19	Africa
10	Nine times	20	A bird

What are the names of these items of laboratory equipment?

Easy

1

2

3

4

Medium

5

6

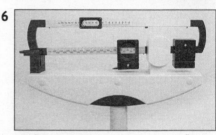

7

8

Hard

Answers to QUIZ 132 – The Olympics

1	1980s (1984)	11	(Track) cycling
2	Last	12	Norway (368) (as at 2020)
3	Italy	13	1970s (1976)
4	Torvill and Dean (1984)	14	Stuart Pearce
5	Berlin (1936)	15	1980s (1984)
6	Jessica Ennis-Hill (heptathlon)	16	100m and 200m
7	Long-distance	17	Three (1916, 1940, 1944)
8	France	18	Yellow
9	The heptathlon	19	Norway (Lillehammer)
10	Paris	20	Four (beam, floor, uneven bars, vault)

1 Danny De Vito played the character of Louie De Palma in which comedy series?

2 What is a *vaquero*?

3 In the name of the animal charity, for what do the letters PDSA stand?

4 Ukraine has a border on which body of water?

5 What activity is featured in the video game *Gran Turismo*?

6 What is a cuckoo pint?

7 Jack Skellington was the main character in which 1993 film?

8 First Direct is part of which larger banking group?

9 Which type of pizza shares its name with a set of concertos by Vivaldi?

10 The French racecourse Longchamp is to the west of which city?

11 What name is given to a regular series of concerts by a group or singer in the same venue, such as in Las Vegas?

12 Is Belize in Central America or South America?

13 What type of pastry is used to make a Beef Wellington?

14 What colour is the background of the Jolly Roger pirate flag?

15 In which year did *Made in Chelsea* first air?

16 The 1942 film *Casablanca* was set during which conflict?

17 What colour is the Professor Plum piece in Cluedo®?

18 What is Barack Obama's middle name?

19 What document format is wider than it is tall?

20 In which decade did David Weir first win the London wheelchair marathon?

Easy

Medium

Hard

Answers to QUIZ 133 – Pot Luck

1	*A Midsummer Night's Dream*	11	Ian Dury
2	5000m	12	Stoicism
3	Its cover	13	Geno Washington
4	39 (17 and 19)	14	Asia and Europe
5	Arthur C Clarke	15	Croydon Airport
6	Canada	16	Nina Ricci
7	Goat	17	The Earth
8	Madagascar	18	*Taxi Driver* (1976)
9	*Eclipse*	19	Wicklow
10	Florida	20	Ferrari

Easy

1 "Don't be fooled by the rocks that I got" is a lyric from which song?

2 "I am serious. And don't call me Shirley" is a line from which film?

3 Which band originally recorded *Don't Stop Believin'*?

4 What word completes the saying "Don't put all your eggs in one ___"?

5 Who starred as Zohan in the 2008 film *You Don't Mess With the Zohan*?

6 Who duetted with Neil Diamond on the 1978 hit *You Don't Bring Me Flowers*?

7 The 1973 film *Don't Look Now* was set in which European city?

8 The ELO single *Don't Bring Me Down* was taken from which 1979 album?

9 Which sitcom, first broadcast in 1983, featured the characters of Tom and Toby Latimer?

10 *Don't Go* was a 1982 hit for which duo?

11 Who hosted the game show *Don't Forget the Lyrics*?

12 What word completes the saying "Don't put the ___ before the horse"?

13 "Tonight I'm gonna have myself a real good time" are the opening lyrics to which 1979 song?

14 Which animal completes the title of the game show, *Don't Scare the ___*?

15 Who recorded the 1956 song *Don't Be Cruel*?

16 The racehorse Don't Push It won which major English race in 2010?

17 "The one you warned me all about" is a line from which 1986 song?

18 In what year did the Pussycat Dolls release *Don't Cha*?

19 What word completes the saying "If it ain't ___, don't fix it"?

20 *I Don't Know How to Love Him* is a song from which 1970 musical?

Answers to QUIZ 134 – Laboratory Equipment

1 Bunsen burner
2 Crucible
3 Pestle and mortar
4 Pipette
5 Calipers
6 Weighing scale
7 Goggles
8 Beaker

1   What "line" do strikers stand on outside their place of work?

2   What is the French word for "mother"?

3   What colour is Frascati wine?

4   The fashion chain Zara is based in which country?

5   What two-word term is the order to a group of soldiers on parade to adopt a relaxed position?

6   What word can mean both "any plant grown for food" and "to reduce the size of an image"?

7   The Welsh athlete Lynn Davies won the gold medal in the 1964 Olympics in which event?

8   Which line precedes "and don't dilly dally on the way" in the famous music-hall song?

9   Who wrote the Foundation series of science-fiction novels, the first of which was published in 1951?

10 A dermatologist specialises in what type of diseases?

11 Spencer Matthews found fame on which UK reality show?

12 Boxer Naseem Hamed adopted which regal nickname?

13 *Never Say Never Again* (1983) was an "unofficial" film featuring which character?

14 Which song was the first no.1 for The Beatles in the UK: - *I Wanna Hold Your Hand, Let It Be* or *From Me To You*?

15 How many hours ahead of GMT is Moscow?

16 In which country was Formula 1 driver Daniel Ricciardo born?

17 Which region has recorded the lowest average temperatures, the Antarctic or the Arctic?

18 Who was appointed Leader of the House of Commons in July 2019?

19 Sergeant Bob Cryer was a character in which long-running TV series?

20 What precedes XXXX in the name of an Australian beer?

Easy

Medium

Hard

Answers to QUIZ 135 – Pot Luck

1	*Taxi*	11	Residency
2	(Horse-mounted) herder	12	Central America
3	People's Dispensary for Sick Animals	13	Puff pastry
4	The Black Sea	14	Black
5	Driving	15	2011
6	A plant (species of Arum)	16	WWII
7	*The Nightmare Before Christmas*	17	Purple
8	HSBC	18	Hussein
9	Four Seasons	19	Landscape
10	Paris	20	2000s (2002)

Easy

1   What do Americans call fish fingers?

2   What type of fish is a brill?

3   Chipmunks are found primarily on which continent?

4   The male of which species of fish has a pouch in which he incubates eggs?

5   Which fish are used to make Worcestershire sauce?

6   What was the profession of the title character in the film *Goodbye, Mr Chips*?

7   Laurence Fishburne played Raymond Langston in which US series?

8   Who created the children's character of Jeremy Fisher?

9   What is a chipotle?

10 What name is given to someone who eats fish but not meat?

11 In the 1988 film *A Fish Called Wanda*, who played Wanda?

12 What colour is the mascot Mr Chips on the game show *Catchphrase*?

Medium

13 The Fisher sea area lies off the west coast of which country?

14 Who played John Actor, star of the fictional drama *Monkfish*, in *The Fast Show*?

15 What type of food item is a chipolata?

16 Something that is easily done is said to be like shooting fish in what container?

17 Carrie Fisher played which character in the Star Wars films?

18 Which motorway is closest to the Wiltshire town of Chippenham?

19 What nationality is actress Isla Fisher?

20 What is the real name of the singer-songwriter known as Fish?

Hard

Answers to QUIZ 136 – Don't

1	*Jenny from the Block* (Jennifer Lopez)	11	Shane Richie
2	*Airplane!*	12	Cart
3	Journey	13	*Don't Stop Me Now*
4	Basket	14	*Hare*
5	Adam Sandler	15	Elvis Presley
6	Barbra Streisand	16	The Grand National
7	Venice	17	*Papa Don't Preach*
8	*Discovery*	18	2005
9	*Don't Wait Up*	19	Broke
10	Yazoo	20	*Jesus Christ Superstar*

1   Which two words that differ only by their last letter mean "group of trees" and "sheep's covering"?

2   Which of these Stanley Kubrick films was released first: *Eyes Wide Shut, Full Metal Jacket* or *The Shining*?

3   The scientific name of which flower means "finger-like"?

4   In relation to the disease, for what do the letters MS stand?

5   In which country was actress Rachel McAdams born?

6   What colour are the outside stripes on the Italian flag?

7   Which UK prime minister resigned in 1976?

8   Is the musk ox found in the northern hemisphere or the southern hemisphere?

9   What is the name given to the point on a football pitch at which a penalty is taken?

10 Which radio show is known by the initials *TMS*?

11 Which Duran Duran single shares its title with a 2006 David Attenborough TV series?

12 The song *More Than a Woman* featured on the soundtrack of which 1977 film?

13 What colour is a packet of Walkers® prawn cocktail crisps?

14 The twins Ryan and Sharpay Evans appeared in which series of films?

15 In the folk tale, how many little pigs built houses?

16 In which decade was *'Allo 'Allo!* first broadcast?

17 Which horse won all of his 14 flat races from 2010 to 2012?

18 In which county was the first Harry Ramsden's fish and chip shop opened?

19 The Broads National Park covers Norfolk and which other county?

20 Which large Asian country had a one-child policy from 1979 to 2015?

Easy

Medium

Hard

Answers to QUIZ 137 – Pot Luck

1	A picket line	11	*Made in Chelsea*
2	*Mère*	12	Prince (Naseem)
3	White	13	James Bond
4	Spain	14	*From Me To You* (1963)
5	At ease	15	Three hours
6	Crop	16	Australia
7	Long jump	17	The Antarctic
8	"My old man said follow the van"	18	Jacob Rees-Mogg
9	Isaac Asimov	19	*The Bill*
10	Skin diseases	20	Castlemaine

ANSWERS ON PAGE 142

1. Which type of workers are represented by the NFU?
2. What was the occupation of Kylie Minogue's character in *Neighbours*?
3. William Sitwell is a writer and critic on what subject?
4. What is the profession at the centre of the TV series *The Split*?
5. Which 1967 hit includes the lyrics "the miller told his tale"?
6. A helmsman steers what type of vehicle?
7. In *My Fair Lady*, what job did Alfred Doolittle have?
8. In the army, for what do the initials CO stand?
9. What was the occupation of the boy in the fable *The Boy Who Cried Wolf*?
10. What was Captain Mainwaring's day job in *Dad's Army*?
11. Jack Tar is a nickname for which profession?
12. Who was appointed the UK's Chief Medical Officer in October 2019?
13. What was Lovejoy's occupation in the TV series of the same name?
14. What was the original occupation of Steve Austin in the TV series *The Six Million Dollar Man*?

15. Which occupation featured in the TV series *Cutting It*?
16. What was the profession of the title character in the TV series *Becker*?
17. "Apothecary" is an old-fashioned term for what occupation?
18. With what type of animals does a farrier work?
19. What is the occupation of people who belong to the trade union NUJ?
20. Which sitcom starred Karl Howman as a house painter?

Answers to QUIZ 138 – Fish and Chips

1	Fish sticks	11	Jamie Lee Curtis
2	A flatfish	12	Yellow or gold
3	North America	13	Denmark
4	Seahorse	14	Simon Day
5	Anchovies	15	A sausage
6	Schoolteacher	16	A barrel
7	*CSI: Crime Scene Investigation*	17	Princess Leia
8	Beatrix Potter	18	The M4
9	A (smoked) chilli	19	Australian
10	Pescatarian	20	Derek Dick

1 "I need some love like I never needed love before" is a lyric from which song?

2 Carrickfergus Castle lies in which county of Northern Ireland?

3 What is six squared?

4 Which fictional sleuth has been played on TV by both Kenneth More and Mark Williams?

5 What does the letter "C" stand for in the netball position?

6 In the traditional bingo call, what number is "Young and Keen"?

7 Which US president took office first: John F Kennedy, Lyndon B Johnson or Richard Nixon?

8 In the phrase "street cred", for what is "cred" short?

9 Yucatán is a state in which country?

10 Line umpires and a chair umpire oversee what type of sports match?

11 Which 1981 film about the Arthurian legend took its title from the name of King Arthur's sword?

12 How is Joe Exotic known in the title of a 2020 Netflix series?

13 In which decade did Australia first appear in the FIFA World Cup finals?

14 Which human teeth are the last to grow?

15 The characters in which TV series had the mission "to explore strange worlds. To seek out new life and new civilisations"?

16 In which decade was *Fame Academy* first broadcast?

17 Used in the Star Wars films, for what is the word "droid" short?

18 What are raced in the game Scalextric®?

19 In the TV series *Hector's House*, what type of animal was Hector?

20 Which group originally recorded the song *Stairway to Heaven*?

Answers to QUIZ 139 – Pot Luck

1	Wood and wool	11	*Planet Earth*
2	*The Shining* (1980)	12	*Saturday Night Fever*
3	Foxglove (*Digitalis*)	13	Pink
4	Multiple sclerosis	14	High School Musical
5	Canada	15	Three
6	Green and red	16	1980s (1982)
7	Harold Wilson (Baron Wilson of Rievaulx)	17	Frankel
8	The northern hemisphere	18	West Yorkshire
9	The spot	19	Suffolk
10	*Test Match Special*	20	China

Easy

1 The Scenic Railway wooden rollercoaster is located at the Dreamland amusement park in which English town?

2 The song *Once Upon a Dream* appeared in which Disney film?

3 *Dream On* (1973) was a hit for which US rock group?

4 Who is the King of the Fairies in Shakespeare's *A Midsummer Night's Dream*?

5 Who sang *I Dreamed a Dream* in the 2012 film *Les Misérables*?

6 In which decade was the DreamWorks studio founded?

7 Which English football stadium is nicknamed "the Theatre of Dreams"?

8 *The Dream of Gerontius* (1900) was written by which English composer?

9 Which group had a 1967 hit with *Daydream Believer*?

10 Which 1984 sci-fi film starred Dennis Quaid as a psychic who can project himself into people's dreams?

Medium

11 Which Disney character sings *A Dream Is A Wish Your Heart Makes*?

12 In the TV series *I Dream of Jeannie*, what type of magical creature was Jeannie?

13 Who played record executive Curtis Taylor Jr in the 2006 film *Dreamgirls*?

14 In which of John Keats' odes did he ask "Was it a vision, or a waking dream"?

15 Which founder of psychoanalysis believed that dreams could be interpreted as unconscious wishes?

16 What words appeared in brackets in the title of the Eurythmics song *Sweet Dreams*?

17 Which civil rights leader made the famous "I Have a Dream" speech in 1963?

18 *The American Dream* is a song from which musical, first staged in London in 1989?

19 What term is given to a dream where the dreamer is aware that they are dreaming?

20 In the 1984 film *Electric Dreams*, what instrument does Lori Singer's character play?

Hard

Answers to QUIZ 140 – Occupations

1	Farmers (National Farmers Union)	11	Sailor
2	Mechanic	12	Chris Whitty
3	Food	13	Antiques dealer
4	Law	14	Astronaut
5	*A Whiter Shade of Pale*	15	Hairdressing
6	A boat	16	Doctor
7	Dustman	17	Pharmacist
8	Commanding officer	18	Horses
9	Shepherd	19	Journalist
10	Bank manager	20	*Brush Strokes*

ANSWERS ON PAGE 145

1   Which film won both the Best Picture and the Best International Feature Film awards at the 2020 Oscar awards ceremony?

2   What geometrical shape is a 50p coin?

3   In wiring, which colour is the neutral wire?

4   What is the name of Natalie J Robb's *Emmerdale* character?

5   Who directed the 2016 film *The BFG*?

6   What product is produced by the Wrigley Company?

7   What is advertised with the slogan: "The trouble is, they taste too good"?

8   *I Only Want to Be With You* was the first song performed on *Top of the Pops*, by which singer?

9   Who had a 1959 hit with the song *Oh! Carol*?

10   In 2014, who became the first cyclist to win the BBC Sports Personality of the Year Lifetime Achievement Award?

11   Which children's character has a cat called Pilchard?

12   What five words follow "How do I love thee?" in the poem by Elizabeth Barratt Browning?

13   Ladybower Reservoir lies in which East Midlands county?

14   What does a sump hold in a car?

15   For what did the letters WRNS stand in the name of a military organisation?

16   Which country did gymnast Olga Korbut represent in the 1972 Olympic Games?

17   The phrase "Cooking doesn't get tougher than this" is associated with which TV competition?

18   In which major US city was the 1995 film *Heat* set?

19   Which US tennis player was beaten by Steffi Graf in the 1989 Wimbledon Ladies' Singles semi-final?

20   Is the Caspian sea mainly a freshwater lake or a saltwater lake?

Answers to QUIZ 141 – Pot Luck

1	*2 Become 1* (The Spice Girls)	11	*Excalibur*
2	County Antrim	12	Tiger King
3	36	13	1970s (1974)
4	*Father Brown*	14	The wisdom teeth
5	Centre	15	*Star Trek*
6	15	16	2000s (2002)
7	John F Kennedy (1961)	17	Android
8	Credibility	18	Toy cars
9	Mexico	19	A dog
10	A tennis match	20	Led Zeppelin

Easy

Medium

Hard

Easy

1   In which city were the BBC's Pebble Mill studios?

2   Leipzig is a city in which country?

3   Which of these cities lies furthest east: Bath, Birmingham or Sunderland?

4   Which is Scotland's third most populous city?

5   The New York thoroughfare of Broadway runs mainly through which borough?

6   John Moores University is situated in which English city?

7   Which Scandinavian capital city is nicknamed "the Venice of the North"?

8   Turin Cathedral is dedicated to which saint?

9   To the nearest 0.25, how many square kilometers is the Vatican City?

10 The city of Wolverhampton lies in which metropolitan county?

11 In which city did the 2019 Tour de France start?

12 Which city, a modern-day county town, was the capital of the Kingdom of Wessex?

13 In which city does the firm Ernst & Young have its headquarters?

14 The game show *Countdown* was originally filmed in which English city?

Medium

15 The city of Alicante borders which body of water?

16 Halifax and Richmond are the names of towns in the UK. In which country are they both names of cities?

17 In 2017, which city was chosen to be the 2021 UK City of Culture?

18 Which brand of cream cheese is named after a Pennsylvanian city?

19 Which city is situated in Lothian on the Firth of Forth?

20 Which of Greater Manchester's districts is alphabetically last?

Hard

Answers to QUIZ 142 – Dreams

1	Margate	11	Cinderella
2	*Sleeping Beauty*	12	A genie
3	Aerosmith	13	Jamie Foxx
4	Oberon	14	*Ode to a Nightingale*
5	Anne Hathaway (as Fantine)	15	Sigmund Freud
6	1990s (1994)	16	*(Are Made of This)*
7	Old Trafford	17	Martin Luther King Jr
8	Sir Edward Elgar	18	*Miss Saigon*
9	The Monkees	19	Lucid dream
10	*Dreamscape*	20	The cello

QUIZ 145 – Pot Luck

ANSWERS ON PAGE 147

1   Who was reputed to have said "I may be drunk, Miss, but in the morning I will be sober and you will still be ugly"?

2   How many players are there in a quintet?

3   In which county is the town of Chesterfield?

4   What number do the Roman numerals VII represent?

5   Who played Laura Nielson in the TV series *Liar*?

6   Who was the UK Leader of the Opposition from 2010 to 2015?

7   How many syllables are there in the word "autobiographical"?

8   How many people are in the group New Kids on the Block?

9   Which of these Brad Pitt films was released first: *Legends of the Fall*, *Meet Joe Black*, or *Thelma and Louise*?

10 William Perry, nicknamed "The Refrigerator", is a former professional in which sport?

11 The "Wainwright Peaks" are found in which National Park?

12 What colour is the cross on the Norwegian flag, on a white background?

13 Who was the US president when Dan Quayle was vice-president?

14 According to the proverb, what is he who hesitates?

15 Which of the Great Lakes is alphabetically last?

16 In the TV series *Last of the Summer Wine*, how was the character of Walter Dewhurst better known?

17 Which two four-letter words that differ only by their last letter mean "a period of time" and "an unwanted plant"?

18 Which wall is an actor said to break, if they talk directly to the audience in a theatre?

19 Who or what was Ballyregan Bob?

20 In relation to the law, for what do the initials JP stand?

Answers to QUIZ 143 – Pot Luck

1	*Parasite*	11	Bob the Builder
2	Heptagon	12	"Let me count the ways"
3	Blue	13	Derbyshire
4	Moira Dingle	14	Oil
5	Steven Spielberg	15	Women's Royal Navy Service
6	Chewing gum	16	The Soviet Union
7	Kellogg's® Crunchy Nut Cornflakes	17	*MasterChef*
8	Dusty Springfield	18	Los Angeles
9	Neil Sedaka	19	Chris Evert
10	Sir Chris Hoy	20	A saltwater lake

Easy

1 What is a Knickerbocker Glory?

2 Which area of London goes with Kensington to form the name of a borough?

3 The term "kitchen-sink drama" was first used to describe plays in which decade?

4 The phrase "Kill the fatted calf" refers to which biblical parable?

5 Who presented the 2020 Channel 4 TV series *Keep Crafting and Carry On*?

6 For what prefix does the letter "k" stand in relation to a measurement of weight?

7 Is Kyle of Lochalsh on the east coast, north coast or west coast of Scotland?

8 Who played Agent K in the Men in Black series of films?

9 In physics, what does the adjective "kinetic" relate to?

10 Kangaroo Island is part of which country?

11 What type of race is the Kentucky Derby?

12 Kuala Lumpur is the capital of which country?

13 What colour is the muppet Kermit?

14 In chess notation, K is used to identify which piece?

Medium

15 In which decade was Kristen Stewart born?

16 A kettledrum is found in which section of an orchestra?

17 Kleptomania is the compulsion to do what?

18 The borough of Knowsley is part of which metropolitan county?

19 In which Irish county is the town of Killarney?

20 Which chemical element has the symbol K?

Hard

Answers to QUIZ 144 – Cities

1	Birmingham	11	Brussels
2	Germany	12	Winchester
3	Sunderland	13	London
4	Aberdeen	14	Leeds
5	Manhattan	15	The Mediterranean Sea
6	Liverpool	16	Canada
7	Stockholm	17	Coventry
8	St John the Baptist	18	Philadelphia
9	0.5 km square kilometers (0.49)	19	Edinburgh
10	West Midlands	20	Wigan

1. As at the end of 2019, which was the UK's second-busiest airport in terms of passenger numbers?

2. Which two words that sound the same but are spelt differently mean "to pour on water" and "to search for water"?

3. For which English team did Eric Cantona play before transferring to Manchester United?

4. The character of Jake the Jailbird appears on which board game?

5. Which two four-letter words that differ only by their last letter mean "a piece of mud" and "a wooden shoe"?

6. For what are the letters HQ an abbreviation?

7. Which of these reality shows was broadcast first: *Big Brother*, *Popstars* or *The X Factor*?

8. "Touching the very part of me, It's making my soul sing" is a lyric from which song?

9. *Europe's Most Wanted* (2012) was the subtitle of the third film in which animated series?

10. Which two words that differ only by their first letter mean "clothes fastener" and "sheep meat"?

11. *People are People* was a 1984 hit for which group?

12. How many times did Jack Nicklaus win The Masters golf championship?

13. What type of animals were *Blue Peter*'s Jack and Jill?

14. The Forest of Bowland lies to the west of which range of hills?

15. What is the name of Robin Wright's character in the 1987 film *The Princess Bride*?

16. The 1970s TV series McCloud was set in which US city?

17. The fabric velour takes its name from a French word for what type of fabric?

18. Which South American desert is the driest in the world?

19. Shea butter is obtained from a tree that is native to which continent?

20. The world's longest road tunnel, as at 2020, is in which Scandinavian country?

Easy

Medium

Hard

Answers to QUIZ 145 – Pot Luck

1	Sir Winston Churchill	11	The Lake District
2	Five	12	Blue
3	Derbyshire	13	George HW Bush
4	Seven	14	Lost
5	Joanne Froggatt	15	Lake Superior
6	Ed Miliband	16	Foggy
7	Seven	17	Week and weed
8	Five	18	The fourth wall
9	*Thelma and Louise* (1991)	19	A greyhound (d.1994)
10	American football	20	Justice of the Peace

Easy

1   What type of garment is a pashmina?

2   What type of hat does Fred Thursday wear in the TV series *Endeavour*?

3   What shapes are used in an Argyle pattern?

4   In the traditional song, what does Yankee Doodle stick in his hat?

5   In which country was the footwear company Crocs, Inc formed?

6   What is the name of the hooded garment worn by monks?

7   The Dr Martens company is best known for what type of clothing?

8   What type of hat is worn by the character Indiana Jones?

9   Which silent film star wore iconic pork-pie hats in many of his films?

10 Which brand makes 501 denim jeans?

11 What type of hat is traditionally worn with a morning suit?

12 Who starred in the 1949 western *She Wore a Yellow Ribbon*?

13 The word "cagoule" is taken from which language?

14 Where would a snood be worn?

15 What item of clothing is a "dicky bow"?

16 Designer Giorgio Armani was born in which country?

17 What type of clothing is a "waspie"?

18 Which type of heel takes its name from a young animal?

19 What is the name of the leather riding breeches worn by cowboys?

20 What name is given to a shoe designed to provide aid for a problematic physical condition?

Medium

Hard

Answers to QUIZ 146 – K

1	An ice cream sundae	11	Horse race
2	Chelsea	12	Malaysia
3	1950s	13	Green
4	The Prodigal Son	14	The king
5	Kirstie Allsopp	15	1990s (1990)
6	Kilo	16	Percussion section
7	The west coast	17	Steal
8	Tommy Lee Jones	18	Merseyside
9	Movement	19	County Kerry
10	Australia	20	Potassium

1 Who won Best New Artist and Song of the Year at the 2020 Brit Awards?

2 Which of these Pixar films was released first: *Cars, The Good Dinosaur* or *The Incredibles*?

3 A golf ball is usually hit the furthest by which type of club?

4 Which car company has the slogan "Built for the road ahead"?

5 What colour are the flowers on the plant cow parsley?

6 MN is the abbreviation for which US state?

7 Matt Baker was the runner-up to which actress on *Strictly Come Dancing*?

8 In which Scottish town does the New Year's Eve celebration involve a parade of large fireballs that are thrown into the harbour?

9 The remains of Hailes Abbey lie in which English county?

10 For which 2012 film did Quentin Tarantino win the Best Screenplay Oscar?

11 What instrument did Sting play in the Police?

12 What does a cricketer specialise in, if they are described as "seam" or "spin"?

13 What does the company Wonga supply?

14 Lake Victoria drains into which major river?

15 In which country was actress Catherine Deneuve born?

16 In the English version of Scrabble®, how many "X" tiles are there?

17 The coyote is native to which continent?

18 Which future prime minister was elected as the MP for Finchley in 1959?

19 In which decade did the comedy series *Hi-De-Hi!* first air?

20 "That'll do, pig. That'll do" is a line from which 1995 film?

Easy

Medium

Hard

Answers to QUIZ 147 – Pot Luck

1	London Gatwick	11	Depeche Mode
2	Douse and dowse	12	Six (1963, 1965, 1966, 1972, 1975, 1986)
3	Leeds United	13	Cats
4	Monopoly™	14	The Pennines
5	Clod and clog	15	Buttercup
6	Headquarters	16	New York
7	*Big Brother* (2000)	17	Velvet
8	*Your Love is King* (Sade)	18	The Atacama Desert
9	*Madagascar*	19	Africa
10	Button and mutton	20	Norway (Leardal Tunnel, 15 miles)

What are the names of these rock bands?

1

2

3

4

5

6

7

8

Easy

Medium

Hard

Answers to QUIZ 148 – Clothing

1	Shawl	11	Top hat
2	A trilby	12	John Wayne
3	Diamonds	13	French
4	A feather	14	On the head
5	The USA (Niwot, Colorado)	15	Bow tie
6	Cowl	16	Italy
7	Footwear (boots)	17	A corset
8	Fedora	18	Kitten heel
9	Buster Keaton	19	Chaps
10	Levi's	20	An orthopaedic shoe

ANSWERS ON PAGE 153

1   What name is given to the upper edge of a boat's side?

2   Which famous poet of the Beat Generation wrote the 1955 poem *Howl*?

3   Actress Reese Witherspoon named her son, born in 2012, after which US state?

4   What is barathea?

5   The activity of "plogging" combines jogging with what activity?

6   Who was the first player from outside the British Isles to captain a European Ryder Cup team?

7   What is a female budgie called?

8   In which decade was the bikini invented?

9   What part of the body is affected by plantar fasciitis?

10 What name is given to a cross between a poodle and a Cavalier King Charles spaniel?

11 In which country is Caribbean Airlines based?

12 Who was elected as the president of FIFA in 2016?

13 Erasmus of Formia, known as St Elmo, is the patron saint of which travellers?

14 What is the main religion of Burma?

15 What unit of time is added to the Chinese calendar at intervals instead of an extra day in a leap year?

16 In Roman mythology, who was the father of Romulus and Remus?

17 Who released the 2019 album *Divinely Uninspired to a Hellish Extent*?

18 What was the title of the second film in the *Road to* series, released in 1941?

19 Reed Richards is a member of which group of superheroes?

20 The ruined mansion of Witley Court, damaged by fire in 1937, lies in which county?

Easy

Medium

Hard

Answers to QUIZ 149 – Pot Luck

1	Lewis Capaldi	11	Bass guitar
2	*The Incredibles* (2004)	12	Bowling
3	Driver	13	Payday loans
4	Ford	14	(White) Nile
5	White	15	France
6	Minnesota	16	One
7	Kara Tointon	17	North America
8	Stonehaven	18	Baroness Margaret Thatcher
9	Gloucestershire (near Winchcombe)	19	1980s (1980)
10	*Django Unchained*	20	*Babe*

Easy

1. As at 2020, how many bridges span the Grand Canal in Venice?

2. Bridge House is a National Trust property in which Lake District town?

3. The Scandinavian crime drama series *The Bridge* featured the police forces in which two cities?

4. Who directed the 1995 film *The Bridges of Madison County*?

5. The Scottish town of Bridge of Allan lies close to which city?

6. The Emma Bridgewater company is known for what type of product?

7. In which decade was the Forth Rail Bridge opened?

8. The Bridgestone company, famous for its tyres, has its headquarters in which country?

9. Which duo recorded the 1966 track *The 59th Street Bridge Song (Feelin' Groovy)*?

10. The Acol bidding system was founded by a club in which city?

11. Beau Bridges played President Ralph Warner in which TV series?

12. The Golden Jubilee footpath bridges across the River Thames lie next to which railway bridge?

Medium

13. Which duo released the 1987 single *Building a Bridge to Your Heart*?

14. Who partnered Frankie Bridge when she appeared on *Strictly Come Dancing*?

15. In which English town is the bridge known as "The Winking Eye Bridge"?

16. To what was the Second Severn Crossing bridge officially renamed in 2018?

17. Who played Mrs Bridges in the 1970s TV series *Upstairs, Downstairs*?

18. What is the real name of the Oxford landmark often called "The Bridge of Sighs"?

19. The book and film *A Bridge Too Far* told the story of which WWII operation?

20. Who directed the 2015 film *Bridge of Spies*?

Hard

Answers to QUIZ 150 – Rock Bands

1. U2
2. Coldplay
3. The Rolling Stones
4. Aerosmith
5. Foo Fighters
6. ZZ Top
7. Muse
8. Guns N' Roses

1 What is the world's most common eye colour?

2 The Ring named "Courage" is a feature of which planet?

3 Which Italian designer (d.1960) popularised the wedge heel?

4 "The Child is Father of the Man" is a line from which poem by William Wordsworth?

5 What is the general name for a beauty treatment that uses seawater and other sea products?

6 The Houston Rockets compete in which sport?

7 What is the currency unit of Montenegro?

8 The TV series *Turn Up Charlie* stars which actor in the title role?

9 The ruins of Dunluce Castle are situated in which county of Northern Ireland?

10 Which band released the 2001 album *We Love Life*?

11 Which real-life mother and daughter starred in the 2015 film *Ricki and the Flash*?

12 In the RAF, what rank is immediately above air marshal?

13 In which year was Mother Teresa canonised?

14 Which city hosted the 2006 Commonwealth Games?

15 Who created the children's character of Beetle Boy?

16 Dalhousie University is in which country?

17 In which month of 1918 did the Battle of Amiens take place?

18 Who wrote the 2018 book *How to be Human: The Manual*?

19 What colour is lycopene?

20 In the Harry Potter novels and films, what type of mythical creature is Buckbeak?

Easy

Medium

Hard

Answers to QUIZ 151 – Pot Luck

1	Gunwale	11	Trinidad and Tobago
2	Allen Ginsberg	12	Gianni (Giovanni) Infantino
3	Tennessee	13	Sailors
4	A fabric	14	Buddhism
5	Litter picking	15	A month
6	Seve Ballesteros (1997)	16	Mars
7	Hen	17	Lewis Capaldi
8	1940s (1946)	18	*The Road to Zanzibar*
9	(Arch of) the foot	19	The Fantastic Four
10	Cavapoo (or Cavoodle)	20	Worcestershire

1   Sleeping, off-string and looping are techniques associated with the use of which toy?

2   Popular in the 1960s, what is the Watusi?

3   Which simple game is also known as Rochambeau?

4   What animals are the baddies in the video game *Angry Birds*?

5   Which comic strip about a boy and his toy tiger was created by Bill Watterson?

6   HO, OO and N are scales of measurement common in which pastime?

7   The National Trust property of Wightwick Manor lies in which metropolitan county?

8   In which country was the world's first commercial bungee jump site built, in 1988?

9   Korg is most famous for manufacturing what kind of musical instruments?

10   What is the technical name for the point on which a seesaw pivots?

11   How many people are in an official tug of war team?

12   Hasselblad is a famous manufacturer of what type of equipment?

13   If you were exercising using the fartlek technique, what would you be doing?

14   The exclusive holiday resort known as The Hamptons is in which US state?

15   Which board game played a major part in the 2018 film *Sometimes Always Never*?

16   What children's game would you be playing if you were using a taw?

17   How many bowls does a player get in an "end" during a standard singles game?

18   In which European city is the Miniatur Wunderland model railway situated?

19   How many dominoes are there in a traditional set?

20   Which basic hit video puzzle game was created by Russian Alexey Pajitnov?

Easy

Medium

Hard

Answers to QUIZ 152 – Bridges

1	Four	11	*Homeland*
2	Ambleside	12	Hungerford Bridge
3	Copenhagen and Malmö	13	Wax
4	Clint Eastwood	14	Kevin Clifton
5	Stirling	15	Gateshead
6	Pottery	16	The Prince of Wales Bridge
7	1890s (1890)	17	Angela Baddeley
8	Japan	18	Hertford bridge
9	Simon and Garfunkel	19	Operation Market Garden
10	London	20	Steven Spielberg

ANSWERS ON PAGE 157

1   Which terrier breed was originally developed by Captain John Edwardes in the county of Pembrokeshire?

2   In which country was singer Jack Savoretti born?

3   Who stars as Sam Fox in the TV series *Better Things*?

4   "The Bhoys" and "The Hoops" are nicknames of which famous football club?

5   Who was *Time* magazine's Person of the Year in 2019?

6   Whose stand-up tours have included *My Family: Not the Sitcom* and *Trolls: Not the Dolls*?

7   The National Museum of Science and Media is situated in which English city?

8   Which band's *Greatest Hits* album had the second-highest UK sales figures of the 1970s?

9   In which English county is the open space of Hindhead Common?

10 Free running is an alternative name for which urban activity?

11 What is a Glanville fritillary?

12 Which bishop is officially known as Dunelm?

13 For what do the initials QVC stand in the name of the shopping channel?

14 Which acid is found in bee stings?

15 Who played Bridget's mother in the Bridget Jones's Diary films?

16 Cass Elliot sang with which famous 1960s band?

17 In which country was athlete Eilidh Doyle born?

18 *Puttanesca* sauce for pasta originated in which Italian city?

19 Who wrote the 1953 sci-fi novel *The Kraken Wakes*?

20 In which year was the word "podcast" first used?

Easy

Medium

Hard

Answers to QUIZ 153 – Pot Luck

1	Brown	11	Meryl Streep and Mamie Gummer
2	Neptune	12	Air chief marshal
3	Salvatore Ferragamo	13	2016
4	*My Heart Leaps Up*	14	Melbourne
5	Thalassotherapy	15	MG Leonard
6	Basketball	16	Canada
7	The euro	17	August
8	Idris Elba	18	Ruby Wax
9	County Antrim	19	Red
10	Pulp	20	A hippogriff

ANSWERS ON PAGE 158

Easy

1   What was the name of the short sword used by Roman legionaries?

2   In which century was the East India company dissolved?

3   The Iceni tribe mainly occupied which two modern-day counties?

4   What was the nickname of the V-1 flying bomb in WWII?

5   In 1947, who became the first pilot to break the sound barrier?

6   What was the regnal number of Ivan the Terrible (d.1584)?

7   The Siege of Paris (1870-71) took place during which war?

8   In which decade were the Dead Sea Scrolls discovered?

9   The Golden Horde was originally part of which ancient empire?

10 Which explorer recorded his travels through Asia in *Book of the Marvels of the World*?

11 In 1852, at which castle in Kent did the Duke of Wellington die?

12 What part of a house was the basis of a UK tax from 1696 until 1851?

13 In 1912, Harriet Quimby became the first woman to fly across which area of water?

14 In which historic county was Oliver Cromwell born?

15 Who drafted the 1942 report *Social Insurance and Allied Services*?

16 In which century was the Battle of Magenta fought?

17 Who was the Kaiser of Germany at the outbreak of WWI?

18 Which famous landmark was built as the entrance arch for the 1889 World's Fair?

19 Which country governed Algeria from 1830 to 1962?

20 Josip Tito became the president of Yugoslavia in which decade?

Medium

Hard

Answers to QUIZ 154 – Leisure Time

1	Yo-yo	11	Eight
2	A dance	12	Photographic
3	Rock paper scissors	13	Interval training
4	Pigs	14	New York
5	Calvin and Hobbes	15	Scrabble®
6	Model railways	16	Marbles
7	The West Midlands	17	Four
8	New Zealand	18	Hamburg
9	Synthesisers and keyboards	19	28
10	Fulcrum	20	*Tetris*

1 In which US state was the writer John Steinbeck born?

2 Who won the men's singles tennis gold medal at the 1996 Summer Olympics?

3 Which religion celebrates the Festival of Holi?

4 What is the main carbohydrate ingredient of the Italian *panzanella* salad?

5 Barafundle Bay lies in which UK county?

6 Who had a hit with *Alone Again (Naturally)* in 1972?

7 Rugby union player Zach Mercer joined which Premiership team in 2015?

8 What is an imbroglio?

9 Which airline is the flag carrier of Hong Kong?

10 In which area of France was the 1955 film *To Catch a Thief* set?

11 Which two creatures combined to form the mythical griffin?

12 The industrial heritage site of Quarry Bank Mill lies in which English county?

13 Which Hollywood actor married Katherine Schwarzenegger in June 2019?

14 Which former capital of Egypt shares its name with a city in Tennessee?

15 Who plays Nurse Shelagh Turner in *Call the Midwife*?

16 The crime novel *The Crow Trap* (1999) was written by which author?

17 "Don't stop, make it pop, DJ blow my speakers up" is a lyric from which 2009 song?

18 The kakapo is native to which island country?

19 Who starred as lawyer Robert Bilott in the 2019 film *Dark Waters*?

20 Who wrote the play on which the 1944 film *This Happy Breed* was based?

Answers to QUIZ 155 – Pot Luck

1	Sealyham	11	A butterfly
2	England (London)	12	The Bishop of Durham
3	Pamela Adlon	13	Quality, Value, Convenience
4	Celtic FC	14	Formic acid
5	Greta Thunberg	15	Gemma Jones
6	David Baddiel	16	The Mamas & the Papas
7	Bradford	17	Scotland (Perth)
8	ABBA	18	Naples
9	Surrey	19	John Wyndham
10	Parkour	20	2004

1   The long-distance path St Cuthbert's Way runs from Melrose in the Scottish Borders to which island?

2   Which children's character was created by Astrid Lindgren?

3   In which province of Ireland is County Longford?

4   Who wrote the 2019 novel *A Long Petal of the Sea*?

5   Which musician topped the charts in 1967 with *Let the Heartaches Begin*?

6   In which type of establishment would someone work if they were dealing with short orders?

7   In metres, what is the maximum range of short-wave broadcasting?

8   In which decade did Isaac Pitman first introduce the PitmanScript form of shorthand?

9   What was the number of the robot in the 1986 film *Short Circuit*?

10   Which soft drink gives a Long Island Iced Tea its colour?

11   What is described as "an absurd little bird" in the song *So Long, Farewell*?

12   Actress Eva Longoria was born in which US state?

13   Adam McKay directed which 2015 film about the 2007-08 financial crisis?

14   Which American set a world record in the men's long jump in 1991, still unbeaten as at 2020?

15   The 1993 film *Short Cuts* was set in which US city?

16   Longbridge, site of the former car factory, is part of which English city?

17   What was the title of the TV series filmed at Longleat from 1998 to 1999 that preceded *Animal Park*?

18   Which famous 1925 novel was set on Long Island?

19   What, in baking, is shortening?

20   Who played the title role in the biographical film *Longford*, first shown on television in 2006?

Answers to QUIZ 156 – History

1	Gladius	11	Walmer Castle
2	19th century (1874)	12	Window
3	Norfolk and Suffolk	13	The English Channel
4	Doodlebug	14	Huntingdonshire (now part of Cambridgeshire)
5	Chuck Yeager	15	William Beveridge (First Baron Beveridge)
6	IV	16	19th century (1859)
7	The Franco-Prussian war	17	Wilhelm II
8	1940s (1946-47)	18	Eiffel Tower
9	The Mongol Empire	19	France
10	Marco Polo	20	1950s (1953)

1 What name is given to the wine bottle that is also known as a double magnum?

2 Which Japanese fencing-like sport uses a split bamboo pole in place of a sword?

3 *The Divine Miss M* was the debut album by which actress and singer?

4 Who wrote the 2004 suspense novel, *Just One Look*?

5 What type of weapon is a katana?

6 Who played Agent 99 in the 2008 film *Get Smart*?

7 In what environment does a bathysphere travel?

8 Who was Dame Joan Plowright's famous second husband?

9 Takeshi Kovacs is the main character in which TV series?

10 What is the name of the membrane sac that contains the human heart?

11 Which year is expressed by the Roman numerals MCMXCIX?

12 What is the surname of the twin brothers Bob and Mike, regarded as one the greatest ever tennis doubles pairings?

13 In Greek mythology, which region of the Peloponnese was home to the god Pan?

14 Who were the two stars of the 1960 comedy *The Apartment*?

15 Which Australian former fast bowler has the nickname "Pigeon"?

16 The word "redolent" relates to which sense?

17 Which rock-and-roller's first single was called *That's All Right* (1954)?

18 Which country was formerly known as East Pakistan?

19 UNESCO has given "intangible" heritage status to the kalpak of Kyrgyzstan. What is a kalpak?

20 Which term for a youth subculture from the 1950s and 1960s in part takes its name from a Russian satellite?

Easy

Medium

Hard

Answers to QUIZ 157 – Pot Luck

1	California	11	Eagle and lion
2	Andre Agassi	12	Cheshire
3	Hinduism	13	Chris Pratt
4	(Stale) bread	14	Memphis
5	Pembrokeshire	15	Laura Main
6	Gilbert O'Sullivan	16	Ann Cleeves
7	Bath	17	TiK ToK (Kesha)
8	A confused situation	18	New Zealand
9	Cathay Pacific	19	Mark Ruffalo
10	The Riviera	20	Sir Noël Coward

Easy

1 Florence Nightingale set up a nursing school at which London hospital in 1860?

2 Who lives at the Apostolic Palace?

3 Which is the second-largest inhabited castle in England?

4 The country house of Rode Hall lies in which county?

5 The Cathedral of Monreale in Sicily is an example of what type of architecture?

6 Duart Castle is situated on which Scottish island?

7 Which castle in Kent is home to the world's only dog collar museum?

8 Which ruler commissioned the Kadriorg Palace, situated in modern-day Estonia?

9 In which building was Edward VI born?

10 In which Spanish city would you see the Torre del Oro (Tower of Gold)?

11 Guildford Cathedral was completed in which decade?

12 Which composer opened the first HMV shop in Oxford Street in 1921?

13 The Chateau Marmont hotel lies on which famous thoroughfare in Los Angeles?

14 In which building in Berlin does the German parliament meet?

Medium

15 *Mezquita* is the Spanish word for what type of building?

16 Until the Chrysler Building in New York City was built in 1930, what was the world's tallest man-made structure?

17 London's only example of what type of building stands at Trinity Buoy Wharf?

18 Which castle in Northern Ireland has one façade that features Georgian Gothic architecture with the opposite façade being in Palladian style?

19 Which building in Fife houses one of the world's oldest real tennis courts?

20 The first purpose-built mosque in the UK, the Shah Jahan Mosque, is situated in which English town?

Hard

---

1   Which crime drama series, first shown in 2019, centres on the character of Daisy Kowalski?

2   Cashmere Lop and Jersey Wooly are breeds of which animal?

3   Who co-starred with Liam Neeson in the 2019 film *Ordinary Love*?

4   In which sport was Casey Stoner twice world champion, in 2007 and 2011?

5   Who recorded the solo albums *...Nothing Like the Sun* (1987) and *If on a Winter's Night...*(2009)?

6   Who became the Mayor of Plymouth in 1581?

7   By what name is singer Enrique Morales (b.1971) better known?

8   Who composed the 1806 *Razumovsky Quartets*?

9   Yohji Yamamoto is famous in which field?

10   Who said "The way to get started is to quit talking and begin doing"?

11   "Little" Nell Trent is a character in which Dickens novel?

12   Which common household device features a magnetron as an integral part?

13   Which mythical creature of Aboriginal mythology is also called the kianpraty?

14   Sora, Kairi and Riku are the main characters in which video game series?

15   Which element is added to steel to make it stainless?

16   For what do the letters SWAT stand in relation to a police team?

17   What type of animal is a hogget?

18   What name is given to the sacred shell beads of some Native American tribes?

19   With which musical instrument is Herb Alpert (b.1935) most associated?

20   A siddur is a prayer book in which religion?

Easy
Medium
Hard

Answers to QUIZ 159 – Pot Luck

1	Jeroboam	11	1999
2	Kendo	12	Bryan
3	Bette Midler	13	Arcadia
4	Harlan Coben	14	Jack Lemmon and Shirley MacLaine
5	Samurai sword	15	Glenn McGrath
6	Anne Hathaway	16	Smell
7	Under the sea	17	Elvis Presley
8	Laurence Olivier (Baron Olivier)	18	Bangladesh
9	*Altered Carbon*	19	Hat
10	Pericardium	20	Beatnik (Sputnik)

1 In which South London town was Tracey Emin born?

2 Which US painter (d.1956) was famous for his drip paintings?

3 Cherubino and Susanna are characters in which Mozart opera?

4 Which sculptor worked at Trewyn Studio in St Ives?

5 Kathakali is a form of dance that originated in which country?

6 Former MP Tristram Hunt became director of which museum in 2017?

7 The Teatro del Silenzio open-air amphitheatre is located in which Italian region?

8 Which French artist (d.1954) said "Creativity takes courage"?

9 In which decade was the Burrell Collection opened in Glasgow?

10 What nationality was the war artist Fortunino Matania (d.1963)?

11 A cerograph is a design on what type of medium?

12 *Le Fils de l'Homme* (1964) is a famous work by which painter?

13 What does the title of Jean Dupas' 1925 work, *Les Perruches,* mean in English?

14 Lucian Freud was born in which capital city?

15 Which artist is believed to have discovered linear perspective?

16 Which artist was also a military engineer for Cesare Borgia?

17 What did Marcel Duchamp add to the *Mona Lisa*?

18 The artist James Whistler used which kind of stylised insect as his signature on his paintings?

19 What was Andy Warhol's surname at birth?

20 Who said, "I do not photograph nature. I photograph my visions"?

Answers to QUIZ 160 – Buildings

1	St Thomas' Hospital	11	1960s (1961)
2	The Pope	12	Sir Edward Elgar
3	Alnwick Castle	13	Sunset Boulevard
4	Cheshire	14	The Reichstag
5	Norman	15	Mosque
6	Mull	16	The Eiffel Tower
7	Leeds Castle	17	Lighthouse
8	Peter the Great of Russia	18	Castle Ward
9	Hampton Court Palace	19	Falkland Palace
10	Seville	20	Woking

ANSWERS ON PAGE **165**

1   Which word is used to describe the bubbly head on a glass of champagne?

2   *HMS Duncan* features in which Channel 5 TV series?

3   Which sport is played by the South African team the Cheetahs?

4   Who played whistleblower Katharine Gun in the 2019 film *Official Secrets*?

5   Which portly schoolboy was created by writer Charles Hamilton under the pen-name Frank Richards?

6   Dianetics is the belief system followed by members of which controversial organisation?

7   Which animals does the biological family *Suidae* cover?

8   Which part of the body concerns a periodontist?

9   The Horizontal Falls are a feature of which country?

10 Which chemical element has the symbol Cd?

11 In terms of the martial arts code, for what do the letters UFC stand?

12 What type of joint is the human elbow?

13 Which common dish gets its name from the Dutch for "cabbage salad"?

14 Which ancient thinker wrote the six works on logic known as *Organon*?

15 Souter Lighthouse is situated in which county?

16 What is the national anthem of Canada?

17 Which actress is the mother of Emily Atack?

18 What was Sir Tom Jones' surname at birth?

19 Larry Bird (b.1956) is a retired professional in which sport?

20 Which iconic item of home furnishings from the 1960-70s was invented by British accountant Edward Craven Walker?

Answers to QUIZ 161 – Pot Luck

1	Jett	11	*The Old Curiosity Shop*
2	Rabbit	12	Microwave oven
3	Lesley Manville	13	Bunyip
4	MotoGP	14	*Kingdom Hearts*
5	Sting	15	Chromium
6	Sir Francis Drake	16	Special Weapons and Tactics
7	Ricky Martin	17	A sheep
8	Beethoven	18	Wampum
9	Fashion design	19	The trumpet
10	Walt Disney	20	Judaism

1   Which rock band had a 1973 UK top twenty hit with *This Flight Tonight*?

2   The composer Vincenzo Bellini was born on which island?

3   South African Zulu musician Solomon Linda wrote which famous song, first recorded in 1939?

4   *Another Suitcase in Another Hall* is a song from which musical?

5   2020 saw which anniversary of Beethoven's birth?

6   A crumhorn is a member of which family of instruments?

7   Which US musician (d.1973) popularised "Cosmic American Music"?

8   According to Frank Sinatra's *The Coffee Song*, where have they "an awful lot of coffee"?

9   Which composer wrote the early 20th-century tone poem *In the Fen Country*?

10 *Love Don't Cost a Thing* was a 2001 hit for which singer?

11 Which 2013 song opened with the line "We clawed, we chained, our hearts in vain"?

12 Which Gilbert and Sullivan comic opera has the subtitle *The Slave of Duty*?

13 Which singer (d.2012) had the real name LaDonna Adrian Gaines?

14 Chad Kroeger is the lead singer of which band?

15 Which band sang the first line on the Band Aid 30 record?

16 In which country is Puccini's opera *Turandot* set?

17 Which US musician recorded the 2014 album *High Hopes*?

18 Musician Daniel Powter was bom in which country?

19 What question did Rihanna ask in the title of a 2012 single?

20 The band Daughtry was formed by a competitor from which TV talent show?

Answers to QUIZ 162 – The Arts

1	Croydon	11	Wax
2	Jackson Pollock	12	Magritte
3	*The Marriage of Figaro*	13	*The Parakeets* (or Parrots)
4	Dame Barbara Hepworth	14	Berlin
5	India	15	Filippo Brunelleschi
6	The V&A Museum	16	Leonardo da Vinci
7	Tuscany	17	A moustache
8	Henri Matisse	18	Butterfly
9	1980s (1983)	19	Warhola
10	Italian	20	Man Ray

1 In which decade did the first televised football match take place?

2 *Dangerous Lady* (1992) was the first published novel of which crime writer?

3 What is the first name of Kim Bodnia's character in the TV series *Killing Eve*?

4 In terms of average size, which is the smallest: a jaguar, a leopard, a lion or a tiger?

5 Tim Cook became the CEO of which computer company in 2011?

6 The genioglossus muscle is responsible for moving which part of the human body?

7 Ayurveda medicine originated in which country?

8 Which type of spook has a name that means "noise-ghost" in German?

9 Which sportswear brand was founded by Adolf Dassler?

10 What is the ceremonial dagger carried by Sikhs called?

11 In which decade was Lancashire CCC founded?

12 What is a Glock?

13 What colour is the volcanic glass obsidian?

14 The left-handed golfer Bob Charles, who won the Open golf tournament in 1963, was from which country?

15 Kookaburras are part of which group of birds?

16 What was the real first name of the President of Haiti who was known as "Papa Doc"?

17 What would you be doing if you were using the entrelac technique?

18 The ancient Mayan city of Chichen Itza is located in which Mexican state?

19 Who had a hit in 1976 with *The Year of the Cat*?

20 The jeweller Tiffany & Co's original catalogue was known as which colour book?

Easy

Medium

Hard

Answers to QUIZ 163 – Pot Luck

1	Mousse	11	Ultimate Fighting Championship
2	*Warship: Life at Sea*	12	A hinge joint
3	Rugby union	13	Coleslaw
4	Keira Knightley	14	Aristotle
5	Billy Bunter	15	Tyne and Wear
6	Scientology	16	*O Canada*
7	Pigs	17	Kate Robbins
8	The gums and teeth	18	Woodward
9	Australia	19	Basketball
10	Cadmium	20	Lava lamp

In which cities are these cathedrals?

1

2

3

4

5

6

7

8

Answers to QUIZ 164 – Music

1	Nazareth	11	*Wrecking Ball* (Miley Cyrus)
2	Sicily	12	*The Pirates of Penzance*
3	*The Lion Sleeps Tonight*	13	Donna Summer
4	*Evita*	14	Nickelback
5	250th anniversary	15	One Direction
6	Woodwind	16	China
7	Gram Parsons	17	Bruce Springsteen
8	Brazil	18	Canada
9	Ralph Vaughan Williams	19	*Where Have You Been?*
10	Jennifer Lopez	20	*American Idol* (Chris Daughtry)

1   What is the national animal of both India and Bangladesh?

2   In the 1954 film *Rear Window*, what caused James Stewart's character to be wheelchair bound?

3   Who wrote the 2019 novel *Anna of Kleve Queen of Secrets*?

4   What is the name of the US Navy's aerobatics team?

5   What was the title of Roger Daltrey's debut solo single, released in 1973?

6   Which starch puts the bubbles into bubble tea?

7   Who wrote the 1864 opera *La damnation de Faust*?

8   Shin Bet is the internal security service of which country?

9   Who played the title role in Lynda La Plante's TV series *The Commander*?

10 What was Fred Astaire's original surname?

11 What would you do at a plebiscite?

12 Which biblical figure slayed an entire army with only the jawbone of an ass?

13 *Lignum* is Latin for which natural material?

14 What is produced by the process of saponification?

15 Who succeeded Caligula as Roman emperor?

16 In which decade was the poet Emily Dickinson born?

17 Which team won the first two Cricket World Cups?

18 The Claddagh is part of which Irish city?

19 Which country is the world's largest producer of cork?

20 What was the title of the radio series of *The Hitchhiker's Guide to the Galaxy* that was first broadcast in 2018?

Answers to QUIZ 165 – Pot Luck

1	1930s (1937)	11	1860s (1864)
2	Martina Cole	12	A pistol
3	Konstantin (Vasiliev)	13	Black
4	Leopard	14	New Zealand
5	Apple Inc	15	Kingfishers
6	Tongue	16	François (Duvalier)
7	India	17	Knitting
8	Poltergeist	18	Yucatán
9	Adidas	19	Al Stewart
10	Kirpan	20	The Blue Book

1. In which decade were yellow balls first used at the Wimbledon tennis championships?

2. The 2019 World Athletics Championships took place in which country?

3. What is the main type of racing held at Cadwell Park in Lincolnshire?

4. What nickname was used to describe the Australian coxless fours team that won Olympic gold in 1992 and 1996?

5. For which football team did Ellen White (b.1989) sign in 2019?

6. What type of sport is taught at a manège?

7. At which club did Stuart Broad begin his professional cricket career in 2005?

8. The Irish Open golf championship was played at which course in 2012?

9. Divock Origi (b.1995) plays football for which international team?

10. Where does the annual six-day long Marathon des Sables take place?

11. Who won the 2020 Masters Snooker Championship?

12. Which sport was not included in the 1960 Winter Olympic Games because too few teams had indicated that they would take part?

13. The bouts of which sport are contested within a dohyō?

14. At which venue were the archery events held at the London Olympics?

15. How many of the NHL's member clubs compete in Canada?

16. How many times did Evonne Goolagong Cawley win the singles title at the Wimbledon tennis tournament?

17. Which sport is played by the Manchester Thunder team?

18. What is the nickname given to the Jamaican Sprinter Yohan Blake?

19. For which team did Luis Figo play from 2000 to 2005?

20. Bouldering is a form of which indoor sport?

Answers to QUIZ 166 – Cities with Cathedrals

1. Cologne
2. Edinburgh (St Giles')
3. St David's
4. Ely
5. Liverpool
6. Rouen
7. Coventry (Anglican)
8. Milan

1 Locust bean gum is made from the seeds of which tree?

2 Which word for a braggart is the name of a boastful character in Spenser's *Faerie Queene*?

3 Who starred as Alice Klieg in the 2014 film *Welcome to Me*?

4 Which journalist and television presenter wrote the 2019 novel *The House by the Loch*?

5 Former cricketer Ashley Giles was nicknamed "the King" of which country following a printing error on a set of mugs?

6 What colour wine is made from the viognier grape?

7 *People, Hell and Angels* was a 2013 posthumous album of work by which legendary guitarist?

8 As at 2019, which country had the highest wealth per adult?

9 What name is given to the smallest size of wine bottle?

10 In Greek mythology, the horn of the goat Amalthaea that suckled Zeus is given what name?

11 Which fictional feline was created by Yuko Shimizu?

12 The Starbucks® coffee chain took its name from a character in which novel?

13 *Music in the Tuileries* was a major early work by which Impressionist artist?

14 Which famous football club's motto is *Droit au But*, meaning "straight to the goal"?

15 Ellen Ternan was famously the mistress of which writer?

16 Which cathedral is described by UNESCO as "the high point of French Gothic art"?

17 Tony Abbot was the prime minister of which country from 2013 to 2015?

18 The Kori bustard is the largest flying bird native to which continent?

19 Jazz musician John Coltrane is associated with which instrument?

20 Ecuador first played in the FIFA World Cup finals in which decade?

Answers to QUIZ 167 – Pot Luck

1	Bengal tiger	11	Vote
2	A broken leg	12	Samson
3	Alison Weir	13	Wood
4	The Blue Angels	14	Soap
5	*Giving It All Away*	15	Claudius
6	Tapioca	16	1830s (1830)
7	Berlioz	17	West Indies
8	Israel	18	Galway
9	Amanda Burton	19	Portugal
10	Austerlitz	20	*The Hexagonal Phase*

1 *All's Well That Ends Well* is set in France and which other country?

2 What is regarded as Shakespeare's first play?

3 Hector, Paris and Agamemnon are characters in which play?

4 How many sonnets did Shakespeare write (to the nearest ten)?

5 In *Measure for Measure*, what relation are Claudio and Isabella?

6 Antonio borrows money from Shylock in *The Merchant of Venice* to aid whom?

7 In which Shakespeare play are Claudio and Hero lovers?

8 "'Tis true that a good play needs no epilogue" is a line from which play?

9 What relation is Sir Toby Belch to Olivia in *Twelfth Night*?

10 Who is mistakenly stabbed in *Hamlet*?

11 What was the first name of Shakespeare's father?

12 Ferdinand, King of Navarre, Don Adriano de Armado and Moth are characters in which Shakespeare play?

13 Which animal completes the title of Shakespeare's 1601 poem, *The Phoenix and the ___*?

14 Who is Brabantio's daughter in *Othello*?

15 In which city is *Titus Andronicus* set?

16 What was the last play that Shakespeare wrote?

17 In which play is there a note that a "spirit like a cat" descends?

18 Casca and Lepidus are characters in which play?

19 Which mythological figure accompanied Venus in the title of a 1593 poem by Shakespeare?

20 "There are more things in heaven and earth, Horatio, than are dreamt of in your philosophy", is a line from which Shakespeare play?

Easy

Medium

Hard

ANSWERS ON PAGE **173**

1   Where would you wear a pantofle?

2   What is the name of the dog in the film *The Call of the Wild*?

3   Tom Kirkman is the leading character in which TV series?

4   Which instrument represents the kangaroo in *The Carnival of the Animals*?

5   Footballer Nick Pope (b.1992) has played in what position for the England national team?

6   Of what is dermatoglyphics the study?

7   The 1952 film *The Snows of Kilimanjaro* was based on a novel by which author?

8   Metis and Leda are moons of which planet?

9   The singer Robyn was born in which country in 1979?

10 Mrs Lovett is a business partner of which fictional killer?

11 Where in the body would you find cementum?

12 What is a cornichon?

13 What does the Chinese company Tsingtao produce?

14 Lake Brienz and Lake Thun lie in which European country?

15 Which element has the lowest boiling point?

16 How many seconds are set on the shot clock in US National Basketball Association games?

17 Alan Scott is the human identity of which superhero?

18 In the Bible, what did Joshua's Israelite army use to destroy the walls of the city of Jericho?

19 Which single was a UK top ten hit for Coast to Coast in 1981?

20 In Greek mythology, how many daughters did the Titan Atlas have?

Answers to QUIZ 169 – Pot Luck

1	Carob tree	11	Hello Kitty
2	Braggadocio	12	*Moby-Dick*
3	Kristen Wiig	13	Manet
4	Kirsty Wark	14	Marseille
5	Spain (it should have been "Spin")	15	Charles Dickens
6	White	16	Chartres
7	Jimi Hendrix	17	Australia
8	Switzerland	18	Africa
9	Piccolo (0.1875 of a litre)	19	Saxophone
10	Cornucopia	20	2000s (2002)

1 Which country is home to the fjord called Doubtful Sound?

2 Which river flows through Christchurch in New Zealand?

3 The town of Boppard lies on which river?

4 The type of vessel known as a felucca is particularly associated with which sea?

5 A canal runs from Bridgwater to which other Somerset town?

6 Which Austrian airport is also referred to as "The Blue Danube" Airport?

7 By what name is the Chinese Huang He river better known?

8 In which country does the Orange River rise?

9 Vientiane, the capital of Laos, lies on which river?

10 Which river forms part of the border between Colombia and Venezuela?

11 Honfleur and Le Havre are situated on the estuary of which river?

12 The port of Ijmuiden is located at the mouth of which Dutch canal?

13 The River Chelmer flows entirely in which county?

14 Which strait separates the South American mainland and Tierra del Fuego?

15 How many rivers in Brazil are called Rio Negro?

16 The name of which river provided a hit single for the group Pussycat in 1976?

17 The city of Venice lies in a lagoon in which sea?

18 In 1914, the SS Ancon was the first ship to officially pass through which waterway?

19 The Anderton Boat Lift links the River Weaver with which canal?

20 The Arabian Sea is part of which ocean?

Answers to QUIZ 170 – Shakespeare

1	Italy	11	John
2	The Two Gentlemen of Verona	12	Love's Labour's Lost
3	Troilus and Cressida	13	Turtle
4	150 (154)	14	Desdemona
5	Brother and sister	15	Rome
6	Bassanio	16	The Tempest
7	Much Ado About Nothing	17	Macbeth
8	As You Like It	18	Julius Caesar
9	Uncle	19	Adonis
10	Polonius	20	Hamlet

1 The ancient structure called Diocletian's Palace lies in which European city?

2 What does the condition hypertrichosis cause an excessive amount of?

3 Who played Pierce Brosnan's ex-wife in the 2013 film *The Love Punch*?

4 What colour is the melon-flavoured liqueur Midori?

5 The Cutler and Gross fashion brand specialises in which field?

6 In terms of the share market, for what do the letters IPO stand?

7 What is the Italian dish of *polpette*?

8 Which city hosted the first summer Olympic Games after WWII?

9 Kaolinite is the main ingredient in which type of ceramics?

10 Turquoise is a mineral comprising mainly which two metals?

11 Which Asian country's flag features a five-pointed gold star on a red background?

12 What colour is uranium ore?

13 What type of person is a panjandrum?

14 How is the common foot ailment Unguis incarnates more commonly known?

15 Which group had a 1976 hit with *Arms of Mary*?

16 Who co-starred with Martin Freeman in the 2020 comedy series *Breeders*?

17 What type of animal is a tick?

18 By which name is the 11th-century Castilian nobleman Rodrigo Díaz de Vivar better known?

19 Freida Pinto made her film debut in which award-winning film of 2008?

20 Which US city hosts the oldest annual marathon?

Answers to QUIZ 171 – Pot Luck

1	On the foot (it's a slipper)	11	The mouth (it covers the roots of teeth)
2	Buck	12	A small gherkin
3	*Designated Survivor*	13	Beer
4	Piano	14	Switzerland
5	Goalkeeper	15	Helium
6	Patterns on the skin, particularly fingerprints	16	24 seconds
7	Ernest Hemingway	17	Green Lantern
8	Jupiter	18	Trumpets
9	Sweden	19	*(Do) The Hucklebuck*
10	Sweeney Todd	20	Seven

1   What is added to the top of a croque-monsieur to turn it into a croque-madame?

2   In which European country do people traditionally eat lentils at New Year in the hope of achieving wealth and happiness?

3   Scotch whisky must be aged for a minimum of how many years?

4   Traditional earthenware vessels called qvevri are still used in the Republic of Georgia to make what drink?

5   What is the eastern Mediterranean cuisine of a series of small dishes to be shared with drinks or as a light meal?

6   What type of meat is the Italian bresaola?

7   In Japanese cookery, what is *panko*?

8   Which process breaks down the fat in milk so that it is evenly spread throughout?

9   The dessert of Bavarian cream is also known by which French name?

10 In baking, what are the three main ingredients of a streusel topping?

11 Melliferous refers to which foodstuff?

12 Ray Kroc was the businessman behind which global food franchise?

13 What is the term for meat cooked slowly in its own fat?

14 The French town of Beaune is associated with the production of which wine?

15 In which town was Quality Street® first manufactured?

16 What colour is the seaweed dulse?

17 What type of condiment is *fleur de sel*?

18 Medronho is a traditional fruit brandy from which European country?

19 What is fermented with bacteria and yeast to make kombucha?

20 Which two main ingredients are added to the filling of a pork pie to make a gala pie?

Easy

Medium

Hard

Answers to QUIZ 172 – Waterways

1	New Zealand	11	The River Seine
2	The River Avon	12	The North Sea Canal
3	The River Rhine	13	Essex
4	The Mediterranean Sea	14	The Strait of Magellan
5	Taunton	15	Six
6	Linz Airport	16	*Mississippi*
7	The Yellow River	17	The Adriatic Sea
8	Lesotho	18	The Panama Canal
9	River Mekong	19	The Trent and Mersey Canal
10	The Orinoco	20	The Indian Ocean

1   In which decade was Florence Nightingale born?

2   What sport is played by the Argentine team La Dolfina?

3   The 1935 novel *The African Queen* was set during which conflict?

4   In the kitchen, how is potassium bitartrate known?

5   What is an escritoire?

6   In which two countries do alligators live?

7   The character of Wolverine has what type of fictional metal in his body?

8   Who was the Roman equivalent of the Greek god Ares?

9   In which city is the world's oldest stock exchange based?

10 How many teams play in the UK Netball Superleague?

11 Tampere is the second largest city, by area, in which nation?

12 Which band released the 2013 album *Mechanical Bull*?

13 What type of creature is a Norfolk hawker?

14 In the Old Testament, who was the great-grandfather of Nimrod?

15 Which flightless birds are of the genus *Apteryx*?

16 In which decade did Uhuru Kenyatta become the president of Kenya?

17 What was the name of James Michael Tyler's character in *Friends*?

18 Which singer's albums include *Music City Soul* (2007) and *Soulsville* (2016)?

19 In poetry, how many lines long is a Sapphic stanza?

20 Which Greek mathematician wrote the work *On Floating Bodies*?

Easy

Medium

Hard

Answers to QUIZ 173 – Pot Luck

1	Split (Croatia)	11	Vietnam
2	Hair	12	Yellowish-grey
3	Dame Emma Thompson	13	A pretentious official
4	Green	14	Ingrown (toe)nail
5	Eyewear	15	Sutherland Brothers & Quiver
6	Initial Public Offering	16	Daisy Haggard
7	(Small) meatballs	17	Arachnid
8	London (1948)	18	El Cid
9	Porcelain	19	*Slumdog Millionaire*
10	Aluminium and copper	20	Boston

1. April 2020 marked which anniversary of William Wordsworth's birth?

2. Which children's writer created the character of Worzel Gummidge?

3. In which Charles Dickens novel is the title character born and raised in the Marshalsea debtors' prison?

4. The novelist David Baldacci was born in which country?

5. The fictional Yorkshire house of Misselthwaite Manor features in which 20th-century children's novel?

6. Which French term describes a novel in which real events and people form the basis for the fiction?

7. The Ernest Hemingway novel *For Whom the Bell Tolls* was set during which conflict?

8. Which novel by Thomas Hardy takes place on the fictitious Egdon Heath?

9. GK Chesterton was born in what decade?

10. CS Lewis Square, containing several Narnia-inspired sculptures, lies in which UK city?

11. The title of Aldous Huxley's novel *Eyeless in Gaza* was taken from a play by which 17th-century poet?

12. Who wrote *Le Morte d'Arthur* (1485)?

13. How old was Mary Shelley when she began writing *Frankenstein*?

14. Which novel of the 1870s has the subtitle *A Study of Provincial Life*?

15. For what does the R stand in the name of the 19th-century writer RM Ballantyne?

16. Which Caribbean island features at the beginning of the 1966 novel *Wide Sargasso Sea*?

17. Who wrote the 2019 novel *The Strawberry Thief*?

18. Which implement features twice on the logo of the Crime Writers' Association?

19. *The Carpet People* (1971) was the first novel by which author?

20. In which decade was *Pride and Prejudice* published?

Answers to QUIZ 174 – Food and Drink

1	A fried egg	11	Honey
2	Italians	12	McDonald's
3	Three years	13	Confit
4	Wine	14	Burgundy
5	Meze	15	Halifax
6	(Air-dried and salted) beef	16	Red
7	(White) breadcrumbs	17	Salt
8	Homogenisation	18	Portugal
9	Bavarois	19	Tea
10	Flour, butter and sugar	20	Chicken and egg

1   The town of Sirmione lies on which Italian lake?

2   Who starred as Debra Callahan in the 2018 film *American Woman*?

3   What method of sealing takes its name from the Greek god Hermes?

4   In the early days of aviation, what name was given to a pilot who performed at country fairs in the US?

5   "Life is what happens when you're busy making other plans" are lyrics in the song *Beautiful Boy (Darling Boy)* from which 1980 album?

6   Rita Wilson (b.1956) married which actor in 1988?

7   How many dancers typically perform the *Dance of the Little Swans* in *Swan Lake*?

8   Who was Matt Damon's female co-star in the 2013 film *Elysium*?

9   Which is South Africa's busiest port?

10 The Miami Heat team plays which sport?

11 East Stonehouse was a town that became part of which city in the UK?

12 Which star of Hollywood's golden era was born Virginia McMath?

13 Which European river flows through the Iron Gates gorge?

14 Ashkenazim members belong to which religion?

15 What does bellicose mean?

16 What colour is an emu's egg?

17 Which part of the human body is also referred to as the antebrachium?

18 Beating England in the final, which team won the Cricket World Cup for the first time in 1992?

19 In which century did the Early Post-Classic period of the Maya Civilisation begin?

20 Which food means "it is sour" in Japanese?

Answers to QUIZ 175 – Pot Luck

1	1820s (1820)	11	Finland
2	Polo	12	Kings of Leon
3	WWI	13	A dragonfly
4	Cream of tartar	14	Noah
5	Writing desk	15	Kiwis
6	USA and China	16	2010s (2013)
7	Adamantium	17	Gunther
8	Mars	18	Beverley Knight
9	Amsterdam	19	Four
10	Ten	20	Archimedes

Easy

Medium

Hard

1   Which seaside resort connects to the M6 via the M55?

2   In which year were tolls abolished on the Skye Bridge?

3   Where in Liverpool are the statues known as Bella and Bertie?

4   In which decade did Christmas lights first appear in Oxford Street in London?

5   Which river flows through the city of Lancaster?

6   Which Northamptonshire town holds an annual Rowell Fair, celebrating the granting of a market charter in 1204?

7   In Cornwall, of what are Geevor and Levant examples?

8   The Vale of White Horse is a local government district in which English county?

9   In which Staffordshire town was Minton pottery produced?

10 An annual Festival of Speed takes place in the grounds of which West Sussex stately home?

11 In which Surrey town is there a stainless steel sculpture known as *The Martian*?

12 Which tax was replaced by VAT in 1973?

13 In which decade was Belfast granted city status?

14 The Isle of Gigha is part of which UK council area?

15 In 1821, King George IV bestowed royal status on the harbour of which Kent town?

16 St Swithin is associated with which English city?

17 "By Land and Sea" is the motto of which Welsh city?

18 Which English town has the third-deepest natural harbour in the world and the deepest in Western Europe?

19 In which Cornish town does the annual festival of 'Obby 'Oss take place?

20 Greene King IPA is based in which English town?

Answers to QUIZ 176 – Literature

1	250th anniversary	11	John Milton (*Samson Agonistes*)
2	Barbara Euphan Todd	12	Sir Thomas Malory
3	*Little Dorrit*	13	18 years old
4	USA	14	*Middlemarch* (George Eliot)
5	*The Secret Garden*	15	Robert
6	*Roman à clef*	16	Jamaica
7	The Spanish Civil War	17	Joanne Harris
8	*The Return of the Native*	18	A dagger
9	1870s (1874)	19	Sir Terry Pratchett
10	Belfast	20	1810s (1813)

1   Perugia is the capital of which Italian region?

2   Daniel Tranter (b.1992) competes for Australia in which sport?

3   Which English city hosted the 1998 Eurovision Song Contest?

4   "Swinging in the backyard, Pull up in your fast car" is a lyric from which 2011 song?

5   What type of food is bocconcini?

6   A sybarite is devoted to what type of life?

7   According to apocryphal writings, in the New Testament, Joachim and Anne are the parents of which figure?

8   *Raise Your Glass* was a 2010 single by which singer?

9   For how many years did the soap *Eldorado* run?

10 How old was Harper Lee at the time of her death?

11 Which US golfer (b.1970) is nicknamed "Lefty"?

12 Taksim Square is a major tourist area in which city?

13 Orang-utans are found in the rainforests of Borneo and which other Indonesian island?

14 Which soul singer had a 1968 hit with *I'd Rather Go Blind*?

15 What colour does calcium burn?

16 "Gravid" is the medical term for being in what condition?

17 Melanie Elizabeth Bownds was the birth name of which Australian comedy actress?

18 What is the character of someone who is described as "panglossian"?

19 To the nearest thousand miles, how long is the Great Wall of China?

20 What is a proa?

Answers to QUIZ 177 – Pot Luck

1	Lake Garda	11	Plymouth
2	Sienna Miller	12	Ginger Rogers
3	Hermetic sealing	13	The River Danube
4	Barnstormer	14	Judaism
5	*Double Fantasy* (John Lennon and Yoko Ono)	15	Warlike or pugnacious
6	Tom Hanks	16	(Very dark) green
7	Four	17	Forearm
8	Jodie Foster	18	Pakistan
9	Durban	19	10th century
10	Basketball	20	Sushi

What are the names of these British Olympic gold medallists?

Easy

Medium

Hard

1

2

3

4

5

6

7

8

9

Answers to QUIZ 178 – The UK

1	Blackpool	11	Woking
2	2004	12	Purchase Tax
3	On top of the Royal Liver Building	13	1880s (1888)
4	1950s (1959)	14	Argyll and Bute
5	River Lune	15	Ramsgate
6	Rothwell	16	Winchester
7	Tin mines	17	Newport
8	Oxfordshire	18	Falmouth
9	Stoke-on-Trent	19	Padstow
10	Goodwood House	20	Bury St Edmunds

ANSWERS ON PAGE 183

1   Gastón Gaudio won which Grand Slam tennis event in 2004?

2   In which country does the jetBlue airline operate?

3   The Costa Smerelda is a coastal area on which Mediterranean island?

4   What was the title of the theme song to the James Bond film *The Spy Who Loved Me*?

5   David Sole (b.1962) played rugby union for which country?

6   What is the name of the helmet-wearing alien that appears in *Looney Tunes* cartoons?

7   Which US author wrote *The Sound and the Fury* (1929)?

8   In which 2013 film does Brad Pitt's character fight zombies?

9   What is the name of the sport derived from ski jumping that involves greater distances?

10 Which long-running series, last aired in 2003, was originally going to be given the title *Meadowcroft*?

11 Lox is a brined form of which fish?

12 What pigment is present in freckles?

13 Which actress has been married to the actors Gary Oldman and Ethan Hawke?

14 What is the main liturgical language of Hinduism?

15 As at the end of 2019, how many times had Peter Carey won the Booker prize?

16 What type of creatures do witchetty grubs become?

17 In Greek mythology who was the famous sister of Castor, Pollux and Clytemnestra?

18 What does the Latin phrase *fiat lux* mean?

19 Which is Canada's most populous province?

20 Gwendoline Christie played which character in *Star Wars: The Force Awakens*?

Easy

Medium

Hard

Answers to QUIZ 179 – Pot Luck

1	Umbria	11	Phil Mickelson
2	Swimming	12	Istanbul
3	Birmingham	13	Sumatra
4	*Video Games* (Lana Del Rey)	14	Etta James
5	Cheese (mozzarella)	15	Orange-red
6	Luxury and pleasure	16	Pregnant
7	Mary	17	Rebel Wilson
8	Pink	18	Overly optimistic
9	One (1992-93)	19	13,000 (13,171) miles
10	89	20	A boat (in the South Pacific)

ANSWERS ON PAGE 184

1 What was the title of the 2019 film about a teenager called Javed who becomes a fan of Bruce Springsteen?

2 Which actress co-starred with Hugh Jackman in the 2001 film *Kate & Leopold*?

3 Bong Joon-ho, winner of the Best Director Oscar at the 2020 award ceremony, was born in which country?

4 What was the title of the 2006 film in the Rocky series?

5 The award-winning 2019 film *Bait* was set in which county?

6 Which actor co-starred with John Wayne in the 1962 film *The Man Who Shot Liberty Valance*?

7 Actress Rosamund Pike made her big screen debut as a Bond girl in which film?

8 Who wrote the novel on which the 2015 film *The Martian* was based?

9 Which actor co-starred with Doris Day in the 1963 film *Move Over, Darling*?

10 Who played Zeus in the 2010 film *Clash of the Titans*?

11 "Fasten your seatbelts. It's going to be a bumpy night" is a quote from which 1950 film?

12 What was the title of the 2003 sci-fi film in which a team were tasked with drilling to the centre of the earth?

13 The screenplay for the 1990 film *Postcards from the Edge*, was written by which actress, based on her own semi-autobiographical novel?

14 In the 2019 film *The Personal History of David Copperfield*, who played Peggotty?

15 Who directed the 2019 film *Cats*?

16 Which sci-fi film of 2019 featured the T-800 and the Rev-9?

17 Judy Garland sang *The Trolley Song* in which 1944 film?

18 In the 1959 film *Expresso Bongo*, who played the character of Bert Rudge?

19 Who wrote and directed the 2017 film *Lady Bird*?

20 Who starred as Amy in the 2015 film *Trainwreck*?

Answers to QUIZ 180 – British Olympic Gold Medallists

1 Max Whitlock (gymnastics)
2 Alistair Brownlee (triathlon)
3 Dame Kelly Holmes (athletics)
4 Adam Peaty (swimming)
5 Dame Katherine Grainger (rowing)
6 Greg Rutherford (long jump)
7 Nicola Adams (boxing)
8 Justin Rose (golf)
9 Geraint Thomas (cycling)

1 The Sulu Sea is part of which ocean?

2 "Cutaneous" refers to which part of the body?

3 Seething Bay is located on which body of the solar system?

4 The Marlowe Theatre can be found in which English city?

5 At which FIFA World Cup did Norman Whiteside become the youngest ever player to feature in the tournament?

6 How many times did Mika Hakkinen win the Formula 1 World Championship?

7 What is the title of the Radio 4 obituary show first broadcast in 2006?

8 Which Asian island country has a name that means "Lion City"?

9 In which decade did Greggs open its first shop?

10 The character of Red Reddington, played by James Spader, appears in which TV series?

11 What edible items have the Latin name *Castanea Sativa*?

12 Which nationality completes the title of the first rule book for contract bridge, ___ *Whist*?

13 Brighton marina was constructed in which decade?

14 The spilling of salt and what other foodstuff is considered to be unlucky in Italy?

15 Opened in 1882, which open space is considered to be England's first nature reserve?

16 In the How to Train Your Dragon film series, what type of dragon is Toothless?

17 Which bird is particularly associated with the RSPB reserve of Loch Garten?

18 The three-point seatbelt was invented by an engineer working for which car manufacturer?

19 Kit Harington starred in which 2014 volcano disaster film?

20 The fictional character Don Quixote is from which part of Spain?

Answers to QUIZ 181 – Pot Luck

1	French Open	11	Salmon
2	USA	12	Melanin
3	Sardinia	13	Uma Thurman
4	*Nobody Does it Better*	14	Sanskrit
5	Scotland	15	Twice (1988 and 2001)
6	Marvin the Martian	16	Moths
7	William Faulkner	17	Helen of Troy
8	*World War Z*	18	Let there be light
9	Ski flying	19	Ontario
10	*Brookside*	20	Captain Phasma

Easy

1 Something described as "aquiline" resembles which creature?

2 Which dog is known as the "King of Terriers" because of its size?

3 What type of creature is a burnet?

4 What type of bird is used at the Wimbledon tennis championships to scare pigeons away?

5 Which breed of dog is associated with firefighters in the US?

6 An old creature of which type can be called a "grimalkin"?

7 Which parts of a Tasmanian Devil noticeably turn red when it is involved in a fight?

8 What is the cause of a sloth's fur turning a green colour?

9 What colour is the blood of a horseshoe crab?

10 The kulan is a species of wild ass native to which continent?

Medium

11 In what environment do kinkajous spend most of their time?

12 Which creatures belong to the genus *Vulpes*?

13 With which part of the body does a butterfly taste its food?

14 A cinnabar moth is black and which other colour?

15 What colour eggs does a song thrush lay?

16 How many eyes does a praying mantis have?

17 What type of creature is an axolotl?

18 Scaly anteater is another name for which creature?

19 Which species of tern shares its name with a Kent town?

20 Which animal is the largest living marsupial?

Hard

Answers to QUIZ 182 – Film

1	*Blinded by the Light*	11	*All About Eve*
2	Meg Ryan	12	*The Core*
3	South Korea	13	Carrie Fisher
4	*Rocky Balboa*	14	Daisy May Cooper
5	Cornwall	15	Tom Hooper
6	James Stewart	16	*Terminator: Dark Fate*
7	*Die Another Day*	17	*Meet Me in St Louis*
8	Andy Weir	18	Sir Cliff Richard
9	James Garner	19	Greta Gerwig
10	Liam Neeson	20	Amy Schumer

1 In 2014, a competition featuring what style of music was added to the BBC Young Musician competition?

2 What was the name of the Scottish terrier in *Lady and the Tramp*?

3 At which British Open golf venue would you have to cross the Barry Burn?

4 Baja California is a state in which country?

5 Mirin is a form of which drink?

6 *Axis: Bold as Love* (1967) and *Electric Ladyland* (1968) were albums by which rock band?

7 Who directed the 2014 film *American Sniper*?

8 Which constellation was named after a vain queen of Greek mythology?

9 Discovered in 1947 in Tanzania, what colour is the Williamson Diamond?

10 Which fragrant decoration takes its name for the French for an "apple of amber"?

11 What is the name of the 102-mile trail that runs from Bath to Chipping Camden?

12 Martin Clunes played Nigel Crabtree in which 1980s sitcom?

13 What are the names of the two conferences into which the US National Hockey League is split?

14 Which compound has the formula H_2O_2?

15 Emilio Largo is the main villain in which James Bond novel?

16 Los Condores (The Condors) is the nickname of the rugby union team of which country?

17 Rikers Island in New York city is the site of what type of establishment?

18 What is the literal translation of the Jewish phrase "mazel tov"?

19 How many years does it take to paint the Blackpool Tower from top to bottom?

20 What nickname, derived from its shape, is given to GCHQ?

Answers to QUIZ 183 – Pot Luck

1	The Pacific Ocean	11	Chestnuts
2	The skin	12	*Russian*
3	The Moon	13	1970s (completed in 1979)
4	Canterbury	14	Olive oil
5	1982	15	Epping Forest
6	Twice	16	A Night Fury
7	*Last Word*	17	The osprey
8	Singapore	18	Volvo (Niels Bohlin)
9	1950s (1951)	19	*Pompeii*
10	*The Blacklist*	20	La Mancha

1. Which term, derived from a native Greenland language, is used to describe an all-weather jacket?

2. What does a misanthrope dislike?

3. Which word meaning "going out" means "thrilling" with the addition of one letter?

4. What word given to an area is derived from the Latin for "field"?

5. If a substance is described as "cereous", what does it resemble?

6. What is limestone turned into when it is marmarised?

7. Which pale yellowish-green colour has a name that is French for "water of the Nile"?

8. The name of which Oriental exercise system means "grand ultimate"?

9. What Scottish word meaning "dip" is used to describe the New Year's Day tradition of outdoor swimming?

10. What type of wool takes its name from the French for "curled"?

11. In Japan, the custom of *hanami* is the enjoyment of what?

12. What word can mean both a unit of speed and a small sandpiper?

13. The word "brouhaha" is derived from which language?

14. When does a matutinal event occur?

15. Which term is used for the action of delaying tactics to hinder the passing of legislative action?

16. What does someone who is described as querulous do?

17. The name of which falcon is taken from the Latin for "wandering"?

18. What term is given to a country that is completely surrounded by another country?

19. To what does the adjective bucolic relate?

20. Of what is zoophobia a fear?

Answers to QUIZ 184 – Animal World

1	An eagle	11	In trees
2	Airedale	12	Foxes
3	A moth	13	The feet
4	A Harris Hawk	14	Red
5	The Dalmatian	15	(Pale) blue
6	A cat	16	Five
7	Ears	17	A salamander
8	Algae	18	Pangolin
9	Blue	19	Sandwich
10	Asia	20	The red kangaroo

1   Operating from 1905 to 1981, what type of company was Midland Red?

2   Who wrote the 2015 novel *The Stranger*, adapted for television in 2020?

3   The Cesarewitch Handicap and which other race were traditionally referred to as the "autumn double"?

4   In which country is Ian Fleming International Airport?

5   Which children's book author coined the term "nerd" in the 1950 book *If I Ran the Zoo?*

6   *Day by Day* and *Light of the World* are songs from which musical?

7   For what do the letters NV stand on a bottle of wine?

8   Which car brand produces high performance models under the AMG marque?

9   The Viktor & Rolf fashion house is based in which country?

10 What is the more common name for the runner's condition medial tibial stress syndrome?

11 Between 2009 and 2019, the Dakar Rally took place on which continent?

12 *Wonderful Crazy Night* was a 2016 album by which musician?

13 Which 2016 film was based on the real-life rescue of the *SS Pendleton* by the US Coast Guard?

14 In which century was Thomas Aquinas made a saint?

15 How many Pulitzer Prizes did Robert Frost win during his lifetime?

16 Who directed the 1972 film *Deliverance?*

17 The founder of Buddhism achieved spiritual enlightenment while sitting under what type of tree?

18 Titania is the largest moon of which planet?

19 The Greek mythological figure Pygmalion was what type of artist?

20 Which investor has been referred to as "The Oracle of Omaha"?

Easy

Medium

Hard

Answers to QUIZ 185 – Pot Luck

1	Jazz	11	The Cotswold Way
2	Jock	12	*No Place Like Home*
3	Carnoustie	13	Eastern and Western
4	Mexico	14	Hydrogen peroxide
5	Sake	15	*Thunderball*
6	The Jimi Hendrix Experience	16	Chile
7	Clint Eastwood	17	Jail (correctional centre)
8	Cassiopeia	18	Good luck
9	Pink	19	Seven years
10	Pomander	20	The Doughnut

Easy

1. The TV series *Good Omens* was based on a novel by Sir Terry Pratchett and which other writer?

2. Mrs Miggins, played by Helen Atkinson-Wood, featured in which TV comedy series?

3. Maurice Minnifield was a character in which 1990s TV series?

4. Police Detective Oskar Reinhardt appeared in which 2019 TV crime series?

5. Who plays Camilla in the TV series *The Windsors*?

6. Who wrote the novels on which the TV series *Outlander* is based?

7. Katie Rushworth and Frances Tophill are amongst the presenters of which makeover show?

8. Which character did Anne Reid play in *Coronation Street*?

9. In which country did *Top Gear* presenter Andrew Flintoff do a bungee jump in a car in the 2020 series?

10. Who wrote the sitcom *Porridge*?

11. Which long-running 1990s US sitcom starred Paul Reiser and Helen Hunt?

12. The TV series *Casualty* and *Holby City* take place in which fictional county?

13. Who played Charles Parnell in the 1991 mini-series *Parnell and the Englishwoman*?

14. In which sci-fi series of the 2000s did Patricia Helfer play the character of Number Six?

15. The crime drama series *Wisting* is set in which country?

16. Who played Dr Beatrice Mason in the 1980s series *Tenko*?

17. What was the title of the UK's first breakfast television programme?

18. Sam Rockwell and Michelle Williams starred as the title characters in which 2019 biographical series?

19. Who finished highest in the first series of *Pop Idol*: Hayley Evetts, Jessica Garlick or Zoe Birkett?

20. In the children's series *Captain Scarlet and the Mysterons*, what was the name of Spectrum's headquarters?

Medium

Hard

Answers to QUIZ 186 – Words

1	Anorak	11	Flowers, particularly cherry blossom
2	All other people	12	Knot
3	Exiting (exciting)	13	French
4	Campus	14	In the morning
5	Wax	15	Filibuster
6	Marble	16	Complain
7	Eau de nil	17	Peregrine falcon
8	Tai chi	18	Enclave
9	Dook	19	The countryside
10	Bouclé	20	Animals

ANSWERS ON PAGE 191

1 Who released the 1979 album *Night Owl*?

2 A two-woman version of which sport was first included in the Winter Olympics in 2002?

3 In the RAF, what rank is immediately below group captain?

4 Of what is vehophobia the fear?

5 The River Hamble flows through which English county?

6 Mountain gorillas are native to which continent?

7 Zinc oxide is the main ingredient in which soothing balm?

8 What name is given to a European wood and canvas structure used as a mobile entertainment venue?

9 The Bell 30 was an early prototype for which form of transport?

10 Footix the cockerel appeared as the official FIFA World Cup mascot in which country?

11 In which decade was the integrated circuit invented?

12 Whiff-whaff was an early name of which sport?

13 What is the name of the prehistoric ground sloth in the Ice Age films?

14 In the name of the liqueur Tia Maria®, what does the Italian word *tia* mean in English?

15 From 1969 to 1974 Mick Taylor was a guitarist with which band?

16 How many series of *Scrubs* were there?

17 What does the Greek word *oxi* translate to in English?

18 Which Hollywood legend wrote the 1928 play *Diamond Lil*?

19 A Nipponophile loves the culture of which country?

20 In the Old Testament, Jacob grasped which part of Esau upon birth?

Easy
Medium
Hard

Answers to QUIZ 187 – Pot Luck

1	Bus company	11	South America
2	Harlan Coben	12	Sir Elton John
3	The Cambridgeshire Handicap	13	*The Finest Hours*
4	Jamaica	14	14th century (1323)
5	Dr Seuss	15	Four (1924, 1931, 1937, 1943)
6	*Godspell*	16	John Boorman
7	Non-vintage	17	A fig tree
8	Mercedes	18	Uranus
9	The Netherlands	19	A sculptor
10	Shin splints	20	Warren Buffett

Easy

1   Veracruz is a state in which country?

2   Which is the second-largest lake in Italy?

3   Agrigento is a province of which Mediterranean island?

4   Azerbaijan is to the west of which body of water?

5   Nevsky Prospect is the main street in which Russian city?

6   The borders of which three Asian countries meet at the area called the Golden Triangle?

7   Which became the largest African country following the break-up of Sudan in 2011?

8   The airport of which city is on the island of Chek Lap Kok?

9   On which famous beach would you be if you could see the extinct volcano Diamond Head?

10   The flag of which African country features an AK-47 rifle?

11   The Amundsen Gulf lies off the coast of which country?

Medium

12   Which pass connects the town of Landi Kotal to the Valley of Peshawar?

13   The Gulf of Honduras is an inlet of which sea?

14   To the nearest 1000 feet, how high is Aconcagua?

15   Which country is the only one to lie entirely within the Alps?

16   Which two countries have an English language name that begins with "The"?

17   The Bismarck Archipelago is part of which country?

18   Which mountain range lies in the three Italian provinces of Belluno, South Tyrol and Trentino?

19   Which Turkish peninsula lies between the Aegean Sea and the Dardanelles?

20   The ancient European city of Worms is in which country?

Hard

Answers to QUIZ 188 – Television

1	Neil Gaiman	11	*Mad About You*
2	*Blackadder (Blackadder the Third)*	12	Wyvern
3	*Northern Exposure*	13	Trevor Eve
4	*Vienna Blood*	14	*Battlestar Galactica*
5	Haydn Gwynne	15	Norway
6	Diana J Gabaldon	16	Stephanie Cole
7	*Love Your Garden*	17	*Breakfast Time* (BBC in 1983)
8	Valerie Barlow	18	*Fosse/Verdon*
9	Switzerland	19	Zoe Birkett
10	Dick Clement and Ian La Frenais	20	Cloudbase

1   The 18th-century house Killerton, owned by the National Trust, lies in which county?

2   Which animal represents the year 2020 in the Chinese zodiac?

3   To the nearest ten years, how many Earth years does it take for Saturn to orbit the Sun?

4   In which state was Andy Warhol born?

5   The Rugby Challenge Cup Man of the Match award is named after which New Zealand-born player?

6   Which is the third-largest city in the UK, by population?

7   In which decade was Roald Dahl born?

8   Who played the lead role in the 1961 film *El Cid*?

9   What would you do with a galantine?

10   Which US singer had a hit with the album *River of Dreams* in 1993?

11   Tripolitania, Fezzan and Cyrenaica are the three main regions of which North African country?

12   Who wrote the 1985 sci-fi novel *Contact*?

13   What is the Antonov An-255 Mriya, the heaviest of its kind in the world?

14   In 2016, Novak Djokovic became the first male tennis player to hold all four major titles at the same time since 1969, when who previously achieved that feat?

15   Which character did Donald Sutherland play in the film *The Hunger Games: Catching Fire*?

16   Which sitcom featured the characters Linda La Hughes and Tom Farrell?

17   "Patriation" was the term coined for the political process that led to which country's transfer of sovereignty from the UK in 1982?

18   Which of these leaders was born first: Charlemagne, Hannibal or Julius Caesar?

19   Saint Agnes of Rome is always depicted with which animal?

20   Which actor (d.1957) was buried with a gold whistle inscribed with the words, "If you want anything, just whistle"?

Easy
Medium
Hard

Answers to QUIZ 189 – Pot Luck

1	Gerry Rafferty	11	1950s (1959)
2	Bobsleigh	12	Table tennis
3	Wing commander	13	Sid
4	Driving	14	Aunt
5	Hampshire	15	The Rolling Stones
6	Africa	16	Nine
7	Calamine	17	No
8	Spiegeltent	18	Mae West
9	Helicopter	19	Japan
10	France (1998)	20	His heel

1 Which chemical element has a name that means "metal of Cyprus"?

2 In which decade did the first public demonstrations of television take place?

3 Which communications company was originally founded in 1865 as a mill producing pulp for the paper industry?

4 The website domain level .tv belongs to which island?

5 As at the end of 2019, which element in the periodic table was alphabetically first?

6 The first industrial robot, Unimate, was originally installed on an assembly line in a factory belonging to which car manufacturer?

7 In physics, what is defined as the number of times a sound or radio wave vibrates within a specified period of time?

8 The modern name of which chemical element is derived from the Swedish for "heavy stone"?

9 Rather than radar's radio wave, what does lidar use to measure range?

10 What does the H stand for in the pH measure of acidity?

11 Which branch of physics is concerned with static charges?

12 "Cal Tech", produced in 1967, was the first prototype version of which electronic device?

13 Tux the penguin is the mascot of which computer operating system?

14 Which chemical element takes its name from the Greek word for foreigner?

15 Which semiconductor device lies at the heart of all integrated circuits and electronic devices?

16 The Rod of Asclepius, a serpent wrapped around a staff, is associated with which science?

17 Mimas is a moon of which planet?

18 What term is given to the energy produced by the motion of a body?

19 Which company developed the 1970s arcade game *Starship 1*?

20 What does a pyrometer measure?

---

1. What was the birth name of actress Julianne Moore?

2. Annette Kellerman (d.1975) helped popularise which water sport in the early 20th century?

3. *Innervisions* (1973) was a classic album by which US musician?

4. What is mastic?

5. What is the secret identity of the fictional character Don Diego de la Vega?

6. *Speak Softly, Love* is the famous theme music from which film?

7. Erik Wallenberg was a Swedish engineer behind which innovative food container?

8. In 1807 Thomas Bowdler produced a sanitised "family" version of which writer's works?

9. Road Town is the capital of which British Overseas Territory?

10. Birds largely evolved during which geological period?

11. What type of meat is used to make a Reuben sandwich?

12. Which everyday items appear on the flag of the Vatican City?

13. Ronaldo won the Golden Boot in the FIFA 2002 World Cup, scoring how many goals?

14. Who presented the 2019 TV series *Equator from the Air*?

15. During which century was the tsardom of Russia established?

16. Michael Starke played which character in *Brookside*?

17. Which US first lady wrote the newspaper column "My Day", from 1935 to 1962?

18. Along with the Grand National, which race forms the traditional "spring double"?

19. The Serpent Sea can be found where in the solar system?

20. What is the main religion of Armenia?

Easy

Medium

Hard

Answers to QUIZ 191 – Pot Luck

1	Devon	11	Libya
2	The rat	12	Carl Sagan
3	30 years (29 years)	13	A (cargo) plane
4	Pennsylvania	14	Rod Laver
5	Lance Todd	15	President Snow
6	Glasgow	16	*Gimme Gimme Gimme*
7	1910s (1916)	17	Canada
8	Charlton Heston	18	Hannibal (247 BC)
9	Eat it (a cold, jellied meat dish)	19	A lamb
10	Billy Joel	20	Humphrey Bogart

What are the names of these British bridges?

Easy

1

2

3

4

Medium

5

6

7

8

Hard

Answers to QUIZ 192 – Science and Technology

1	Copper	11	Electrostatics
2	1920s (1925)	12	Pocket calculator
3	Nokia	13	Linux
4	Tuvalu	14	Xenon
5	Actinium	15	Transistor
6	General Motors	16	Medicine
7	Frequency	17	Saturn
8	Tungsten	18	Kinetic energy
9	Lasers	19	Atari®
10	Hydrogen (power of hydrogen)	20	High temperatures

ANSWERS ON PAGE 197

1   Which singer had a 1996 hit with *Spinning the Wheel*?

2   The quality of which product is measured using a lactoscope?

3   Which designer label makes the Kelly bag, named after Grace Kelly?

4   Which Verdi opera is about a Nubian princess?

5   In Greek myth, who was Hero's ill-fated lover?

6   What was the name of the character voiced by Dame Angela Lansbury in *Beauty and the Beast* (1991)?

7   Penhold and shakehand are grips used in which sport?

8   Which French term is used to describe the preparation of ingredients for a dish ready for use?

9   Who won her second BBC Women's Footballer of the Year Award in 2020?

10   "Thus with a kiss I die," are the last words of which Shakespearean character?

11   In Greek mythology, Apollo gave King Midas the ears of which animal?

12   Who composed the 19th-century opera *Manon Lescaut*?

13   The Catalans Dragons rugby team are based in which French city?

14   Which US state has the lowest population?

15   Vermiculture is the cultivation of which creatures?

16   What was the first European beer to be imported into America after Prohibition?

17   What is the nickname of the main character in the series *True Detective*?

18   Which meat is traditionally part of eggs Benedict?

19   In which country was the actress Sofia Vergara born?

20   In Portugal, what is a *quinta*?

Answers to QUIZ 193 – Pot Luck

1	Julie Anne Smith	11	Corned beef
2	Synchronised swimming	12	Keys
3	Stevie Wonder	13	Eight
4	Tree resin	14	Gordon Buchanan
5	Zorro	15	16th century (1547)
6	*The Godfather*	16	Sinbad
7	Tetra Pak®	17	Eleanor Roosevelt
8	Shakespeare	18	The Lincoln Handicap
9	British Virgin Islands	19	The Moon
10	Jurassic	20	Christianity

1   U2's *With or Without You* (1987) was the lead single from which album?

2   To the nearest half-hour, how long is the film *Gone with the Wind*?

3   The autobiographical novel *Cider with Rosie* by Laurie Lee was set in which county?

4   In which city was the 1955 film *Rebel Without a Cause* set?

5   Who played prison governor Faye Boswell in the 1970s TV series *Within These Walls*?

6   Which actress played Stands With a Fist in the 1990 film *Dances with Wolves*?

7   George Emerson and Cecil Vyse are characters in which 1908 novel, adapted for the big screen in 1985?

8   Marianne Jean-Baptiste played Special Agent Vivian Johnson in which US TV series, first shown in 2002?

9   In which year was *Come Dine with Me* first broadcast?

10 Who played Jan Vermeer in the 2003 film *Girl with a Pearl Earring*?

11 *Without You*, sung by Roger and Mimi, is a song from which 1990s musical?

12 Who sang the theme to the Bond film *From Russia with Love*?

13 In which decade was the Jennifer Aniston film *Just Go With It* released?

14 *With a Girl Like You* was a 1966 chart-topping single for which band?

15 Who starred as teacher Mark Thackeray in the 1967 film *To Sir, with Love*?

16 Which group released the 1978 single *Angels with Dirty Faces*?

17 Reese Witherspoon was nominated for an Oscar for her perfomance in which 2014 film?

18 Which Doobie Brothers single includes the refrain "Without love, where would you be now"?

19 Who co-wrote the 1976 single *You See the Trouble with Me* with Barry White?

20 The 1987 film *Withnail and I* was set in London and which county?

Answers to QUIZ 194 – Crossings

1   Tamar Bridge
2   The Clyde Arc
3   Blackfriars Bridge
4   Pulteney Bridge, Bath
5   Menai Bridge
6   Humber Bridge
7   Queensferry Crossing
8   Tarr Steps, Exmoor

QUIZ 197 – Pot Luck

ANSWERS ON PAGE **199**

1   Which river flows through the Wachau valley?

2   *Fairytale* was a 1976 single by which Eurovision winner?

3   What is the name of Jack Nicholson's character in *The Shining*?

4   Miu Miu is a subsidiary of which fashion house?

5   In which Canadian province is the city of London?

6   Which 1956 film was the last to star Grace Kelly?

7   Who officially opened the Sydney Opera House?

8   Which sport was a five-man competition at the 1928 Winter Olympic Games but has since been a two or four man event?

9   Quarrelling composers George Frideric Handel and Giovanni Bononcini were famously likened to which literary duo?

10 The Central American dish *gallo pinto* has which two main ingredients?

11 What is the more common name for the beetles *lampyridae*?

12 Who played Colonel Irina Spalko in the 2008 film *Indiana Jones and the Kingdom of the Crystal Skull*?

13 Lucknow is the capital of which Indian state?

14 How many Grand Slam tennis finals did David Nalbandian reach during his playing career?

15 Batman's enemy Harvey Dent is known by which nickname?

16 What is a tumbrel?

17 Which TV series, first shown in 2005, was set in the FBI's Behavioral Analysis Unit?

18 What is the smallest country on the African continent, nearly entirely surrounded by Senegal?

19 Which French painter produced the 19th-century work *The Boy in the Red Vest*?

20 David Wenham played which character in Peter Jackson's The Lord of the Rings trilogy?

Answers to QUIZ 195 – Pot Luck

1	George Michael	11	An ass or donkey
2	Milk	12	Puccini
3	Hermès	13	Perpignan
4	*Aida*	14	Wyoming
5	Leander	15	Worms
6	Mrs Potts	16	Heineken®
7	Table tennis	17	Rust (Rustin Cohle)
8	*Mise en place*	18	Bacon
9	Lucy Bronze	19	Colombia
10	Romeo	20	Estate (such as a vineyard or olive grove)

ANSWERS ON PAGE 200

1 After Mexico, which was the second nation to host the World Cup twice?

2 Which country hosted the first World Cup to be played in Eastern Europe?

3 The World Cup was first held in Europe in which decade?

4 By what scoreline did Brazil beat Germany in the 2002 final?

5 César Luis Menotti managed which nation in the 1978 tournament?

6 Which country hosted the first Women's World Cup, in 1999?

7 England first played in the World Cup in which decade?

8 Davor Šuker scored six goals for which nation at the 1998 tournament?

9 How many teams contested the 1982 World Cup Finals?

10 Cameroon and which other African country made their debuts in the 1982 finals?

11 How many goals did Gerd Müller score in the 1970 tournament to win the Golden Boot?

12 In which decade did Germany, as West Germany, first win the tournament?

13 Goleo the Lion was the official mascot in which year?

14 Which South American team was the first to win the Fair Play Award, in 1978?

15 Megan Rapinoe won the Golden Ball award at the 2019 Women's World Cup, representing which team?

16 The England team reached the semi-finals of the tournament in 2018 for the first time since which year?

17 Despite starring in the tournament, who missed the final penalty in the 1994 final?

18 In 2018, which three countries were announced as joint hosts of the 2026 tournament?

19 Thibaut Courtois won the Golden Glove award in 2018 for his performance with which team?

20 In which decade did the players' shirts first include their names at the finals?

Answers to QUIZ 196 – With It

1	*The Joshua Tree*	11	Rent
2	Four hours (three hours, 58 minutes)	12	Matt Monro
3	Gloucestershire	13	2010s (2011)
4	Los Angeles	14	The Troggs
5	Googie Withers	15	Sidney Poitier
6	Mary McDonnell	16	Sham 69
7	*A Room with a View*	17	Wild
8	*Without a Trace*	18	*Long Train Runnin*
9	2005	19	Ray Parker Jr
10	Colin Firth	20	Cumbria

1 Fred Astaire and Ginger Rogers first appeared on screen together in which 1933 film?

2 The 16th-century country house The Vyne lies in which English county?

3 By what name was Mark Feld (d.1977) better known?

4 What is indicated in Formula 1 by a red and yellow flag?

5 Keith Brymer Jones is a judge on which TV competition?

6 Which sport does James Bond play against the title character in the film *Goldfinger*?

7 Which Shakespeare comedy features the marriage of Theseus to Hippolyta?

8 On what would a petroglyph be carved?

9 Which American author wrote the 1869 travel book *The Innocents Abroad*?

10 Pasticho is a Greek dish similar to which Italian dish?

11 In 2012, MTV re-made which UK sitcom, first shown in 2008, for the US audience?

12 Which drug is named after the Greek god of dreams?

13 In which year was Blur's *Parklife* released?

14 Who is the author of the novels *Digital Fortress* (1998) and *Deception Point* (2001)?

15 What, on the face, is the glabella?

16 The Steve McQueen film *Bullitt* was mainly set in which US city?

17 What is the main component of egg and snail shells?

18 *Still Open All Hours* is set in a suburb of which town?

19 Who was Angelina Jolie's first husband?

20 In which decade was the shooting distance in the biathlon reduced to 50m?

Easy
Medium
Hard

Answers to QUIZ 197 – Pot Luck

1	River Danube	11	Fireflies
2	Dana	12	Cate Blanchett
3	Jack Torrance	13	Uttar Pradesh
4	Prada	14	One (Wimbledon)
5	Ontario	15	Two-Face
6	*High Society*	16	Two-wheeled cart
7	Queen Elizabeth II	17	*Criminal Minds*
8	Bobsleigh	18	The Gambia
9	Tweedledum and Tweedledee	19	Paul Cézanne
10	Rice and beans	20	Faramir

1 Who were Department S looking for in the title of a 1980 song?

2 For which event did Hale and Pace release *The Stonk* in 1991?

3 What was the full title of the act that released 1981's *Shaddap You Face*?

4 "Aquarius, and my name is Ralph" was a line from which 1977 song?

5 A techno version of the Charleston was released in 1994 by which Dutch duo, named the same as the single?

6 In which decade did actor Richard Harris originally have a hit with *MacArthur Park*?

7 What was the title of CW McCall's 1975 novelty hit?

8 What was everybody free to wear in the title of a 1999 single by Baz Luhrmann?

9 The Tommy Dorsey Orchestra had a 1958 hit with *Tea for Two*, taken from which musical?

10 Which musician's only solo UK hit single was *How Wonderful You Are* (2001)?

11 Partners in Kryme had a 1990 hit with the theme from which film?

12 "I was working in the lab late one night" was the opening line of which 1973 novelty record?

13 Where did The Flower Pot Men suggest going in the title of a 1967 song?

14 Which French musician, real name Quentin Dupieux, had a 1999 hit with *Flat Beat*?

15 The cover of *Mad World* by Michael Andrews and Gary Jules featured on the soundtrack of which 2001 cult film?

16 Whose only hit single was 1979's *One Day at a Time*?

17 *Skyscraper* (2013) was the only hit for which winner of *The X Factor*?

18 What nationality were the sisters who formed Las Ketchup, singers of 2002's *The Ketchup Song*?

19 What was the title of PhD's only UK hit, released in 1982?

20 Which group was *Big in Japan* in 1984?

Answers to QUIZ 198 – World Cup Football

1	Italy	11	10
2	Russia	12	1950s (1954)
3	1930s (1934)	13	2006
4	2-0	14	Peru
5	Argentina	15	USA
6	China	16	1990
7	1950s (1950)	17	Roberto Baggio
8	Croatia	18	USA, Canada and Mexico
9	24	19	Belgium
10	Algeria	20	1990s (1994)

1. Audrey Hepburn was associated with the fashion of which designer?
2. What type of animal is a gelada?
3. Melania Trump was born in which country?
4. Which sauce of Italian cuisine takes its name for the Italian word for "sailor"?
5. Which comedian is the star of the sitcom *King Gary*?
6. How many people are there in a synchronised diving team?
7. *The Last Tycoon* was an unfinished novel by which author (d.1940)?
8. In which decade was the Unknown Warrior buried in Westminster Abbey?
9. Syntagma Square is the central square in which European capital city?
10. Which notable feminist was the mother of author Mary Shelley?
11. Blue John is a form of which mineral?
12. Who starred as Newton Knight in the 2016 film *Free State of Jones*?
13. What colour is the Rosetta Stone?
14. China first played in the FIFA World Cup in which year?

15. In astrology, which planet is regarded as exerting a positive influence, giving its name to a word meaning "happy"?
16. In which US state is Brigham Young University?
17. Which real-life couple starred in the 1966 film *Who's Afraid of Virginia Woolf*?
18. Ecuador is bordered by which two countries?
19. The Pandora jewellery company is based in which country?
20. How much does one cubic centimetre of water weigh?

Answers to QUIZ 199 – Pot Luck

1	*Flying Down to Rio*	11	*The Inbetweeners*
2	Hampshire	12	Morphine (Morpheus)
3	Marc Bolan	13	1994
4	Oil on the track (or water)	14	Dan Brown
5	*The Great Pottery Throw Down*	15	The space between the eyebrows
6	Golf	16	San Francisco
7	*A Midsummer Night's Dream*	17	Calcium carbonate
8	A rock	18	Doncaster
9	Mark Twain	19	Jonny Lee Miller
10	Lasagne	20	1970s (1978)

1   Who designed the rock garden at Chatsworth House in 1842 and built the famous Emperor Fountain two years later?

2   How many Californian National Parks are named after trees?

3   Which conservation organisation has reserves at Arundel and Llanelli?

4   What type of landscape would you see in a region described as "montane"?

5   The peaks of Haven Brow and Rough Brow are part of which series of chalk cliffs in the South Downs?

6   Which is Canada's oldest National Park?

7   In the USA, chaparral is the name given to an area of dense shrubs or trees, particularly evergreen trees of what type?

8   In which county is the nature reserve of Wicken Fen?

9   What is the name of the second-largest National Park in Ireland?

10 In which English county is the Knepp Castle Estate, home to a noted rewilding project?

11 What name is given in Scotland to a small loch?

12 The hill known as Haystacks lies in which UK National Park?

13 In which county is Trebah garden?

14 The Magilligan peninsula lies at the entrance to which lough?

15 A garden at Guatiza on Lanzarote is particularly noted for its extensive collection of which plants?

16 The Saints' Way is an ancient trackway and long-distance footpath in which county?

17 Wilkes Land is a large area of which continent?

18 Which organisation was set up in 1919 to increase the amount of British woodland?

19 The Cumberland Mountains are part of which US mountain range?

20 Which canal runs approximately 60 miles from Inverness to Corpach near Fort William?

Easy

Medium

Hard

1 Who wrote the 1972 play *Jumpers*?

2 What type of food item is sopressa?

3 The single *Tears on My Pillow* was taken from which 1989 Kylie Minogue album?

4 What is the name of the region containing the countries of Djibouti, Eritrea, Ethiopia and Somalia?

5 Who played the lead role in the 2015 film *Woman in Gold*?

6 Which sport is played by the Japanese team Suntory Sungoliath?

7 In which decade was Milton Friedman awarded the Nobel Prize in Economic Sciences?

8 In 1967, which became the first sporting event to be broadcast in colour in the UK?

9 Amrit Sanchar is a baptism ceremony in which religion?

10 Which Victorian poet wrote the lines: "Tis better to have loved and lost, Than never to have loved at all"?

11 Little France is a suburb of which UK city?

12 Which TV series set in the fictional town of Neptune starred Kristen Bell as a teenage sleuth?

13 Absolut Vodka is made in which country?

14 In which century was Giacomo Casanova born?

15 Which elementary particle takes its name for the Greek for "first"?

16 Who presents the Radio 4 current affairs series *Broadcasting House*, first aired in 1998?

17 Ayrton Senna won three Formula 1 World Championships with which team?

18 Arthralgia is pain in which body parts?

19 Which fabric used to make sacks is named after a German state?

20 What is a baby elk called?

Easy

Medium

Hard

Answers to QUIZ 201 – Pot Luck

1	(Hubert de) Givenchy	11	Fluorite
2	A baboon	12	Matthew McConaughey
3	Slovenia (formerly part of Yugoslavia)	13	Dark grey
4	Marinara	14	2002
5	Tom Davis	15	Jupiter (jovial)
6	Two	16	Utah
7	F Scott Fitzgerald	17	Dame Elizabeth Taylor and Richard Burton
8	1920s (1920)	18	Colombia and Peru
9	Athens	19	Denmark
10	Mary Wollstonecraft	20	One gram

ANSWERS ON PAGE 206

1 In which country do new nurses take the "Nightingale Pledge"?

2 What is notable about the majority of firefighters in Chile?

3 What was the profession of David Tennant's character in the TV series *Deadwater Fell*?

4 Former US president Jimmy Carter was originally a farmer of which crop?

5 What was the occupation of Charles Stent, after whom a medical device was named?

6 The profession of orthoptics is concerned with which part of the human body?

7 Akram Khan is a well-known name in which branch of the performing arts?

8 The 2017 biographical drama *Only the Brave* featured people in which profession?

9 Originally, and in modern times since 1984, the Poet Laureate's salary has included a quantity of what drink?

10 What is the occupation of Starveling in *A Midsummer Night's Dream*?

11 Philanthropist Andrew Carnegie made his fortune in which business?

12 What is the profession of Ai Weiwei?

13 The mining of which metal is featured in Joseph Conrad's novel *Nostromo*?

14 Which Hollywood actors played sailors Clarence Doolittle and Joe Brady in the 1945 film *Anchors Aweigh*?

15 On a film or television set, what does a wrangler handle?

16 Which mathematician delivered the 2019 Royal Institution Christmas lectures?

17 In Graham Greene's *Our Man in Havana*, what does the character James Wormold sell?

18 Before becoming involved in politics, what was Joseph Stalin training to become?

19 What is the occupation of Leerie in a poem by Robert Louis Stevenson?

20 A sutler was a merchant who sold goods to people in which occupation?

Answers to QUIZ 202 – The Great Outdoors

1	Joseph Paxton	11	Lochan
2	Three (Joshua Tree, Redwood and Sequoia)	12	The Lake District
3	The Wildfowl and Wetlands Trust	13	Cornwall
4	Mountainous	14	Lough Foyle
5	The Seven Sisters	15	Cacti
6	Banff National Park	16	Cornwall
7	Oak	17	Antarctica
8	Cambridgeshire	18	The Forestry Commission
9	Glenveagh	19	The Appalachian Mountains
10	West Sussex	20	The Caledonian Canal

1   What colour is the blood of the Star Trek character Dr Spock?

2   A hinny is the offspring of a female ass or donkey, and what male animal?

3   What are the three main ingredients of the Spanish dish piperade?

4   What was the nationality of the mathematician David Hilbert (d.1943)?

5   Which group released the 1995 single *Wake Up Boo!*?

6   Which aircraft manufacturer produced the world's first commercial jet engine?

7   Gads Hill Place in Kent was the country home of which author?

8   The Dante Stakes, named after a famous Derby winner, takes place at which racecourse?

9   *Kiss Me Once* (2014) was an album by which pop star?

10 What type of bird is the main character in the Rio films?

11 The 2009 novel *And Another Thing* by Eoin Colfer was the final instalment in which sci-fi series written by another author?

12 What does the "Para" stand for in the Paralympic Games?

13 The Shakespeare play *Coriolanus* is set mainly in which city?

14 In 1903, Panama seceded from which country?

15 Princess Diana of Themyscira is an alterego of which superhero?

16 Which religion has a name that translates as "submission" in English?

17 What fibre is used to make velveteen?

18 Which is the only country outside of Africa to have native lions?

19 Which part of the Vatican was named after the pope who commissioned it, Sixtus IV?

20 Which fictional feline was owned by the Marquis of Carabas?

Easy

Medium

Hard

Answers to QUIZ 203 – Pot Luck

1	Sir Tom Stoppard	11	Edinburgh
2	Salami	12	*Veronica Mars*
3	*Enjoy Yourself*	13	Sweden
4	The Horn of Africa	14	18th century (1725)
5	Dame Helen Mirren	15	Proton
6	Rugby union	16	Paddy O'Connell
7	1970s (1976)	17	McLaren
8	Wimbledon tennis championships	18	Joints
9	Sikhism	19	Hessian
10	Alfred, Lord Tennyson	20	Calf

Easy

1   The former kingdom of Galicia was in the north-west part of which modern-day European country?

2   Which Irish city became one of the European Capitals of Culture in January 2020?

3   In which country was the Schengen Agreement signed, enabling free movement between participating European countries?

4   In which Italian city are the unique features known as the *sassi* found?

5   In which decade of the 20th century did Finland declare independence?

6   What type of establishment is the Tiergarten Schönbrunn in Vienna?

7   What do Spaniards traditionally eat 12 of at midnight on New Year's Eve, one for each chime of the midnight bells?

8   The Predjama Castle, built into the mouth of a cave, is situated in which European country?

9   The area known as Temple Bar, famed for its nightlife, is part of which European capital city?

Medium

10   What is the largest city in Switzerland?

11   In which area of France is a form of Celtic language spoken?

12   The town of Menaggio lies on which Italian lake?

13   Which city became Ireland's first National City of Culture, in 2014?

14   The kabanos sausage originated in which European country?

15   Which territory left the then EEC in 1985?

16   Which Swedish city hosted the 2013 Eurovision Song Contest?

17   Maria-Theresien-Platz is a famous public square in which European capital city?

18   Which European country's capital city has an airport with the code TIA?

19   Which is the largest German state, by land area?

20   Suomenlinna is a district of which European capital city?

Hard

Answers to QUIZ 204 – Occupations

1	USA	11	Steel
2	They are volunteers	12	Artist
3	GP	13	Silver mining
4	Peanuts	14	Frank Sinatra and Gene Kelly
5	He was a dentist	15	Animals
6	Eye	16	Hannah Fry
7	Dance	17	Vacuum cleaners
8	Firefighting	18	A priest
9	Sherry	19	A lamplighter
10	Tailor	20	Soldiers

1   Which 1990s prime-time TV drama began life as a spin-off from the teen hit *Beverly Hills 90210*?

2   Of what is the outer cover of Edam cheese made?

3   Telesto is a moon of which planet?

4   *Living History* (2003) and *Hard Choices* (2014) are memoirs by which former US First Lady?

5   Asafoetida is used widely as a digestive aid in the cuisine of which country?

6   Who was Burt Reynolds' co-star in *Smokey and the Bandit* (1977)?

7   The Wright Brothers made their first flight near Kitty Hawk in which US state?

8   *The Murder of Gonzago* is a play within which Shakespeare play?

9   How many gears are there on a speedway motorcycle?

10 By which nickname was American bank robber Lester Gillis better known?

11 How many points is a free throw worth in basketball?

12 In which decade was Emily Brontë born?

13 Cape St Vincent is the most south-westerly point on which continent?

14 In which European capital city is the Belvedere art museum?

15 Until the end of the 19th century, Cuba belonged to which country?

16 Which fruity drink has a name that comes from the Sanskrit for five, after its five original ingredients?

17 Which origami animal signifies peace?

18 In the title of a 1939 film, James Stewart's character Jefferson Smith goes to which US city?

19 Agrippina the Younger was the mother of which Roman emperor?

20 Dame Katherine Grainger won five Olympic medals, making her one of the most decorated British female Olympians. With which tennis player does she share this record?

Answers to QUIZ 205 – Pot Luck

1	Green	11	*The Hitchhiker's Guide to the Galaxy* (Douglas Adams)
2	A horse		
3	Onions, peppers and tomatoes	12	Parallel
4	German	13	Rome
5	The Boo Radleys	14	Colombia
6	de Havilland (the Comet)	15	Wonder Woman
7	Charles Dickens	16	Islam
8	York	17	Cotton
9	Kylie Minogue	18	India
10	Macaw	19	The Sistine Chapel
		20	Puss in Boots

1   *Mangifera indica* is the Latin name for which fruit?

2   Which green vegetable was once known as "poor man's bread"?

3   Noble rot affects which fruit?

4   Which vitamin is most prominent in a swede?

5   Which part of the salsify plant is eaten as a vegetable?

6   Fig trees are part of which family?

7   Lemons are native to which country continent?

8   Which fruit takes its name from the Latin for "seeded apple"?

9   Which popular apple is a cross between a Granny Smith and a Lady Hamilton?

10 In the 16th century, which country introduced the tomato to Europe?

11 What type of fruit grows on a Frantoio tree?

12 Kale is noted for its high content of what vitamin?

13 What fruit or vegetable has a variety called a bush crop?

14 Which fruit is used to make amchoor powder?

15 What is the main grape used in Chianti wine?

16 Giant of Sicily is a variety of which salad item?

17 Which is the largest producer of Brussels sprouts in Europe?

18 Who painted the 1885 work *The Potato Eaters*?

19 The winter melon is native to which continent?

20 Chopped carrots, onions and which other vegetable combine to form a mirepoix, the basis for many dishes and sauces in French cuisine?

Answers to QUIZ 206 – Europe

1	Spain	11	Brittany
2	Galway	12	Lake Como
3	Luxembourg	13	Limerick
4	Matera (they are houses built into the rocks)	14	Poland
5	1910s (1917)	15	Greenland
6	A zoo	16	Malmö
7	Grapes	17	Vienna
8	Slovenia	18	Albania (Tirana)
9	Dublin	19	Bavaria
10	Zürich	20	Helsinki

1   Which private investigator featured in the 2014 novel *The Silkworm*?

2   *Out Among the Stars* (2014) was a posthumous album of work by which musician?

3   The 1970 film *Hercules in New York* marked the big screen debut of which actor?

4   In 1792, Claude Joseph Rouget de Lisle wrote which iconic anthem?

5   With whom did Usher duet on the 2004 song *My Boo*?

6   Idris Elba was born in which London borough?

7   How many bones are there in the human skull?

8   The ring ouzel is a member of which family of birds?

9   Which pop star played Colorado in the 1959 western *Rio Bravo*?

10 In which decade were the first laws of the game of cricket drafted?

11 In the Bible, Samson found honey in the dead body of which animal?

12 Who was put on trial first: Galileo, Joan of Arc or Sir Thomas More?

13 Bacchus is the Roman name for which Greek god?

14 The String of Pearls is a feature of which planet?

15 On which golf course would you find the Road Hole?

16 What word completes the title of the 2013 Taylor Swift single, *I Knew You Were ___*?

17 Nisshōki is the official name of the flag of which country?

18 In The Hunger Games novels and films, how many surviving districts are there believed to be in Panem at the beginning of the first novel?

19 In which decade did the Republic of Ireland join the EEC?

20 The fictional company Waystar Royco features in which TV series?

Answers to QUIZ 207 – Pot Luck

1	*Melrose Place*	11	One point
2	Wax	12	1810s (1818)
3	Saturn	13	Europe
4	Hillary Rodham Clinton	14	Vienna
5	India	15	Spain
6	Sally Field	16	Punch
7	North Carolina	17	Crane
8	*Hamlet*	18	Washington (*Mr Smith Goes to Washington*)
9	One	19	Nero
10	Baby Face Nelson	20	Kitty Godfree

What are the names of these comedians?

Easy

1

2

3

Medium

4

5

6

Hard

7

8

9

---

1   Who had a hit in 1979 with *Contact*?

2   How is Tyrone Lindo better known?

3   The 1980s TV series *Dynasty* was set in which US city?

4   Which brand of sweets has a name based on those of its creators, Forrest Mars and Bruce Murrie?

5   How many teams contested the 1998 FIFA World Cup, a first for the event?

6   Which 2007 film about the USA's support of the mujahedin during the Soviet war in Afghanistan starred Tom Hanks, Julia Roberts and Philip Seymour Hoffman?

7   Who succeeded Abraham Lincoln as president of the USA?

8   What was the title of One Direction's second album?

9   Coleen Nolan was runner-up to which other contestant on *Celebrity Big Brother* in 2012?

10 *Shenzhou 5*, the first manned Chinese space flight, occurred in which decade?

11 What is the most popular religion in Sri Lanka?

12 The lager Budweiser® takes its name from a town in which country?

13 What is the old fashioned name for a club similar to a No.2 wooden golf club, taken from the material used for the sole?

14 In the Four Horsemen of the Apocalypse, what does the pale green horse represent?

15 Merrion Square, famous for its Georgian architecture, is in which capital city?

16 What is the largest island off the west coast of North America?

17 What name is given to a solid figure with eight plane surfaces?

18 Which US author (d.1916) lived at Lamb House in Rye, East Sussex?

19 Which character was played in *Coronation Street* by Brian Capron?

20 What term is given to the minimum number of people that a committee must have to carry out its business?

Easy

Medium

Hard

Answers to QUIZ 209 – Pot Luck

1	Cormoran Strike	11	A lion
2	Johnny Cash	12	Joan of Arc (1431)
3	Arnold Schwarzenegger	13	Dionysus
4	*La Marseillaise*	14	Saturn
5	Alicia Keys	15	St Andrews
6	Hackney	16	*Trouble*
7	22	17	Japan
8	Thrush family	18	12
9	Ricky Nelson	19	1970s (1973)
10	1740s (1744)	20	*Succession*

ANSWERS ON PAGE **214**

Easy

1   In 1912, in which town (now a city) was a statue known as "The Peace Statue" unveiled as a memorial to Edward VII?

2   What relation was Margaret Douglas, Countess of Lennox (d.1578) to Henry VIII?

3   What is the name of the Sandringham church traditionally attended by the Royal Family?

4   In which English county is the village of Indian Queens?

5   Lady Jane Grey was briefly queen of England following the death of which monarch?

6   Queen Elizabeth I made her famous address to the troops in 1588 at which English port?

7   In which decade did Edward VI become king of England?

8   The city of Charlottesville in Virginia was named after the wife of which king?

9   In which decade was King Farouk overthrown in Egypt?

10 Which king put his seal to the 1217 Charter of the Forest to establish rights of access to royal forests?

11 How many times had Wallis Simpson been married at the time of King Edward VIII's abdication?

12 Princess Feodora of Leiningen was the half-sister of which English queen?

Medium

13 Which country has the oldest continuing hereditary monarchy in the world?

14 Who was the second wife of James II?

15 The Cullinan Diamond, discovered in South Africa, was presented to which monarch?

16 The Countess of Castlemaine was the mistress of which English king?

17 Which Scottish king was nicknamed "The Red King"?

18 Prince Albert II of Monaco competed in which sport at five winter Olympics?

19 The ship *Queen Anne's Revenge* was famously captained by which pirate?

20 What was the name of the horse owned by Queen Elizabeth II that won the Ascot Gold Cup in 2013, the first winner to be owned by a reigning monarch?

Answers to QUIZ 210 – Comedians

Hard

1   Ellie Taylor
2   Kevin Bridges
3   Adil Ray
4   Russell Howard
5   Sara Pascoe
6   Rhod Gilbert
7   Aisling Bea
8   Geoff Norcott
9   Shappi Khorsandi

ANSWERS ON PAGE 215

1 To the nearest ten minutes, how many minutes does it take for the International Space Station to orbit the Earth?

2 In which decade was the Hungry Hungry Hippos™ game first sold?

3 The Spanish city of San Sebastián lies on which bay?

4 *Tainted Love* by Soft Cell won the BRIT Award for Best Single in which year?

5 What is lampblack, traditionally used to make Indian ink?

6 The crushed spice and nut mixture known as Dukkah originated in which country?

7 The characters of Beans, Roadkill and Bad Bill featured in which 2011 animated film?

8 What is the name of a muscle that turns a limb to face downwards?

9 What is a male giraffe called?

10 The character of Jango Fett first appeared in which of the Star Wars films?

11 Which 1990s sitcom featured two flatmates who lived on the dole in Hammersmith?

12 Which winter sport includes an "Aerials" event?

13 The canton of Valais lies in which European country?

14 What relation are the characters of Rosalind and Celia in Shakespeare's *As You Like It*?

15 What would you be suffering if you had a graphospasm?

16 US president Lyndon B Johnson was sworn into office while travelling in which mode of transport?

17 Which city is the administrative capital of the Laconia region in Greece?

18 Who played Dr John W Thackery in the TV series *The Knick*?

19 What nickname is given to racing driver Sergio Pérez (b.1990)?

20 In which decade did the poet William Wordsworth die?

Easy

Medium

Hard

Answers to QUIZ 211 – Pot Luck

1	Edwin Starr	11	Buddhism
2	Big Narstie	12	Czech Republic/Czechia
3	Denver, Colorado	13	Brassie
4	M&M's	14	Death
5	32	15	Dublin
6	*Charlie Wilson's War*	16	Vancouver Island
7	Andrew Johnson	17	Octahedron
8	*Take Me Home*	18	Henry James
9	Julian Clary	19	Richard Hillman
10	2000s (2003)	20	Quorum

Easy

1   In which month can the Geminids meteor shower be seen?

2   Which is the only planet whose name comes from Greek, rather than Roman, mythology?

3   As at 2020, how many people have walked on the Moon?

4   An AU (astronomical unit) approximately measures the distance from the Sun to which planet?

5   The Bay of Dew can be found on which body within the solar system?

6   The moon Himalia is a satellite of which planet?

7   To the nearest ten years, how many earth years does it take for Neptune to orbit the Sun?

8   In 1631 Pierre Gassendi obtained the first set of data of the transit of which planet across the Sun?

9   Erda was the Anglo-Saxon name for which planet?

10 What is the second-most abundant gas element on Jupiter?

11 The *Venera* space probes were sent to explore which planet?

12 The number 134340 precedes the name of which body in the solar system?

13 Which gas makes up 96% of the atmosphere on Venus?

Medium

14 Approximately how many minutes short of 24 hours does it take the earth to rotate on its axis?

15 In 1968, Edward Guinan was one of the first people to discover the rings around which planet?

16 The *Phoenix* sampled water ice on which planet in the solar system in 2008?

17 In which month does the Full Buck Moon occur?

18 Which heavenly bodies are sometimes referred to as "dirty snowballs", as they are made mostly of ice?

19 Which astronaut wrote the 1973 autobiography *Return to Earth*?

20 To the nearest ten miles, how many miles above the Earth does the International Space Station orbit?

Hard

Answers to QUIZ 212 – Royalty

1	Brighton	11	Twice
2	Niece	12	Queen Victoria
3	St Mary Magdalene	13	Japan
4	Cornwall	14	Mary of Modena
5	Edward VI	15	Edward VII
6	Tilbury	16	Charles II
7	1540s (1547)	17	Macbeth
8	George III	18	Bobsleigh
9	1950s (1952)	19	Blackbeard (Edward Teach)
10	Henry III	20	Estimate

1   Who lived across the hall from Jerry in the TV series *Seinfeld*?

2   Which US actor was born Alphonso D'Abruzzo in 1936?

3   The Encke Gap is a feature of which planet?

4   According to the 2019 Global Peace Index, what was the world's most peaceful country?

5   Who played the female lead role in the film *The Switch* (2010)?

6   What is the name of the lead singer of Kings of Leon?

7   *Curtain Call* was a 2005 greatest hits album by which rapper?

8   Who was pope during WWII and beyond, from 1939 to 1958?

9   What type of fabric covering takes its name from the French for "white"?

10 In which city state do car registration plates begin with the letters SCV?

11 Which three colours are on the Russian flag?

12 Which sport is contested at the Louis Armstrong Stadium in New York?

13 The Barossa Valley is primarily known for the production of which variety of wine?

14 The Bradford art gallery Salts Mill is particularly associated with the works of which artist?

15 In which decade was AstroTurf® invented?

16 The football club RSC Anderlecht is based in which country?

17 A statue of which Poet Laureate stands at St Pancras station?

18 Which US state capital lies on the Hudson River?

19 Inveraray Castle lies on the shore of which Scottish loch?

20 What gas is released when a diamond burns?

Easy
Medium
Hard

Answers to QUIZ 213 – Pot Luck

1	90 minutes (92 minutes)	11	*Bottom*
2	1970s (1978)	12	Freestyle skiing
3	The Bay of Biscay	13	Switzerland
4	1982	14	Cousins
5	A black pigment made from soot	15	Writer's cramp
6	Egypt	16	Aeroplane (Air Force One)
7	*Rango*	17	Sparta
8	Pronator	18	Clive Owen
9	A bull	19	Checo
10	*Attack of the Clones*	20	1850s (1850)

1 How would a chicken be cooked if it was served as a spatchcock?

2 The interchange nicknamed Spaghetti Junction is where the M6 meets the A5127 and which other A road?

3 The 1945 crime fiction novel *Sparkling Cyanide* was written by which author?

4 Spaghetti carbonara was originally created in which region of Italy?

5 The misleadingly-named Spanish Moss belongs to which family of plants?

6 What was the title of the last Spandau Ballet single to reach the UK top ten?

7 What colour are the upper parts of a male sparrowhawk?

8 The 1960 film *Spartacus* was nominated for how many Oscars, winning four of them?

9 What gives sparkling wine its sparkle?

10 Which tool takes its name from the German for "to stretch"?

11 For which 1980 film did Sissy Spacek win the Best Actress Oscar?

12 Spangles sweets first went on sale in which decade?

13 Feldspar is what type of substance?

14 Which 1974 single was Sparks' biggest UK hit, peaking at no. 2?

15 What was the name of the space shuttle that flew its final mission in 2011?

16 The Belgian town of Spa is in which province?

17 In relation to politics, what is a spad?

18 The name of the fabric spandex is an anagram of what word?

19 Spalding in Lincolnshire lies on which river?

20 The Spanish vegetable *cebolla* has what English name?

Answers to QUIZ 214 – Astronomy

1	December	11	Venus
2	Uranus	12	Pluto
3	12	13	Carbon dioxide
4	Earth	14	4 minutes
5	The Moon	15	Neptune
6	Jupiter	16	Mars
7	160 years (164 years)	17	July
8	Mercury	18	Comets
9	Earth	19	Buzz Aldrin
10	Helium	20	250 miles (248)

1   What is Sigourney Weaver's real first name?

2   Which drummer composed the music to the 1983 film *Rumble Fish*?

3   In which century was Sikhism founded?

4   "My tea's gone cold and I'm wondering why I got out of bed at all" is a lyric from which 2000 song?

5   In which English city is the educational establishment of Ruskin College?

6   Who played the title role in the TV series *The Trial of Christine Keeler*?

7   In anatomy, what would you find on either side of a vomer?

8   In the 2008 film *Bolt*, what is the name of Bolt's co-star in his TV show?

9   Which author wrote *The Witches of Eastwick*?

10 In which decade did South Africa first acquire test cricket status?

11 Which two cities does the Trans-Siberian Railway link?

12 Which member of The Beatles wrote *Here Comes The Sun*?

13 In terms of the human body, for what do the letters BMR stand?

14 What are poblanos?

15 The *RMS Lusitania* was sunk off the coast of which country in 1915?

16 The Gold Logie Award is presented to the most popular person on TV in which country?

17 By which name is a renal calculus more commonly known?

18 The Vince Lombardi Trophy is awarded to the team that wins which game?

19 Which RHS annual garden show features the "Back to Back" gardens?

20 The word "cromlech" is given to a prehistoric tomb or circle of standing stones in which country of the UK?

Answers to QUIZ 215 – Pot Luck

1	(Cosmo) Kramer	11	Red, white and blue
2	Alan Alda	12	Tennis
3	Saturn	13	Shiraz
4	Iceland	14	David Hockney
5	Jennifer Aniston	15	1960s (1965)
6	Caleb Followill	16	Belgium
7	Eminem	17	Sir John Betjeman
8	Pope Pius XII	18	Albany (New York)
9	Blanket	19	Loch Fyne
10	Vatican City	20	Carbon dioxide

1   Sarah Palin was the governor of which US state from 2006 to 2009?

2   As what was the Statue of Liberty used from 1886 until 1902?

3   In which US city is there a pathway known as "the Freedom Trail", which passes 16 historically significant sites?

4   In which decade was the Grand Canyon officially declared a National Park?

5   Which US state capital has an airport with the code SLC?

6   For what does the acronym DEFCON stand?

7   The National Civil Rights Museum can be found in which US city?

8   In which US city is the Louis Armstrong Park?

9   The plantation of Monticello belonged to which US president?

10 The US Republican Party is often referred to as the GOP. For what do these letters stand?

11 In what decade was the Green jacket first presented to winners of the Masters golf championship?

12 The *Grand Theft Auto V* video game is based in the south of which US state?

13 The Detroit Red Wings compete in which sport?

14 To the nearest ten, how many episodes of *Friends* were made?

15 In which month of 1917 did the USA declare war on Germany?

16 Artist Edward Hopper was born in which US state?

17 In 1931, which US city was founded to house workers on the Hoover Dam?

18 Who wrote *American Notes,* an account of his 1842 visit to the USA?

19 According to legend, as a child, what type of tree did George Washington chop down?

20 In which US state is the Wild West frontier city of Dodge?

Answers to QUIZ 216 – Spa Day

1	Split open and grilled	11	*Coal Miner's Daughter*
2	A38	12	1950s (1950)
3	Dame Agatha Christie	13	A mineral
4	Lazio	14	*This Town Ain't Big Enough for Both of Us*
5	Bromeliads	15	*Atlantis*
6	*Through the Barricades* (1986)	16	Liège
7	Bluish-grey	17	Special adviser
8	Six	18	Expands
9	Carbon dioxide	19	The River Welland
10	Spanner	20	Onion

1 Who wrote the 2001 novel *The Corrections*?

2 What was the subtitle of the revamped version of the TV series *Softly, Softly*?

3 The town of Desenzano lies on which Italian lake?

4 What is rillettes?

5 Which singer said, "We need fantasy to survive reality"?

6 What is the title of the Radio 4 literary review presented by Mariella Frostrup?

7 Henry Cavill and Armie Hammer starred in which 2015 big-screen remake of a hit 1960s TV show?

8 Which of these English kings reigned the earliest: Henry II, John, or Richard I?

9 What is a female bear called?

10 Which architect designed Covent Garden square and Lincoln's Inn?

11 In which country is the northernmost point of the Andes?

12 On what surface was the US Open tennis championship contested when it began in 1881?

13 What is the second-largest city of Austria?

14 Which rapper released the 2018 single *God's Plan*?

15 In which decade did Scotland appoint its first Poet Laureate?

16 Which is the longest swimming event at the Olympics?

17 What nationality was ice-skater Ulrich Salchow, after whom the jump was named?

18 Which composer wrote the 1791-92 symphony known as "the Surprise Symphony"?

19 The comet Shoemaker–Levy 9 collided with which planet in 1994?

20 A group of which big cats is called a leap?

Answers to QUIZ 217 – Pot Luck

1	Susan	11	Moscow and Vladivostok
2	Stewart Copeland (of the Police)	12	George Harrison
3	15th century (1490s)	13	Basal metabolic rate
4	*Stan* (Eminem featuring Dido)	14	Chilli peppers
5	Oxford	15	Ireland
6	Sophie Cookson	16	Australia
7	The nostrils	17	Kidney stone
8	Penny	18	The Superbowl
9	John Updike	19	Tatton
10	1880s (1889)	20	Wales

Easy

1　Who plays Logan Roy in the TV series *Succession*?

2　What is the name of Luke Skywalker's mother in the Star Wars films?

3　At the beginning of the Poldark novels and TV series, the title character had returned from which war?

4　Which best-selling novel of 1977, set on an Australian sheep station, focused on Meggie Cleary and her family?

5　What was the title of the 1993 sequel to the 1991 film *The Addams Family*?

6　*Breaking Up is Hard to Do* and *Walking in the Rain* were chart hits for which fictional family?

7　What was the first name of Alan's wife in the TV series *The New Statesman*?

8　*The House of the Spirits* (1982), telling the story of the de Valle family, was the debut novel by which author?

9　Which fictional Scottish family lives in a flat at 10 Glebe Street?

10　In the TV series *Family Guy*, what type of dog is Brian Griffin?

11　Jor-El and Lara are the parents of which superhero?

12　Who provides the voice of Mrs Incredible in the animated films?

13　The Lupertazzi family featured in which US TV series?

Medium

14　Who played Fred and George, the Weasley twins, in the Harry Potter films?

15　*Hold the Dream* (1985) was a sequel to which best-selling novel by Barbara Taylor Bradford?

16　What was the first name of Jack Osborne's first wife in the TV series *Hollyoaks*?

17　Which Denzel Washington film of 2016, based on a stage play, features the Maxson family?

18　Which TV series features Kate, Kevin and Randall, nicknamed "The Big Three"?

19　In *To Kill a Mockingbird*, what is the nickname of Scout's brother?

20　Known as Yara in the TV series *Game of Thrones*, what is the name of Theon Greyjoy's sister in the original novels by George RR Martin?

Hard

Answers to QUIZ 218 – The USA

1	Alaska	11	1940s (1949)
2	Lighthouse	12	California
3	Boston	13	Ice hockey
4	1910s (1919)	14	240 (236)
5	Salt Lake City (Utah)	15	April
6	Defense readiness condition	16	New York
7	Memphis	17	Boulder City
8	New Orleans	18	Charles Dickens
9	Thomas Jefferson	19	Cherry tree
10	Grand Old Party	20	Kansas

1 Who was the ruling Roman emperor at the time of Boudicca's revolt?

2 Sarawak is a state in which country?

3 Which actor has performed musically under the stage name "Russ Le Roq"?

4 In which decade did the Eurovision Song Contest first feature two semi-finals?

5 Which creature features in the Sherlock Holmes short story *The Speckled Band*?

6 The sweet bread or cake known as *babka* is associated with which religion?

7 What was the name of the town in which the 1996 film *Brassed Off* was set?

8 "Osmic" refers to which sense?

9 Which was the first country to retain the FIFA World Cup?

10 Which actor directed the 2016 film *Hacksaw Ridge*?

11 Brandy takes its name from the word for "burnt wine" in which language?

12 The Millennium Sundial can be found in which London park?

13 Which 2020 crime series starred Jason Watkins and Tala Gouveia?

14 Which African animal is also known as the forest giraffe and the zebra giraffe?

15 How were Hansel and Gretel described in the title of a 2013 film?

16 Which property of a liquid can be measured on the Baumé scale?

17 Kansas City is the largest city in which US state?

18 Daisy Buchanan is a character in which 1925 novel?

19 In Roman mythology, on which hill did Remus want to build Rome?

20 In which decade did the women's marathon become an Olympic event?

Easy

Medium

Hard

Answers to QUIZ 219 – Pot Luck

1	Jonathan Franzen	11	Venezuela
2	*Taskforce*	12	Grass
3	Lake Garda	13	Graz
4	Paté made from minced pork	14	Drake
5	Lady Gaga	15	2000s (2004)
6	*Open Book*	16	1500m (freestyle)
7	*The Man from U.N.C.L.E*	17	Swedish
8	Henry II (1154-89)	18	Haydn
9	Sow	19	Jupiter
10	Inigo Jones	20	Leopards

1   Carlos Valderrama captained which side in the FIFA World Cup?

2   Designer Vera Wang was born in which country?

3   Vincent D'Onofrio and Julia Roberts starred in which 1988 film set around a fast-food restaurant?

4   How was Richard Steven Valenzuela (d.1959) better known?

5   What colour is the drink Vimto®?

6   The Valley of the Kings is on the opposite side of the River Nile to which city?

7   Hervé Villechaize was famous for his role as Tattoo on which TV series?

8   The Vall de Núria Rack Railway is situated in which European mountain range?

9   What word beginning with "v" can be used to describe a simple fraction?

10   The vervet monkey is native to which continent?

11   The 2003 film *Touching the Void* takes place in which mountain range?

12   Vänern, the largest lake in the EU, is in which country?

13   The English translation of which food item means "flight in the wind"?

14   What is the profession of Vicki Vale in the Batman story?

15   *Uncle Vanya*, by Anton Chekhov, received its premier in which decade?

16   What is the usual abbreviation for the Latin phrase *videre licet*, meaning "it is possible to see"?

17   The Verdi opera *Giovanna d'Arco* is about which French national icon?

18   What is the name of the cartoon Viking created by Dik Browne?

19   The leaves of the Virginia creeper turn what colour in autumn?

20   What name beginning with "v" is given to the ability to throw your voice?

Answers to QUIZ 220 – Fictional Families

1	Brian Cox	11	Superman
2	Padmé (Amidala)	12	Holly Hunter
3	American War of Independence	13	*The Sopranos*
4	*The Thorn Birds*	14	James and Oliver Phelps
5	*Addams Family Values*	15	*A Woman of Substance*
6	The Partridge Family	16	Celia
7	Sarah	17	*Fences*
8	Isabel Allende	18	*This is Us*
9	*The Broons*	19	Jem
10	A (white) labrador	20	Asha

1 What was the name of the fox in the 1981 film *The Fox and the Hound*?

2 Who was the lead singer with the band that had a hit with *Lady Marmalade* in 1974?

3 In describing diamonds, the four "C"s are clarity, colour, cut and what other word?

4 Who wrote the 1929 novel *The Good Companions*?

5 Which actress was born Deborah Trimmer in 1921?

6 Built in 1930, in which US state is the only remaining Shell filling station built in the shape of a shell?

7 What colour is the adult Amazon river dolphin?

8 In the human body, what is the more common name for the axilla?

9 Maggie Wheeler played which recurring character in the TV series *Friends*?

10 The winner of the Indianapolis 500 motor race celebrates with which drink?

11 What is the world's largest landlocked country?

12 What was the title of Eminem's first UK top ten single?

13 The 1929 film *Untamed* was the first "talkie" to star which actress?

14 Which dessert do the French refer to as a "Norwegian omelette"?

15 What type of substance is a monosaccharide?

16 Reid Hoffman co-founded which networking website in 2002?

17 Which city was once nicknamed "Linenopolis"?

18 Who composed the 1724 opera *Giulio Cesare*?

19 Which Belgian city hosted the 1920 Summer Olympics?

20 The spectacled bear is native to which continent?

Easy

Medium

Hard

Answers to QUIZ 221 – Pot Luck

1	Nero	11	Dutch (*brandewijn*)
2	Malaysia	12	Greenwich Park
3	Russell Crowe	13	*McDonald & Dodds*
4	(2000s) 2008	14	Okapi
5	A snake	15	*Witch Hunters*
6	Judaism	16	Density
7	Grimley	17	Missouri
8	Smell	18	*The Great Gatsby*
9	Italy (1934 and 1938)	19	The Aventine Hill
10	Mel Gibson	20	1980s (1984)

Easy

1   Which Australian animal is classified as a subspecies of the grey wolf?

2   Who was prime minister earliest: Andrew Fisher, Sir Edmund Barton or James Scullin?

3   Which two state and territory capitals are not named after people?

4   Under what name is Hugh Jackman's character billed in the film *Australia*?

5   Jason Day (b.1987) plays which sport?

6   What is the national gemstone of Australia?

7   HBA is the airport code for which city?

8   Who captained Australia to victory in the 1958-59 Ashes series?

9   In which state does the Murray River reach the sea?

10 Who was the first Australian to win the Booker Prize?

11 The River Torrens flows through which city?

12 The *XXXX* brand of beer originated in which city?

13 The Spencer Gulf is a body of water of which state?

Medium

14 Who was Australia's shortest-serving PM, for eight days between 6-13 July, 1945?

15 Which Australian state capital was named after the Fourth Earl of Buckinghamshire?

16 Alicia Vikander and Michael Fassbender starred in which 2016 romantic drama set in Australia?

17 South Australia borders how many other states and territories?

18 How many hours is Sydney ahead of GMT?

19 "The Honey Badger" is the nickname of which former Australian rugby union player?

20 Porpoise Spit, Queensland was the home town of the main character in which 1994 film?

Hard

Answers to QUIZ 222 – V

1	Colombia	11	The (Peruvian) Andes
2	USA	12	Sweden
3	*Mystic Pizza*	13	Vol-au-vent
4	Ritchie Valens	14	A journalist
5	Purple	15	1890s (1899)
6	Thebes (modern Luxor)	16	Viz
7	*Fantasy Island*	17	Joan of Arc
8	The Pyrenees	18	Hägar the Horrible
9	Vulgar	19	Red (crimson)
10	Africa	20	Ventriloquism

ANSWERS ON PAGE 227

1   Who released the 1978 single *Just for You*?

2   Which Roman emperor reigned at the time when the Roman Empire was at its largest?

3   Bootham Bar and Micklegate Bar can be found in which English city?

4   In which decade does George Bernard Shaw's play *Arms and the Man* take place?

5   Which region of Italy is nicknamed "Chiantishire"?

6   In the children's TV series *Rag, Tag and Bobtail*, what type of animal was Tag?

7   In which month of 1906 did San Francisco experience a devastating earthquake?

8   Jon Bon Jovi had a recurring role on which TV drama first broadcast in 1997?

9   Of what was Phobos the personification in Greek mythology?

10   In Jewish legend, who was Adam's first wife?

11   In the human body, the portal vein feeds which organ?

12   Who played the title role of Jane Austen in the 2007 film *Becoming Jane*?

13   To the nearest ten years, how many Earth years does it take for Uranus to orbit the Sun?

14   In 1994 Oleg Salenko became the first player to score how many goals in a single FIFA World Cup match?

15   The Commonwealth Parliament, or Federal Parliament is the governing body in which country?

16   How many of its nominated eleven Oscars did *The Color Purple* (1985) win?

17   Which stone is used to produce stonewashed denim?

18   Which Arab state has a name that means "two seas"?

19   Anne-Sophie Mutter (b.1963) is associated with which musical instrument?

20   Marsala wine originates from which Mediterranean island?

Easy

Medium

Hard

Answers to QUIZ 223 – Pot Luck

1	Tod	11	Kazakhstan
2	Patti LaBelle (with her band LaBelle)	12	*My Name Is*
3	Carat	13	Joan Crawford
4	JB Priestley	14	Baked Alaska
5	Deborah Kerr	15	A (simple) sugar
6	North Carolina	16	LinkedIn™
7	Pink	17	Belfast
8	Armpit	18	Handel
9	Janice	19	Antwerp
10	Milk	20	South America

1   Which author invented the tengwar script?

2   Who wrote the poetry collection entitled *Satires of Circumstance* (1914)?

3   As at 2020, which was the second-largest library in the world, measured by the number of items catalogued?

4   Which novel of 2004 included the story entitled *Letters from Zedelghem*?

5   Who wrote the early 16th-century work *Discourses on Livy*?

6   What type of writing takes its name from the Italian for "little scratch"?

7   Diarist Samuel Pepys served as an MP for which two East Anglian wards?

8   Who wrote the fantasy novel *Howl's Moving Castle* (1986)?

9   Which Biblical character held a feast during which a hand appeared and wrote on the wall?

10   Who wrote the 2001 novella *Rabbit Remembered*?

11   In which decade was Bertrand Russell (Third Earl Russell) awarded the Nobel prize in Literature?

12   What name is given to the room in a monastery set aside for writing?

13   Which English poet wrote the 1843 poem *The Cry of the Children*?

14   What is the term for a single symbol that represents a word or phrase, such as a Chinese character?

15   The satirical poem *The True Born Englishman* (1701) was written by which author?

16   Dante's *Divine Comedy* is divided into how many cantos?

17   What type of person is the hero of a picaresque novel?

18   Which novelist shared the 2019 Booker Prize with Margaret Atwood?

19   In which decade was the Pulitzer Prize for Fiction (originally for a novel) first awarded?

20   What German word is used to describe a novel dealing with a person's formative years and development?

Answers to QUIZ 224 – Australia

1	Dingo	11	Adelaide
2	Sir Edmund Barton (1901-03)	12	Castlemaine
3	Canberra and Perth	13	South Australia
4	The Drover	14	Francis Forde
5	Golf	15	(Robert) Hobart
6	Opal	16	*The Light Between Oceans*
7	Hobart	17	Five (every state except Tasmania)
8	Richie Benaud	18	Ten hours
9	South Australia	19	Nick Cummins
10	Thomas Keneally	20	*Muriel's Wedding*

1   Which English town was the first in the world to achieve Fairtrade Town status?

2   Which singer (d.1984) was nicknamed "Mr Excitement!"?

3   What name is given to someone who polishes and cuts gemstones?

4   The Cerberus Fossae is found on which planet?

5   Who directed the 2014 film *Noah*?

6   The UNESCO World Heritage Site of Trogir lies in which modern-day country?

7   For what do the initials "APH" stand in the name of the agency APHA, part of Defra?

8   Historically, who would have used a portolan?

9   What unit of currency is used in the Seychelles?

10   What was the title of the UK's 2011 Eurovision Song Contest entry, sung by Blue?

11   In which year did Cuba lift a ban on owning mobile phones?

12   Derventio Coritanorum was the Roman name for a settlement near which modern English city?

13   An ard is a simple version of what type of implement?

14   The Bab is a key figure in which religion?

15   Hetty Sorrel is a major character in which 1859 novel?

16   What emotion did the herb basil symbolise to ancient Greeks?

17   In Arthurian legend, what was the name of Gawain's horse?

18   Which company has been the primary developer of the *Call of Duty* franchise since 2003?

19   Which team won the first Superbowl in 1966?

20   *Full Fathom Five* was a 1947 painting by which artist?

Easy

Medium

Hard

Answers to QUIZ 225 – Pot Luck

1	Alan Price	11	The liver
2	Trajan	12	Anne Hathaway
3	York	13	80 years (84 years)
4	1880s (1885) (the Serbo-Croatian War)	14	Five
5	Tuscany	15	Australia
6	A mouse	16	None
7	April	17	Pumice
8	*Ally McBeal*	18	Bahrain
9	Fear	19	The violin
10	Lilith	20	Sicily

1. What was the name of the horse that won the first official Grand National in 1839?

2. How many games does each team play in a regular US National Hockey League season?

3. In which country was the boxer Teófilo Stevenson born?

4. The Knickerbocker rules govern which sport?

5. In 1978, which team became the first team from Africa to win a game in the FIFA World Cup finals, beating Mexico 3-1?

6. Kerstin Palm (b.1946) competed in every Summer Olympic games from 1964 to 1988 in which sport?

7. As at 2020, how many countries are eligible to compete in the Pan American Games?

8. Lucha Libre is s style of wrestling most associated with which country?

9. In which sport was Mária Mednyánszky (d.1978) a five-times world champion?

10. What is the maximum number of gates on the course in men's alpine skiing events?

11. As at 2020, who was the most capped player in the Australian rugby league team's history?

12. Jamie Chadwick won which inaugural motorsport championship in 2019?

13. Antonio Carbajal (b.1929) played in five FIFA World Cup finals for which nation?

14. In which country did speed skating originate?

15. Graham Hill was driving for which team when he won the 1962 Formula 1 World Championship?

16. In 1862, who became the first person to retain The Open golf championship title?

17. In which sport do players contest the Thomas Cup?

18. Which sport did Peyton Manning (b.1976) play?

19. Which cyclist has the nickname "the First Queen of BMX"?

20. In which decade was the US Open tennis championship first played?

Answers to QUIZ 226 – The Written Word

1	JRR Tolkien	11	1950s (1950)
2	Thomas Hardy	12	Scriptorium
3	The Library of Congress (Washington DC)	13	Elizabeth Barrett Browning
4	Cloud Atlas (David Mitchell)	14	Logogram
5	Niccolò Machiavelli	15	Daniel Defoe
6	Graffiti	16	100
7	Castle Rising and Harwich	17	A rogue
8	Diana Wynne Jones	18	Bernardine Evaristo
9	Belshazzar	19	1910s (1918)
10	John Updike	20	Bildungsroman

1   The Kinabatangan River is the second-longest river in which country?

2   Which organisation awards the Copley Medal for scientific research?

3   Plants with the Latin name *sambucus nigra* produce which fruit?

4   The Sansad is a general term used in several Asian countries for what type of institution?

5   Which 2010 film centred on a villain who defeated Metro Man and ruled Metro City?

6   Who was the Greek goddess of strife and discord?

7   Formerly used in Russia and Ukraine, what was a gudok (also known as a hudok)?

8   The word "littoral" relates to what area of land?

9   Who was the head coach of the Scottish national rugby union team from 1988 to 1993?

10 The card game canasta was invented in which country?

11 Bo Bruce and Tyler James have been contestants on which television competition?

12 John Wilson were the real first and last names of which writer (d.1993)?

13 Bradley International Airport is located in which US state?

14 Which US company was formed in 1945 by Harold Matsen and Elliot Handler and originally sold picture frames?

15 Which tourist attraction on the Isle of Man is also known as Lady Isabella?

16 Which composer was born in Pesaro in Italy in February 1792?

17 What was the title of the 2014 album released by David Guetta?

18 The Cameron Highlands is a region in which Asian country?

19 Which Kent castle is the official home of the Lord Warden of the Cinque Ports?

20 For what do the initials ZIP stand in the US mail system?

Answers to QUIZ 227 – Pot Luck

1	Garstang (Lancashire)	11	2008
2	Jackie Wilson	12	Derby
3	Lapidary	13	A plough
4	Mars	14	Bahá'í
5	Darren Aronofsky	15	*Adam Bede*
6	Croatia	16	Hate
7	Animal and Plant Health	17	Gringolet
8	A sailor (it is a sea chart)	18	Infinity Ward
9	(Seychellois) rupee	19	Green Bay Packers
10	*I Can*	20	Jackson Pollock

Easy

1   *Chicken Little* (2005) was set in which fictional town?

2   What was the first name of the title character in the 1963 *film Dr No*?

3   Which 2001 crime thriller centres on the character of Stanley Jobson, played by Hugh Jackman?

4   In the Star Wars films, what is the name of Chewbacca's home planet?

5   Which singer won the Best Actor Oscar for his role in the 1944 film *Going My Way*?

6   In the film *Black Narcissus*, to which region do the nuns travel to set up a school?

7   Which 2014 film had "He's leaving his mark on history" as one of its tag lines?

8   Who composed the musical score for *The Lion King*?

9   Richard Attenborough played which character in the 1947 film *Brighton Rock*?

10   Which film won Best Documentary at the 2020 BAFTA film awards?

Medium

11   What was the name of Oliver Reed's character in the 1969 film *Women in Love*?

12   *Hero* by Chad Kroeger and Josey Scott featured on the soundtrack of which 2002 film?

13   Who directed the 1975 political thriller *Three Days of the Condor*?

14   The 1963 film *Move Over, Darling* was a remake of which 1940 film?

15   In which 1991 film does the character of Mike Waters suffer from narcolepsy?

16   For which 1935 film did Bette Davis win her first Best Actress Oscar?

17   Which Royal Ballet principal dancer played Victoria in the 2019 film *Cats*?

18   Who played the character of Enobaria in *The Hunger Games: Catching Fire* (2013)?

19   The 1960 film *An Honourable Murder* was based on which Shakespeare play?

20   Who won a Best Supporting Actor Oscar for his debut in the 1984 film *The Killing Fields*?

Hard

Answers to QUIZ 228 – Sport

1	Lottery	11	Darren Lockyer
2	82	12	W Series
3	Cuba	13	Mexico
4	Baseball	14	The Netherlands
5	Tunisia	15	BRM
6	Fencing	16	Tom Morris Snr
7	42	17	Badminton
8	Mexico	18	American football
9	Table tennis	19	Mariana Pajón
10	75	20	1880s (1881)

1   Which actress won the Best Juvenile Oscar for her performance in the 1960 film *Pollyanna*?

2   The country of Georgia celebrates St George's Day in April and which other month?

3   What type of creature is a springtail?

4   The temple complex of Tōdai-ji lies in which Japanese city?

5   Discovered in 2005, where in the solar system is the body known as Makemake?

6   In which decade did Larry Mize win the US Masters golf championship?

7   Located in Mexico, what is the Cantarell Complex?

8   On which island is the World Heritage Site of the volcanic peaks called the Pitons?

9   For what does the "S" stand in the name of CS Gas?

10   Which is the second-largest uninhabited island in the Isles of Scilly?

11   Which language became the 24th official language of the European Union in 2013?

12   Cornell Iral Haynes Jr is the real name of which popstar?

13   Who was the father of Xerxes I of Persia?

14   The aromatherapy oil petitgrain has what scent?

15   In an episode of *Father Ted*, what was the title of the Eurovision entry written by Ted and Dougal?

16   What nickname was given to the Triumph Model H motorcycle during WWI?

17   In which present-day country was artist Marc Chagall born?

18   The 1951 novels *Molloy* and *Malone Dies* were written by which author?

19   How many years does a quinquennial anniversary mark?

20   The company Bulova, subject of the first paid advertisement to be broadcast on TV in 1941, sold what products?

Easy

Medium

Hard

Answers to QUIZ 229 – Pot Luck

1	Malaysia	11	*The Voice UK*
2	The Royal Society	12	Anthony Burgess
3	Elderberries	13	Connecticut
4	Assembly or parliament	14	Mattel Inc.
5	*MegaMind*	15	The Laxey Wheel
6	Eris	16	Rossini
7	A musical instrument (stringed)	17	*Listen*
8	The coast	18	Malaysia
9	Sir Ian McGeechan	19	Walmer Castle
10	Uruguay	20	Zone Improvement Plan

Easy

1 Which pop star won the *Most Promising Newcomer* Golden Globe award for his role in the 1961 film *Come September*?

2 What was the name of the horse that won the first Cheltenham Gold Cup, run in 1924?

3 The Chief Scout of which country presents the Golden Pheasant Award for long service to scouting?

4 What was Rose's surname in the TV series *The Golden Girls*?

5 The golden lion tamarin is native to which country?

6 Who wrote the 1962 novel *The Golden Notebook*?

7 In which US state did the Golden Delicious apple originate?

8 What was the title of Andrew Gold's first UK top twenty single, released in 1977?

9 In Greek mythology, what was the name of the ancient country in which the Golden Fleece was held?

10 Which group had a 1974 and 1982 top thirty single with their version of Neil Young's *After the Gold Rush*?

11 In which decade was the Golden Gate Bridge opened?

Medium

12 What is the name of the protagonist in Donna Tartt's 2013 novel *The Goldfinch*?

13 What motto appears on a tin of Lyle's Golden Syrup?

14 Who created the 1990s TV series *Band of Gold*?

15 Golders Green station lies between which two Underground stations on the Northern Line?

16 Who directed the 1995 James Bond film *GoldenEye*?

17 Who hosted the 2008-09 version of the quiz show *Going for Gold*?

18 Sir Francis Drake renamed his ship *The Pelican* as *The Golden Hind* in honour of which politician's coat of arms?

19 In which discipline did American Charles Jewtraw win the first ever gold medal at the Winter Olympics in 1924?

20 Which novel by Oliver Goldsmith is subtitled *A Tale, Supposed to be Written by Himself*?

Hard

Answers to QUIZ 230 – Film

1	Oakey Oakes	11	Gerald Crich
2	Julius	12	*Spider-Man*
3	*Swordfish*	13	Sydney Pollack
4	Kashyyyk	14	*My Favorite Wife*
5	Bing Crosby	15	*My Own Private Idaho*
6	The Himalayas	16	*Dangerous*
7	*Mr Peabody & Sherman*	17	Francesca Hayward
8	Hans Zimmer	18	Meta Golding
9	Pinkie Brown	19	*Julius Caesar*
10	*For Sama*	20	Haing S Ngor

ANSWERS ON PAGE 235

1   The "Summer White House" of which US president was situated in the town of Kennebunkport in Maine?

2   For what do the letters AGM stand in relation to plants in the UK?

3   For which Brazilian football club did Pelé play from 1956 to 1974?

4   What word meaning "a large number" is derived from the Greek term for ten thousand?

5   In which country was golfer Nelly Korda born in 1998?

6   Who was the Norse god of daytime?

7   Who succeeded Pope Stephen III and preceded Pope Leo III?

8   Juan Vucetich (d.1925) pioneered what investigative method in the late 19th century?

9   In Shakespeare's *The Winter's Tale*, Polixenes is the king of which historical region?

10   What type of food are shimeji?

11   Who starred as Max Vatan in the 2016 film *Allied*?

12   *All We Know is Falling* was the 2005 debut album by which band?

13   In relation to astronomy, what is the 3753 Cruithne?

14   In which US state is the Emily Dickinson Museum?

15   The TV series *Vienna Blood* was based on novels by which author?

16   Thomas Aquinas was born in which modern-day Italian region in 1225?

17   Zenkō Suzuki served two years as Japanese Prime Minister in which decade?

18   Which was the first company in the world to make production aeroplanes?

19   In Greece, the day of which saint is celebrated in early January with a bread or cake called vasilopita?

20   What is the name given to the smallest unit of sound that is significant in a language?

1	Hayley Mills	11	Croatian
2	November (23)	12	Nelly
3	An insect	13	Darius I
4	Nara	14	Orange
5	The Kuiper Belt	15	*My Lovely Horse*
6	1980s (1987)	16	The Trusty
7	An oilfield	17	Belarus
8	St Lucia	18	Samuel Beckett
9	Stoughton	19	Five
10	Annet	20	Clocks and watches

1   The Karoo is a semi-desert region of which country?

2   What is the geological term for the process of one tectonic plate sliding under another?

3   A stretch of which body of water in the UK is known as "The Swellies"?

4   What term is used to describe rocks formed from the solid fragments from a volcanic eruption?

5   What adjective describes a plant that has the male and female reproductive organs in separate flowers on the same plant?

6   The giant viper's bugloss plant is native to which group of islands?

7   What is the term for the measurement of the elevation of land above sea level?

8   The Tayrona National Natural Park includes an area of which sea?

9   What is the *khamsin*, in Egypt?

10 What is the common name of the tree *Quercus suber*?

11 In which European city are the Castellana Caves located?

12 The islands known as the Cumbraes lie in which body of water?

13 In which country is the Valley of Geysers, home to the second-largest collection of geysers in the world?

14 What is the name of the highest peak in the Canadian Rocky Mountains?

15 The River Manifold flows through which English county?

16 The *altiplano* is the name given to the widest part of which mountain range?

17 What is a maar?

18 The word "ffridd" describes a mixed habitat for wild creatures in which country?

19 As at the end of 2019, in which country did the most powerful earthquake ever recorded take place?

20 Lake Constance (Bodensee) has shorelines in Bavaria and which other German state?

Answers to QUIZ 232 – Gold

1	Bobby Darin	11	1930s (1937)
2	Red Splash	12	Theodore (Theo) Decker
3	Japan	13	Out of the strong came forth sweetness
4	Nylund	14	Kay Mellor
5	Brazil	15	Brent Cross and Hampstead
6	Doris Lessing	16	Martin Campbell
7	West Virginia	17	John Suchet
8	*Lonely Boy*	18	Sir Christopher Hatton
9	Colchis	19	Speed skating
10	Prelude	20	*The Vicar of Wakefield*

1 Burgas Airport is located in which European country?

2 Chad Smith became the drummer for which group in 1988?

3 "For king and the law" is the motto of which city in the UK?

4 The lunate bones are found in which part of the human body?

5 By what name is the motor racing track Circuit de Nevers better known?

6 *You Bring Me Joy* (2012) was a single from which *The X Factor* contestant?

7 The word "niksen", meaning the concept of doing nothing, is taken from which language?

8 What is the real first name of actress Tilda Swinton?

9 What type of edible item is a "Bonnie Lad"?

10 Ustad Ahmad Lahauri is best known for designing which world-famous building?

11 Aquincum was the Roman name for which European city?

12 Toshio Iue founded which electronics company in the 1940s?

13 To the nearest one percent, the Sun makes up what percentage of the solar system's mass?

14 The Itria Valley is located in which region of Italy?

15 In Roman mythology, who was the mother of Romulus and Remus?

16 Which South American capital city was originally founded under the name "City of Kings"?

17 *Echoes, Silence, Patience & Grace* is a 2007 album by which band?

18 Elizabeth Petrovna was the ruler of which country from 1741 to 1762?

19 *The King of Thieves* (1996) was a sequel to which Disney film?

20 What was the middle name of the author Sir Kingsley Amis?

Easy

Medium

Hard

Answers to QUIZ 233 – Pot Luck

1	George HW Bush	11	Brad Pitt
2	Award of Garden Merit	12	Paramore
3	Santos	13	An asteroid
4	Myriad *(myrias)*	14	Massachusetts
5	USA	15	Frank Tallis
6	Dagr	16	Lazio
7	Pope Adrian I	17	1980s (1980-82)
8	Fingerprinting	18	Short Brothers (Belfast)
9	Bohemia	19	Basil
10	Mushrooms	20	Phoneme

What are the names of these former Conservative or coalition Cabinet ministers?

Easy

1

2

3

Medium

4

5

6

7

8

9

Hard

Answers to QUIZ 234 – Natural World

1	South Africa	11	Bari (Italy)
2	Subduction	12	The Firth of Clyde
3	Menai Strait	13	Russia
4	Pyroclastic	14	Mount Robson
5	Monoecious	15	Staffordshire
6	The Canary Islands	16	The Andes
7	Hypsometry	17	A volcanic crater (formed by an explosion)
8	The Caribbean Sea	18	Wales
9	A hot, dry wind	19	Chile (1960)
10	Cork oak	20	Baden-Württemberg

1. In relation to the Paris transport network, for what do the initials RER stand?

2. In which year was the International Space Station launched?

3. By what name is actress Margaret Hyra (b.1961) better known?

4. A town in the eastern part of the island of Newfoundland shares its name with which male creature?

5. Mussorgsky's *Pictures at an Exhibition* was based on the work of which Russian artist and designer?

6. Who wrote the 2002 cyberpunk novel *Altered Carbon*, which was adapted for television in 2018?

7. Which two countries were involved in the brief "Football War" in 1969?

8. Recep Tayyip Erdoğan became president of which country in 2014?

9. What is the first name of the brother of Titus Andronicus in the Shakespeare play?

10. In which country does the Yabloko political party operate?

11. What name is given to the giant carved heads found on Rapa Nui (Easter Island)?

12. What is the name of the musical wing of the Royal Navy?

13. *Jaded* was a 2000 single by which US rock band?

14. In which decade did the Salem Witch Trials take place in Massachusetts?

15. What flower shares its name with a powder known as jeweller's rouge, which is used to polish metal?

16. Who was the mother of Henry V?

17. Which team did Liverpool beat in the 2005 Champions League final?

18. What is the American word for a terraced house?

19. *Nuns and Soldiers* was a 1980 novel by which author?

20. How old was the Roman Emperor Nero when he committed suicide?

Easy

Medium

Hard

Answers to QUIZ 235 – Pot Luck

1	Bulgaria	11	Budapest
2	The Red Hot Chili Peppers	12	Sanyo
3	Leeds	13	99% (approximately 99.8%)
4	The hands	14	Apulia (south-east Italy)
5	Magny-Cours	15	Rhea Silvia
6	Amelia Lily	16	Lima
7	Dutch	17	Foo Fighters
8	Katherine	18	Russia
9	A broad bean	19	*Aladdin*
10	Taj Mahal	20	William

QUIZ 238 – Gordon

1 With which football club did Gordon Strachan begin his playing career?

2 What was the first name of the British Army officer known as "Chinese Gordon" (d.1885)?

3 Former prime minister Gordon Brown studied which subject at Edinburgh University?

4 In the TV series *Gotham*, who portrayed James Gordon?

5 Which cartoonist created the character of Flash Gordon?

6 The Gordon Rugby Football Club is based in which city?

7 What was the title of Peter and Gordon's second single, released in 1964?

8 Who was the first member of the Royal Family to be educated at Gordonstoun school?

9 What was the title of Gordon Ramsay's second memoir, published in 2008?

10 In which 1953 film did Gordon MacRae play the character of Paul Bonnard?

11 What was the title of the 1991 sitcom that starred John Gordon Sinclair as Robert Neilson?

12 How many caps did Gordon Banks win for England?

13 In which decade was Gordon's gin first produced?

14 The Gordon Highlanders were amalgamated with which other regiment in 1994?

15 What number engine is Gordon in the series of books by the Reverend William Awdry?

16 Who portrayed the character of Tony Gordon in *Coronation Street*?

17 How do competitors in the race for the current Gordon Bennett Cup travel?

18 In the lyrics of the 1978 song *Jilted John*, what was the name of the girlfriend who left John for Gordon?

19 The character of Gordon Tracy in *Thunderbirds* was named after which US astronaut?

20 Who released the 1970s albums *Don Quixote* and *Sundown*?

Answers to QUIZ 236 – Cabinet Ministers

1 Kenneth Baker (Baron Baker of Dorking)
2 Justine Greening
3 Danny Alexander
4 William Waldegrave (Baron Waldegrave of North Hill)
5 Virginia Bottomley
6 Peter Lilley
7 David Gauke
8 Esther McVey
9 Chris Patten (Baron Patten of Barnes)

1 What is the capital of the Spanish region of Cantabria?

2 In 2003, Ann Daniels and Caroline Hamilton became the first all-female expedition to complete what feat?

3 What was the name of the Lunar Module pilot on the *Apollo* 12 space mission?

4 Who directed the 2019 film *Military Wives*?

5 What is a Trinidad scorpion?

6 What is the medical term for pins and needles?

7 In Turkey, what is a gulet?

8 What was the first name of Neville Chamberlain's father, who was also a politician?

9 The European Parliament established a Freedom for Thought prize in 1988 in honour of which scientist and activist?

10 In 2007 Claire Buckfield was runner-up when which other celebrity won *Dancing on Ice*?

11 As at the end of 2019, who was the only person to have won three Kate Greenaway medals for illustrating children's books?

12 Who was the blacksmith of the gods in Greek mythology?

13 Who released the 1990 single *Black Cat*?

14 Diego Pérez (b.1962) and Marcel Felder (b.1984) have played in the Davis Cup for which nation?

15 Of what is eleutherophobia the fear?

16 Which golfer (b.1991) is known by the nickname "The Bashful Prince"?

17 The Flaminian Way connected Rome and which other location?

18 What nationality was the explorer Jacob Roggeveen?

19 On what substance is the protein sericin found?

20 Founded in 1894, Spillers in Cardiff is the world's oldest shop selling what items?

Easy

Medium

Hard

Answers to QUIZ 237 – Pot Luck

1	Réseau Express Régional	11	*Moai*
2	1998	12	The Royal Marines Band Service
3	Meg Ryan	13	Aerosmith
4	Gander	14	1690s (1692)
5	Viktor Hartmann	15	Crocus
6	K Richard Morgan	16	Mary de Bohun
7	El Salvador and Honduras	17	AC Milan
8	Turkey	18	Rowhouse
9	Marcus	19	Dame Iris Murdoch
10	Russia	20	30

Easy

1   The inner city district of Dingle was the setting for which sitcom?

2   What was the name of the constable in the 1960s children's series *The Herbs*?

3   Rolando Villazón was a judge on which 2010 talent show?

4   Who played Annie Cartwright in *Life on Mars*?

5   What was the name of the fictional planet on which the 2011 series *Outcasts* was set?

6   Superintendents James McKay and Kevin Dunne appeared in which crime drama series?

7   The first Bradshaw's guide to railway timetables, the basis for Michael Portillo's travel series, was published in which decade?

8   What was the name of Lance's ex-wife in *Detectorists*?

9   Who was in third place in the 2019 BBC Sports Personality of the Year award?

10 Which long-running BBC programme has previously been broadcast at The Magnolias and Clack's Farm?

Medium

11 Who composed the theme music for *Coronation Street*?

12 Which 2014 Australian drama series featured the brothers Jesse and Ned Banks?

13 Who played Detective Chief Constable Mike Dryden in *Line of Duty*?

14 Greg Sumner, played by William Devane, was a character in which US series?

15 Who created the historical fantasy drama series *Britannia*?

16 Which college won the 2020 series of *University Challenge*?

17 What was the name of Michael Sheen's character in *Good Omens*?

18 In which year did *The Chase* game show first air on ITV?

19 Which city was the setting for the crime drama series *Motive*, first broadcast in 2013?

20 Who presented the series *Britain's Greatest Bridges* (2016) and *The World's Greatest Bridges* (2017)?

Hard

Answers to QUIZ 238 – Gordon

1	Dundee FC	11	*An Actor's Life for Me*
2	Charles	12	73
3	History	13	1760s (1769)
4	Ben McKenzie	14	The Queen's Own Highlanders
5	Alex Raymond	15	4
6	Sydney	16	Gray O'Brien
7	*Nobody I Know*	17	By gas balloon
8	Prince Philip, Duke of Edinburgh	18	Julie
9	*Playing With Fire*	19	Leroy Gordon Cooper
10	*The Desert Song*	20	Gordon Lightfoot

ANSWERS ON PAGE 243

1   Which singer played Johnny Fontane in The Godfather series of films?

2   The Eredivisie is the highest league of football in which country?

3   On what day is the Gaelic festival of Beltane?

4   In which decade did the uprising known as the Pilgrimage of Grace take place in England?

5   Of what is batrachophobia the fear?

6   What were the first names of the writer EB White (d.1985)?

7   The Great Pit of Carkoon was located near which character's palace in the Star Wars films?

8   Which people worshipped Illapa, a god of thunder and lightning?

9   Approximately how many degrees Celsius is the temperature at the Sun's core?

10 Which group's only UK chart single was *A Teenager in Love* (1959)?

11 According to a 2019 report by the United Nations, which country is the happiest in the world?

12 Which plant has the nickname "butter and eggs" because of the colour of its flowers?

13 Lella Lombardi (d.1992) competed in which sport from 1974 to 1976?

14 What is the name given to the unit of measurement 10^{-6}?

15 "Temblor" is an alternative name for what type of event?

16 Philosopher Ludwig Wittgenstein was born in which decade?

17 *The Red House Mystery* (1922) was the only crime story written by which author?

18 To what does the adjective "sidereal" relate?

19 Who released the 1983 song *Break My Stride*?

20 Lauren Lambert won the 2013 series of which TV show?

Answers to QUIZ 239 – Pot Luck

1	Santander	11	Chris Riddell
2	Walking to the North Pole and the South Pole	12	Hephaestus
3	Alan Bean	13	Janet Jackson
4	Peter Cattaneo	14	Uruguay
5	A chilli pepper	15	Freedom
6	Paraesthesia	16	Ryo Ishikawa
7	A (wooden) sailing boat	17	Rimini (Ariminum)
8	Joseph	18	Dutch
9	Andrei Sakharov	19	Raw silk
10	Kyran Bracken	20	Records

Easy

Medium

Hard

1 Which musician (d.2008) was nicknamed "The Originator"?

2 Which composer influenced the work of Friedrich Nietzsche?

3 The cuatro is the national instrument of which nation?

4 Which singer released both an album and an autobiography entitled *Thursday's Child*?

5 The Famous Flames was the backing group for which singer?

6 *First Impressions of Earth* was a 2006 album released by which band?

7 *My Son, My Son* (1954) was the only UK chart-topping single for which singer?

8 Which composer's music was used as the theme for the TV series *The New Statesman*?

9 What was the title of Brotherhood of Man's follow-up single to *Save Your Kisses for Me*?

10 "Like ghosts they want me to make 'em all, They won't let go" is a lyric from which 2014 song?

11 *There You'll Be*, featured on the soundtrack of the 2001 film *Pearl Harbor*, was recorded by which singer?

12 How does a chordophone instrument produce sound?

13 *Dookie* (1994) and *Insomniac* (1995) were albums by which US band?

14 The Bellini opera *Norma* is set in which historical region?

15 What name is given to the middle pedal on a piano that allows selected notes to be sustained?

16 What was the real surname of singer Ray Charles?

17 By what name are the singer Tunde Baiyewu and the keyboard player Paul Tucker known?

18 What type of instruments are the Japanese *taiko*?

19 AJ McLean is an original member of which vocal group?

20 What musical term indicates that something is to be played in a flexible tempo?

---

1. In Greek mythology, who was the mother of Apollo and Artemis?

2. What is the name for a unit of measurement of the intensity of pain?

3. Which layer of the Sun lies between the photosphere and the corona?

4. Who wrote the 1958 opera *Noye's Fludde*?

5. What was the name of André the Giant's character in the 1987 film *The Princess Bride*?

6. Bert Patenaude scored the first hat trick in FIFA World Cup history whilst playing for which nation?

7. Mount Kinabalu lies on which island?

8. In which decade did the Battle of Plassey take place in Bengal?

9. What was the name of King Alfred's wife?

10. Caterine Ibargüen won the gold medal in which athletics event at the 2016 Olympic Games?

11. Vindobona was the Roman name for which European capital city?

12. Who released the 2010 single *Bulletproof*?

13. Who played Lieutenant Crocker in the 1970s TV series *Kojak*?

14. "It ain't my fault that I'm out here getting loose" is a lyric from which 2019 song?

15. In which country is the 1995 sculpture known as *Men at Sea*, or *Man Meets the Sea*?

16. What type of creature is a prion?

17. Inventor John Logie Baird was born in which decade?

18. Hattusa was the capital of which empire, which lasted from the 15th century BC until the 8th century BC?

19. What was the name of Sally Hawkins' character in the 2010 film *Made in Dagenham*?

20. Who commanded the German fleet at the Battle of Jutland in 1916?

Easy

Medium

Hard

Answers to QUIZ 241 – Pot Luck

1	Al Martino	11	Finland
2	The Netherlands	12	Yellow toadflax
3	May Day	13	Formula 1
4	1530s (1536)	14	Micrometre
5	Amphibians	15	An earthquake
6	Elwyn Brooks	16	1880s (1889)
7	Jabba the Hutt	17	AA Milne
8	The Incas	18	Stars
9	15 million degrees Celsius	19	Matthew Wilder
10	Dion and the Belmonts	20	*Britain's Next Top Model*

Easy

1   *Orchard Tambourines* was a 1999 set of woodcuts by which English artist?

2   For what does the "C" stand in the name of the Dutch graphic artist MC Escher?

3   In which decade was the COBRA art movement founded?

4   The fresco of *The Assumption of the Virgin* by Antonio da Correggio decorates the dome of which cathedral?

5   During his lifetime, which artist was known by many different names including Shunrō and Tawaraya Sōri?

6   Tamara De Lempicka (d.1980) was born in which European capital city?

7   In which US state was artist Jasper Johns born in 1930?

8   Which West Sussex country house is noted for its collection of paintings by JMW Turner?

9   In what branch of the arts was Laurent Delvaux (d.1778) famous?

10 The art critic Louis Leroy (d.1885) coined what term that was subsequently adopted by an artistic movement?

11 Who painted the 1740s series of pictures entitled *Marriage A-la-Mode*?

12 Which technique employed by Max Ernst involved layering oil paint on a canvas over a textured object then scraping off the paint?

Medium

13 *Whaam!* was a 1963 work by which artist?

14 The fibreglass artwork *Repetition 19* was created by which artist?

15 How was the artistic group The Blue Rider known in the country in which it was founded?

16 Le Corbusier (d.1965) was born with which double-barrelled first name?

17 What name is given to the item that artists use to rest their brush hand when painting?

18 Which British architect designed the Hepworth Wakefield art museum, opened in 2011?

19 Who painted the work *The Water Seller of Seville* (c.1622)?

20 What was Pablo Picasso's middle name?

Answers to QUIZ 242 – Music

Hard

1	Bo Diddley	11	Faith Hill
2	Richard Wagner	12	By the vibration of strings
3	Puerto Rico	13	Green Day
4	Eartha Kitt	14	Gaul
5	James Brown	15	The sostenuto pedal
6	The Strokes	16	Robinson
7	Dame Vera Lynn	17	The Lighthouse Family
8	Modest Mussorgsky	18	Drums
9	*My Sweet Rosalie*	19	Backstreet Boys
10	*Ex's & Oh's* (Elle King)	20	Rubato

1   Anthony Carelli (b.1974) competed in WWE under what name?

2   What is the first name of Inspector Montalbano's housekeeper?

3   Who was the father of Odin in Norse mythology?

4   Suzanne Berne won the 1999 Orange Prize for Fiction for which novel?

5   In *The Comedy of Errors*, what is the name of the Merchant of Syracuse?

6   *Winter with Flowers* was the original working title of which sitcom?

7   The Phong Nha Cave lies in which Asian country?

8   What name is given to someone who has memorised the entire Koran?

9   Which 2018 film featured the character of Meg Murry trying to find her missing father?

10 On what is a paradiddle played?

11 What was the nationality of the 1946 Masters golf championship winner Herman Keiser?

12 In 1929, which golf club became the first British club to host the Ryder Cup?

13 Walden Robert Cassotto was the real name of which singer (d.1973)?

14 Spitsbergen is the largest island in which archipelago?

15 In the Just William books, what were the names of his three friends with which he formed the gang The Outlaws?

16 Dan Reynolds is best known as the lead vocalist of which band?

17 Kalimantan is the name given to the Indonesian part of which island?

18 Which horse won the Champion Hurdle at the Cheltenham Festival in 2014?

19 Joan of Acre was the daughter of which English king?

20 Something described as "reticulate" resembles or takes the form of what?

Answers to QUIZ 243 – Pot Luck

1	Leto	11	Vienna
2	Dol	12	La Roux
3	The chromosphere	13	Kevin Dobson
4	Sir Benjamin Britten	14	*Juice* (Lizzo)
5	Fezzik	15	Denmark (Esbjerg)
6	USA	16	A bird (a petrel)
7	Borneo	17	1880s (1888)
8	1750s (1757)	18	The Hittite Empire
9	Ealhswith	19	Rita O'Grady
10	Triple jump	20	Reinhard Scheer

1 Cream of Saskatchewan is a variety of which fruit?

2 *Aemono* is the Japanese term for which type of dish?

3 What is the name given to the malt liquid created during the process of making whisky and beer?

4 Which restaurant chain was founded in 1965 by Fred DeLuca and Peter Buck?

5 The mango is a member of which family of plants?

6 What were the first names of Mr Heinz, founder of the food company?

7 Old Forester is a brand of what type of drink?

8 In which country is the wine-producing region of Casablanca Valley?

9 *Fortunella Margarita* is the Latin name for which fruit?

10 The name of which US state appears in the alternative name of the dish Hoppin' John?

11 From what is the Italian liqueur Nocino made?

12 Which tropical fruit's name means "Indian date"?

13 The seeds of which plant are an ingredient of an Abernethy biscuit?

14 Laplap is the national dish of which island country?

15 Mexican restaurateur Ignacio Anaya is credited with inventing what dish?

16 What are the main two ingredients of the Sicilian dish crocchè?

17 Which fish is traditionally the centrepiece of a Polish Christmas Eve meal?

18 By what name is the meat dish brawn known as in the US?

19 The Thai dessert *kluai buat chi* consists of which fruit in coconut milk?

20 In which country was the furmint grape originally grown?

Answers to QUIZ 244 – Art

1	Sir Terry Frost	11	William Hogarth
2	Cornelis	12	Grattage
3	1940s (1948)	13	Roy Lichtenstein
4	Parma (Italy)	14	Eva Hesse
5	Hokusai	15	*Der Blaue Reiter* (Germany)
6	Warsaw	16	Charles-Édouard
7	Georgia	17	Maulstick
8	Petworth House	18	Sir David Chipperfield
9	Sculpture	19	Diego Velázquez
10	Impressionists	20	Ruiz

1   What was measured using the ancient device known as a clepsydra?

2   Which type of pasta derives its name from the Italian word for "corkscrew"?

3   Of what is agrostology the study?

4   Los Ticos is the nickname of which country's national football team?

5   Who played Zeus in the 2010 film *Percy Jackson and the Lightning Thief*?

6   "Ain't that Mr Mister on the radio, stereo" is a lyric from which 2009 song?

7   Who, with assistance from her gardener, created the Minack Theatre in Cornwall in the early 1930s?

8   In July 2019, a street in which Welsh town was measured by the Guinness Book of World Records as being the steepest in the world, a record it later lost to a street in New Zealand?

9   Perdita falls in love with which character in Shakespeare's *The Winter's Tale*?

10 What type of creature is an albacore?

11 Oeschinen Lake lies in which European country?

12 Bo Bice and Diana DeGarmo have been runners up on which long-running musical talent show?

13 What was the original name of the company that built the first Jaguar cars?

14 Who played Colonel Lucas in the 1979 film *Apocalypse Now*?

15 What name was given to the NASA rover that landed on Mars in 1997?

16 The former kingdom of Dahomey is part of which modern-day African country?

17 Founded in 1898 and closed in 1969, Studley College for Women taught which two subjects?

18 What adjective is given to a computer program that uses rules based on previous experience to solve a problem?

19 In sport, for what is a Zamboni machine used?

20 The TV series *Grantchester* is based on a collection of short stories by which author?

Easy

Medium

Hard

Answers to QUIZ 245 – Pot Luck

1	Santino Marella	11	American
2	Adelina	12	Moortown
3	Borr	13	Bobby Darin
4	*A Crime in the Neighborhood*	14	Svalbard
5	Aegeon	15	Douglas, Ginger and Henry
6	*As Time Goes By*	16	Imagine Dragons
7	Vietnam	17	Borneo
8	Hafiz	18	Jezki
9	*A Wrinkle in Time*	19	Edward I
10	A drum	20	A net

1   In which branch of science was Herophilos a famous Greek figure?

2   Maxwell Montes is a mountain massif on which planet?

3   What is the name of the largest carpal bone in the hand?

4   Which Austrian physicist was awarded the Nobel Prize in Physics in 1945?

5   Which part of the human digestive system shares its name with the currency unit of Costa Rica?

6   Kazimierz (or Casimir) Funk (d.1967) published a book on what constituent of the human diet in 1912?

7   In 1868, Jules Janssen became one of the first people to discover which element?

8   What is the name of the largest object in the asteroid belt between Mars and Jupiter?

9   Comedo is the medical name for what skin disorder?

10 As at the end of 2019, which was the only element in the periodic table with a name beginning with "V"?

11 The ethmoid bone is located at the roof of which part of the body?

12 In botany, what name is given to the process whereby a green plant becomes white through lack of sunlight?

13 Spodumene is a source of which metallic element?

14 Skathi is a moon of which planet?

15 In 1846, which French astronomer and mathematician correctly predicted the location of Neptune?

16 The fovea centralis is a part of which organ?

17 Which inventor (d.2011) was nicknamed "The Grandfather of Robotics"?

18 What is the name of the thin fluid layer of the Earth that is part of the mantle and lies directly beneath the lithosphere?

19 What other surname sometimes precedes the name of the Kuiper Belt?

20 An analeptic drug works on which part of the body?

Answers to QUIZ 246 – Food and Drink

1	Watermelon	11	(Unripe) walnuts
2	Salad (or its sauce)	12	Tamarind
3	Wort	13	Caraway
4	Subway	14	Vanuatu
5	Cashew family	15	Nachos
6	Henry John	16	Mashed potato and eggs
7	Bourbon whiskey	17	Carp
8	Chile	18	Head cheese
9	Kumquat	19	Bananas
10	Carolina (peas and rice)	20	Hungary

1   What was the first name at birth of Mexican revolutionary Pancho Villa (d.1923)?

2   In which US state was the poet Ezra Pound born?

3   "Hail Great Mother" is the motto of which city in the UK?

4   Who wrote the 1748 book *An Enquiry Concerning Human Understanding*?

5   The Gulf of Gökova is part of which sea?

6   What name is given to the reigning emperor of Japan?

7   What does it mean if someone is described as an autodidact on a subject?

8   *Mr Vain* was a 1993 chart-topper for which German group?

9   The breakfast food cachitos, similar to croissants, are traditionally eaten in which country?

10   "Mother says I was a dancer before I could walk" is a lyric from which pop song?

11   Who played Minister Mason in the 2013 film *Snowpiercer*?

12   In what year did San Marino and Azerbaijan make their first appearances in the Eurovision Song Contest?

13   Who won the 1961 French Formula 1 Grand Prix on his debut but never won another race?

14   In numbers, what is a milliard?

15   Who played the Viking warrior Bloodhair in the TV series *The Last Kingdom*?

16   What is the largest moon in the solar system?

17   Which city was the capital of the Inca Empire?

18   Nataraja is an alternative name of which god?

19   What was the middle name of author Doris Lessing?

20   In which decade was Marks & Spencer founded?

Answers to QUIZ 247 – Pot Luck

1	Time	11	Switzerland
2	Cavatappi	12	*American Idol*
3	Grasses	13	Swallow Sidecar Company
4	Costa Rica	14	Harrison Ford
5	Sean Bean	15	*Sojourner*
6	*Hey, Soul Sister* (Train)	16	Benin
7	Rowena Cade	17	Horticulture and agriculture
8	Harlech (Ffordd Pen Llech)	18	Heuristic
9	Florizel	19	Resurfacing an ice rink
10	A fish	20	James Runcie

1   The island of Ortygia is part of which Italian city?

2   What is the name of Mexico's highest mountain?

3   Locarno is a district in which Swiss canton?

4   Fiordland National Park is in which country?

5   How long is the coastline of Brazil: 3,655, 4,155 or 4,655 miles?

6   How are the islands of Borneo, Sulawesi, Sumatra and Java collectively known?

7   The Sapsan high-speed train runs in which country?

8   Which European country has 443 named islands?

9   Shimla is the capital of which Indian state?

10 Which is the lowest capital city in the world, at around 92 feet below sea level?

11 Which Asian country is nicknamed "the Land of the eternal blue sky"?

12 Which country formerly used the austral as its unit of currency?

13 Hirta is the largest island in which archipelago?

14 The Sherman Minton Bridge spans which river?

15 Mtskheta is the former capital of which former Soviet country?

16 Alfonso Bonilla Aragón International Airport is located in which South American country?

17 The A888 is the only classified road on which UK island?

18 Which is the largest of the Japanese Fuji Five Lakes?

19 What is the fourth-smallest country in the world, by area?

20 In which US state is the Kancamagus Highway?

Answers to QUIZ 248 – Science

1	Anatomy (a physician)	11	The nose
2	Venus	12	Etiolation
3	Capitate bone	13	Lithium
4	Wolfgang Pauli	14	Saturn
5	Colon	15	Urbain Le Verrier
6	Vitamins	16	The eye
7	Helium	17	George Devol
8	Ceres (dwarf planet)	18	Asthenosphere
9	Blackhead	19	Edgeworth
10	Vanadium	20	The central nervous system

1   What is the official name of the tax known as "car tax" or "road tax"?

2   The town of North Shields lies in which English Metropolitan county?

3   How many adult teeth does a dog usually have (to the nearest ten)?

4   How many seasons are there in a year?

5   Which brand of coffee was advertised by Anthony Head and Sharon Maughan?

6   Which city was home to Charles Rennie Mackintosh?

7   In which decade was the TV series *I'm Alan Partridge* first broadcast?

8   Who was the first football player from the UK to win the European Golden Boot award?

9   What is a snake's head fritillary?

10 What are the two home colours of St Helens RFC?

11 How many hours ahead of GMT is Berlin?

12 In which country was the English king Richard II born?

13 Which Israeli communal agricultural settlement takes its name from the Hebrew for "gathering"?

14 For what crime was Dick Turpin executed in 1739?

15 Which fashion house created the *J'Adore* perfume?

16 What colour was the Roman coin the denarius?

17 What is the name of the title character in the 1967 film *The Graduate*?

18 Who was the US president when *Apollo 11* landed on the Moon?

19 Neurons are part of which system of the body?

20 *One Love* was a 2002 hit for which boy band?

Answers to QUIZ 499 – Pot Luck

1	Ferrari	11	A priest
2	Bullfinches	12	Chemical elements
3	Kings of Leon	13	*The Sixth Sense*
4	Inti	14	Montana
5	John	15	Mauritian rupee
6	Pastels	16	William
7	Hammond	17	Torino
8	Stockholm	18	David Sassoli
9	Amelia (Wren)	19	René Descartes
10	17 hours (17 hours 14 minutes)	20	Croatia, and Boznia and Herzegovina

1   Which children's author invented the game of Poohsticks?

2   What name is given to the outdoor game of finding objects left by others using GPS technology?

3   Who wrote the short story *The Little Match Girl*?

4   How many tiles does a player have at the start of a game of Scrabble®?

5   Which New York river and district is named after colonial settler Jonas Bronck?

6   What title is given to the head electrician on a film set?

7   Who directed the 1955 film *Set a Thief To Catch a Thief*?

8   In which decade was the reference to "Empire" removed from the name of the Commonwealth Games?

9   What shape is a set square?

10 In the game rock, paper, scissors, what does a fist represent?

11 Queen's gambit is an opening move in which game?

12 What is the maximum number of players in a game of tennis?

13 "Set me free, why don't cha, babe?" is a line from which 1986 hit for Kim Wilde?

14 How long are the breaks between rounds in a boxing match?

15 What type of animal is the video game character Donkey Kong?

16 Which company makes Matchmakers® chocolates?

17 How long is a standard half of a football match?

18 Match play is a scoring system in which sport?

19 What part of the body might a harsh noise be said to set on edge?

20 Who would use a setting lotion as part of their work?

Answers to QUIZ 500 – Film

1   *The Hummingbird Project*
2   Fergus
3   *The Sand Pebbles*
4   Minnie Driver
5   Sir Daniel Day-Lewis
6   The Huntress
7   Mafalda (Hopkirk)
8   *Sin City*
9   *The Lavender Hill Mob*
10 *Remember the Titans*
11 *Withnail and I*
12 Elmer Bernstein
13 Winklevoss
14 *How to Make an American Quilt*
15 Hugo (Barrett)
16 Jennifer Connelly
17 *Hercules*
18 *The Cocoanuts*
19 *Panic Room*
20 EM Forster

1 Which two colours appear in the logo of American Airlines?

2 What is 48 in Roman numerals?

3 Balmoral Castle lies in which Scottish county?

4 Who played Crowley in the TV series *Good Omens*?

5 The 1887 comic opera *Ruddigore* was written by which duo?

6 Who became Chancellor of the Exchequer in July 2019, resigning in February 2020?

7 Which first-class cricket club plays its home games at Sophia Gardens in Cardiff?

8 What name is given to a baby ferret?

9 What is bombazine?

10 In 1966, which Australian racing driving became the first person to win a race in a car of his own design?

11 Which type of flower has a candelabra variety?

12 In the 2006 film *Miami Vice*, who played Crockett?

13 Which couple presented the 2020 Channel 4 book review *Keep Reading and Carry On*?

14 What is between the tee and the green on a golf course?

15 The TV series *Tenko* was set in which country?

16 Which is the most northerly main island of Japan?

17 How many feet are there in five fathoms?

18 Which two words, that differ only by their first letter, mean "a bet" and "keen"?

19 As what was David Bowie dressed in the video to *Ashes to Ashes*?

20 Which footballer was an original team captain on the panel show *They Think It's All Over*?

Answers to QUIZ 251 – Pot Luck

1	Vehicle Excise Duty	11	One hour
2	Tyne and Wear	12	France
3	40 (42)	13	Kibbutz
4	Four	14	Horse theft
5	Gold Blend™	15	Dior
6	Glasgow	16	Silver
7	1990s (1997)	17	Benjamin Braddock
8	Ian Rush (1984)	18	Richard Nixon
9	A flower	19	The nervous system
10	White and red	20	Blue

Easy

1 Which film won Best Picture at the 2020 BAFTA Film awards?

2 Who plays the lead role of Toula in the My Big Fat Greek Wedding films?

3 What was the subtitle of the 2017 film in the Alien series?

4 Which 2019 film, starring Emilia Clarke, took its name from a hit by *Wham!*?

5 Jodie Foster and Scott Baio were the child stars of which 1976 musical?

6 Which planet completes the title of the 2015 film, ___ *Ascending*?

7 Which actor starred as a poltergeist in the 1988 film *Beetlejuice*?

8 *Ordinary People* (1980) was the first film directed by which Hollywood actor?

9 Which 1920s silent-film star made the films *The Sheik* and *Blood and Sand*?

10 Which of these Pixar films was released first: *Cars*, *Finding Nemo* or *WALL-E*?

11 Which actor was originally cast as the voice of Paddington in the 2014 film of the same name?

12 Richard Hannay and Mr Memory are characters in which classic 1959 film?

13 Which 1984 film starring Patrick Swayze was remade in 2012 with Chris Hemsworth in the same role?

Medium

14 Which technology guru (d.2011) did Michael Fassbender play in a 2015 biopic?

15 Who won the Best Actor Oscar for his portrayal of Claus von Bulow in the 1990 film *Reversal of Fortune*?

16 For which 1994 film did Quentin Tarantino win the Best Original Screenplay Oscar?

17 How were Chevy Chase, Martin Short and Steve Martin referred to in the title of a 1986 comedy film?

18 Who played Jo in the 2019 film *Little Women*?

19 Which film directed by Sir Alfred Hitchcock sees the main character conquer his fear of heights to reach the roof of a bell tower in a crucial scene?

20 The 1966 film *Funeral in Berlin* featured Sir Michael Caine as which fictional spy?

Hard

Answers to QUIZ 252 – Game, Set and Match

1	AA Milne	11	Chess
2	Geocaching	12	Four
3	Hans Christian Andersen	13	*You Keep Me Hangin' On*
4	Seven	14	One minute
5	The Bronx	15	A gorilla
6	Gaffer	16	Nestlé
7	Sir Alfred Hitchcock	17	45 minutes
8	1970s (1970)	18	Golf
9	Triangular	19	Your teeth
10	Rock	20	A hairdresser

1   What colour is a packet of Walkers® ready salted crisps?

2   In 2020, who hosted the Brit Awards for the third time?

3   What is the first name of Tanya Branning's sister in *EastEnders*, played by Tanya Franks?

4   What is the meaning of the name Octavius?

5   In 2018, the world record for which men's athletic event was set at 9,126 points?

6   *Walk Like a Man* was a 1963 hit for which group?

7   What does it mean if a creature is on the IUCN Red List?

8   In which decade was the TV series *Rugrats* first aired?

9   What colour is Gavi wine?

10 In what sport are the Klitschko brothers famous names?

11 Who played FBI agent Sean Archer in the 1997 film *Face/Off*?

12 Which Lincolnshire town is famous for its tulip-growing?

13 John Arlott (d.1991) commentated on which sport?

14 In the comic strip Peanuts, who has a booth offering psychiatric help?

15 TN is the abbreviation for which US state?

16 Which two words that differ only by their first letter mean "correspond" and "unoriginal"?

17 "Pay no attention to that man behind the curtain" is a line from which film?

18 What are the two official languages of the island of Puerto Rico?

19 Which Canadian province is alphabetically first?

20 In 1992, who succeeded Neil Kinnock (Baron Kinnock) as leader of the Labour Party?

Answers to QUIZ 253 – Pot Luck

1	Blue and red	11	Primula
2	XLVIII	12	Colin Farrell
3	Aberdeenshire	13	Richard and Judy
4	David Tennant	14	The fairway
5	Gilbert and Sullivan	15	Japan
6	Sajid Javid	16	Hokkaido
7	Glamorgan CCC	17	30 feet
8	Kit	18	Wager and eager
9	A fabric (made of cotton or wool)	19	A Pierrot (clown)
10	Jack Brabham	20	Gary Lineker

Easy

1. "Hosanna in excelsis" is a line from which Christmas carol?

2. What word follows "hydrogen" in the name of a bleaching agent?

3. What was the name of Ron Howard's character in *Happy Days*?

4. With which country are hieroglyphics associated?

5. "Here we are now, entertain us" is a lyric from which song?

6. What is the usual abbreviation for the county of Hertfordshire?

7. In the Harry Potter series, Gringotts Bank is staffed mainly by which type of creatures?

8. What animal completes the phrase about enjoyment: "Have a ___ of a time"?

9. Is Highgate Cemetery in the east, north or west of London?

10. The Hilton Park services in Staffordshire is on which motorway?

11. Are *hors d'ouevres* served before or after a meal?

12. In which decade did Helen Sharman become the first British woman to go into space?

Medium

13. Who played Jonathan Hart in the TV series *Hart to Hart*?

14. What shape is the UK road containing a warning of a humpback bridge or road humps?

15. Huckleberry Finn is a friend of which fictional character?

16. What is the medical name for the complaint known as "housemaid's knee"?

17. Haverfordwest is the county town of which Welsh county?

18. Of what is hydrology the study?

19. What is someone doing too rapidly if they are hyperventilating?

20. Which fruit juice is an ingredient of Hollandaise sauce?

Hard

1 Who won his second Oscar for his supporting role in the 2019 film *Once Upon a Time...in Hollywood*?

2 In which decade did the county cricket championship first become a two-tier competition?

3 "And watches the ships that go sailing" is a lyric from which song?

4 In which county is the town of Burton-on-Trent?

5 How many hours are there in four days?

6 In which series of films does Liam Neeson's character claim to have "a very particular set of skills"?

7 Rosyth Dockyard is situated in which historic county of Scotland?

8 Which of these reality shows was broadcast first: *Britain's Got Talent, Popstars* or *The X Factor* ?

9 What type of food is Limburger?

10 In which year did Facebook™ implement the ability to choose a reaction to a post?

11 What was the name of the family featured in *Butterflies*?

12 Which actress starred in the 1963 film *The Birds*?

13 Which two European countries have black, red and yellow stripes on their flags?

14 What cabinet position was held by Sir John Nott during the Falklands War?

15 "All that glisters is not gold" is a line from which Shakespeare play?

16 What adjective describes a creature that feeds mostly on insects?

17 Which remote continent is sometimes referred to as "The Last Frontier"?

18 How many syllables are there in the word "customary"?

19 What type of marine creature is a bowhead?

20 Which composer was born in Leipzig in 1813?

Answers to QUIZ 255 – Pot Luck

1	Red	11	John Travolta
2	Jack Whitehall	12	Spalding
3	Rainie	13	Cricket
4	Eighth	14	Lucy (van Pelt)
5	Decathlon	15	Tennessee
6	The Four Seasons	16	Write and trite
7	It is threatened with extinction	17	*The Wizard of Oz*
8	1990s (1991)	18	Spanish and English
9	White	19	Alberta
10	Boxing	20	John Smith

Easy

1 What bird features on the crest of Tottenham Hotspur FC?

2 In which season would you hear a cuckoo in the UK?

3 Someone who is considered to be a coward might be given the name of which farmyard bird?

4 Who wrote the 2013 novel *The Goldfinch*?

5 Which group had a 1986 hit with *Happy Hour*?

6 The New York club Birdland is associated with which type of music?

7 In what sort of tree does the kookaburra sit, in the traditional Australian song?

8 What bird is featured on the Barclays Bank logo?

9 Where do kittiwakes make their nests?

10 Which bird shares its name with a movement of the throat?

11 In the nursery rhyme *Who Killed Cock Robin*, who saw him die?

12 Abbotsbury in Dorset is home to a large nesting colony of which type of bird?

13 In the TV series *Game of Thrones*, which birds were used to send messages?

Medium

14 Which bird was associated with Minerva, the Roman goddess of wisdom?

15 Who wrote the 1992 novel *The Crow Road*?

16 The name of which bird is often applied to someone who collects things?

17 Which chess piece can also be referred to by the name of a bird?

18 Who is the main presenter of the TV series *The Repair Shop*?

19 According to the proverb, sauce for the goose is also sauce for what?

20 Which Irish group recorded the 1984 song *Robin (The Hooded Man)*?

Hard

Answers to QUIZ 256 – H

1	*Ding Dong Merrily on High*	11	Before a meal
2	Peroxide	12	1990s (1991)
3	Richie Cunningham	13	Robert Wagner
4	Egypt	14	Triangular
5	*Smells Like Teen Spirit* (Nirvana)	15	Tom Sawyer
6	Herts	16	Bursitis
7	Goblins	17	Pembrokeshire
8	Whale	18	Water (of the Earth)
9	The north	19	Breathing
10	The M6	20	Lemon juice

1   Who was the star of the 1948 western *The Treasure of the Sierra Madre*?

2   Which TV series starring Robbie Coltrane took its name from a song by Little Richard?

3   What does the word "Kinder" mean in the brand Kinder Egg?

4   Pamela Stephenson was born in which country?

5   Bob Odenkirk is the star of which TV drama, a spin-off from *Breaking Bad*?

6   Which US president took office first: Gerald Ford, Jimmy Carter or Richard Nixon?

7   Barry Island is in which Welsh county borough?

8   What is Canderel®?

9   Who was the king at the time of the Great Fire of London?

10 What are you said to have coming out of your ears, if you are very angry?

11 Which group released the 2005 single *Superman*?

12 The 1899 novel *Heart of Darkness* follows a voyage along which African river?

13 Which actor played outlaw Roy O'Bannon in the 2000 film *Shanghai Noon*?

14 From what is paprika made?

15 Terry Butcher (b.1958) played which sport for England?

16 Which two motorways cross the River Severn?

17 To what part of the body does the adjective "lumbar" refer?

18 By what name are the combined regiments of the Blues and Royals and the Lifeguards known?

19 In what environment do lugworms live?

20 The majority of the Pyramids in Egypt lie on which river?

Answers to QUIZ 257 – Pot Luck

1	Brad Pitt	11	Parkinson
2	2000s (2000)	12	Tippi Hedren
3	*Beyond the Sea* (*La Mer*) (Bobby Darin)	13	Belgium and Germany
4	Staffordshire	14	Secretary of State for Defence
5	96	15	*The Merchant of Venice*
6	Taken	16	Insectivorous
7	Fife	17	Antarctica
8	*Popstars* (2001)	18	Four syllables
9	Cheese	19	A whale
10	2016	20	Richard Wagner

ANSWERS ON PAGE **262**

Easy

1 The TV series *Grange Hill* was set in which city?

2 What qualification does someone hold if they have the letters MSc after their name?

3 "We don't need no education" is a line from which single?

4 What is the name of the headmaster in *The Simpsons*?

5 "Swami" is the title for a teacher in which religion?

6 What is the occupation of Rita in the film *Educating Rita*?

7 How is the Office for Standards in Education more commonly known?

8 In the Harry Potter books and films, who is the head of Ravenclaw House?

9 What is the name of the main school bully in *The Simpsons*?

10 Mr Creakle is a headmaster in which novel by Charles Dickens?

Medium

11 Which chef campaigned to remove junk food, particularly Turkey Twizzlers, from school menus?

12 Which English university features in the 2009 film *An Education*?

13 What is the French word for a school?

14 In which century did Richard Brinsley Sheridan write the play *School for Scandal*?

15 What subject did Tony Blair study at university?

16 Which 2003 film features the fictional Horace Green prep school?

17 Which two former *University Challenge* contestants present the TV series *Genius Guide to Britain*?

18 In which country did the school strikes for climate change begin in 2018?

19 For what do the letters NVQ stand?

20 "No more pencils, no more books" is a line from which 1972 single?

Hard

Answers to QUIZ 258 – Birds

1	A cockerel	11	The fly
2	Spring	12	(Mute) swan
3	Chicken	13	Ravens
4	Donna Tartt	14	An owl
5	The Housemartins	15	Iain Banks
6	Jazz	16	Magpie
7	Old gum tree	17	Castle (rook)
8	An eagle	18	Jay Blades
9	On cliffs	19	The gander
10	Swallow	20	Clannad

1   Which animated character has the email address ChunkyLover53@aol?

2   *Psychodrama* won the Album of the Year at the 2020 Brit Awards. Who recorded it?

3   "You're gonna need a bigger boat" is a line from which film?

4   Which is the only word in the radio phonetic alphabet that is the name of a sport?

5   Who starred as Frank Sheeran in the 2019 film *The Irishman*?

6   Sir Garfield Sobers played Test cricket for which team?

7   Which of these was the last to be made a city: Bradford, Leeds or Wolverhampton?

8   Which character in *Brookside* was played by Anna Friel?

9   Which is the second-smallest planet in the solar system?

10 What is the name of the rebel leader in District 13 in *The Hunger Games: Mockingjay*?

11 Which two words that differ only by their first letter mean "furniture wood" and "part of a bird's mouth"?

12 GR is the international car registration for which country?

13 What position did Gordon Banks play in the 1966 England FIFA World Cup team?

14 Who played the title character in the TV series *Becker*?

15 Was the apatosaurus (previously called "brontosaurus") a carnivore or a herbivore?

16 What was the most popular name for a baby boy in the UK in 2019: Leo, Muhammad or Oliver?

17 The town of Abingdon lies in which county?

18 Which two words that differ only by their last letter mean "enthusiastic" and "retain"?

19 Which two members of The Beatles were left-handed?

20 What was the name of Laurence Fishburne's character in The Matrix series of films?

Answers to QUIZ 259 – Pot Luck

1	Humphrey Bogart	11	The Stereophonics
2	*Tutti Frutti*	12	The River Congo
3	Children	13	Owen Wilson
4	New Zealand	14	(Dried) peppers
5	*Better Call Saul*	15	Football
6	Richard Nixon (1969)	16	M4 and M48
7	Vale of Glamorgan	17	The (lower part of) the back
8	An artificial sweetener	18	The Household Cavalry
9	Charles II	19	Sand
10	Steam	20	The River Nile

Easy

Medium

Hard

Easy

1 What is Canada's national winter sport?

2 What colour is between the blue and gold rings on an archery target?

3 Which is the heavier division in boxing: middleweight or welterweight?

4 In which sport do Australia and New Zealand compete against each other in the Chappell–Hadlee Trophy?

5 Eight ball is a form of which sport?

6 How many numbered bases are there in baseball?

7 What do the letters "GS" stand for in the netball position?

8 What nationality was the snooker player Eddie Charlton (d.2004)?

9 Swimmer Adam Peaty specialises in which stroke?

10 In which year did tennis player Björn Borg win the last of his five Wimbledon singles titles?

Medium

11 Which football club has a bantam on its crest, giving rise to its nickname?

12 The Sussex Stakes horse race is run at which racecourse?

13 What was the full name of the athlete nicknamed Flo-Jo?

14 Which Spanish golfer was the European Tour's Golfer of the Year in 2019?

15 Which Premiership rugby union team plays home games at the Recreation Ground?

16 The madison is an event in which sport?

17 What shape is a badminton court?

18 What name is given to the device that connects a ski to a ski boot?

19 In which aquatic sport might a handstand be required before starting?

20 In which country did volleyball originate?

Hard

Answers to QUIZ 260 – Education

1	London	11	Jamie Oliver
2	Master of Science	12	Oxford
3	*Another Brick in the Wall (Part 2)*	13	*École*
4	Principal Seymour Skinner	14	18th century (1777)
5	Hinduism	15	Law
6	Hairdresser	16	*School of Rock*
7	Ofsted	17	(Eric) Monkman and (Bobby) Seagull
8	Filius Flitwick	18	Sweden
9	Nelson Muntz	19	National Vocational Qualification
10	*David Copperfield*	20	*School's Out* (Alice Cooper)

1   "I really want to see you, really want to be with you" is a lyric from which song?

2   Which two words that differ only by their first letter mean "behind time" and "entrance"?

3   What is seven squared?

4   What general conditions are antihistamines used to treat?

5   Who played the title role in the 2012 film *Django Unchained*?

6   As at the end of 2019, how many times had Phil Mickleson won The Masters golf championship?

7   Which two six-letter words that differ only by their first letter mean "an open shoe" and "a wrecker"?

8   Perrie Edwards is a member of which group?

9   Are the stripes on the flag of the Republic of Ireland horizontal or vertical?

10 What was the name of the out-takes show originally presented by Denis Norden?

11 What type of creature is Gimli in The Lord of the Rings novels and films?

12 Dr Julius Hibbert is a character from which TV series?

13 Which colloquial name for a constellation shares its name with a large Canadian lake?

14 Who succeeded William Hague (Baron Hague of Richmond) as UK Foreign Secretary?

15 What is the opposite of dystopian?

16 Mr Dixon the postman and Mr Ellis the museum curator were characters in which children's series?

17 In which decade did the International Cricket Council change its name from the International Cricket Conference?

18 Which apple shares its name with a term for a swimming competition?

19 How many kings of England were sons of Henry II and Eleanor of Aquitaine?

20 Baboons are mostly found on which continent?

Answers to QUIZ 261 – Pot Luck

1	Homer Simpson	11	Teak and beak
2	Dave	12	Greece
3	*Jaws*	13	Goalkeeper
4	Golf	14	Ted Danson
5	Robert de Niro	15	A herbivore
6	The West Indies	16	Muhammad
7	Wolverhampton (2000)	17	Oxfordshire
8	Beth Jordache	18	Keen and keep
9	Mars	19	Sir Paul McCartney, Sir Ringo Starr
10	President Coin	20	Morpheus

What are the names of these film stars who have won two or more Oscars for acting?

Easy

1

2

3

Medium

4

5

6

7

8

9

Hard

Answers to QUIZ 262 – Sport

1	Ice hockey	11	Bradford City AFC
2	Red	12	Goodwood
3	Middleweight	13	Florence Griffith Joyner
4	Cricket	14	Jon Rahm
5	Pool	15	Bath Rugby
6	Three	16	Track cycling
7	Goal shooter	17	Rectangular
8	Australian	18	Binding
9	Breaststroke	19	Diving
10	1980	20	USA

1 For which English county cricket team did Jofra Archer sign in 2016?

2 Which was the youngest and shortest of the Teletubbies?

3 Which celebrity was the runner-up in the 2020 series of *Dancing on Ice*?

4 What word completes the title of the 2010 Michael Bublé hit, *Haven't Met You ___*?

5 How many bones are there in the typical human rib cage?

6 The town of Wallasey lies on which river?

7 What facial feature might be a "walrus"?

8 Which of these Stephen King novels was published first: *Carrie*, *Cujo* or *The Shining*?

9 Which 2000s song was no. 1 in the UK first: *Dakota*, *Patience* or *Vertigo*?

10 Albert Stroller and Mickey Stone were characters in which TV series, first broadcast in 2004?

11 In 1920, Douglas Fairbanks was the first actor to play which swashbuckling hero on film?

12 Who was elected Speaker of the House of Commons in November 2019?

13 As at the end of 2019, which was the UK's busiest airport in terms of passenger numbers?

14 *O What a Circus* was a 1978 hit for which singer?

15 The sitcom *Bottom* first aired in which decade?

16 *Coch* is Welsh for which colour?

17 The name for the first note of a musical scale shares its name with which mixer drink?

18 Eva Longoria advertises products for which cosmetics company?

19 What is the name of the girl to whom Andy's toys are given at the end of *Toy Story 3*?

20 Which of Enid Blyton's Famous Five is alphabetically first?

Easy

Medium

Hard

Answers to QUIZ 263 – Pot Luck

1 *My Sweet Lord* (George Harrison)
2 Late and gate
3 49
4 Allergies
5 Jamie Foxx
6 Three (2004, 2006, 2010)
7 Sandal and vandal
8 Little Mix
9 Vertical
10 *It'll Be Alright on the Night*

11 A dwarf
12 *The Simpsons*
13 Great Bear
14 Philip Hammond
15 Utopian
16 *Bob the Builder*
17 1980s (1989)
18 Gala
19 Two (Richard I and John)
20 Africa

1. What name is given to the shock barriers at the end of a railway track?

2. In which decade did the Docklands Light Railway open?

3. Grand Central Terminal lies in which borough of New York?

4. What name is given to the short track beside a main railway line where trains are kept when they are not in use?

5. Portsmouth Harbour is the nearest mainland station to which island?

6. What two-word term is given to all the engines and carriages that are used on a railway?

7. A heritage railway runs from Totnes to Buckfastleigh in which English county?

8. What is carried on a freight train?

9. Milford Haven is the most westerly station in which country of the UK?

10. The first inter-city railway in the world was built between Manchester and which other city?

11. Which is the largest mainline station in Birmingham?

12. Railway tracks are usually made from which alloy?

13. King's Lynn is the most northerly mainline station in which county?

14. What is the name for the substance that forms the bed for railway tracks?

15. Central and Queen Street are the two main stations in which Scottish city?

16. Which funfair ride shares its name with the term for an empty train?

17. What is the French word for "station"?

18. Which London station is the terminus for the Great Western main line?

19. In which decade was the first public railway opened, between Stockton and Darlington?

20. What name is given to a train that only stops at major stations?

Answers to QUIZ 264 – Multiple Oscar-winning Actors

1. Denzel Washington
2. Meryl Streep
3. Tom Hanks
4. Dame Elizabeth Taylor
5. Mahershala Ali
6. Sally Field
7. Sean Penn
8. Jodie Foster
9. Jack Nicholson

1   Which 2000s song was no. 1 in the UK first: *Grace Kelly*, *Greatest Day* or *Viva La Vida*?

2   Former boxer Marvin Hagler was born in which country?

3   Craig Charles and Dara Ó Briain have both presented which TV engineering competition?

4   Which actress won the Best Actress Oscar first: Grace Kelly, Dame Elizabeth Taylor or Ingrid Bergman?

5   What is the French word for "son"?

6   In the story of the Nativity, the Three Wise Men travelled from which direction?

7   *Hushabye Mountain* is a song from which 1968 musical film?

8   What word was coined in 2020 to refer to a cocktail made during a period of isolation?

9   What is 56 in Roman numerals?

10 The name of which month is also a word for "stately"?

11 In which decade was the sitcom *Waiting For God* first broadcast?

12 The island of St Lucia lies in which sea?

13 NE is the postcode for which English city?

14 San Miguel beer originated in which country?

15 Which film musical won the Razzie Award for Worst Picture in 2019?

16 Which two London boroughs have names beginning with "E"?

17 Who was the second Tudor monarch?

18 Sergeant Troy is a character in which Thomas Hardy novel?

19 In which 1979 song was "the Sweeney doing 90"?

20 Which 1970s toys were advertised with the phrase: "___ wobble, but they don't fall down"?

Answers to QUIZ 265 – Pot Luck

1	Sussex	11	Zorro (*The Mark of Zorro*)
2	Po	12	Sir Lindsay Hoyle
3	Perri Kiely	13	Heathrow
4	*Yet*	14	David Essex
5	24	15	1990s (1991)
6	River Mersey	16	Red
7	A moustache	17	Tonic
8	*Carrie* (1974)	18	L'Oréal
9	*Vertigo* (U2, 2004)	19	Bonnie
10	*Hustle*	20	Anne

1 In which year did Apple introduce the first iPhone?

2 How many bones are there in the middle ear?

3 In which decade was the first ever text message sent?

4 Which astronomical device was launched into orbit aboard the space shuttle *Discovery* in April 1990?

5 What name is given to the temporary alteration of Google's logo to mark a specific event?

6 Osteoarthritis affects which part of the human body?

7 The parietal lobe can be found in which part of the human body?

8 How is the non-stick coating polytetrafluoroethylene better known?

9 What was the name of the research programme that developed the first atomic bomb?

10 In medicine, for what do the letters IVF stand?

11 What causes thermoplastic to soften?

12 The liver and the spleen are contained in which part of the body?

13 Which term is used to describe somebody who gains unauthorised access to a computer system?

14 On a standard keyboard, on which number is the dollar sign?

15 Which substance found in plants has a name meaning "green leaf"?

16 How many pairs of chromosomes are there in a human cell?

17 Which planet is usually the third-brightest body in the solar system?

18 What branch of physics is abbreviated to QM?

19 What four-letter word is spelt out by the chemical symbols for nitrogen, oxygen and neon?

20 What is the name of the brand of smart displays launched by Facebook™ in 2018?

Easy

Medium

Hard

Answers to QUIZ 266 – Trains

1	Buffers	11	Birmingham New Street
2	1980s (1987)	12	Steel
3	Manhattan	13	Norfolk
4	Siding	14	Ballast
5	Isle of Wight	15	Glasgow
6	Rolling stock	16	Ghost train
7	Devon	17	*Gare*
8	Goods	18	Paddington Station
9	Wales	19	1820s (1825)
10	Liverpool	20	Express train

ANSWERS ON PAGE **271**

1. Which Coldplay single was released first: *Fix You*, *The Scientist* or *Viva La Vida*?

2. What colour did the front of the British passport change to in March 2020?

3. What are the three air signs of the zodiac?

4. Oliver Barrett IV and Jenny Cavilleri were the main characters in which 1970 film?

5. Which measurement is abbreviated to "hp"?

6. In which country was Michael J Fox born?

7. Which two parties entered into the UK Coalition Government in 2010?

8. Which long-running series was set in Cabot Cove?

9. Which *Britain's Got Talent*-winning act shares its name with a 1945 film directed by Sir Alfred Hitchcock?

10. What is the name of the lower chamber of parliament in Australia, the Netherlands and the USA, amongst other countries?

11. Belize has a coastline on which sea?

12. Which football team did Tony Pulis manage from 2017 to 2019?

13. The term "tinny", to describe a can of beer, comes from which country?

14. Who is Peter Pan's arch-enemy?

15. The Paisley textile pattern is named after a town in which country?

16. Which singer released the 2016 album *Lemonade*?

17. In 1940, which king instituted the George Cross?

18. What is the English translation of the Spanish word *madre*?

19. In the revived version of *Who Wants to Be a Millionaire?*, the only specified safety net is set at which sum of money?

20. Oakland and Bakersfield are cities in which US state?

Easy

Medium

Hard

Answers to QUIZ 267 – Pot Luck

1	*Grace Kelly* (Mika, 2007)	11	1990s (1990)
2	USA	12	The Caribbean Sea
3	*Robot Wars*	13	Newcastle-upon-Tyne
4	Ingrid Bergman (1944)	14	Spain
5	*Fils*	15	Cats
6	The East	16	Ealing and Enfield
7	*Chitty Chitty Bang Bang*	17	Henry VIII
8	Quarantini	18	*Far from the Madding Crowd*
9	LVI	19	*Cool for Cats* (Squeeze)
10	August	20	Weebles

1   For which type of metal cookware is the French company Le Creuset famous?

2   What is the major ingredient used to make traditional gnocchi?

3   What name is given to the point in a restaurant where the waiting staff collect the dishes from the kitchen?

4   What type of food is sold under the Amoy® brand?

5   What foodstuff can be caster, granulated or icing?

6   In which decade was Pyrex™ cookware first sold?

7   What kind of cooker hob uses magnetism to heat food?

8   Into what is something briefly dipped to blanch it?

9   What colour is a chanterelle mushroom?

10   What general name is given to carrots, parsnips and potatoes?

11   What is the main ingredient in the French sauce *beurre noisette*?

12   The name of which brand of cooker is a three-letter palindrome?

13   What type of pastry takes its name from the Greek word for "leaf"?

14   The part of a kettle that heats the water has what name?

15   What nautical term is given to the container used to serve gravy?

16   What is the full name of the appliance usually referred to as a "fridge"?

17   Which cooking oil has an "extra-virgin" variety?

18   The "jerk" style of cooking originated in which country?

19   What is a tagine?

20   What is the collective name for a team of kitchen workers in a restaurant?

Answers to QUIZ 268 – Science and Technology

1	2007	11	Heat
2	Three	12	The abdomen
3	1990s (1992)	13	Hacker
4	The Hubble Space Telescope	14	Four
5	Google Doodle	15	Chlorophyll
6	Joints	16	23
7	The brain	17	Jupiter
8	Teflon	18	Quantum mechanics
9	Manhattan Project	19	None
10	In vitro fertilisation	20	Portal

1. In the song *The Twelve Days of Christmas*, which was the first day on which people were given?
2. What is the fourth-largest planet in the solar system?
3. Beppe de Marco was a character in which long-running series?
4. How were Bobbie, Peter and Phyllis described in the title of a 1906 novel by Edith Nesbit?
5. What religion is followed by the majority of the population in Iraq?
6. What relative to you is your sister's son's son?
7. What type of creature is a smew?
8. Which Leonardo DiCaprio film was released first: *The Great Gatsby*, *The Departed* or *The Wolf of Wall Street*?
9. Is Derby in the East Midlands or the West Midlands?
10. The TV series *Mad Men* was set on which New York thoroughfare?
11. In which building are Geoffrey Chaucer, Robert Browning and Rudyard Kipling buried?
12. Who trained the 1983 Grand National winner Corbiere?
13. The name of which Fiat model means "point" in English?
14. In the Star Wars films, which character first intimates that Luke has a sister?
15. The song *No Matter What*, a hit for Boyzone, features in which musical?
16. Which part of the cardamom plant is used as a spice?
17. With which sci-fi series was the phrase "Save the cheerleader, save the world" associated?
18. By population, which is the largest city in Spain?
19. Which chess piece is alphabetically first?
20. Who succeeded John Adams as president of the USA?

Easy

Medium

Hard

Answers to QUIZ 269 – Pot Luck

1	*The Scientist* (2002)	11	The Caribbean Sea
2	Navy blue	12	Middlesbrough
3	Gemini, Libra and Aquarius	13	Australia
4	*Love Story*	14	Captain Hook
5	Horsepower	15	Scotland
6	Canada (Edmonton)	16	Beyoncé
7	Conservatives and Liberal Democrats	17	King George VI
8	*Murder, She Wrote*	18	Mother
9	Spellbound	19	£1,000
10	House of Representatives	20	California

Easy

1 "Laying everybody low with a love song that he made" is a lyric from which song?

2 For what do the letters AOR stand in relation to music?

3 The song *Danny Boy* is sung to which tune?

4 What word completes the title of the 2004 Maroon 5 hit, *She Will Be___*?

5 Which singer (d.1998) was nicknamed "The Voice"?

6 Traditionally, which material was used to make white piano keys?

7 "Long ago, high on a mountain in Mexico" are the opening lyrics to which song?

8 Who had a hit with *Just the Way You Are (Amazing)* in 2010?

9 What type of instrument is a vibraphone?

10 Which section is nearest the front of an orchestra: brass, violins or woodwind?

11 How often does the BBC Young Musician competition take place?

12 Who was the lead singer with The Pips?

13 In which decade was the first *Now That's What I Call Music!* album released?

Medium

14 Who composed the 1790 opera *Così Fan Tutte*?

15 Who sang the UK's 1971 Eurovision entry, *Jack in the Box*?

16 "But how strange the change from major to minor" is a line from which Cole Porter song?

17 Which of these composers was born first: Frédéric Chopin, Johannes Brahms or Ludwig van Beethoven?

18 Which percussion instrument derives its name from the Spanish word for "chestnut"?

19 Who was the lead guitarist in the Police?

20 In 1981, which Frenchman became the first Western musician officially invited to play in China?

Hard

Answers to QUIZ 270 – In the Kitchen

1	Cast iron	11	Butter
2	Potatoes	12	Aga™
3	The pass	13	Filo pastry
4	Oriental	14	Element
5	Sugar	15	(Gravy) boat
6	1910s (1915)	16	Refrigerator
7	Induction	17	Olive oil
8	Boiling water	18	Jamaica
9	Yellow	19	A heavy cooking pot (or the Arabic dish named after it)
10	Root vegetables	20	A brigade

1. Proverbially, what can faith move?

2. What number is reached by adding the digits of the US emergency telephone number together?

3. In February 2020, who became the first person to receive a VIP "black card" from the Greggs bakery chain?

4. The pub The Waterhole features in which TV series?

5. Which is the UK's busiest container port?

6. Which of these Martin Scorsese films was released first: *The Aviator*, *The Color of Money* or *The Wolf of Wall Street*?

7. What number is obtained by adding the number four to the numbers either side of it on a dartboard?

8. How many hours behind GMT is Miami?

9. What sport do the Exeter Chiefs play?

10. The singer Lemar first found fame on which reality show?

11. Thandie Newton named her daughter Ripley after a character in which series of sci-fi films?

12. Which company makes the Cheerios® brand of breakfast cereal?

13. In which year of the 1970s did the final Apollo mission take place?

14. Which Northern Ireland golfer won his second Major at the 2012 US PGA?

15. Who played Sophie Chapman in the TV series *Peep Show*?

16. Who preceded Jack Straw as UK Foreign Secretary?

17. What type of creature is a koala?

18. For what do the letters POW stand?

19. What is the international car registration code for Mexico?

20. Which two words that differ only by their first letter mean "lair" and "writing implement"?

Answers to QUIZ 271 – Pot Luck

1. The eighth day
2. Neptune
3. *EastEnders*
4. *The Railway Children*
5. Islam
6. Great-nephew
7. A bird (duck)
8. *The Departed* (2006)
9. East Midlands
10. Madison Avenue
11. Westminster Abbey (Poets' Corner)
12. Jenny Pitman
13. Punto
14. Yoda
15. *Whistle Down the Wind*
16. The seeds
17. *Heroes*
18. Madrid
19. Bishop
20. Thomas Jefferson

Easy

1   Which Australian state is alphabetically first?

2   Which is the largest peninsula in the world?

3   What is the second-largest city in China, by population?

4   Uluru (or Ayers Rock) is in which Australian state?

5   Which shape appears on the Israeli flag?

6   Europe has how many volcanoes measuring over 10,000 ft in height?

7   Which airport is known as the Costa del Sol Airport?

8   Which country has the largest area: Iceland, Liechtenstein or Nepal?

9   Roughly what shape is India on a map?

10 Which US state has a coastline that stretches for 1350 miles?

11 How many independent states make up the United Arab Emirates?

12 What colour is the background of the Turkish flag?

13 Which city lies furthest north: Newcastle-upon-Tyne, Nottingham or Sunderland?

14 What is the county town of the Isle of Wight?

15 Into which ocean does the Limpopo River flow?

16 The name of which South American country means "little Venice" in Spanish?

17 Which English county is closest to France?

18 Which of the Great Lakes has the shortest name?

19 The area known as the Piedmont plateau lies in which country?

20 Which Canadian province is also a word in the radio phonetic alphabet?

Answers to QUIZ 272 – Music

1	*Romeo and Juliet* (Dire Straits)	11	Every two years
2	Adult-oriented rock	12	Gladys Knight
3	*Londonderry Air*	13	1980s (1983)
4	*Loved*	14	Mozart
5	Frank Sinatra	15	Clodagh Rodgers
6	Ivory	16	*Ev'ry Time We Say Goodbye*
7	*Angelo* (Brotherhood of Man)	17	Ludwig van Beethoven (1770)
8	Bruno Mars	18	Castanets
9	Percussion instrument	19	Andy Summers
10	Violins	20	Jean-Michel Jarre

1   Paul Merson played for which football club from 1985 to 1997?

2   In which type of building was the 1980s TV series *St Elsewhere* set?

3   Who was the first president of the Russian Federation?

4   Which talent show introduced a golden buzzer in 2014?

5   What food group do eggs belong to?

6   In which decade was the Guinness World Records book first published?

7   What is a delphinium?

8   What is the name of author Sir Arthur Conan Doyle's most famous creation?

9   Which meteorological condition completes the title of the musical featuring the work of the Proclaimers, ___ *on Leith*?

10   The 2003 novel *Private Peaceful* was set during which conflict?

11   Which two words, that differ only by their last letter, mean "idiot" and "12 inches"?

12   Which English city has the postcode area code GL?

13   Who plays Caroline, Countess of Brockenhurst in the TV series *Belgravia*?

14   If you have a large quantity, it is more than you can shake what at?

15   What name is given to the hairstyle formed by small plaits worn close to the head?

16   What part of the body is treated by a pedicure?

17   The lesser horseshoe and greater horseshoe are types of which mammal?

18   Who played Annie Walker in the 2011 film *Bridesmaids*?

19   What is organdie?

20   Which was the first country outside of Europe and the USA to host the Summer Olympic Games?

Easy

Medium

Hard

Answers to QUIZ 273 – Pot Luck

1	Mountains	11	Alien
2	11 (911)	12	Nestlé
3	Stormzy	13	1972 (*Apollo 17*)
4	*Neighbours*	14	Rory McIlroy
5	Felixstowe (Suffolk)	15	Olivia Colman
6	*The Color of Money* (1986)	16	Robin Cook
7	35 (18 and 13)	17	A marsupial
8	Five hours	18	Prisoner of war
9	Rugby union	19	MEX
10	*Fame Academy*	20	Den and pen

Easy

1 In which country is the TV series *Hidden* set?

2 Which professional chef joined the judges of *Britain's Best Home Cook* for the 2020 series?

3 Which business was central to the TV series *Howards' Way*?

4 What was the stage name of the winner of the 2020 UK series of *The Masked Singer*?

5 Which former politician has presented the documentary series *Travels in Trumpland* and *Travels in Euroland*?

6 Kerry and Kurtan Mucklowe are the main characters in which sitcom?

7 What is the first name of James Nesbitt's *Cold Feet* character?

8 Who presents the TV series *Make a New Life in the Country*?

9 Which *Line of Duty* character said "I didn't float up the Lagan in a bubble"?

10 Who became the host of the BBC programme *Football Focus* in the 2009-10 season?

Medium

11 Todrick Hall appeared as a captain in the 2020 series of which talent show?

12 Julia Smith co-created *EastEnders* with which other writer?

13 Who played Miles Stewart in the 1990s TV series *This Life*?

14 Who played Joyce Temple-Savage in the TV series *Benidorm*?

15 On which programme might a contestant receive "a Hollywood handshake"?

16 *Mork & Mindy* was a spin-off from which hit US sitcom?

17 Which channel aired the TV series *Albion Market*?

18 Neil Sutherland was a character in which sitcom, first broadcast in 2008?

19 What was the first name of Sally Lindsey's character in *Coronation Street*?

20 What was the name of the UK TV subscription service launched by the BBC and ITV in November 2019?

Hard

Answers to QUIZ 274 – Geography

1	New South Wales	11	Seven
2	The Arabian peninsula	12	Red
3	Beijing	13	Newcastle-upon-Tyne
4	Northern Territories	14	Newport
5	Star of David	15	The Indian Ocean
6	One (Mount Etna)	16	Venezuela
7	Malaga	17	Kent
8	Nepal (56,100 square miles)	18	Erie
9	Triangular	19	USA
10	Florida	20	Quebec

ANSWERS ON PAGE 279

1   Who played the title role in the 2019 film *The Personal History of David Copperfield*?

2   Which colour lies between orange and green in a rainbow?

3   "You've gone too far this time, but I'm dancing on the Valentine" is a lyric from which song?

4   What word completes the title of the 2011 Lady Gaga hit, *The Edge of ___*?

5   Guillaume is the French equivalent of what English name?

6   Which English actor played Rupert Giles in the TV series *Buffy the Vampire Slayer*?

7   *I Get Around* was a 1964 UK hit for which group?

8   What colour jersey is awarded to the best sprinter in the Tour de France race?

9   What kind of animal is Marty in the *Madagascar* films?

10   Chad is the largest landlocked country on which continent?

11   What is the name of the tiger in the Winnie-the-Pooh stories?

12   Which king ordered the execution of Sir Walter Raleigh?

13   In which decade did it become compulsory for drivers to wear a seatbelt in the UK?

14   What name was given to the group of settlers who arrived in America on the *Mayflower* in 1620?

15   Which US city is furthest east: Baltimore, Baton Rouge or Boston?

16   The *Orient Express* originally ran between Istanbul and which European capital city?

17   In which decade did the comedy *Citizen Smith* first air?

18   Which school did David Cameron and Boris Johnson both attend?

19   Which is larger, a stoat or a weasel?

20   Which cartoon canine was, according to his theme tune, "number one super guy" and "quicker than the human eye"?

Answers to QUIZ 275 – Pot Luck

1	Arsenal FC	11	Fool and foot
2	A hospital	12	Gloucester
3	Boris Yeltsin	13	Dame Harriet Walter
4	*Britain's Got Talent*	14	A stick
5	Proteins	15	Cornrow
6	1950s (1955)	16	The feet
7	A flower	17	Bat
8	Sherlock Holmes	18	Kristen Wiig
9	*Sunshine*	19	A (thin cotton) fabric
10	WWI	20	Australia (Melbourne, 1956)

1. How many digits are there in a UK bank sort code?

2. At what age does someone become a septuagenarian?

3. How many odd numbers are there between two and 20?

4. What is five squared?

5. How many ounces are there in six pounds?

6. What number do the Roman numerals XXV represent?

7. Which shape has the largest number of faces: a dodecahedron, an octahedron or a tetrahedron?

8. How many hours are there in a day and a half?

9. How many *Questions* did 50 Cent have in the title of a 2003 single?

10. What, theoretically, is the minimum number of colours required to colour a map so that no adjacent regions have the same colour?

11. In the traditional bingo call, what number is "Torquay in Devon"?

12. What imperial measurement is equal to 0.305 metres?

13. What number is opposite six on a die?

14. How many points is the letter M worth in a game of Scrabble®?

15. What number do you get if you add the number of seats on four tandems to the number of wheels on three unicycles?

16. What is a dozen dozen?

17. What number is obtained by adding the number ten to the numbers either side of it on a dartboard?

18. How many coins were there in the fountain in the title of the 1954 film?

19. How many syllables are there in the word "cinematographer"?

20. Which two shirt numbers do strikers in a football team traditionally wear?

Answers to QUIZ 276 – Television

1	Wales	11	*The Greatest Dancer*
2	Angela Hartnett	12	Tony Holland
3	A boatyard	13	Jack Davenport
4	Queen Bee	14	Sherrie Hewson
5	Ed Balls	15	*The Great British Bake Off*
6	*This Country*	16	*Happy Days*
7	Adam	17	ITV
8	Ben Fogle	18	*The Inbetweeners*
9	Ted Hastings	19	*Shelley*
10	Dan Walker	20	BritBox

1 What is the name of Charles Collingwood's character in the radio series *The Archers*?

2 Which two counties of the Republic of Ireland have four letters in their names?

3 Who was the English monarch at the time of the Spanish Armada?

4 What relative to you is your sister's daughter?

5 In which decade was Jody Scheckter a Formula 1 World Champion?

6 Morocco has a coastline on the Mediterranean Sea and which other body of water?

7 What is a female giraffe called?

8 Treebeard is a character in which series of fantasy novels?

9 Which actor was Angelina Jolie's second husband?

10 Which political ideology advocates the abolition of government?

11 On the quiz show, which of the Chasers has the nickname of a female fox?

12 In the name of the sporting body, for what does the "P" stand in PGA?

13 Is something described as "ubiquitous" rare or common?

14 In which county is the TV series *Vera* set?

15 Which naturalist featured on the Bank of England £10 note prior to Jane Austen?

16 Springboks are native to which continent?

17 Kevin McCallister is the central character in which film franchise?

18 In which decade was the National Exhibition Centre opened?

19 The character of Peter Perfect was a competitor in which TV series?

20 Oscar Peterson was associated with which musical instrument?

Answers to QUIZ 277 – Pot Luck

1	Dev Patel	11	Tigger
2	Yellow	12	James I
3	*The Reflex* (Duran Duran)	13	1980s (1983)
4	*Glory*	14	The Pilgrim Fathers
5	William	15	Boston
6	Anthony Head	16	Paris
7	The Beach Boys	17	1970s (1977)
8	Green	18	Eton
9	Zebra	19	A stoat
10	Africa	20	Hong Kong Phooey

What are the names of these fruit and vegetables?

1

2

3

4

5

6

7

8

9

Answers to QUIZ 278 – Numbers

1	Six	11	87
2	70	12	A foot
3	Eight	13	One
4	25	14	Three points
5	96	15	11 (eight + three)
6	25	16	144
7	Dodecahedron (12 faces)	17	31 (6 and 15)
8	36	18	*Three (Three Coins in the Fountain)*
9	21	19	Six
10	Four	20	Nine and ten

Easy

Medium

Hard

ANSWERS ON PAGE 283

1   Who played Mark Easterbrook in the 2020 TV adaptation of Agatha Christie's *The Pale Horse*?

2   What part of the body is called *nez* in French?

3   What are the cattle doing in *Away in a Manger*?

4   *Be Back Soon* is a song from which 1968 musical film?

5   Which 1960s figure did Ellie Bamber portray in the TV series *The Trial of Christine Keeler*?

6   In which decade did Madonna release *Justify My Love*?

7   Who demands a pound of flesh in *The Merchant of Venice*?

8   What is the name of the Bristol Premiership rugby union team?

9   What colour are the two outside stripes on the Canadian flag?

10 Which company manufactures the Aircross car model?

11 Which mythical creature appeared on the logo of the Midland Bank?

12 VT is the abbreviation for which US state?

13 What is four squared?

14 Which tree was named after the French botanist Pierre Magnol?

15 Theresa May was elected as the MP for which constituency in 1997?

16 Where on a boat is the prow?

17 Which actress was married to Roger Vadim, Tom Hayden and Ted Turner?

18 LV is the international car registration for which European country?

19 How often does a sexennial event happen?

20 Which Cluedo® character has an army rank?

Easy

Medium

Hard

Answers to QUIZ 279 – Pot Luck

1	Brian Aldridge	11	Jenny Ryan (The Vixen)
2	Cork and Mayo	12	Professional
3	Elizabeth I (1588)	13	Common
4	Niece	14	Northumberland
5	1970s (1979)	15	Charles Darwin
6	The Atlantic Ocean	16	Africa
7	A cow	17	*Home Alone*
8	The Lord of the Rings	18	1970s (1976)
9	Billy Bob Thornton	19	*Wacky Races*
10	Anarchism	20	Piano

Easy

1   What term beginning with "t" was given to former Russian rulers?

2   Pervez Musharraf was a military dictator of which country?

3   Quotations from which political leader were published in *The Little Red Book*?

4   After which US president is NASA's famous launch operations space centre named?

5   Jonathan Sacks held which religious post from 1991 until 2013?

6   The words "Workers of all lands unite" are inscribed on the tomb of which revolutionary (d.1883)?

7   Which US president issued a pardon to the former president Richard Nixon?

8   How many times did William Gladstone serve as prime minister in the 19th century?

9   Who was Europe's first female prime minister?

10 Which UK prime minister described Russia as "a riddle, wrapped in a mystery, inside an enigma"?

Medium

11 Who was the governor of California from 2003 to 2011?

12 What name given to Mohandas Gandhi derives from the Sanskrit for "great soul"?

13 Hamid Karzai was the president of which country from 2001 to 2014?

14 In which decade did Nikita Khrushchev become the leader of the Soviet Union?

15 Which US president was depicted in the video for Frankie Goes to Hollywood's *Two Tribes*?

16 Who was the first Pope to visit the White House?

17 Who was the UK Leader of the Opposition from 1997 to 2001?

18 Who preceded François Mitterrand as President of France?

19 In which decade did Sirimavo Bandaranaike become the world's first non-hereditary female head of state?

20 Which UK prime minister introduced the "Citizen's Charter"?

Hard

Answers to QUIZ 280 – Fruit and Vegetables

1   Pumpkin
2   Celery
3   Avocado
4   Fennel
5   Watermelon
6   Broccoli
7   Pomegranate
8   Asparagus
9   Rhubarb

1   On a meeting agenda, for what do the letters AOB stand?

2   Which airline merged with United Airlines in 2012?

3   "Stupid is as stupid does" is a line from which film?

4   What word can refer to both a duck's noise and an unskilled doctor?

5   Which of these cities is most easterly: Bristol, Derby or Leeds?

6   Stuart Sutcliffe was an early member of which band?

7   In musical notation with the treble clef, what note is written on the middle line of a stave?

8   Who played Bubbles DeVere in *Little Britain*?

9   In which decade was the Second Severn Crossing opened?

10 Which country hosted the 2015 Rugby World Cup?

11 Who was the only female judge on the *Strictly Come Dancing* panel when the show started?

12 In relation to the smallest room in the house, for what do the letters WC stand?

13 What colour is the background of the label on a standard tin of Heinz baked beans?

14 What nationality was the actress Greta Garbo?

15 The International Court of Justice is part of which organisation?

16 What religion is followed by the majority of the population in India?

17 According to the proverb, what is one man's meat?

18 What was the title of the first James Bond film of the 21st century?

19 What colour is the background of the Hong Kong regional flag?

20 "Rising up, back on the street" is the opening lyric from which song?

Answers to QUIZ 281 – Pot Luck

1	Rufus Sewell	11	A Griffin
2	The nose	12	Vermont
3	Lowing	13	16
4	*Oliver!*	14	Magnolia tree
5	Mandy Rice-Davies	15	Maidenhead
6	1990s (1990)	16	The front
7	Shylock	17	Jane Fonda
8	Bristol Bears	18	Latvia
9	Red	19	Every six years
10	Citroën	20	Colonel Mustard

Easy

1   In which country was the former boxer Sugar Ray Leonard born?

2   Five-spice powder is most associated with the cuisine of which country?

3   Sugar "Kane" Kowalczyk is a character in which 1959 film?

4   Which spice shares its name with a ceremonial object kept in the Houses of Parliament?

5   How many Spice Girls were there in the original group?

6   In which decade did The Archies have a hit with *Sugar, Sugar*?

7   Journalist Kate Spicer is particularly associated with writing on which subject?

8   What brown confection is made by boiling sugar?

9   Which dried flower buds used as a spice are pushed into oranges to make a Christmas decoration?

10 In which decade was Alan Sugar (Baron Sugar) given a life peerage?

11 The term "Spice Boys" was applied in the mid 1990s to a group of players from which football club?

12 In the saying, what do you sugar if you make something bad seem less so?

13 Which TV presenter followed *The Spice Trail* in 2011?

Medium

14 How many corners are there on a sugar cube?

15 Which part of a house completes the title of a programme which has been presented by Lorne Spicer, *Cash in the ___*?

16 What is sugar soap most commonly used for in decorating?

17 What colour is barley sugar?

18 At which famous London concert venue did the Spice Girls perform in the 1997 film *Spice World*?

19 Which group had a 1971 hit with *Brown Sugar*?

20 The name of which Essex town reflects its previous status as an area where a yellow spice was grown?

Hard

Answers to QUIZ 282 – Leaders

1	Tsar	11	Arnold Schwarzenegger
2	Pakistan	12	Mahatma
3	Mao Zedong	13	Afghanistan
4	John F Kennedy	14	1950s (1953)
5	Chief Rabbi	15	Ronald Reagan
6	Karl Marx	16	John Paul II (1979)
7	Gerald Ford	17	William Hague (Baron Hague of Richmond)
8	Four times (1868-74, 1880-85, 1886, 1892-94)	18	(Valéry) Giscard d'Estaing
9	Baroness Margaret Thatcher	19	1960s (1960)
10	Sir Winston Churchill	20	Sir John Major

1   According to the former advertising slogan, which lager stays "sharp till the bottom of the glass"?

2   How many atoms are there in a water molecule?

3   In 2018, a judge in Missouri ordered that a deer poacher should watch which film once a month during his year-long jail sentence?

4   What shape is an oculus window?

5   The town of Walsall is in which metropolitan county?

6   How many days are there in 26 weeks?

7   Which version of the Android operating system was released in February 2020?

8   The name of which month is also a word meaning "has permission to"?

9   Who stars in the reality TV series *First Time Mum*?

10 Which manager of Manchester United (1945-69) began his playing career with Manchester City?

11 What was the name of the warrior princess in the spin-off series from *Hercules: The Legendary Journeys*?

12 What single word can follow "common", "dress" and "sixth" to make three phrases?

13 The ackee is the national fruit of which Caribbean country?

14 Which is further away from the earth: the ozone layer or the stratosphere?

15 Warthogs are native to which continent?

16 Which two words that differ only by their last letter mean "end of a pen" and "fool"?

17 The character Raquel Watts was a barmaid in which fictional pub?

18 What colour are the flowers on the shrub gorse?

19 *Dream Baby (How Long Must I Dream)* was a 1962 hit for which US singer?

20 Someone referred to as a "fresher" is in which year at a university?

Easy

Medium

Hard

Answers to QUIZ 283 – Pot Luck

1	Any other business	11	Arlene Phillips
2	Continental Airlines	12	Water closet
3	*Forrest Gump*	13	Blue
4	Quack	14	Swedish
5	Leeds	15	United Nations
6	The Beatles	16	Hinduism
7	B	17	Another man's poison
8	Matt Lucas	18	*Die Another Day* (2002)
9	1990s (1996)	19	Red
10	England	20	*Eye of the Tiger* (Survivor)

Easy

1. Sports journalist Tom Fordyce and radio presenter Chris Stark present a podcast alongside which footballer?

2. What is the title of the newspaper in the Harry Potter novels and films?

3. Which channel aired the soap opera *Crossroads*?

4. Which DJ began presenting the *Sounds of the 80s* show on Radio 2 in 2018?

5. Which UK publication is the world's oldest Sunday paper?

6. In June 2020, which English actress became the oldest person to appear on the front cover of *Vogue*?

7. What is the real first name of the radio presenter Mr Jensen, nicknamed "Kid"?

8. Which term for the display of moving visual media comes from the Latin for "I see"?

9. Lord Beaverbrook was associated with which daily newspaper?

10. Which newspaper did Piers Morgan edit from 1995 to 2004?

11. What radio station broadcasts *The Archers*?

12. Kate Thornton was an editor of which music magazine, first published in 1978?

13. Which magazine shares its name with a cocktail made from vodka and cranberry juice?

14. *National Geographic* was first published in which century?

15. What replaced the BBC's iPlayer radio service in 2018?

16. What type of content is broadcast on the ESPN channel?

17. In which decade did the *Radio Times* begin publishing TV listings?

18. In 1861, which daily newspaper was the first to publish a weather forecast?

19. Which former MP became editor of the *London Evening Standard* in 2017?

20. Who took over from Chris Moyles on the Radio 1 breakfast show in 2012?

Answers to QUIZ 284 – Sugar and Spice

1	USA	11	Liverpool FC
2	China	12	The pill
3	*Some Like it Hot*	13	Kate Humble
4	Mace	14	Eight
5	Five	15	*Attic*
6	1960s (1969)	16	Cleaning paintwork
7	Food	17	Amber
8	Caramel	18	The Royal Albert Hall
9	Cloves	19	The Rolling Stones
10	2000s (2009)	20	Saffron Walden

1 For what does the letter "S" stand in the name of the organisation UNESCO?

2 "Looking out a dirty old window" is the opening line from which song?

3 The town of Shaftesbury lies in which county?

4 The kidneys are found in which part of the human body?

5 In the Middle-Eastern tales, how many voyages did Sinbad the Sailor make?

6 What is the national flower of England?

7 The Dingle family made their debut in *Emmerdale* in which decade?

8 Lt is an abbreviation for which army rank?

9 Belgium, The Netherlands and which other country make up the Low Countries?

10 In which country was the Kawasaki company founded?

11 Which two words that differ only by their first letter mean "entrance" and "human"?

12 Who succeeded Sir Roger Moore as James Bond?

13 Which comedy trio released the 1975 song *Black Pudding Bertha*?

14 According to the proverb, what does haste make?

15 What is four in Roman numerals?

16 If something is described as "prosaic", is it exciting or dull?

17 What number was the warehouse in the title of a sci-fi series first broadcast in 2009?

18 Which two words that differ only by their last letter mean "a bed covering" and "an old writing implement"?

19 Martin Kaymer (b.1984) plays which sport?

20 Who took over from Nick Grimshaw on the Radio 1 breakfast show?

Easy

Medium

Hard

Answers to QUIZ 285 – Pot Luck

1	Harp	11	Xena
2	Three (two hydrogen, one oxygen)	12	Sense
3	*Bambi*	13	Jamaica
4	Round	14	The stratosphere
5	West Midlands	15	Africa
6	182	16	Nib and nit
7	Android 11	17	Rovers Return
8	May	18	Yellow
9	Ferne McCann	19	Roy Orbison
10	Sir Matt Busby	20	First year

1   Of what is a cucumber mainly composed?

2   What food group does milk belong to?

3   Catsup is another name for what foodstuff?

4   What is the English translation of *cavolo nero*?

5   Which fruit is harvested predominately by flooding the vines so the loosened fruit then floats on top of the water?

6   Baked beans from a can commonly use which variety of pulse?

7   Le Puy-en-Velay in France is famous for the production of which pulse?

8   Banana, spaghetti and butternut are all types of which vegetable?

9   Which non-alcoholic drink is used to flavour the dessert tiramisu?

10 Traditionally, which dried fruit put the "spots" into a spotted dick pudding?

11 Which culinary setting agent is made from collagen?

12 What gives black pudding its colour?

13 Native to North America, the *acer saccharum* plant is the primary source of which sweet substance?

14 Müller Corner® is a brand of which type of food?

15 *Passiflora edulis* is the Latin name of which fruit?

16 The drink Aperol originated in which country?

17 Bento boxes are part of the cuisine of which country?

18 From what type of milk is Manchego cheese made?

19 Which staple Scottish food did Samuel Johnson say "in England is generally given to horses"?

20 What colour is a kalamata olive?

Answers to QUIZ 286 – Media

1	Peter Crouch	11	Radio 4
2	*The Daily Prophet*	12	*Smash Hits*
3	ITV	13	*Cosmopolitan*
4	Gary Davies	14	19th century (1888)
5	*The Observer*	15	The BBC Sounds app
6	Dame Judi Dench	16	Sport
7	David	17	1930s (1936)
8	Video	18	*The Times*
9	*Daily Express*	19	George Osborne
10	*The Daily Mirror*	20	Nick Grimshaw

1   Who had a 2010 hit with *Only Girl (In The World)*?

2   Who co-starred with Windsor Davies in the sitcom *Never the Twain*?

3   In which decade did Emerson Fittipaldi first win the Formula 1 World Championship?

4   Before 2004, what colour was used in wiring to indicate the live wire?

5   Who succeeded Michael Heseltine (Baron Heseltine) as the UK's Deputy Prime Minister?

6   Which city is furthest north: Aberdeen, Glasgow or Inverness?

7   What is the name of William Roache's *Coronation Street* character?

8   *The Sign* (1994) was a single by which group?

9   What was the name of the housekeeper in the TV series *Dr Finlay's Casebook*?

10 Which two words that differ only by their first letter, mean "a building block" and "deception"?

11 What colour is SpongeBob SquarePants?

12 The phrase "Live long and prosper" is associated with which sci-fi series?

13 Which restaurant does Andy visit on his birthday in *Toy Story*?

14 Which common childhood illness has a name that comes from the Latin for "reddish"?

15 How many legs did the tyrannosaurus rex have?

16 Meerkats are native to which continent?

17 How many fluid ounces are there in quarter of a pint?

18 What geometrical shape is a 20p coin?

19 For how long did the Owl and the Pussycat sail away?

20 Which company introduced the Chrome web browser in 2008?

Easy

Medium

Hard

Answers to QUIZ 287 – Pot Luck

1	Scientific	11	Portal and mortal
2	*Kids in America* (Kim Wilde)	12	Timothy Dalton
3	Dorset	13	*The Goodies*
4	The abdomen	14	Waste
5	Seven	15	IV
6	The rose	16	Dull
7	1990s (1994)	17	*Warehouse 13*
8	Lieutenant	18	Quilt and quill
9	Luxembourg	19	Golf
10	Japan	20	Greg James

Easy

1 New York City is divided into how many boroughs?

2 How many spikes are there on the crown of the Statue of Liberty?

3 Which letter does not appear in the name of any US state?

4 Which former US presidential candidate was awarded a Nobel Prize in 2007 for his work on climate change awareness?

5 Which state is mentioned in the John Denver song *Take Me Home, Country Roads*?

6 How long is a term served by most members elected to the US House of Representatives?

7 Which state's coastline, at 6,640 miles, is longer than the coastlines of all the other US states combined?

8 In which state was Barack Obama born?

9 Which Nobel Peace Prize winner was Secretary of State under President Nixon and President Ford?

10 In which US state is the city of Waco?

11 What is used to make the US dish "grits"?

12 Michael R Bloomberg and Rudy Giuliani are both former mayors of which US city?

13 Which US state has a name that ends with three vowels?

14 What do Americans call a launderette?

15 How many rows of stars are there on the American flag?

16 In which state did the first self-service launderette open in 1934?

17 What is Armistice Day called in the US?

18 In which century did the Brooklyn Bridge open?

19 Which 20th-century US president started the Great Society initiatives?

20 What is referred to as the "lungs" of New York City?

Answers to QUIZ 288 – Food and Drink

1	Water	11	Gelatine
2	Dairy	12	(Animal) blood
3	Ketchup	13	Maple syrup
4	Black cabbage	14	Yogurt
5	Cranberries	15	Passion fruit
6	Haricot bean	16	Italy
7	Lentil	17	Japan (as takeaways)
8	Squash	18	Sheep's milk
9	Coffee	19	Oats
10	Currants	20	(Dark) purple

1   "The Real Deal" is the nickname of which former boxer?

2   What relation is Goneril to Regan in Shakespeare's *King Lear*?

3   What is Ellie Goulding's full first name?

4   The company Chanel was founded in which country?

5   From what do greyhounds start a race?

6   Is Cowes on the east, north or west coast of the Isle of Wight?

7   Which former *Doctor Who* star played Radagast the Brown in The Hobbit films?

8   *Since You've Been Gone* was a 1979 UK hit for which rock band?

9   In which decade was Angela Merkel born?

10 The character of Gwendolen Fairfax appears in which Oscar Wilde play?

11 In which city was the TV series *Cutting It* set?

12 Who is the master of ceremonies on *The Muppet Show*?

13 Who succeeded Richard the Lionheart as king of England?

14 Which company released what was then called the Kindle Fire tablet in 2011?

15 The London Marathon finishes on which thoroughfare?

16 Which bird features on the logo of Nando's restaurant chain?

17 In which decade was the sitcom *Porridge* first broadcast?

18 Faro is the main city of which Portuguese region?

19 The name of which vegetable means "eat all" in French?

20 The ship the *Mary Rose* was launched in which century?

Easy

Medium

Hard

Answers to QUIZ 289 – Pot Luck

1	Rihanna	11	Yellow
2	Sir Donald Sinden	12	*Star Trek*
3	1970s (1972)	13	Pizza Planet
4	Red	14	Rubella
5	John Prescott (Baron Prescott)	15	Two
6	Inverness	16	Africa
7	Ken Barlow	17	Five fluid ounces
8	Ace of Base	18	Heptagon
9	Janet	19	A year and a day
10	Brick and trick	20	Google

Easy

1   What term is given to a vision of something in a desert that is further away than it seems or does not exist?

2   "Mizzle" is a dialect word for what type of weather?

3   Famous for its carvings, Mount Rushmore is formed from what type of stone?

4   The chalk ridge known as the Purbeck Hills lies in which southern county of England?

5   Which weather event takes its name from the Greek for "to revolve"?

6   What term is given to low-lying cloud that reduces visibility to less than one kilometre?

7   Which is the shallowest and smallest of the five major oceans?

8   Two US states have a glacier called the Columbia Glacier: Washington and which other state?

9   In what environment does eelgrass grow?

10 In nature, what is a scabious?

Medium

11 What name is given to a build-up of salt in soil?

12 What two-word term is given to the slow movement of the Earth's continents?

13 Of what type of rock is the Australian landmark Uluru formed?

14 What name for a narrow piece of land derives from the Latin for "almost island"?

15 Which continent is nicknamed "the White Continent"?

16 Which two creatures spend their juvenile stages as caterpillars?

17 The glacier named the *Mer de Glace* is in which European country?

18 What colour are the flowers on the shrub broom?

19 Does a "mackerel sky" usually precede a cold front or a warm front?

20 The valleys of Great Langdale and Little Langdale lie in which English National Park?

Hard

Answers to QUIZ 290 – The USA

1	Five	11	Ground maize
2	Seven	12	New York
3	Q	13	Hawaii
4	Al Gore	14	Laundromat
5	West Virginia	15	Nine
6	Two years	16	Texas (Fort Worth)
7	Alaska	17	Veterans Day
8	Hawaii	18	19th century (1883)
9	Henry Kissinger	19	Lyndon B Johnson
10	Texas	20	Central Park

ANSWERS ON PAGE 295

1   For what purpose is a bursary awarded?

2   In relation to car ownership, what is a SORN?

3   The name of which pasta means "little tongues"?

4   Which author created the character of Horace Rumpole?

5   The Costa Brava is in which region of Spain?

6   The LaserJet brand of printers is produced by which company?

7   In which decade did the UEFA Cup rebrand as The Europa League?

8   With what is a Nice biscuit flavoured?

9   *This Ain't a Love Song* was a 1995 hit for which rock band?

10 The programme *Loose Ends* is broadcast on which radio station?

11 Which star of *The Expendables* directed and co-wrote the first film in the series?

12 What is the term for a word or phrase that is repeated during meditation?

13 Cambridge, Norfolk and which other county border Suffolk?

14 What was Romesh Ranganathan's occupation before turning to comedy full-time?

15 What type of supernatural beings feature in the TV series *The Walking Dead*?

16 Which alcoholic drink is normally used to make a hot toddy?

17 LAO is the international car registration for which country?

18 What word can refer to both a short news report and a regular leaflet produced by an organisation?

19 To which "beast" does the famous film quotation "It was beauty killed the beast" refer?

20 What part of a car provides the power to the starter?

Easy

Medium

Hard

Answers to QUIZ 291 – Pot Luck

1	Evander Holyfield	11	Manchester
2	Sister	12	Kermit the Frog
3	Elena	13	King John
4	France	14	Amazon
5	The traps	15	The Mall
6	The north coast	16	A rooster
7	Sylvester McCoy	17	1970s (1974)
8	Rainbow	18	The Algarve
9	1950s (1954)	19	Mangetout
10	*The Importance of Being Earnest*	20	16th century (1511)

What are the makes and models of these cars?

1

2

3

4

5

6

7

8

Answers to QUIZ 292 – Natural World

1	Mirage	11	Salinisation
2	Drizzle	12	Continental drift
3	Granite	13	Sandstone
4	Dorset	14	Peninsula
5	Cyclone	15	Antarctica
6	Fog	16	Butterfly and moth
7	The Arctic Ocean	17	France
8	Alaska	18	Yellow
9	Marine environment (salt water)	19	A warm front
10	A plant	20	The Lake District

1   Which word relating to the universe derives from the Latin word for "heaven"?

2   Which city lies furthest north: Leeds, Lincoln or Liverpool?

3   What colour are the home shirts of Leicester City FC?

4   Sarah Churchill, Duchess of Marlborough, was a close friend of which monarch?

5   Which term for someone who creates a fake online identity is taken from the title of a 2010 documentary film?

6   Who sang the theme tune to *New Tricks*?

7   "Feeding my fantasy, give me a kiss or three" is a lyric from which 2004 song?

8   What name is given to an open lattice used to support plants?

9   Which animals advertise the Compare the Market website?

10   What shape is a whorl?

11   Which clothing brand does the Devil wear in the title of a 2006 film?

12   In which English county is Ellesmere Port?

13   What is the name of the scientific study of how the body works?

14   Who co-starred with David Tennant in the 2020 TV series *Staged*?

15   What colour are elderberries?

16   Which bean is named after an organ of the body?

17   What word completes the famous quotation by Benjamin Franklin: "In this world, nothing can be certain except death and ___"?

18   Harlem is an area of which borough of New York?

19   What was the first name of the wife of George V?

20   Which arteries in the neck carry blood to the head?

Easy

Medium

Hard

Easy

1   Which song title was shared by a Boney M record of 1976 and a Darts record of 1977?

2   "Young man, I was once in your shoes" is a lyric from which disco classic?

3   *Discothèque* and *The Fly* were 1990s chart-toppers for which band?

4   *The Emancipation of Mimi* was a 2005 hit album for which artist?

5   Which female pop star had a 2006 hit with *Unfaithful*?

6   Which band released the 1973 single *Hell Raiser*?

7   *Break Up Song* was a 2020 single by which girl group?

8   Donnie Wahlberg was a founding member of which boy band?

9   Did singer James Blunt serve in the British Army, the British Navy, or the Royal Air Force?

10 On which British TV talent show did One Direction find fame?

11 Francis Rossi co-founded which rock band?

12 From which country were the singers in the 1970s duo Baccara?

13 Which singer released the 2013 song *Just Give Me a Reason*?

14 "You must understand though the touch of your hand makes my pulse react" are the opening lines to which 1984 song?

15 Who released the 2006 album *Back to Black*?

16 In which country was the band Imagine Dragons formed?

17 Which singers duetted on the 2020 single *Stuck with U*?

18 With which boy band did Justin Timberlake find fame?

19 Who released the 1987 single *Who's That Girl*?

20 What was the name of the band who released the 1969 single *Give Peace a Chance*?

Answers to QUIZ 294 – Cars

1   Citroën 2CV
2   Ford Capri
3   DeLorean DMC
4   VW Beetle
5   BMW Mini
6   Jaguar E-type
7   Lotus Elan
8   Morris Minor

1   For what do the initials ICU stand in the name of a hospital department?

2   "I'm having an old friend for dinner" is a line from which film?

3   What is the name of Tony Benn's son, who became MP for Leeds Central in 1999?

4   Does Argentina lie north or south of the Equator?

5   Which of these musicals was performed first: *Sunset Boulevard*, *The Phantom of the Opera* or *The Woman in White*?

6   *Somebody to Love* was a 1976 hit for which rock band?

7   Mark Wing-Davey played which character in both the radio and TV adaptations of *The Hitchhiker's Guide To The Galaxy*?

8   In 2011, which comedian impersonated Ken Bruce for an entire radio show on April Fool's Day?

9   Journalist Chris Mason (b.1980) reports on what subject?

10 If someone is described as profligate, are they extravagant or mean?

11 What is a corncockle?

12 The Parker Pen company was founded in which country?

13 From what fabric was satin originally made?

14 *Kingston Town* was a 1990 hit for which band?

15 The ferry port of Rosslare is in which Irish county?

16 Who was appointed captain of the Scotland national football team in 2018?

17 What nationality was composer Alexander Borodin?

18 Which company manufactured the Hawk Moth and Mosquito planes?

19 The city of San Antonio is in which US state?

20 Who wrote the 2015 children's novel *Grandpa's Great Escape*?

Answers to QUIZ 295 – Pot Luck

1	Celestial	11	Prada
2	Leeds	12	Cheshire
3	Blue	13	Physiology
4	*Queen Anne*	14	Michael Sheen
5	Catfish	15	Black
6	Dennis Waterman	16	Kidney bean
7	*Love Machine* (Girls Aloud)	17	Taxes
8	Trellis	18	Manhattan
9	Meerkats	19	Mary
10	A spiral	20	The carotid arteries

Easy

1 Which of Greater Manchester's boroughs has the shortest name?

2 What is the English equivalent of the Spanish name Miguel?

3 What was the name of the talking cat in the TV series *Sabrina the Teenage Witch*?

4 Of the seven London boroughs that have names beginning with "H", which is alphabetically first?

5 What are the surnames of comedy duo Vic and Bob?

6 Which branch of mathematics takes its name from the Greek for "to measure the land"?

7 What was the name of Rodney's wife in *Only Fools and Horses*?

8 Which former footballer (b.1968) has the nickname "Razor"?

9 By what name is a third molar more commonly known?

10 What is the Italian equivalent of the English name Andrew?

11 Which dinosaur takes its name from the Greek for "three-horned face"?

12 The names of how many of the Great Lakes start and end with the same letter?

13 What was the name of the housekeeper in *Father Ted*?

Medium

14 Which sea creature has a Latin name that is the same as the name for part of the brain?

15 What is the name of the stone historically used in the coronation of Scottish monarchs?

16 Which UK prime minister was nicknamed "The British Bulldog"?

17 *My Name is Tallulah* is a song from which 1976 musical film?

18 What was the first name of Keeley Hawes' character in the TV series *The Durrells*?

19 What is the common name of a species of garden plant called *Nicotiana*?

20 What were the first names of the TV detectives Dalziel and Pascoe?

Hard

Answers to QUIZ 296 – Pop Music

1	*Daddy Cool*	11	Status Quo
2	Y.M.C.A. (Village People)	12	Spain
3	U2	13	Pink
4	Mariah Carey	14	*What's Love Got to Do with It* (Tina Turner)
5	Rihanna	15	Amy Winehouse
6	The Sweet	16	USA
7	Little Mix	17	Ariana Grande and Justin Bieber
8	New Kids on the Block	18	NSYNC
9	The British Army	19	Madonna
10	*The X Factor*	20	The Plastic Ono Band

1   Who took over the role of Dotty Cotton in *EastEnders* in 2019?

2   What name is given to someone who worries unnecessarily about their health?

3   What type of animal was Elsa in the 1960 book *Born Free*?

4   The 2019 series *The Capture* was set in which city?

5   Who preceded Charles Kennedy as Leader of the Liberal Democrats?

6   Shaznay Lewis was a member of which group from 1993 until 2001?

7   Which of these Keanu Reeves films was released first: *Parenthood, Point Break* or *Street Kings*?

8   In which country is *I'm a Celebrity…* filmed?

9   The butter brand Lurpak® was founded in which country?

10   Lancashire County Cricket Club plays most home games at which ground?

11   In which decade did tie-dyeing become popular in Western fashion?

12   Which two other girls' names are anagrams of Coraline?

13   In which country was Kim Cattrall born?

14   How many players are there in an octet?

15   "Mrs Trellis" is a fictional correspondent on which radio show?

16   Which part of a shoe shares its name with a type of fish?

17   The St Lawrence River forms part of the border between which two countries?

18   The French phrase *bon anniversaire* would be said to someone on what occasion?

19   In which decade did the Women's Royal Air Force merge with the RAF?

20   In which country was the band Van Halen formed?

Easy

Medium

Hard

Answers to QUIZ 297 – Pot Luck

1	Intensive Care Unit	11	A plant (with pink flowers)
2	*The Silence of the Lambs*	12	USA
3	Hilary Benn	13	Silk
4	South	14	UB40
5	*The Phantom of the Opera* (1986)	15	County Wexford
6	Queen	16	Andy Robertson
7	Zaphod Beeblebrox	17	Russian
8	Rob Brydon	18	de Havilland
9	Politics	19	Texas
10	Extravagant	20	David Walliams

1 Who was the first prime minister to occupy 10 Downing Street?

2 The Kelpies sculptures, near Falkirk, are based on which animal?

3 In which decade was the National Cyber Security Centre established in the UK?

4 Which Wiltshire monument is a focal point for the celebration of the summer and winter solstices?

5 Who was the UK Leader of the Opposition from 2001 to 2003?

6 The UK's 1969 Eurovision-winning song *Boom Bang-a-Bang* was performed by which singer?

7 In which decade did the Tyne and Wear Metro light rail network open?

8 Which UK rugby union team plays home games at the Liberty Stadium?

9 *Gwyn* is Welsh for which colour?

10 The Melon Yard and Pineapple Pit are features of which famous Cornish gardens?

11 In which decade did the *Flying Scotsman* make its first journey?

12 What is the minimum age at which someone can legally ride a motorcycle (not a moped) in the UK?

13 Who was the UK's first Prince Consort?

14 The oldest underwater tunnel in the world lies under which English river?

15 The early May Bank Holiday was moved to a Friday in 2020 to mark the 75th anniversary of what event?

16 What is the postcode area code for Glasgow?

17 The town of Caerphilly lies in which historic county of Wales?

18 In relation to employment, for what do the initials SSP stand?

19 Golden and white-tailed are the two species of which bird of prey found in the wild in the UK?

20 Which river forms much of the border between County Antrim and County Down?

Answers to QUIZ 298 – Names

1	Bury	11	Triceratops
2	Michael	12	Two (Erie and Ontario)
3	Salem	13	Mrs Doyle
4	Hackney	14	Seahorse (hippocampus)
5	Reeves and Mortimer	15	The Stone of Scone
6	Geometry	16	Sir Winston Churchill
7	Cassandra	17	*Bugsy Malone*
8	Neil Ruddock	18	Louisa
9	Wisdom tooth	19	Tobacco plant
10	Andrea	20	Andy and Peter

1 In 2019, which member of Fleetwood Mac became the first female singer to be inducted into the Rock and Roll Hall of Fame twice?

2 Which famous children's character lives at 4 Privet Drive in Little Whinging when he is first introduced?

3 Leigh-Anne Pinnock is a member of which group?

4 Which of these Tom Cruise films was released first: *Magnolia*, *Vanilla Sky* or *War of the Worlds*?

5 Which two words that differ only by their last letter mean "cleansing bar" and "rise quickly"?

6 The hotel company Best Western® was founded in which country?

7 Which German city is the largest city on the River Rhine?

8 Who played headmaster Ian George in the TV series *Hope and Glory*?

9 What is the term in fencing for a move that deflects an attack?

10 In which decade did the first Isle of Man TT race take place?

11 What is the female equivalent of "patriarch"?

12 According to the saying, which animal never forgets?

13 Opera singer Katherine Jenkins was born in which country of the UK?

14 The island of Capri is part of which Italian region?

15 *Grace & Favour* was a sequel to which sitcom?

16 What is *Jumanji* in the title of the film franchise?

17 How many US states begin with the letter "W"?

18 In which county is the town of Burnley?

19 Which way of serving potatoes takes its name from the French verb "to crunch"?

20 What name is given to a raised shelter where racing pigeons are kept?

Easy

Medium

Hard

Answers to QUIZ 299 – Pot Luck

1	Milly Zero	11	1960s
2	Hypochondriac	12	Caroline and Cornelia
3	A lion (lioness)	13	England (Liverpool)
4	London	14	Eight
5	Paddy Ashdown (Baron Ashdown of Norton-sub-Hamdon)	15	*I'm Sorry I Haven't a Clue*
		16	Sole
6	All Saints	17	Canada and the USA
7	*Parenthood* (1989)	18	Their birthday
8	Australia	19	1990s (1994)
9	Denmark	20	USA (Pasadena)
10	Old Trafford		

Easy

1   The adjective ferrous refers to which metal?

2   Which two four-letter words that differ only by their last letter mean "an oven" and "an item of Scottish clothing"?

3   What does a dipsomaniac crave?

4   If something is described as "orthodox", is it traditional or unconventional?

5   "Aurora" is a poetic word for what time of day?

6   How many syllables are there in the word "entrepreneurialism"?

7   What is the characteristic of someone who is described as "insouciant"?

8   What word can mean both "isolated" and "TV controller"?

9   The name of which material can be made from the Roman numeral for fifty and the name of a top value playing card?

10 What name is given to the study of epidemics?

Medium

11 Which two words, that differ only by their first letter, mean "envious" and "over-enthusiastic"?

12 Which term for eating outdoors means "in the cool" in Italian?

13 What name is given to the form of a language that is only spoken in a particular area?

14 In the US, for what is "condo" short?

15 Which French word, generally used in a disapproving way to describe the typical middle-class, means "town-dweller"?

16 Which of Canada's provinces and territories is alphabetically last?

17 Which type of beer is an anagram of "regal"?

18 Civic, peep and radar are examples of what type of word?

19 If someone is described as sapient, are they wise or foolish?

20 What Latin word is a name for the male head of a family?

Hard

Answers to QUIZ 300 – The UK

1	Sir Robert Walpole	11	1860s (1862)
2	Horse	12	17
3	2010s (2016)	13	Prince Albert (1857)
4	Stonehenge	14	River Thames (Rotherhithe to Wapping)
5	Sir Iain Duncan Smith	15	VE Day
6	Lulu	16	G
7	1980s (1980)	17	Glamorgan
8	Ospreys	18	Statutory Sick Pay
9	White	19	Eagle
10	The Lost Gardens of Heligan	20	The River Lagan

1 "I'm not bad, I'm just drawn that way" is a line from which 1988 film?

2 The word for which meat product can also mean "more foolhardy"?

3 Which is lowest in a standing human: the cranium, the humerus or the tarsals?

4 Andy Pipkin and Lou Todd were characters in which comedy series?

5 What does Ariel sacrifice to be given human legs in *The Little Mermaid*?

6 What is three cubed?

7 In the English version of Scrabble®, how many "H" tiles are there?

8 Which is the first ghost to visit Scrooge in the novel *A Christmas Carol*?

9 In the 2014 Winter Olympics, in which alpine sport were women allowed to compete for the first time?

10 The Ben Sherman® clothing brand was founded in which country?

11 In which decade was the TV licence introduced in the UK?

12 Which singer embarked on the Blonde Ambition tour in 1990?

13 In which English county is the River Taw?

14 If someone is described as gullible, are they cynical or easily fooled?

15 What was the name of Paul Whitehouse's football pundit on *The Fast Show*?

16 What type of creature is a reed bunting?

17 Who presents the Radio 1 show *Rhythm Nation*?

18 On a standard keyboard, which letter is between I and P?

19 On which continent is Angola?

20 In which New Testament gospel is the story of Lazarus?

Easy

Medium

Hard

Answers to QUIZ 301 – Pot Luck

1	Stevie Nicks	11	Matriarch
2	Harry Potter	12	An elephant
3	Little Mix	13	Wales
4	*Magnolia* (1999)	14	Campania
5	Soap and soar	15	*Are You Being Served?*
6	USA	16	A board game
7	Cologne	17	Four (Washington, West Virginia, Wisconsin and Wyoming)
8	Sir Lenny Henry		
9	Parry	18	Lancashire
10	1900s (1907)	19	Croquette
		20	A loft

Easy

1   Who was the quizmaster on the 2020 TV series *Very Hard Questions*?

2   In which quiz show can contestants select the Eye of Horus as an option?

3   Who portrayed Chris Tarrant in the 2020 miniseries *Quiz*?

4   Which entertainer succeeded Bob Monkhouse as host of the game show *Family Fortunes*?

5   Michael Rodd was the original host of which children's film-based game show?

6   *Who Wants to Be a Millionaire?* takes its title from a song from which 1956 musical film?

7   Which snooker player captained a team on *A Question of Sport* opposite Ally McCoist?

8   Who was the original presenter of the television panel show *They Think It's All Over*?

9   What trophy is presented to the winner of *Mastermind*?

10 Which anniversary did the *Eggheads* quiz show celebrate in 2013?

Medium

11 In which decade was the quiz show *Sale of the Century* first broadcast?

12 What was the booby prize on *3-2-1*?

13 Who hosted the game show *Name That Tune* from 1976 to 1983?

14 The Gold Run featured in which quiz show?

15 Which game show, first broadcast in 1979, included the Supermatch game?

16 In which show do the games "Broken Karaoke" and "I'm Terrible at Dating" feature?

17 Who was the host of *Take Your Pick!* from 1992 to 1999?

18 The question-setters on which show are sometimes referred to as elves?

19 How many pairs start a game of *Pointless*?

20 What was the title of the 2020 variation of *The Chase*, which saw The Chasers teaming up against one contestant?

Hard

Answers to QUIZ 302 – Words

1	Iron	11	Jealous and zealous
2	Kiln and kilt	12	Alfresco
3	Alcohol	13	Dialect
4	Traditional	14	Condominium
5	Dawn	15	Bourgeois
6	Eight	16	Yukon
7	Unconcerned	17	Lager
8	Remote	18	Palindrome
9	Lace (L-ace)	19	Wise
10	Epidemiology	20	*Paterfamilias*

1   *Emmerdale* is set in which area of England?

2   The Mackenzie River flows into which ocean?

3   How many Graces were there in Greek mythology?

4   In *The House that Jack Built*, which animal worried the cat?

5   Which US state capital is nicknamed "The Big Pineapple"?

6   Who played Kate in the 2020 TV series *Kate and Koji*?

7   A tom is the male of which animal?

8   Mr Freeze is an enemy of which superhero?

9   Which of these shapes has the most sides: a pentagon, a triangle or a trapezoid?

10 Pete the Eagle is the mascot of which south London football team?

11 Who played the title role in the 1965 film *Cat Ballou*?

12 Which bank uses the advertising slogan "Get a little Xtra help"?

13 "Simply the Best" is the nickname of which former boxer?

14 In the USA, for what do the initials NRA stand in the name of the lobbying group?

15 Who topped the charts in 1996 with *Because You Loved Me*?

16 Who was elected as the MP for Uxbridge and South Ruislip in 2015?

17 What word can be applied to both the breaking of an egg and the solving of a code?

18 What colour were postboxes when they were first introduced to mainland Britain in 1850?

19 What number is opposite three on a die?

20 On which island was the singer Ricky Martin born?

Answers to QUIZ 303 – Pot Luck

1	*Who Framed Roger Rabbit* (said by Jessica)	11	1940s (1946)
2	Rasher	12	Madonna
3	The tarsals (ankle bones)	13	Devon
4	*Little Britain*	14	Easily fooled
5	Her voice	15	Ron Manager
6	27	16	A bird
7	Two	17	Trevor Nelson
8	Jacob Marley	18	O
9	Ski jumping	19	Africa
10	England (Brighton)	20	Gospel of John

1   What form of transport is an autogyro?

2   Caledonian MacBrayne provides what type of transport?

3   In 1819, the *SS Savannah* became the first steamship to cross which body of water?

4   Which car brand has been advertised with the slogan "The drive of your life"?

5   Carlisle Airport is named after which National Park?

6   In which decade was the first Severn Bridge opened?

7   The 113-mile-long Overseas Highway is a major road in which US state?

8   J is the international car registration for which country?

9   What is the full name of the main station in Devon's county town?

10   Which airport has the code INV?

11   In which decade was the 70mph maximum speed limit introduced in the UK?

12   What type of vessel has a name that means "under water"?

13   Which vehicle rental company shares its name with a unit of measurement?

14   What does the letter "R" stand for on an automatic gearbox?

15   In Germany, what is an autobahn?

16   Which is the only city between London and Birmingham that is close to the M40?

17   Which company manufactures the Boxster sports car?

18   By what name is the Midlands Expressway also known?

19   Datsun is a brand owned by which car manufacturer?

20   Which US city is nicknamed "Motor City"?

Answers to QUIZ 304 – Quiz and Game Shows

1	Jon Snow	11	1970s (1971)
2	*Only Connect*	12	Dusty Bin
3	Michael Sheen	13	Tom O'Connor
4	Max Bygraves	14	*Blockbusters*
5	*Screen Test*	15	*Blankety Blank*
6	*High Society*	16	*Richard Osman's House of Games*
7	John Parrott	17	Des O'Connor
8	Nick Hancock	18	*QI*
9	A glass bowl	19	Four
10	Tenth anniversary	20	*Beat the Chasers*

1   Which book of the New Testament is alphabetically first?

2   Mike Hazelwood (b.1958) was a world champion twice in the 1970s in which sport?

3   In the 1963 film *Cleopatra*, who played Mark Antony?

4   The 1960s TV series featuring Skippy was set in which country?

5   Who won the 2019 Wimbledon men's singles title?

6   The Centauri, Minbari and Narn races appeared in which sci-fi series?

7   Oporto is the second-largest city in which European country?

8   *The Boys are Back in Town* was a 1976 hit for which band?

9   For what do the letters PA stand in a voice amplification system?

10 What part of an item of clothing might be in a "batwing" style?

11 What is the occupation of Stephen and Daniel from *Gogglebox*?

12 Is the Rhondda Valley in North Wales, South Wales or West Wales?

13 The TikTok social network service was developed in which country?

14 *Under a Blood Red Sky* was a 1983 live album by which band?

15 What is a nasturtium?

16 What type of confection can be tempered?

17 Which old tailoring measurement was equal to approximately 45 inches?

18 How many ounces are there in three pounds?

19 What word can mean both "having plenty of money" and "to clean out with water"?

20 If an event is described as serendipitous, is it lucky or unlucky?

Easy
Medium
Hard

Answers to QUIZ 305 – Pot Luck

1	The Yorkshire Dales	11	Jane Fonda
2	The Arctic Ocean	12	The Halifax
3	Three	13	Chris Eubank
4	The dog	14	National Rifle Association (of America)
5	Honolulu (Hawaii)	15	Céline Dion
6	Brenda Blethyn	16	Boris Johnson
7	Cat	17	Cracking
8	Batman	18	Green
9	A pentagon (five)	19	Four
10	Crystal Palace FC	20	Puerto Rico

Easy

1 Which recording artist famously changed his name to a symbol during a dispute with his recording label?

2 What colour is the "l" in the Google logo?

3 Which tree features on the flag of Lebanon?

4 The symbol for which sign of the zodiac is a stylised version of the Roman numerals II?

5 What colour is the background of the Ford logo?

6 The "smiley" emoji is usually what colour?

7 Which rugby union team has a striped insect as its logo?

8 What colour is the star on a Heineken® label?

9 The symbol for which planet of the solar system is also a symbol for the male gender?

10 Which flower was associated with Flanders in WWI?

Medium

11 On a motorway sign, which two items of cutlery are used to indicate catering facilities?

12 Which communications application has a logo of a blue circle with a white "S" in the centre?

13 On the logo on Apple products, on which side is the apple incomplete?

14 Which amphibian features on the logo of the Rainforest Alliance?

15 What is indicated by the hazard symbol of a skull and crossbones?

16 Which two colours appear on the FedEx® logo?

17 Mathematically, what is indicated by the symbol "<"?

18 Which luxury brand of watch features a crown as its logo?

19 Si is the symbol for which chemical element?

20 How many coloured squares are there on the Microsoft® logo?

Hard

Answers to QUIZ 306 – Getting Around

1	An aircraft (similar to a helicopter)	11	1960s (temporarily in 1965, permanently in 1967)
2	Ferries	12	Submarine
3	The Atlantic Ocean	13	Hertz
4	Peugeot	14	Reverse
5	The Lake District	15	A motorway
6	1960 (1966)	16	Oxford
7	Florida	17	Porsche
8	Japan	18	The M6 toll road
9	Exeter St Davids	19	Nissan
10	Inverness	20	Detroit (Michigan)

1   County Sligo has a coastline on which body of water?

2   As at 2020, how many times had Ed Sheeran won the British Album of the Year Brit Award?

3   What type of company is William Hill?

4   In the US legal system, for what do the letters "DA" stand?

5   In which 1998 film did Bruce Willis play Harry S Stamper, who was tasked with preventing an asteroid destroying the Earth?

6   Which retired cricket commentator is nicknamed "Blowers"?

7   Who wrote the music to the 1937 song *They Can't Take That Away from Me*?

8   On which continent is the country of Jordan?

9   The STV North TV franchise was formerly named after which mountain range?

10   What is the official language of Uruguay?

11   What type of fish is a skate?

12   Buckland Abbey in Devon was the home of which famous seafarer?

13   The game "One Song to the Tune of Another" appears on which radio show?

14   Which wild flower is associated with making "chains"?

15   What is the occupation of the Muppet Bunsen Honeydew?

16   The mnemonic "Richard of York gained battles in vain" is used to assist the remembering of what?

17   For what do the letters HR stand on a UK road sign?

18   What type of drink was the brand Top Deck?

19   What is 73 in Roman numerals?

20   Which future Star Wars actor appeared as Bob Falfa in the 1973 film *American Graffiti*?

Easy

Medium

Hard

Answers to QUIZ 307 – Pot Luck

1	Acts	11	Hairdressers
2	Water-skiing	12	South Wales
3	Richard Burton	13	China
4	Australia	14	U2
5	Novak Djokovic	15	A (trailing) plant
6	*Babylon 5*	16	Chocolate
7	Portugal	17	Ell
8	Thin Lizzy	18	48
9	Public address	19	Flush
10	A sleeve	20	Lucky

1   What was the first name of Joanne Froggatt's *Downton Abbey* character?

2   Who succeeded John Prescott (Baron Prescott) as the UK's Deputy Prime Minister?

3   What is a jalopy?

4   "Just keep swimming" is a line from which 2003 animated film?

5   What accompanies Jack in the title of a pantomime?

6   The town of Jarrow lies in which metropolitan county?

7   CC Jitters is a coffee shop in which US TV series?

8   What type of creature was Beatrix Potter's Jemima?

9   What word beginning with "J" can mean both "a milky dessert" and "a trip taken by officials at public expense"?

10 In which country was the Jehovah's Witnesses denomination founded?

11 Jeddah is a seaport in which country?

12 What type of creature is a jerboa?

13 "Here's Johnny" is a line from which film?

14 In which country did the martial art of ju-jitsu originate?

15 John Altman played which *EastEnders* villain?

16 Jamborees are associated with which organisation?

17 What are jodphurs?

18 "Jackhammer" is the American term for what tool?

19 Where in the body is the jugular vein?

20 Who played Jay Gatsby in the 2013 version of *The Great Gatsby*?

Answers to QUIZ 308 – Symbols and Logos

1	Prince	11	A fork and spoon
2	Green	12	Skype
3	A cedar tree	13	The right-hand side
4	Gemini	14	A frog
5	Blue	15	Poison
6	Yellow	16	Purple and orange
7	Wasps	17	Less than
8	Red	18	Rolex
9	Mars	19	Silicon
10	The poppy	20	Four (orange-red, green, blue and yellow)

1   With which modern-day county is William Wordsworth associated?

2   Which of these was the first to be made a city: Inverness, Lisburn or Newry?

3   For what do the initials VSO stand in the name of the non-profit making organisation?

4   What substance is traditionally associated with a fifth wedding anniversary?

5   Which English football club's home ground is the Riverside Stadium?

6   Which actress played singer Susie Diamond in the 1989 film *The Fabulous Baker Boys*?

7   The Kent town of Sheerness lies at the mouth of which river?

8   Crawley is in which English county?

9   In which decade was the red tractor food assurance scheme launched?

10 The name of which city can precede "artichoke" to make a type of vegetable?

11 In which winter sport is ice swept with a broom during play?

12 *Take Me I'm Yours* (1978) was the first single released by which British band?

13 In which country was actress Tuppence Middleton born?

14 How many people make up a triumvirate?

15 In the traditional pictures of the US character Uncle Sam, what type of hat is he wearing?

16 Which member of the Pussycat Dolls released the 2013 single *Boomerang*?

17 In the Harry Potter novels and films, who kills Sirius Black?

18 Which chocolate bar was advertised with the slogan "The sweet you can eat between meals"?

19 The first dukedom was created in 1337, for which English county?

20 In relation to the EU, what is the CAP?

Easy

Medium

Hard

Answers to QUIZ 309 – Pot Luck

1	The Atlantic Ocean	11	A (marine) flatfish
2	Once (for x, in 2015)	12	Sir Francis Drake
3	Bookmaker	13	*I'm Sorry I Haven't a Clue*
4	District Attorney	14	Daisy
5	*Armageddon*	15	Scientist
6	Henry Blofeld	16	Colours of the rainbow
7	George Gershwin	17	Holiday route
8	Asia	18	Shandy
9	Grampian Mountains (Grampian Television)	19	LXXIII
10	Spanish	20	Harrison Ford

What are the names of these chefs and cooks?

1

2

3

4

5

6

7

8

9

Answers to QUIZ 310 – J

1	Anna	11	Saudi Arabia
2	Sir Nick Clegg	12	A rodent
3	An old car	13	*The Shining*
4	*Finding Nemo*	14	Japan
5	*The Beanstalk*	15	Nick Cotton
6	Tyne and Wear	16	The Scouts
7	*The Flash*	17	Trousers (worn by a horse rider)
8	A duck (Puddle-Duck)	18	Pneumatic drill
9	Junket	19	The neck
10	USA	20	Leonardo DiCaprio

QUIZ 313 – Pot Luck

ANSWERS ON PAGE 315

1 Who won the Female British Solo Artist Brit award in 2020?

2 For which film did Laura Dern win the Best Supporting Actress Oscar at the 2020 award ceremony?

3 What is the name of Beverley Callard's *Coronation Street* character?

4 In January 2020, it was announced that which rugby union club would be relegated from the Premiership after breaching the salary cap?

5 Whom did Fiona Bruce succeed as presenter of *Antiques Roadshow*?

6 In which decade did Mariah Carey release her debut single, *Vision of Love*?

7 Which English football club won the European Cup Winner's Cup in 1991?

8 *All the Things She Said* and *Sanctify Yourself* were 1986 hits for which band?

9 How many days are there in four weeks?

10 Tom Parker Bowles is a critic and writer on which subject?

11 Which US president took office before the others: Bill Clinton, George Bush Senior or Gerald Ford?

12 What is the capital city of Brazil?

13 NM is the abbreviation for which US state?

14 What military term is given to the moving of troops or their assignment to a different task?

15 In which year did Red Rum win his first Grand National?

16 The song *Rise Like a Phoenix* was the winning entry in which 2014 competition?

17 Cheam and Carshalton are part of which London borough?

18 The Stackpole Estate, managed by the National Trust, is part of which UK National Park?

19 How many points is the letter Y worth in a game of Scrabble®?

20 In musical notation with a treble clef, which note is written immediately below the bottom line on a stave?

Answers to QUIZ 311 – Pot Luck

1	Cumbria	11	Curling
2	Inverness (2000)	12	Squeeze
3	Voluntary Service Overseas	13	England (Bristol)
4	Wood	14	Three
5	Middlesbrough FC	15	A top hat
6	Michelle Pfeiffer	16	Nicole Scherzinger
7	River Medway	17	Bellatrix Lestrange
8	West Sussex	18	Milky Way ™
9	2000s (2000)	19	Cornwall
10	Jerusalem	20	Common Agricultural Policy

Easy

1 The joining of the English and Scottish parliaments in 1707 took place during the reign of which monarch?

2 The first battle of the American Civil War took place in which US state?

3 Henry VIII is buried in the chapel of which Berkshire castle?

4 Which country ruled the Orkney Islands before it became part of Scotland in 1472?

5 Who was the first vice-president of the United States?

6 How many wheels were there on a Roman chariot?

7 In which battle of WWI did the British first use tanks?

8 Which geological period came first, the Jurassic or Cretaceous?

9 The Roman province of Lusitania covered part of which two European countries?

10 The Most Noble Order of the Garter was founded in which century?

11 To the nearest ten years, how old was Edward VII when he became king?

12 What name describes the period from 1837 to 1901 in the UK?

13 Who was leader of the Soviet Union earliest: Brezhnev, Khrushchev or Stalin?

Medium

14 Members of which clan were killed at Glencoe in 1692?

15 Which royal house succeeded the Tudors?

16 George II was born in which modern-day country?

17 In which country was Marie Antoinette born?

18 Canute was king of England in which century?

19 Which of the three orders of Greek architecture was developed last?

20 Which future leader wrote the 1925 book *Mein Kampf*?

Hard

Answers to QUIZ 312 – Chefs and Cooks

1   John Torode
2   Nigella Lawson
3   Gordon Ramsay
4   Lorraine Pascale
5   Prue Leith
6   Mary Berry
7   Jamie Oliver
8   Nadiya Hussain
9   Dave Myers

ANSWERS ON PAGE 317

1 "My morals got me on my knees, I'm begging please stop playing games" is a lyric from which 2008 song?

2 In which city was the 2020 TV series *The Nest* mostly set?

3 What number do the Roman numerals LXXVIII represent?

4 Was the 1571 Battle of Lepanto fought on land or at sea?

5 The name of which percussion instrument means "little drum"?

6 Did Brendan Foster compete in sprint, middle-distance or long-distance races during his athletics career?

7 In the title of the 2003 film, what type of animal was *Seabiscuit*?

8 Which city is furthest south: Bolton, Carlisle or Leeds?

9 Which Scottish actor played ex-KGB agent Valentin Zhukovsky in *GoldenEye* and *The World is Not Enough*?

10 The National Trust property of Basildon Park lies in which county?

11 What word means both a time signal and a fruit seed?

12 What name is given to a nurse trained to deliver babies?

13 What was the currency unit of Italy before the euro?

14 Who played Head of Deliverance Ian Fletcher in the TV series 2012 *Twenty Twelve*?

15 Which type of alcoholic drink is sometimes added to batter to make it lighter?

16 What colour light is emitted by computer and smartphone screens?

17 In which area of London was Arsenal FC founded?

18 Which car company makes the Almera model?

19 Which US president said "Speak softly and carry a big stick" in relation to foreign policy?

20 *Shoes Upon the Table* is a song from which musical by Willy Russell?

Easy

Medium

Hard

Answers to QUIZ 313 – Pot Luck

1	Mabel	11	Gerald Ford (1974)
2	*Marriage Story*	12	Brasilia
3	Liz McDonald	13	New Mexico
4	Saracens	14	Redeployment
5	Michael Aspel	15	1973
6	1990s (1990)	16	The Eurovision Song Contest (for Austria)
7	Manchester United FC	17	Sutton
8	Simple Minds	18	Pembrokeshire Coast National Park
9	28	19	Four points
10	Food	20	D

ANSWERS ON PAGE 318

Easy

1. In which decade was the crime series *Softly, Softly* first broadcast?
2. Which organisation operates the 0800 555 111 number allowing members of the public to anonymously pass on information about crime?
3. Who played Detective Sergeant George Carter in the 1970s TV series *The Sweeney*?
4. Commissioner Selwyn Patterson is a character in which TV crime drama series?
5. Which item of police equipment features in the term for an inducement for an employee to stay with a company over a period of time?
6. In which country are the Harry Hole crime novels set?
7. What two-word term for home-made alcohol was first used in the US during the prohibition era?
8. Mr Barraclough and Mr Mackay were warders in which fictional prison?
9. Which organisation formerly had the telephone number Whitehall 1212?
10. In which city did Cagney and Lacey fight crime?

Medium

11. Which 1944 crime film took its two-word name from a clause in US insurance policies relating to accidental death?
12. Which crime drama series focused on the work of the Unsolved Crime and Open Case Squad?
13. What colour is the armband worn by military police in the UK?
14. The International Criminal Court sits in which city?
15. Who presented the long-running series *Police 5*?
16. Which writer created the character of Myron Bolitar?
17. What was the surname of Finn and his family in the 2020 drama series *Gangs of London*?
18. In 2018, the Independent Office for Police Conduct replaced which UK organisation?
19. Which is the next rank up from constable in the UK police?
20. In which city was the TV series *The Bill* set?

Hard

Answers to QUIZ 314 – History

1. Queen Anne
2. South Carolina (Fort Sumter)
3. Windsor Castle
4. Norway
5. John Adams
6. Two
7. The Battle of the Somme
8. Jurassic
9. Portugal and Spain
10. 14th century (1348)
11. 60 (59)
12. Victorian
13. Stalin (1922)
14. The MacDonald clan
15. The Stuarts
16. Germany
17. Austria
18. 11th century (1016-35)
19. Corinthian
20. Adolf Hitler

1 In the song *The Twelve Days of Christmas*, what were the ladies doing?

2 Carisbrooke Castle lies on which UK island?

3 Which two words that differ only by their first letter mean "dress" and "earthenware vessel"?

4 In which decade did Jack Brabham make his Formula 1 debut?

5 Lindsey Coulson played which character in *EastEnders*?

6 Who played Queen Elizabeth in the 2010 film *The King's Speech*?

7 Which team won the 2019 rugby Super League championship?

8 The city of Louisville is in which US state?

9 Who played Major George Cowley in the TV series *The Professionals*?

10 Which Scottish city has the postcode area code DD?

11 Who played pilot "Whip" Whitaker in the 2012 film *Flight*?

12 What name is given to the wife of a raja?

13 As at 2020, which snooker player holds the record for the most career century breaks?

14 What does the German phrase *Guten tag* mean?

15 In which decade was the original *Dirty Harry* film released?

16 What name is given to the act of driving closely behind another vehicle?

17 Jools Holland has a regular music programme on which radio station?

18 Which grain is traditionally thrown at weddings?

19 For what product is the Eveready® brand famous?

20 Who succeeded Michael Howard as the UK Home Secretary?

Easy

Medium

Hard

Answers to QUIZ 315 – Pot Luck

1	*Mercy* (Duffy)	11	Pip
2	Glasgow	12	Midwife
3	78	13	Lira
4	At sea (off the west coast of Greece)	14	Hugh Bonneville
5	Tambourine	15	Beer
6	Long-distance	16	Blue
7	A horse	17	Woolwich
8	Bolton	18	Nissan
9	Robbie Coltrane	19	Theodore Roosevelt
10	Berkshire	20	*Blood Brothers*

Easy

1 Which group had a 1980 hit with *Special Brew*?

2 What status is given by public regulators in the UK to an organisation that falls short of expected standards?

3 What was the title of the first UK no.1 for The Specials?

4 On which channel does the pre-school children's programme *Something Special* air?

5 Which football manager is nicknamed "The Special One"?

6 In which decade was the TV series *Special Branch* first shown?

7 What is the name of Mariska Hargitay's character in *Law and Order: Special Victims Unit*?

8 In the UK, which organisations have a department known as the Special Branch?

9 Dina Carroll released the single *Special Kind of Love* in which decade?

10 A "special relationship" has historically existed between the UK and which other country?

11 Who played Special Agent Dana Scully in *The X-Files*?

Medium

12 "You float like a feather in a beautiful world. I wish I was special" are lyrics from which 1992 song?

13 Paloma Faith sang "Make your own kind of music, sing your own special song" in an advert for which car brand?

14 In the entertainment world, for what do the letters SFX stand?

15 In the UK, are special constables paid staff or volunteers?

16 Which country singer released the 1995 album *Something Special*?

17 For what do the initials SEN stand in relation to schooling?

18 Which company makes the Special K® brand of breakfast cereal?

19 In which decade did Kylie Minogue and Jason Donovan top the charts with *Especially For You*?

20 What is the full name of the organisation usually referred to as the SAS?

Hard

Answers to QUIZ 316 – Crime

1	1960s (1966)	11	*Double Indemnity*
2	Crimestoppers (Trust)	12	*New Tricks*
3	Dennis Waterman	13	Red (with the letters MP in black)
4	*Death in Paradise*	14	The Hague
5	Handcuffs (golden handcuffs)	15	Shaw Taylor
6	Norway	16	Harlan Coben
7	Bathtub gin	17	Wallace
8	HMP Slade (*Porridge*)	18	IPCC (Internal Police Complaints Commission)
9	Scotland Yard	19	Sergeant
10	New York	20	London

ANSWERS ON PAGE 321

1   The Manchester Ship Canal connects Manchester to which body of water?

2   Which actress played Evelyn Abbott in the 2018 horror film *A Quiet Place*?

3   Is the Peloponnese peninsula in the north or the south of Greece?

4   Which team were runners-up in the 2019 FA Community Shield?

5   How many hours ahead of GMT is Capetown?

6   In which city was the 1988 film *Working Girl* set?

7   Which musical instrument might you be said to be as fit as?

8   In which country was the sci-fi series *Fringe* set?

9   What type of headache is often accompanied by visual disturbance?

10 What is a maxim?

11 Which telecommunications company has a red speech mark as its logo?

12 What is an agapanthus?

13 If something is anathema to you, do you dislike it or like it?

14 In which country was athlete Zola Budd born?

15 Romesh Ranganathan and which other comedian appear in the *Vs* series?

16 In the TV series *Last of the Summer Wine*, what was Clegg's first name?

17 Who wrote the 2012 novel *Four Children and It*, based on the 1902 novel *Five Children and It* by Edith Nesbit?

18 How many goals must be scored in football to claim a hat trick?

19 In which county is the town of Beaconsfield?

20 What number do the Roman numerals LXXXVI represent?

Easy

Medium

Hard

Answers to QUIZ 317 – Pot Luck

1	Dancing	11	Denzel Washington
2	The Isle of Wight	12	Rani
3	Crock and frock	13	Ronnie O'Sullivan (over 1000)
4	1950s (1955)	14	Good day
5	Carol Jackson	15	1970s (1971)
6	Helena Bonham Carter	16	Tailgating
7	St Helens	17	Radio 2
8	Kentucky	18	Rice
9	Gordon Jackson	19	Batteries
10	Dundee	20	Jack Straw

Easy

1 Which title character of a Shakespearean play "loved not wisely but too well"?

2 What is the profession of the character of Robbie Hart in the title of a 1998 film?

3 Which title character of a film said "Life is like a box of chocolates"?

4 Which boxer did Russell Crowe portray in the film *Cinderella Man*?

5 How were the characters of Lloyd Christmas and Harry Dunne described in the title of a 1994 comedy film?

6 What nationality was the girl in the title of the 2015 film starring Eddie Redmayne?

7 Who played the title role in the 2018 film *Christopher Robin*?

8 Which singer played the title character in the 1976 film *The Man Who Fell to Earth*?

9 The Bergens are the enemies of which title characters of a 2016 film?

10 What is the name of the school in the High School Musical series of films?

11 Which punk rocker did Gary Oldman portray in a 1986 film?

12 How was Skippy described in the title of the TV series?

13 Who had a hit with the title song to the 1999 film *Wild Wild West*?

Medium

14 The title character of which TV series was represented in the opening titles by a stick man with a halo?

15 What is the name of the princess in the title of the 1871 Verdi opera set in Egypt?

16 Which name is shared by Liam Neeson's character in the title of a 1996 film and an *Apollo 11* astronaut?

17 Who was *The Man with the Golden Gun* in the James Bond film?

18 In which decade was the TV series *Sherlock* first broadcast?

19 In the 1970s TV series *Nanny and the Professor*, who played Nanny?

20 What is the first name of the title character in the Bourne series of films?

Hard

Answers to QUIZ 318 – Special

1	Bad Manners	11	Gillian Anderson
2	Special measures	12	*Creep* (Radiohead)
3	*Too Much Too Young* (1980)	13	Škoda (Karoq)
4	Cbeebies	14	Special effects
5	José Mourinho	15	Volunteers
6	1960s (1969)	16	Dolly Parton
7	(Captain) Olivia Benson	17	Special Educational Needs
8	Police forces	18	Kellogg's
9	1990s (1992)	19	1980s (1988)
10	The USA	20	Special Air Service

1   Who starred as army veteran Frank McCloud in the 1948 film *Key Largo*?

2   What does a barometer measure?

3   In which TV quiz might you phone a friend?

4   Charlotte is a variety of which root vegetable?

5   What relation was tennis player Tim Gullikson (d.1996) to Tom Gullikson?

6   The River Rhône flows into which sea?

7   Which satirical magazine did Alan Coren edit from 1977 to 1987?

8   What nationality was the artist Claude Monet?

9   A harvest moon occurs in which season of the year?

10 Which former *Friends* actress plays a TV anchor in the series *The Morning Show*?

11 Which Latin phrase means "a terrible year"?

12 If you eschew an activity do you participate in it or shun it?

13 With what is a tom-tom usually played?

14 Who plays Carolyn Martens in the TV series *Killing Eve*?

15 In which country was the 1989 film *Dead Calm* set?

16 What fraction is indicated by the prefix "hemi"?

17 What is gelignite?

18 Which blood disorder may be described as "pernicious"?

19 WLG is the airport code for the capital city of which country?

20 As at 2020, which golfer was the only person to have won the BBC Sports Personality of the Year Lifetime Achievement Award twice, in 1997 and 2009?

Answers to QUIZ 319 – Pot Luck

1	The Irish Sea	11	Vodafone
2	Emily Blunt	12	A flowering plant
3	The south	13	Dislike it
4	Liverpool FC	14	South Africa
5	One hour	15	Rob Beckett
6	New York	16	Norman
7	A fiddle	17	Dame Jacqueline Wilson
8	USA	18	Three
9	Migraine	19	Buckinghamshire
10	A rule or principle (or pithy saying)	20	86

1   ZRH is the code for the main airport in which European country?

2   Within the EU, what type of organisation is the ECB?

3   The island of Naxos is part of which country?

4   What is the second-largest city in Germany, by population?

5   The Tuileries Garden lies in which European capital city?

6   *Domingo* is Spanish for what day of the week?

7   Freddie Ljungberg played international football for which team?

8   Which French island lies just north of Sardinia?

9   Gavi wine comes from which country?

10   RO is the international car registration for which European country?

11   How many hours ahead of GMT is Oslo?

12   The name of which European city completes the title of the 1969 comedy film ___ *or Bust!?*

13   What was the currency unit of Austria before the euro?

14   How many official languages does Belgium have?

15   Which German band released the 1974 album *Autobahn*?

16   Which bird appears on the coat of arms of Poland?

17   Are the stripes on the French flag horizontal or vertical?

18   Which Italian golfer was the European Tour's Golfer of the Year in 2018?

19   Which European car company made the Cinquecento model?

20   Who succeeded François Hollande as president of France?

Answers to QUIZ 320 – Top Billing

1	Othello	11	Sid Vicious (*Sid and Nancy*)
2	*The Wedding Singer*	12	*The Bush Kangaroo*
3	Forrest Gump	13	Will Smith
4	James J Braddock	14	*The Saint*
5	*Dumb and Dumber*	15	*Aida*
6	Danish (*The Danish Girl*)	16	*Michael Collins*
7	Ewan McGregor	17	(Francisco) Scaramanga
8	David Bowie	18	2010s (2010)
9	Trolls	19	Juliet Mills
10	East High School	20	Jason

QUIZ 323 – Pot Luck

1 Which of these Rolling Stones albums was released first: *A Bigger Bang, Exile On Main Street or Tattoo You*?

2 Which photographic term can also refer to the harmful effect of cold weather on the body?

3 Which gas makes up over 96% of Saturn's atmosphere?

4 In which sport might a player take on the role of nightwatchman?

5 Which two letters followed "Windows" in the name of the operating system released in 2001?

6 What is the occupation of Arnold Schwarzenegger's character in the 1994 film *True Lies*?

7 The mazurka is one of the national dances of which European country?

8 Which Caribbean island was named by Christopher Columbus to mark his third voyage?

9 What instrument does Roger Taylor play in the band Queen?

10 In which place did Susan Boyle finish on the 2009 final of *Britain's Got Talent*?

11 What word means to throw goods overboard to lighten the load of a ship?

12 Zayn Malik found fame with which boy band?

13 Is an arid region very dry or very wet?

14 How many ounces are there in four pounds?

15 Nogbad the Bad was a character in which children's TV series?

16 What colour are mangetout?

17 Mycenae was a major centre of the ancient civilisation in which country?

18 Who was the Greek god of music and poetry, amongst other things?

19 Which engineer did Sir Kenneth Branagh portray at the 2012 Olympics opening ceremony?

20 Which of these structures was completed first: St Paul's Cathedral, Tower Bridge or Westminster Abbey?

Easy

Medium

Hard

Answers to QUIZ 321 – Pot Luck

1	Humphrey Bogart	11	*Annus horribilis*
2	Air pressure	12	Shun it
3	*Who Wants to Be a Millionaire?*	13	The hands
4	Potato	14	Fiona Shaw
5	(Twin) brother	15	Australia
6	The Mediterranean	16	Half
7	*Punch*	17	An explosive
8	French	18	Anaemia
9	Autumn	19	New Zealand (Wellington)
10	Jennifer Aniston	20	Seve Ballesteros

Easy

1   What word can precede "doll", "time" and "trade" to make three words or phrases?

2   What word can precede "beetle", "night" and "party" to make three phrases?

3   What word can precede "front", "horse" and "shore" to make three words or phrases?

4   What word can precede "horn", "string" and "tree" to make three words or phrases?

5   What word can precede "number", "sale" and "some" to make three words or phrases?

6   What word can precede "circle", "fox" and "ocean" to make three words or phrases?

7   What word can follow "fringe", "lecture" and "operating" to make three phrases?

8   What word can precede "freeze", "fry" and "rooted" to make three phrases?

9   What word can precede "mural", terrestrial" and "time" to make three phrases?

10 What word can follow "bell", "ivory" and "watch" to make three phrases?

11 What word can precede "fibre", "majority" and "support" to make three phrases?

12 What word can precede "branch", "green" and "oil" to make three phrases?

13 What word can follow "mirror", "public" and "spitting" to make three phrases?

14 What word can precede "aunt", "coat" and "Lakes" to make three phrases?

15 What word can precede "circle", "colon" and "quaver" to make three new words?

16 What word can precede "eyed", "light" and "spark" to make three phrases?

17 What word can follow "fund", "hair" and "self" to make three new words or phrases?

18 What word can precede "class", "dress" and "primrose" to make three phrases?

19 What word can follow "flying", "jump" and "kick" to make three phrases?

20 What word can precede "hat", "soldier" and "whistle" to make three phrases?

Medium

Hard

Answers to QUIZ 322 – Europe

1	Switzerland (Zürich)	11	One hour
2	A bank (European Central Bank)	12	Monte Carlo
3	Greece	13	Schilling
4	Hamburg	14	Three (Dutch, French and German)
5	Paris	15	Kraftwerk
6	Sunday	16	An eagle
7	Sweden	17	Vertical
8	Corsica	18	Francesco Molinari
9	Italy	19	Fiat
10	Romania	20	Emmanuel Macron

1   Cheryl first found fame on which talent show?

2   What two-word name is given to the senior official at a tennis match?

3   The guinea pig is native to which continent?

4   In which decade did *The Fall and Rise of Reginald Perrin* first air on television?

5   Peter Mandelson (Baron Mandelson) represented which constituency from 1992 to 2004?

6   In the 1997 film *The Lost World: Jurassic Park*, a Tyrannosaurus Rex escapes in which US state?

7   Which of these is the correct spelling: minuscule, minusscule or minnuscule?

8   Who were the two original presenters of *Dancing on Ice*?

9   Steve Staunton (b.1969) earned 102 caps playing for which international football team?

10 What name is given to a length of canvas or net that is suspended at either end and used as a bed?

11 Which of these disaster films was released first: *Armageddon*, *Dante's Peak* or *Twister*?

12 In which century was the US president James Garfield assassinated?

13 What qualification does someone hold if they have the letters BA after their name?

14 Which piece of music did Torvill and Dean skate to when they received the highest ever score in ice dance?

15 Which two words that differ only by their first letter mean "cleanse" and "money"?

16 In which decade did Mary Hopkin top the charts with *Those Were the Days*?

17 What colour are the stars on the Chinese flag?

18 What animal appears on the left-hand side of the front cover of a British passport?

19 Which organisation runs the Neptune Coastline Campaign?

20 For what does the letter "C" stand in the name of the organisation UNESCO?

Easy

Medium

Hard

Answers to QUIZ 323 – Pot Luck

1	*Exile on Main Street* (1972)	11	Jettison
2	Exposure	12	One Direction
3	Hydrogen	13	Very dry
4	Cricket	14	64
5	XP (eXPerience)	15	*Noggin the Nog*
6	Spy	16	Green
7	Poland	17	Greece
8	Trinidad	18	Apollo
9	Drums	19	Isambard Kingdom Brunel
10	Second place (to Diversity)	20	Westminster Abbey (1065)

What are the names of these Italian landmarks?

Easy

1

2

3

4

Medium

5

6

7

8

Hard

Answers to QUIZ 324 – Take Three

1	Rag	11	Moral
2	Stag	12	Olive
3	Sea	13	Image
4	Shoe	14	Great
5	Whole	15	Semi
6	Arctic	16	Bright
7	Theatre	17	Raising
8	Deep	18	Evening
9	Extra	19	Start
10	Tower	20	Tin

1   Which Welsh football team is nicknamed "the Bluebirds"?

2   Meat Loaf released *I Would Do Anything for Love* in which decade?

3   What is the French word for "daughter"?

4   Who co-starred with Vince Vaughan in the 2013 film *The Internship*?

5   Which fictional vehicle has the serial number NCC 1701?

6   "Phizog" is a slang term for which part of the body?

7   Which former *Dragons' Den* investor took part in the 2020 series of *The Real Marigold Hotel*?

8   In which decade did Classic FM launch?

9   What name is given to a book in which accounts are kept?

10 In which decade was the Crimean War fought?

11 Meghan Markle guest-edited an edition of which magazine in September 2019?

12 In which 1982 film did Richard Gere play Zack Mayo?

13 Eddie Royle was the landlord of which TV pub from 1990 to 1991?

14 Which car company made the Carlton model?

15 What is eight squared?

16 Which group sang *You Should be Dancing* on the soundtrack of *Saturday Night Fever*?

17 On which continent is Syria?

18 What colour are the flowers of most evening primrose plants?

19 What was the title of Mungo Jerry's first UK no.1 single, released in 1970?

20 Proverbially, what is blood thicker than?

Easy

Medium

Hard

Answers to QUIZ 325 – Pot Luck

1	*Popstars: The Rivals*	11	*Twister* (1996)
2	Chair umpire	12	19th century (1881)
3	South America	13	Bachelor of Arts
4	1970s (1976)	14	*Boléro* (Ravel)
5	Hartlepool	15	Wash and cash
6	California (San Diego)	16	1960s (1968)
7	Minuscule	17	Yellow
8	Phillip Schofield and Holly Willoughby	18	A lion
9	Republic of Ireland	19	The National Trust
10	Hammock	20	Cultural

Easy

1 What number is obtained by adding the number 11 to the numbers either side of it on a dartboard?

2 If a game of tennis is at deuce, what is the total number of points scored?

3 What number is obtained by multiplying the points value of the yellow snooker ball by the points value of the green ball?

4 What is the maximum score with one ball in cricket multiplied by four?

5 In rugby union, what number is obtained by subtracting the points value of a try from the number of players in a team?

6 In Olympic swimming events, what number is obtained by adding the length of the pool in metres to the number of lanes?

7 What number is obtained by subtracting the number of goalkeepers on the pitch in a football match from the number in one team?

8 How many people play in a curling match?

9 In golf, what number is obtained by adding the number of holes on a championship course to the number of teams that contest the Ryder Cup?

10 How many hurdles are jumped in a 110m race?

11 What number is obtained by subtracting the points for a try in rugby league from the points for a try in rugby union?

12 How many points are five touchdowns worth in American football?

13 How many individual Olympic gold medals did Usain Bolt win?

Medium

14 In netball, what number is obtained by subtracting the number of positions on a team named as defence from the total number of people in a team?

15 How many guineas are there in total in the names of the five British classic horse races?

16 In football, what number is obtained by multiplying the number of teams in the Premier League by the number of teams usually relegated in a season?

17 In the 2010s, which Formula 1 team won the constructor's championship six years in a row?

18 What number is obtained by multiplying the number of rings on the Olympic flag by the number of different coloured medals awarded in the Games?

19 How many people are there in four field hockey teams?

20 In Olympic diving, how many metres high is the platform?

Hard

Answers to QUIZ 326 – Italian Landmarks

1 Rialto Bridge (Venice)

2 The Pantheon (Rome)

3 The Leaning Tower (Pisa)

4 The Ponte Vecchio (Florence)

5 Trevi Fountain (Rome)

6 The Doge's Palace (Venice)

7 Cathedral of Santa Maria del Fiore (Florence)

8 The Colosseum (Rome)

ANSWERS ON PAGE 331

1   Royal Birkdale Golf Club lies in which metropolitan county?

2   In the traditional bingo call, what number is "All the fives"?

3   Which of these Russell Crowe films was released first: *3:10 to Yuma*, *Cinderella Man* or *LA Confidential*?

4   What name describes the period from 1558 to 1603 in the UK?

5   Which two words that differ only by their first letters mean "dish" and "roof tile"?

6   In which country is the TV series *Blood* set?

7   What type of food is a pistachio?

8   If something is indigenous to a country, has it been imported or is it native to that country?

9   The band Nickelback was formed in which country?

10 Who succeeded Bill Clinton as US president?

11 Which chef joined Fred Sirieix and Gino D'Acampo on a road trip in an ITV series?

12 Is Robin Hood's Bay on the east, south or west coast of England?

13 Which of these is the correct spelling: inocculate, innocullate, or inoculate?

14 The film *The Wolverine* (2013) is set in which country?

15 Devon, Somerset, Wiltshire and which other county border Dorset?

16 According to the proverb, what gets the grease?

17 What type of animal is a hamster?

18 What poison completes the title of the 1944 black comedy film ___ *and Old Lace*?

19 In a table place setting, which item of cutlery is placed to the right?

20 The flowers of which fragrant plant are traditionally dried and placed in sachets to scent the home?

Easy
Medium
Hard

Answers to QUIZ 327 – Pot Luck

1	Cardiff City FC	11	*Vogue*
2	1990s (1993)	12	*An Officer and a Gentleman*
3	*Fille*	13	The Queen Vic (*EastEnders*)
4	Owen Wilson	14	Vauxhall
5	The *USS Enterprise* (*Star Trek*)	15	64
6	The face	16	The Bee Gees
7	Duncan Bannatyne	17	Asia
8	1990s (1992)	18	Yellow
9	Ledger	19	*In the Summertime*
10	1850s (1853-56)	20	Water

Easy

1 "It might seem crazy what I'm 'bout to say" is the opening lyric from which song?

2 Gavin Williamson became Secretary of State for which department in July 2019?

3 What was the title of William Golding's debut (and most famous) novel, published in 1954?

4 Who preceded William Hague (Baron Hague of Richmond) as UK Foreign Secretary?

5 Who was the runner-up in the 2019 Wimbledon ladies' singles championship?

6 In which century did William McKinley become US president?

7 The National Wallace Monument, commemorating William Wallace, overlooks which Scottish town?

8 Leith Hill Place in Surrey, now managed by the National Trust, was the childhood home of which English composer (d.1958)?

9 *Life thru a Lens* was the 1997 solo debut album of which singer?

10 Which character in the Just William books threatened to "thcream and thcream"?

11 William III was married to which English queen?

Medium

12 Which Scottish tourist destination lies at the north-eastern end of Loch Linnhe?

13 In which decade did Amy Williams win an Olympic gold medal in the skeleton?

14 Who starred in the 2006 film *Man of the Year*?

15 What nationality was the poet William Blake?

16 The MP William Wilberforce (d.1833) famously campaigned to abolish what?

17 What was the name of Maisie Williams' character in the TV series *Game of Thrones*?

18 Will.i.am has been a judge on which UK TV talent show since its first series in 2012?

19 Which character in *Pride and Prejudice* has the first name Fitzwilliam?

20 In which century did William the Conqueror invade Britain?

Hard

Answers to QUIZ 328 – Sporting Numbers

1	33 (8 and 14)	11	One (five – four)
2	80 (40 all)	12	30 points
3	Six (two x three)	13	Six
4	24	14	Five (seven – two)
5	Ten (15 – five)	15	3000 (1000 and 2000)
6	58 (50 + eight)	16	60 (20 x three)
7	Nine (11 – two)	17	Mercedes
8	Eight (two teams of four)	18	15 (five x three)
9	20 (18 + two)	19	44
10	Ten	20	10m

1. In which decade did Colin Cowdrey (Baron Cowdrey of Tonbridge) make his England Test cricket debut?

2. *Hooky Street* was the closing theme for which sitcom?

3. Which two words that differ only by their last letter mean "pig meat" and "small skin opening"?

4. Who played sisters Elinor and Marianne Dashwood in the 1995 film *Sense and Sensibility*?

5. BSA is a famous British brand of what type of transport?

6. Which of these cities is most easterly: Cardiff, Coventry or Gloucester?

7. Which team won Team of the Year at the BBC Sports Personality awards in 2019?

8. Which two words that differ only by their last letter mean "couch" and "gentle"?

9. How many hours ahead of GMT is Beijing?

10. What type of dog was Eddie in the TV series *Frasier*?

11. To the nearest 50 miles, how long is the coastline of Texas?

12. The song *Chim Chim Cher-ee* is from which musical?

13. The harp belongs to which section of an orchestra?

14. In what century did the Battle of the Boyne take place?

15. *Équinoxe* was a 1978 album by which musician?

16. Mario Balotelli plays football for which international team?

17. In the traditional bingo call, what number is "Goodbye Teens"?

18. What name is given in law to someone who assists with a crime?

19. What foodstuff are you said to have on your face, if you are made to look foolish?

20. Jamie Cullum presents a weekly jazz programme on which radio station?

Answers to QUIZ 329 – Pot Luck

1	Merseyside	11	Gordon Ramsay
2	55	12	East coast (North Yorkshire)
3	*LA Confidential* (1997)	13	Inoculate
4	Elizabethan	14	Japan
5	Plate and slate	15	Hampshire
6	Republic of Ireland	16	The squeaky wheel
7	A nut	17	A rodent
8	Native	18	Arsenic
9	Canada	19	The knife
10	George W Bush	20	Lavender

Easy

1 Which 1992 Quentin Tarantino film features a gang of diamond thieves?

2 Which item of jewellery is also a word for a boxing arena?

3 Which of these birthstones is associated with the month that is the earliest in the calendar year: diamond, opal or ruby?

4 The 1984 TV series *The Jewel in the Crown* was set in which country?

5 What item of jewellery may be made in a fish hook style?

6 Which gemstone takes its name from Turkey, from where it was originally imported into Europe?

7 The name of which lettuce sounds like a small precious stone?

8 Which children's author created the Emerald City?

9 What name is given to a "stone" in an item of jewellery that can change colour?

10 What name is given to a ring that contains a small seal, originally used to mark documents?

Medium

11 If a couple married in 2020, in what year would they celebrate their ruby wedding?

12 Which actress starred in the 2001 film *The Affair of the Necklace*?

13 Who played the sister of Jimmy Jewel's character in the 1968-73 sitcom *Nearest and Dearest*?

14 The Jewel Garden belongs to which *Gardeners' World* presenter?

15 London's Hatton Garden is particularly famous for its trade in which precious stone?

16 "I'll buy you a diamond ring, my friend" is a line from which 1964 song?

17 The Jewellery Quarter is an area of which English city?

18 In which building are the Crown Jewels kept?

19 The 1985 film *The Jewel of the Nile* was a sequel to which film?

20 Ruby Rose played Stella Carlin in which prison drama series, first broadcast in 2013?

Hard

1 What was the subtitle of the 2019 *Maleficent* film?

2 Which Welsh county is bordered by Carmarthenshire and Ceredigion?

3 Which of Enid Blyton's Famous Five is alphabetically last?

4 Who moved in with Monica in the first episode of *Friends*?

5 In which year was the band One Direction formed?

6 Which US actress made a cameo appearance in *Casualty* in 2020 as surgeon Zsa Zsa Harper-Jenkinson?

7 In the Mr Men books, what colour is Mr Sneeze?

8 What colour are the feathers on a robin's back?

9 Which county has Trowbridge as its county town?

10 Which of these Stanley Kubrick films was released first: *A Clockwork Orange*, *The Shining* or *Spartacus*?

11 David Campese (b.1962) played rugby union for which international team?

12 What does the letter "D" stand for on an automatic gearbox?

13 How many kings of England, prior to Elizabeth I, were called Charles?

14 What was the currency unit of Belgium before the euro?

15 In the national motto of France, *Liberté, égalité, fraternité*, what does *fraternité* mean?

16 On which farm does Shaun the Sheep live?

17 In the English version of Scrabble®, how many "G" tiles are there?

18 The River Stour flows through which two South of England counties?

19 What nationality is Formula 1 driver Carlos Sainz Jr?

20 In the New Testament, which of the four gospels is alphabetically last?

Easy

Medium

Hard

Answers to QUIZ 331 – Pot Luck

1	1950s (1954)	11	350 miles (367 miles)
2	*Only Fools and Horses*	12	*Mary Poppins*
3	Pork and pore	13	The strings
4	Dame Emma Thompson and Kate Winslet	14	17th century (1690)
5	Motorcycle	15	Jean-Michel Jarre
6	Coventry	16	Italy
7	England cricket team	17	19
8	Sofa and soft	18	An accessory
9	Seven hours	19	Egg
10	A Jack Russell	20	Radio 2

Easy

1. Which long-running US drama followed a Depression-era family living in the Virginia mountains?

2. What is the surname of the family in the TV series *Friday Night Dinner*?

3. In which 2013 film in the Die Hard series did John McClane team up with his son, Jack?

4. Which father and son appear in the TV series *Breaking Dad*?

5. What name is given in Scotland to a group of families with a common surname and ancestor?

6. Which cartoon family lives at 742 Evergreen Terrace?

7. In which TV series did Clive Swift play long-suffering husband Richard?

8. The Sylvanian Families™ toys were first sold in which decade?

9. What is the occupation of father and son Barry and Eddie Hearn?

10. What was the family name of the brothers who marketed the first domestic spa bath?

Medium

11. What relation are Lisa and Zack Loveday in *Hollyoaks*?

12. The word "avuncular" refers to what relative?

13. What relation to you is your grandmother's brother?

14. Which of the siblings in the TV series *Outnumbered* is the youngest?

15. Which 1977 novel by Alex Haley was subtitled *The Saga of an American Family*?

16. In *Only Fools and Horses*, which relative moved in with Del and Rodney following the death of Grandad?

17. Which family group starred in the 1930 film *Animal Crackers*?

18. Which character, son of David, did Alice marry in *The Vicar of Dibley*?

19. In the TV series *The Royle Family*, what relation was Jim to Antony?

20. What is the name of Ron Weasley's mother in the Harry Potter books and films?

Hard

1   AR is the abbreviation for which US state?

2   Filbert Fox is the mascot of which Premier League football team?

3   Jeff Buckley (d.1997) was particularly associated with which instrument?

4   Which singer had a 1991 hit with *All the Man That I Need*?

5   What is the official language of Brazil?

6   *The Liberty Bell* march was associated with which TV comedy series, first broadcast in 1969?

7   Who was leader of the Soviet Union earliest: Andropov, Brezhnev or Chernenko?

8   The 1978 film *The Deer Hunter* was set during which conflict?

9   The letter N is in which position in the alphabet?

10 From which Australian city did Adam Hills present *The Last Leg: Locked Down Under*?

11 What is 82 in Roman numerals?

12 Brian Lara played cricket for which English county side from 1994 to 1998?

13 What eight-letter word is given to solid matter that settles at the bottom of a liquid?

14 "Electric" is a bright shade of which colour?

15 How many hours ahead of GMT is Ankara?

16 S is the postcode area code for which English city?

17 What name is given to a male goat?

18 The 2006-07 TV series *Life on Mars* was set in which decade?

19 Senegal has a coastline on which body of water?

20 In what century was the Spanish Inquisition finally abolished?

Easy

Medium

Hard

Answers to QUIZ 333 – Pot Luck

1	*Mistress of Evil*	11	Australia
2	Pembrokeshire	12	Drive
3	Timmy (the dog)	13	None
4	Rachel	14	Belgian franc
5	2010	15	Brotherhood
6	Sharon Gless	16	Mossy Bottom Farm
7	Blue	17	Three
8	Brown	18	Dorset and Wiltshire
9	Wiltshire	19	Spanish
10	*Spartacus* (1960)	20	Matthew

1   What characteristic does someone described as "tenacious" display?

2   Is Tennessee in the east or the west of the USA?

3   What two colours of tennis ball are approved for use by the International Tennis Federation?

4   The island of Tenerife lies in which body of water?

5   What is three tenths expressed as a decimal?

6   Which voice range is immediately below tenor?

7   Who hosts the TV quiz show *Tenable*?

8   Do tench live in fresh water or salt water?

9   David Tennant played John Knox in which historical film released in 2018?

10 In which decade was the ten pence piece introduced to the UK?

11 Who starred as composer George Webber in the 1979 film *10*?

12 What line follows "She's a perfect ten" in the song *Perfect Ten* by the Beautiful South?

13 Who moved out of 10 Downing Street in July 2019?

14 In which year was the Windows® 10 operating system released?

15 Which girl group released the album *10* in 2012, marking the tenth anniversary of the group being formed?

16 Which is the tenth month of the year?

17 Who played Moses in the 1956 film *The Ten Commandments*?

18 In woodwork, what is a tenon?

19 The 1934 novel *Tender is the Night* was written by which US author?

20 Which Hollywood actor (b.1969) is half of the comedy rock duo Tenacious D?

Answers to QUIZ 334 – Families

1	*The Waltons*	11	Sister and brother
2	Goodman	12	Uncle
3	*A Good Day to Die Hard*	13	Great uncle
4	Bradley and Barney Walsh	14	Karen
5	Clan	15	*Roots*
6	The Simpsons	16	Uncle Albert
7	*Keeping Up Appearances*	17	The Marx Brothers
8	1980s (1985)	18	Hugo (Horton)
9	Sports promotion	19	Father
10	Jacuzzi	20	Molly

1 What type of transport have you just exited if you need to pull a ripcord?

2 Which actor played arms dealer Owen Davian in *Mission: Impossible III*?

3 What type of creature is the puppet Soo, a friend of Sooty and Sweep?

4 Limoges porcelain is made in which country?

5 Which *Minder* character was always looking for a "nice little earner"?

6 In which century was the firearms company Smith & Wesson® formed?

7 The Lloyd's Register lists what type of transport?

8 Australia, South Africa and which other country originally took part in the Tri Nations rugby league competition?

9 The settler Captain John Smith (d.1631) was portrayed in which 1995 animated Disney film?

10 Who is the father of Alfie and Lilly Allen?

11 Bonn was the capital of which former republic?

12 Alberto Tomba (b.1966) is a former Olympic champion in which winter sport?

13 Which company that originally sold posters and prints shares its name with the Greek goddess of wisdom?

14 Shropshire, Worcestershire and which other English county border Herefordshire?

15 Which word, the name of an Audi car model, indicates that it is four-wheel drive?

16 In which decade was the novel *The Lovely Bones* published?

17 The Alto Douro region of Portugal is famous for producing what drink?

18 Dennis Haysbert played President David Palmer in which US TV series?

19 Which two words that differ only by their last letter mean "chair" and "scorch"?

20 Which Oasis single was released first: *Go Let It Out*, *Supersonic* or *Wonderwall*?

Answers to QUIZ 335 – Pot Luck

1	Arkansas	11	LXXXII
2	Leicester City FC	12	Warwickshire
3	Guitar	13	Sediment
4	Whitney Houston	14	Blue
5	Portuguese	15	Three hours
6	*Monty Python's Flying Circus*	16	Sheffield
7	Brezhnev (1964)	17	Billy
8	The Vietnam War	18	1970s
9	14th	19	The Atlantic Ocean
10	Melbourne	20	19th century (1834)

Easy

1 The knight Bedivere appears in stories about which legendary figure?

2 Gerda is the main character in which tale by Hans Christian Andersen?

3 What type of creature is Jiminy in the story of Pinocchio?

4 The name of which Chinese technology company is taken from the name of a character from Middle-Eastern folk tales?

5 Leprechauns are part of the folklore of which island?

6 How many Billy Goats Gruff are there in the Norwegian folk tale?

7 The siren known as Lorelei was associated with which European river?

8 The yeti is associated with which range of mountains?

9 In the fairy-tale of Hansel and Gretel, what is their father's occupation?

10 Traditionally, what colour is a unicorn?

11 The name of which creature in Scandinavian mythology is also a verb meaning "to move in an unhurried way"?

12 The phrase "the Midas touch", referring to someone who is financially successful, originates from a character in mythology who turned everything he touched into what metal?

13 Which legendary outlaw had a band of "Merry Men"?

14 The "huffing and puffing" Big Bad Wolf appears in which folk tale?

15 In a song from the film *Hans Christian Andersen*, which creature "went with a quack and a waddle and a quack"?

16 Which ancient Greek philosopher was the first to write about the legend of Atlantis?

17 The creature known as a selkie appears in the folklore of which country?

18 Which legendary sea monster is controlled by Davy Jones in the Pirates of the Caribbean series of films?

19 The line "The tower, the tower! Rapunzel, Rapunzel!" appears in which 1980 spoof disaster film?

20 The logo of which luxury car company is also the weapon of the god of the sea in Roman and Greek mythology?

Answers to QUIZ 336 – Ten

1	Determination or persistence	11	Dudley Moore
2	The east	12	"But she wears a 12"
3	White and yellow	13	Theresa May
4	The Atlantic Ocean	14	2015
5	0.3	15	Girls Aloud
6	Baritone	16	October
7	Warwick Davis	17	Charlton Heston
8	Fresh water	18	A joint (that fixes into a mortise)
9	*Mary Queen of Scots*	19	F Scott Fitzgerald
10	1960s (1968)	20	Jack Black

ANSWERS ON PAGE 341

1   Skipjack is a type of which fish?

2   Susanna Reid came runner-up to which fellow competitor on *Strictly Come Dancing*?

3   Which of the Spice Girls was nicknamed "Baby Spice"?

4   How many laps of an athletics track are completed in an 800m race?

5   The name of what drink follows the word "small" to indicate that something is not important?

6   *Paranoid Android* was a 1997 single by which English rock band?

7   The city of Nizhny Novgorod hosted FIFA World Cup matches in which year?

8   What was the first name of Felicity Huffman's character in *Desperate Housewives*?

9   In 2004, which newspaper became the first UK paper to publish Sudoku puzzles?

10 In the nursery rhyme *Sing a Song of Sixpence*, what did the blackbird remove from the maid?

11 Montgomery is the capital of which US state?

12 Which Asian country had the world's second-largest economy in 2019?

13 Breeds of which type of dog are associated with King Charles II?

14 Which actor played Raoul Duke in the 1998 film *Fear and Loathing In Las Vegas*?

15 The card game canasta was invented on which continent?

16 Which of these major conflicts began earliest: the Korean War, the Spanish Civil War or WWII?

17 In 1981, which West Midlands football team became the first English team to have an all-seater stadium?

18 What are you said to have drawn, if you are selected for a task you will not enjoy doing?

19 The characters Kirsty Tate and Rachel Walker appear in which series of children's books?

20 What colour is Yoda in the Star Wars films?

Easy

Medium

Hard

Answers to QUIZ 337 – Pot Luck

1	An aeroplane (a ripcord is part of a parachute)	11	West Germany
2	Philip Seymour Hoffman	12	Skiing (slalom)
3	A panda	13	Athena
4	France	14	Gloucestershire
5	Arthur Daley	15	Quattro
6	19th century (1856)	16	2000s (2002)
7	Ships	17	Wine
8	New Zealand	18	24
9	*Pocahontas*	19	Seat and sear
10	Keith Allen	20	*Supersonic* (1994)

What are the names of these castles found in the United Kingdom?

Easy

1

2

3

4

Medium

5

6

7

8

Hard

Answers to QUIZ 338 – Legends and Tales

1	King Arthur	11	Troll
2	The Snow Queen	12	Gold
3	A cricket	13	Robin Hood
4	Alibaba	14	*The Three Little Pigs*
5	Ireland	15	The Ugly Duckling
6	Three	16	Plato
7	The Rhine	17	Scotland
8	The Himalayas	18	The Kraken
9	Woodcutter	19	*Airplane!*
10	White	20	Maserati (trident)

1 In which city was the TV series *Dixon of Dock Green* set?

2 The two-word name of which US state capital is French for "red stick"?

3 Which rapper plays Tej Parker in the Fast and Furious series of films?

4 In the New Testament, who freed the prisoner Barabbas?

5 Which of the *Outnumbered* siblings is the oldest?

6 Which US car company makes the Corvette?

7 "We're a thousand miles apart but you know I love you" is a lyric from which Take That song?

8 Which Estée Lauder men's fragrance, introduced in 1964, shares its name with one of the Three Musketeers?

9 Rickenbacker is a maker of which instruments?

10 In relation to human biology, what are A, B and rhesus?

11 *Love Me Like You Do* was a 2015 single by which singer?

12 Which African country has three designated capital cities?

13 Who provided the voice of Buzz Lightyear in the Toy Story films?

14 Which sport is played by the Castleford Tigers?

15 What name is given to a roof that is shaped like a dome?

16 What does a stevedore do?

17 The Rijksmuseum is situated in which European capital city?

18 What is the decimal equivalent of the binary number 10?

19 Which metal can precede orange, red and yellow in the name of artists' pigments?

20 The Winter Olympics host cities Sapporo (1972) and Nagano (1998) are in which country?

Easy

Medium

Hard

Answers to QUIZ 339 – Pot Luck

1	Tuna	11	Alabama
2	Abbey Clancy	12	China
3	Emma Bunton	13	Spaniel
4	Two	14	Johnny Depp
5	Beer	15	South America (Uruguay)
6	Radiohead	16	Spanish Civil War (1936)
7	2018	17	Coventry City FC
8	Lynette (Scavo)	18	The short straw
9	*The Times*	19	Rainbow Magic
10	Her nose	20	Green

Easy

1   In which decade was the consumer affairs programme *Watchdog* first broadcast?

2   The city of Wakefield is in which English county?

3   What colour is the name on a Waitrose store?

4   Which Irish singer had a 1964 hit with *Walk Tall*?

5   In which 1983 film does Matthew Broderick's character hack into a government computer to play *Global Thermonuclear War*?

6   Water ice is another name for which dessert?

7   Waterloo Station lies in which London borough?

8   The song *The Happy Wanderer* was originally written in which language?

9   Which chemical element has the symbol W, taken from its old name of wolfram?

10 In which decade was Wikipedia® launched?

11 What is indicated by the waving of a white flag?

12 What was the name of Jodie Whittaker's character in the TV series *Broadchurch*?

13 Which Australian actress starred in the TV series *Wanderlust*?

14 What is winceyette?

Medium

15 From which city was the Wife in Chaucer's *The Canterbury Tales*?

16 *Woman in Love* was a 1980 hit single for which US singer?

17 Wisconsin lies to the east of Minnesota and which other US state?

18 Where on the body would you find a widow's peak?

19 The town of Weymouth has a coastline on which body of water?

20 Which wild creature features in the title of an 1884 play by Henrik Ibsen?

Hard

Answers to QUIZ 340 – Castles

1   Edinburgh Castle
2   Tintagel Castle
3   Windsor Castle
4   Stirling Castle
5   Conwy Castle
6   Balmoral Castle
7   Belfast Castle
8   Caernarfon Castle

ANSWERS ON PAGE 345

1   What colour flag would a Formula 1 driver who has been disqualified be shown?

2   Rafael Nadal was born in which decade?

3   Which Fawlty Towers character was noted for saying "I know nothing"?

4   Which US president was the subject of a 2012 Oscar-winning film?

5   Is Llandudno in North Wales, South Wales or West Wales?

6   Which former *The X Factor* contestant won *Celebrity Big Brother* in 2013?

7   Nicky Byrne is a member of which group?

8   Which two words that sound the same but are spelt differently mean "an opening" and "complete"?

9   Which 1946 festive film starring James Stewart was based on the short story *The Greatest Gift* by Philip Van Doren Stern?

10 Hannibal Smith was a character in which 1980s action-adventure TV series?

11 Books by which US author topped the list of those borrowed from UK libraries in 2018-19?

12 Which English king was nicknamed "the Hammer of the Scots"?

13 What two-word term is given to a thief who enters houses by climbing the walls?

14 The airport that serves the European city of Basel is operated by which two countries?

15 Which of the Wombles was named after a Russian city?

16 Augustus Gloop is a character in which children's book?

17 Which singer topped the charts in the UK in 2012 with *This is Love*, featuring Eva Simons and *Scream and Shout*, featuring Britney Spears?

18 In the nursery rhyme *Oranges and Lemons*, where is the Great Bell?

19 Which boxer has the nickname "Pac-Man"?

20 Which chef married Lisa Faulkner in 2019?

Answers to QUIZ 341 – Pot Luck

1	London	11	Ellie Goulding
2	Baton Rouge (Louisiana)	12	South Africa (Bloemfontein, Cape Town and Pretoria)
3	Ludacris	13	Tim Allen
4	Pontius Pilate	14	Rugby league
5	Jake	15	Cupola
6	Chevrolet	16	Load and unload ships
7	*Everything Changes*	17	Amsterdam
8	*Aramis*	18	Two
9	Electric guitars	19	Cadmium
10	Blood groups	20	Japan

Easy

1. What departed from Waterloo Station for the first time on November 14, 1994?
2. The Human Genome Project, launched in 1990, was set up to analyse what substance?
3. Who played the daughter of Cher's character in the 1990 film *Mermaids*?
4. In which year did the UK hand over sovereignty of Hong Kong to China?
5. What was the name of the bright comet that was visible from the Earth in 1997?
6. The Baseball Ground was the home ground of which football team until 1997?
7. Seal won the 1995 Grammy for Record of the Year for which song?
8. Which country was the beaten finalist in the 1998 FIFA World Cup?
9. Which TV series starring Robbie Coltrane, first aired in the 1990s, was created by Jimmy McGovern?
10. What was the title of the first James Bond film of the 1990s?
11. In 1996, which boxer won the first BBC Sports Personality of the Year Lifetime Achievement Award?
12. *Fairground* was the only UK no.1 single of the 1990s for which band?
13. Who played Molly Jensen in the film *Ghost*?

Medium

14. Which conflict, that began in August 1990, was codenamed Operation Desert Shield?
15. Christy Turlington and Linda Evangelista were amongst the so-called "Big Five" in which profession?
16. In 1995, which former US actor was found not guilty of murder but subsequently held liable in a civil case?
17. What was the highest-grossing film of the 1990s?
18. Which twin skyscrapers became the tallest building in the world when they opened in Malaysia in 1998?
19. Who was released on February 11, 1990 after spending 27 years in prison?
20. Who captained the England rugby union team to three Grand Slams, in 1991, 1992 and 1995?

Hard

Answers to QUIZ 342 – W

1	1980s (1985)	11	Surrender
2	West Yorkshire	12	Beth Latimer
3	Green	13	Toni Collette
4	Val Doonican	14	(Cotton) fabric
5	*Wargames*	15	Bath
6	Sorbet	16	Barbra Streisand
7	Lambeth	17	Iowa
8	German	18	On the head (hairline)
9	Tungsten	19	The English Channel
10	2000s (2001)	20	Duck (*The Wild Duck*)

ANSWERS ON PAGE **347**

1   What is the name of the Northampton rugby union team?

2   In which country was the 2020 series of *First Dates Hotel* filmed?

3   Chinchillas are native to which continent?

4   Which two words that differ only by their first letter mean "look after" and "tie"?

5   The US state of Alabama has a short coastline on which body of water?

6   Which actress played Harrison Ford's wife in the 2000 film *What Lies Beneath*?

7   Who beat John Parrott by a record 18 games to three in the final of the 1989 World Snooker Championship?

8   In an employment context, for what do the letters HR stand?

9   What bacterium is named after the scientist Joseph Lister?

10   In which year did WWI begin?

11   Which football team won the 2019-20 Premier League title?

12   Kandahar is the second-largest city in which country?

13   Which celebrity game show shares its name with the title of a 1985 Eurythmics hit?

14   Who wrote the 1986 TV series *The Singing Detective*?

15   In mathematics, what shape is a hyperbola?

16   What is a flibbertigibbet?

17   At what three levels of par are the holes on a championship golf course?

18   The programme *Music Matters* is broadcast on which radio station?

19   Tourmaline and which other stone are the birthstones for October?

20   How many decades are there in 90 years?

Easy

Medium

Hard

Answers to QUIZ 343 – Pot Luck

1	Black	11	James Patterson
2	1980s (1986)	12	Edward I
3	Manuel	13	Cat burglar
4	Abraham Lincoln (*Lincoln*)	14	France and Switzerland
5	North Wales	15	Tomsk
6	Rylan Clark-Neal	16	*Charlie and the Chocolate Factory* (Roald Dahl)
7	Westlife	17	Will.i.am
8	Hole and whole	18	Bow
9	*It's a Wonderful Life*	19	Manny Pacquiao
10	*The A-Team*	20	John Torode

QUIZ 346 – Abbreviations

1 "Cm" is the abbreviation for what unit of length?

2 To what is the word pianissimo abbreviated on a piece of music?

3 In the name of the Met Office, for what is "Met" short?

4 For what is "Sr" an abbreviation, if it follows someone's name?

5 "Oxon" is the abbrevation for which county?

6 The French abbreviation *Mlle* is short for which form of address?

7 "Bart" is an abbreviation for which member of the peerage?

8 By what abbreviation is the former National Biscuit Company now known?

9 What two words are usually abbreviated to "mod cons"?

10 Adm is an abbreviation for which navy rank?

11 DE is the abbreviation for which US state?

12 The term "guv" is short for what word?

13 To what four letters is "abbreviated" usually abbreviated?

14 In relation to a financial statement, what does the abbreviation "dr" mean?

15 "V" is an abbreviation for which word meaning "against"?

16 For what is "c/o" an abbreviation on an address?

17 To what is the Latin phrase *et cetera*, meaning "and so on" abbreviated?

18 "Tbs" is the abbreviation for which measurement used in cookery?

19 What does the word "no" indicate when used as an abbreviation?

20 For what is the US company suffix "Inc" short?

1. Which Irish jockey was flat racing Champion Jockey 11 times between 1974 and 1996?

2. What nut is used to flavour the liqueur Disaronno®?

3. Which two words that differ only by their last letter mean "hygienic" and "tidy away"?

4. Which constellation is named after a winged horse in Greek mythology?

5. In the TV series *Dallas*, which character returned after his death was explained away by occurring in a dream?

6. On which "Sea" did the *Apollo 11* lunar module land?

7. Which singer is backed by The Machine?

8. What is the more usual name for a continental quilt?

9. The School Certificate was abolished in the UK in 1950 after the introduction of what exam?

10. "Maybe I'm foolish, maybe I'm blind" are lyrics from which 2016 song?

11. What name is given to a hot spring that discharges boiling water and steam at intervals?

12. The line "It's just a flesh wound" is from which Monty Python film?

13. Which two English counties lie next to the Scottish Borders?

14. Liam Brady (b.1956) played international football for which team?

15. The Lady of the Lake is associated with which legendary character?

16. What is four cubed?

17. What type of number is expressed as a numerator over a denominator?

18. How many points is the letter "T" worth in a game of Scrabble®?

19. In the Terminator series of films, Kyle Reese is the father of which character?

20. In which decade did Eva Perón die?

Answers to QUIZ 345 – Pot Luck

1	Northampton Saints	11	Liverpool FC
2	Italy	12	Afghanistan
3	South America	13	*Would I Lie to You?*
4	Mind and bind	14	Dennis Potter
5	The Gulf of Mexico	15	A curve
6	Michelle Pfeiffer	16	An irresponsible person
7	Steve Davis	17	Three, four and five
8	Human resources	18	Radio 3
9	Listeria	19	Opal
10	1914	20	Nine

Easy

1. In which decade did Gabrielle have a UK no.1 single with *Rise*?

2. What word completes the title of the novel by Evelyn Waugh, ___ *and Fall*?

3. Is Kensal Rise in North London or South London?

4. What word for ripened fruit blown from a tree can also refer to an unexpected financial gain?

5. Who provided the voice of Jack Frost in the 2012 film *Rise of the Guardians*?

6. "You're hiding from me now. There's something in the way that you're talking" is a lyric from which 1991 song?

7. What was the surname of Frances de la Tour's character in the TV series *Rising Damp*?

8. What are you said to fall flat on, if you make an embarrassing mistake?

9. The Order of the Rising Sun is presented for distinguished achievements in which country?

10. Lucy Fallon played which character in Coronation Street from 2015 until 2020?

11. In which decade was the film *Rise of the Planet of the Apes* released?

Medium

12. Who played serial killer Paul Spector in the TV series *The Fall*?

13. Which company made the 1970s powdered orange juice drink Rise & Shine?

14. Which of these Brad Pitt films was released first: *Legends of the Fall*, *Ocean's Eleven* or *Mr and Mrs Smith*?

15. Which post-punk group released the 1986 single *Rise*?

16. What part of your body is affected if you suffer from fallen arches?

17. The greeting "He is risen" is used in the Christian church during which festival?

18. Who starred as stunt man Colt Seavers in the 1980s TV series *The Fall Guy*?

19. Who directed the film *Star Wars: The Rise of Skywalker*?

20. Proverbially, which of the seven deadly sins comes before a fall?

Hard

Answers to QUIZ 346 – Abbreviations

1	Centimetre	11	Delaware
2	pp	12	Governor
3	Meteorological	13	Abbr
4	Senior	14	Debit
5	Oxfordshire	15	Versus
6	Mademoiselle	16	Care of
7	Baronet	17	Etc
8	Nabisco®	18	Tablespoonful
9	Modern conveniences	19	Number
10	Admiral	20	Incorporated

1   In which century did Sir Francis Drake circumnavigate the globe?

2   How are leafy vegetables served if they are referred to as "chiffonade"?

3   What is eight multiplied by nine?

4   Who played Lady Jane Felsham in the TV series *Lovejoy*?

5   Which of these actors was born first: Charles Bronson, James Coburn or Yul Brynner?

6   County Durham, Tyne and Wear and which other English county border Northumberland?

7   Which actor played Gale Hawthorne in The Hunger Games series of films?

8   In which decade were identity cards abolished in the UK?

9   What type of creature is a pied flycatcher?

10   *New Moon on Monday* was a 1984 single by which band?

11   In the card game Happy Families, what is Mr Bones' occupation?

12   In the DC comics, in which city is *The Daily Planet* newspaper based?

13   The island of Guadeloupe lies in which body of water?

14   Trinity House is the official authority for what type of coastal building?

15   Which Cluedo® character shares a name with a condiment?

16   What word can mean both "a series of musical notes" and "size"?

17   What type of drink is sold under the Bulmers™ brand?

18   Kevin Ashman is a regular team member on which quiz show?

19   Which comedian said "Garlic bread, it's the future, I've tasted it"?

20   Who recorded the 1977 hit *Lovely Day*?

Answers to QUIZ 347 – Pot Luck

1	Pat Eddery	11	Geyser
2	Almond	12	*Monty Python and the Holy Grail*
3	Clean and clear	13	Cumbria and Northumberland
4	Pegasus	14	Republic of Ireland
5	Bobby Ewing	15	King Arthur
6	Sea of Tranquillity	16	64
7	Florence (Welch)	17	A fraction
8	Duvet	18	One point
9	GCE O Level	19	John Connor
10	*Human* (Rag'n'Bone Man)	20	1950s (1952)

Easy

Medium

Hard

Easy

1. How many London Underground lines are there?
2. In which London museum can the Roman vase known as the Portland Vase be seen?
3. Is Notting Hill in East London, North London or West London?
4. The Tower 42 building was originally named after which bank?
5. In which century was the post of Lord Mayor of London founded?
6. Which historical ship, on display in London, was damaged by fire in 2007 and again in 2014?
7. Stanmore and Stratford are termini on which Underground line?
8. Somerset House is situated on which major London thoroughfare?
9. *The Lambeth Walk* is a song from which 1937 musical, set in London?
10. Which London airport has the code LCY?
11. The first Selfridges store opened on which street in 1908?
12. What colour is the tarmac on The Mall?

Medium

13. Which is the only London bridge that can be raised?
14. The Landmark Hotel was originally built to service which main line railway station?
15. The Royal Marsden Hospital in London specialises in treating which disease?
16. Which is the only London borough that has a name beginning with "I"?
17. Which entertainment venue is nicknamed "the Tent"?
18. What type of creature was London Zoo's famous resident Chi Chi?
19. In which decade was The Shard completed?
20. The Albert Memorial is situated in which Royal Park?

Hard

ANSWERS ON PAGE 353

Easy

1   In 2010, which Northern Irish golfer became the first European to win the US Open tournament in 40 years?

2   The town of Keighley is in which English county?

3   Which two words that differ only by their first letter mean "a type of cushion" and "cricket bat wood"?

4   Who played villain Max Zorin in the 1985 film *A View to a Kill*?

5   Is the Algarve in the north or the south of Portugal?

6   Who created the TV series *Last Tango in Halifax*?

7   On the flag of the USA, how many points does each star have?

8   For what do the letters "IP" stand in the phrase "IP address"?

9   What name is given to the occupation of someone who maintains and repairs chimneys?

10 Leinster rugby club is based in which city?

11 In which decade did ring pulls first appear on drinks cans?

12 In what century was the pirate Edward Teach, nicknamed Blackbeard, born?

13 Vatersay is the most southerly island in which Scottish island chain?

14 Is an angle of 38 degrees an acute angle or an obtuse angle?

15 In physics, what is obtained by dividing mass by density?

16 Which Israeli-born chef wrote the 2010 cookbook *Plenty*?

17 Which two-word Latin term is used to refer to the existing state of affairs?

18 In the nursery rhyme, what did Old King Cole call for, before his bowl?

19 "My love has taken a tumble" is a lyric from which song?

20 Sophie Hinchcliffe, known as "Mrs Hinch", is famous for carrying out what activity?

Medium

Hard

Answers to QUIZ 349 – Pot Luck

1	16th century (1577-80)	11	Butcher
2	Thinly sliced	12	Metropolis
3	72	13	The Caribbean Sea
4	Phyllis Logan	14	Lighthouse
5	Yul Brynner (1920)	15	Colonel Mustard
6	Cumbria	16	Scale
7	Liam Hemsworth	17	Cider
8	1950s (1952)	18	*Eggheads*
9	A bird	19	Peter Kay
10	Duran Duran	20	Bill Withers

1   What is the subtitle of the fourth novel in the Harry Potter series?

2   Who played the Green Fairy in the film *Moulin Rouge!*?

3   Who played the mysterious Daryl Van Horne in the 1987 film *The Witches of Eastwick*?

4   In The Lord of the Rings series directed by Peter Jackson, what was the name of Andy Serkis' character?

5   Who played the sister of Sandra Bullock's character in the 1998 film *Practical Magic*?

6   In which 2019 film sequel do the main characters journey to the Enchanted Forest?

7   Which 2014 musical film starred James Corden and Emily Blunt as a baker and his wife seeking to remove a curse?

8   The fairies Fauna, Flora and Merryweather featured in which 1959 Disney film?

9   Who played the evil Queen Narissa in the 2007 film *Enchanted*?

10 Which 1988 film starring Warwick Davis shares its name with a tree?

11 The 2012 film *Mirror Mirror* was based on which fairy-tale?

12 In the 1964 film *Mary Poppins*, what was unusual about the parrot's head on the end of her umbrella?

13 Who plays Newt Scamander in the Fantastic Beasts films?

14 In 2008, what was the title of the second film to be released in the Chronicles of Narnia series?

15 In the 1985 film *Ladyhawke*, who played the title character?

16 Mickey Mouse featured as The Sorcerer's Apprentice in which Disney film?

17 Who played the title character in the 2004 film *Ella Enchanted*?

18 In which 1988 film is Josh Baskin transformed by a fairground fortune-telling machine?

19 Which former *Downton Abbey* actor played the Beast in the 2017 live action film *Beauty and the Beast*?

20 Who played the star in the 2007 film *Stardust*?

Answers to QUIZ 350 – London

1	11	11	Oxford Street
2	British Museum	12	Red
3	West London	13	Tower Bridge
4	NatWest (NatWest Tower)	14	Marylebone (as the Hotel Great Central)
5	12th century (1189)	15	Cancer
6	The *Cutty Sark*	16	Islington
7	The Jubilee Line	17	The O2
8	The Strand	18	A giant panda
9	*Me and My Girl*	19	2010s (2012)
10	London City Airport	20	Kensington Gardens

1 Which major sporting tournament takes place at Flushing Meadow?

2 Published from 1992 to 1997, which series of children's books was written by RL Stine?

3 In which Berkshire town is the London Irish rugby union team based?

4 What name is given to a song for a leading singer in an opera?

5 Gordon Taylor (b.1944) became Chief Executive of which sporting body in 1981?

6 What relation is Bridget Fonda to Jane Fonda?

7 In which ocean did the Battle of Trafalgar take place?

8 What is 60% of 80?

9 The historical location of Runnymede is four miles south-east of which royal residence?

10 Which car company manufactures the Insight hybrid?

11 Albert Bridge connects Battersea with which area of south-west London?

12 Which phrase relating to fireworks means taking an action that will cause an angry or excited reaction?

13 In which county is the town of Chorley?

14 Is a sycamore tree deciduous or evergreen?

15 Which of the stars of the 1969 film *Easy Rider* also directed it?

16 Which girl group had a hit in 2003 with *Scandalous*?

17 Which of these events occurred earliest: the Battle of Hastings, the completion of the Bayeux Tapestry or the commissioning of the Domesday Book?

18 Who played Sergeant Wilson in the TV series *Dad's Army*?

19 Moët & Chandon champagne is produced in which country?

20 What type of animal is a Russian Blue?

Answers to QUIZ 351 – Pot Luck

1	Graeme McDowell	11	1960s (1962)
2	West Yorkshire	12	17th century (1680)
3	Pillow and willow	13	The Outer Hebrides
4	Christopher Walken	14	An acute angle
5	The south	15	Volume
6	Sally Wainwright	16	Yotam Ottolenghi
7	Five	17	*Status quo*
8	Internet Protocol	18	His pipe
9	Steeplejack	19	*Sweet Little Mystery* (Wet Wet Wet)
10	Dublin	20	(House) cleaning

What are the names of these items of arts and crafts equipment?

1

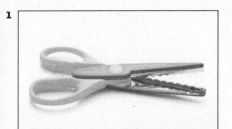

2

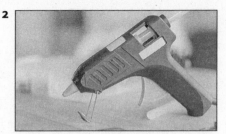

3

4

5

6

7

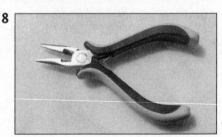

8

Answers to QUIZ 352 – Magical Films

1	*The Goblet of Fire*	11	Snow White
2	Kylie Minogue	12	It talked
3	Jack Nicholson	13	Eddie Redmayne
4	Gollum	14	*Prince Caspian*
5	Nicole Kidman	15	Michelle Pfeiffer
6	*Frozen II*	16	*Fantasia*
7	*Into the Woods*	17	Anne Hathaway
8	*Sleeping Beauty*	18	*Big*
9	Susan Sarandon	19	Dan Stevens
10	Willow	20	Claire Danes

1   Which former politician took part in the 2020 UK series of *The Masked Singer*?

2   The pulmonary arteries link the heart with which organs of the body?

3   Which of these was made a city most recently: Bristol, Chester or Preston?

4   Princess Beatrice (b.1857) was the youngest child of which monarch?

5   What is the name of the Reverend in *The Simpsons*?

6   How many of Enid Blyton's Secret Seven were girls?

7   Sporting teams from which country are often nicknamed "Les Bleus"?

8   The A38 and which other road are the only two main roads in Cornwall?

9   To which Hollywood actor was Ali MacGraw married from 1973 to 1978?

10 Who plays Dr Lydia Fonseca in the TV series *The Good Karma Hospital*?

11 Which planet in the solar system is named after the Roman god of agriculture?

12 What type of vehicles take part in the Isle of Man TT races?

13 The lions Stamford and Bridget are mascots for which Premier League football team?

14 On a standard keyboard, which letter is between V and N?

15 Which two words that differ only by their first letter mean "crush" and "waist band"?

16 Accessorize is a companion store to which clothing outlet?

17 Which rock singer played Bob Paulson in the 1999 film *Fight Club*?

18 Which US president (d.1972) said: "Wherever you have an efficient government you have a dictatorship"?

19 The Khmer Rouge seized power in which country in 1975?

20 The name of which country completes the saying "for all the tea in ___"?

Easy

Medium

Hard

Answers to QUIZ 353 – Pot Luck

1	The US Open tennis tournament	11	Chelsea
2	Goosebumps	12	Light the (blue) touchpaper
3	Reading	13	Lancashire
4	Aria	14	Deciduous
5	The PFA (Professional Footballers' Association)	15	Dennis Hopper
6	Niece	16	Mis-Teeq
7	The Atlantic Ocean	17	The Battle of Hastings (1066)
8	48	18	John Le Mesurier
9	Windsor Castle	19	France
10	Honda	20	A cat

Easy

1   The character of Norman Fletcher first appeared in which series?

2   Su Pollard played which role in *Hi-de-Hi!*?

3   In which city was *The Likely Lads* set?

4   *To The Manor Born* was first broadcast in which decade?

5   Who played Rebecca Howe in *Cheers*?

6   Vincent and Penny were the leading characters in which 1980s sitcom?

7   With which show would you associate Betty, Frank and Jessica?

8   What was the first name of the frantic hotel owner in *Fawlty Towers*?

9   "You stupid boy" is a phrase associated with which sitcom?

10   Which 1989-98 show was remade in 2014 by ITV?

11   *The Royle Family* was first shown on TV in which decade?

12   What was the name of Wolfie's girlfriend in the TV series *Citizen Smith*?

13   The 1980s sitcom *Duty Free* was set in which country?

14   What name did Trigger call Rodney in *Only Fools and Horses*?

Medium

15   In which decade did *Yes Minister* first air on British TV?

16   In the TV series *Last of the Summer Wine*, how was the character of William Simmonite better known?

17   Which character in *Friends* worked within the fashion industry?

18   The village of Nouvion was the setting for which sitcom?

19   The title characters of which sitcom were played by Wilfred Brambell and Harry H Corbett?

20   Corporal, later Sergeant, Klinger appeared in which series first shown in 1972?

Hard

Answers to QUIZ 354 – Arts and Crafts Equipment

1   Pinking shears

2   Glue gun

3   (Beading) loom

4   Stencil

5   Crochet hooks

6   Knitting needles

7   Embroidery hoop

8   (Jewellery) pliers

QUIZ 357 – Pot Luck

ANSWERS ON PAGE 359

1 Who wrote the 19th-century collection of poems *Idylls of the King*?

2 The word "omnishambles" was first used in which TV comedy series?

3 Is Belgium a monarchy or a republic?

4 Jack Sugden was a character in which long-running series?

5 What was the title of Taylor Swift's album released in August 2019?

6 Aardvarks are native to which continent?

7 Shinzo Abe was appointed prime minister of which country in 2012?

8 Which is the furthest east: Chichester, Hastings or Portsmouth?

9 Who co-starred with Sir Ian McKellen in the 2019 film *The Good Liar*?

10 In which century was the London store Liberty founded?

11 St George's Channel lies off which coast of Ireland?

12 With what fruit is James associated in the title of a Roald Dahl book?

13 The River Ouse and which other river meet at the Humber Estuary?

14 The Isle of Wight town of Cowes is famous for what type of racing?

15 Which two-word phrase can mean both "continue" and "make a fuss"?

16 Who was named the Premier League Manager of the Season for 2018-19?

17 In Canada, do motorists drive on the left or the right of the road?

18 What is the name of Riff Raff's sister in *The Rocky Horror Picture Show*?

19 With whom did Ben Fogle row across the Atlantic in 2005-06?

20 How many UK general elections were held between 2000 and 2010?

Easy

Medium

Hard

Answers to QUIZ 355 – Pot Luck

1	Alan Johnson	11	Saturn
2	The lungs	12	Motorcycles
3	Preston (2002)	13	Chelsea FC
4	Queen Victoria	14	B
5	Reverend Lovejoy	15	Mash and sash
6	Three (Barbara, Janet and Pam)	16	Monsoon
7	France	17	Meat Loaf
8	The A30	18	Harry S Truman
9	Steve McQueen	19	Cambodia
10	Amanda Redman	20	China

Easy

1 How many original members were there in the Eagles?

2 In which decade were U2 inducted into the Rock and Roll Hall of Fame?

3 Which group covered the Bee Gees' *Tragedy* in 1998?

4 *Symphony*, featuring Zara Larsson and *Solo*, featuring Demi Lovato, were UK no.1 hits for which band?

5 The Chicks, formerly The Dixie Chicks, perform what genre of music?

6 Nick Mason and Roger Waters were among the founder members of which band?

7 The 1970s band the Bay City Rollers came from which country?

8 After what was the band UB40 named?

9 Which group recorded the mix of Blondie's *One Way or Another* and the Undertones' *Teenage Kicks* for Comic Relief in 2013?

10 Which of these ABBA albums was released first: *Arrival, Ring Ring* or *Super Trouper*?

11 What relation is Dan Hawkin to Justin Hawkin in the band The Darkness?

12 Which continent did Toto sing about in 1982?

13 *Everyday Life* (2019) is the eighth studio album by which rock group?

Medium

14 The Queen albums *A Day at the Races* and *A Night at the Opera* took their titles from films by which family group?

15 The Moody Blues were formed in which English city?

16 Dave Rowntree (b.1964) is the drummer with which rock band?

17 *Rapture* was a 1981 hit for which band?

18 The Shadows were formed as a backing band for which singer?

19 *Go Let it Out* was the first UK no.1 hit of the 21st century for which band?

20 Easther and Vernie Bennett were founder members of which group, formed in 1992?

Hard

ANSWERS ON PAGE 361

1   Which was discovered first: penicillin or a vaccine for polio?

2   The Admiral Benbow Inn features in which adventure novel?

3   In which decade was the original series of *The Likely Lads* first shown on television?

4   *Twilight of the Gods*, or *Götterdämmerung*, is the final opera in the Ring cycle by which composer?

5   *TOWIE* was first broadcast in which decade?

6   The Amityville Horror series of films were set in which US state?

7   Sir Matthew Bourne is a famous name in which branch of the arts?

8   Which of these is the correct spelling: leiase, liaese, or liaise?

9   SG is the postcode area for which English town?

10 Aarhus is the second-largest city in which Scandinavian country?

11 Which author created the sinister character of Mrs Coulter?

12 What is the name of the racing stables in Newmarket owned by the Royal Family of Dubai?

13 The sign for which currency unit is a capital S with a vertical line through it?

14 Which prestigious trophy did Kauto Star win in 2007 and 2009, becoming the first horse to win it again after a loss?

15 The deltoid muscle is so named because it is shaped like which Greek letter?

16 Which country experienced its most powerful earthquake in 2011, with a magnitude of approximately 9.0?

17 What is the four-word nickname of Dumfries, after which its football team is named?

18 Which two words that differ only by their first letter mean "a type of stone" and "sing"?

19 The country of Botswana lies on which continent?

20 In which century did Genghis Khan die?

Answers to QUIZ 357 – Pot Luck

1	Alfred, Lord Tennyson	11	The east coast
2	*The Thick of It*	12	A (giant) peach (*James and the Giant Peach*)
3	A monarchy	13	The River Trent
4	*Emmerdale*	14	Yacht racing
5	*Lover*	15	Carry on
6	Africa	16	Pep Guardiola
7	Japan	17	The right
8	Hastings	18	Magenta
9	Dame Helen Mirren	19	James Cracknell
10	19th century (1875)	20	Three (2001, 2007, 2010)

Easy

Medium

Hard

Easy

1 What word for the value of an asset is also a word meaning "impartiality"?
2 What two-word term is given to the situation where the value of a country's exported goods is less than the cost of its imported goods?
3 London's Lombard Street takes its name from an area of which European country?
4 What two-word term for a monetary system related to a metal, also refers to a supreme example of something?
5 What animal is mentioned in the two-word term for an economy that is growing rapidly, particularly one in Asia?
6 The term for a person or business appointed by law to manage the affairs of a failing business is also used to refer to which part of an old telephone handset?
7 What word for the increase in value of something over time is also a word meaning "gratitude"?
8 What is the name of the US daily index of stock exchange, taken from the surnames of two statisticians?
9 What word can refer to both a statement of support for an organisation and a penalty on a driving licence?
10 Which board game shares its name with a company that is the only one providing a product or service?

Medium

11 In a Dutch auction are prices gradually increased or gradually decreased?
12 What word beginning with "e" means to steal money from a company?
13 What term for investing in a potentially risky venture also refers to guessing or theorising about a situation?
14 Which soporific two-word term refers to someone who has put money into a company but does not take an active part in running it?
15 What word for a company's readily available cash or assets is also a word for a property of water?
16 The name of which currency unit is also a word for a place where cars seized by the police are kept?
17 What is the opposite of an asset?
18 What two-word term describing safe but profitable investments shares its name with the highest token in gambling?
19 What is the meaning of the Latin phrase *pro rata*?
20 Which two words that differ only by their last letter mean "a type of stocks or security" and "to cover in a thin layer of gold"?

Hard

Answers to QUIZ 358 – Bands and Groups

1	Four	11	Brother
2	2000s (2005)	12	*Africa*
3	Steps	13	Coldplay
4	Clean Bandit	14	The Marx Brothers
5	Country music	15	Birmingham
6	Pink Floyd	16	Blur
7	Scotland	17	Blondie
8	An unemployment benefit form	18	Sir Cliff Richard
9	One Direction	19	Oasis
10	*Ring Ring* (1973)	20	Eternal

ANSWERS ON PAGE 363

1   In the TV series *After Life*, what is the first name of Ricky Gervais' character?

2   Mitzi Gaynor played Nellie Forbush in which 1958 musical film?

3   The island of Montserrat lies in which sea?

4   Who played terrorist Castor Troy in the 1997 film *Face/Off*?

5   Who starred in the 1980s TV series *Nanny*?

6   A metal clip with interlocking edges, used for creating a temporary electrical connection, is named after which reptile?

7   What substance does the adjective "glacial" describe?

8   What is the name of the Good Witch of the South, created by L Frank Baum?

9   Which title character of a Shakespeare play is particularly associated with jealousy?

10 Bob Paisley managed which football team from 1974 to 1983?

11 Which British artist directed the video for Blur's *Country House* in 1995?

12 According to the proverb, what is in the eye of the beholder?

13 The Bow Street Runners, founded in 1749, are considered to be Britain's first professional version of which organisation?

14 Chilli and a little chocolate are key ingredients of which Mexican sauce?

15 The Bad Seeds are the backing band for which Australian singer?

16 What word precedes "Campden" and "Norton" in the names of towns in the Cotswolds?

17 The Buick car company was founded in which country?

18 Dame Kelly Holmes served in which of the British armed forces?

19 Which future monarch was born at Kensington Palace on May 24, 1819?

20 Linz is the third-largest city in which European country?

Easy

Medium

Hard

Answers to QUIZ 359 – Pot Luck

1	Penicillin (1928)	11	Sir Philip Pullman (*His Dark Materials* trilogy)
2	*Treasure Island*	12	Godolphin
3	1960s (1964)	13	Dollar
4	Richard Wagner	14	Cheltenham Gold Cup
5	2010s (2010)	15	Delta (a triangle)
6	New York state	16	Japan
7	Dance (he is a choreographer)	17	Queen of the South
8	Liaise	18	Marble and warble
9	Stevenage	19	Africa
10	Denmark	20	13th century (1227)

Easy

1 Which was the second of Jane Austen's novels to be published?

2 What is the more common name for parentheses?

3 In the French and Spanish languages, is a cedilla mark placed above or below a letter?

4 What do Americans call the exclamation mark?

5 Who wrote the 1819 poem *Ode on Melancholy*?

6 Which golfer wrote the autobiography *The Way of the Shark* (2006)?

7 In which decade was John Grisham's first novel published?

8 What word completes the title of the book on punctuation by Lynne Truss, *Eats, ___ & Leaves*?

9 The name for what part of a book is also the name for a human finger?

Medium

10 Does the adjective "sylvan" describe earth, trees or water?

11 What do the letters *cf* mean in a written work?

12 The title character of which 1861 George Eliot novel is a weaver by trade?

13 Which comedienne wrote the 2017 book *Daily Dose of Such Fun!*?

14 In which decade was the Booker Prize first awarded (as the Booker–McConnell Prize)?

15 *The BMJ* is a publication for people in which profession?

16 The Kindle e-reader was launched in which decade?

17 Who wrote *The Pilgrim's Progress* (1678)?

18 Which writer and broadcaster (d.2019) wrote the 1980 *Unreliable Memoirs*?

Hard

19 How many dots are there in the ellipsis punctuation mark?

20 Which US writer wrote the 1990 history of the English language, *The Mother Tongue*?

Answers to QUIZ 360 – Trade Terms

1 Equity
2 Trade deficit
3 Italy (Lombardy)
4 Gold standard
5 Tiger economy
6 Receiver
7 Appreciation
8 Dow Jones
9 Endorsement
10 Monopoly™
11 Gradually decreased
12 Embezzle
13 Speculating
14 Sleeping partner
15 Liquidity
16 Pound
17 A liability
18 Blue chip
19 By proportion
20 Gilt and gild

1 Who played Andrew Earlham in the TV series *Liar*?

2 The Equator passes through how many continents?

3 Skinny and bootleg are styles of which item of clothing?

4 In the Bible, with what did David kill Goliath?

5 Who portrayed US TV star Fred Rogers in *A Beautiful Day in the Neighborhood*?

6 What word referring to a state of lawlessness derives from the Greek for "without a ruler"?

7 *The Hotel Inspectors* was an episode of which classic sitcom?

8 In Greek mythology, in what environment was Triton found?

9 At what is an orator skilled?

10 Which was the only Grand Slam tennis singles tournament won by Michael Stich?

11 In which country was the playwright George Bernard Shaw born?

12 What word for a period of isolation derives from the Italian for "40 days"?

13 Which country hosted and won the 1995 Rugby World Cup?

14 Who played the title character in the 2001 film *Mike Bassett: England Manager*?

15 Isabella, the wife of Edward II, was known as "the She-Wolf" of which country?

16 On which food covering are you said to be walking, if you are being very diplomatic?

17 On an OS map, what type of transport would make use of the feature represented by an H in a circle?

18 The main ingredients of which dip are chickpeas, tahini, garlic and lemon juice?

19 What does an aqueous cream have as its base?

20 The Enid Blyton Malory Towers series of books is set in which county?

Answers to QUIZ 361 – Pot Luck

1	Tony (Johnson)	11	Damien Hirst
2	*South Pacific*	12	Beauty
3	The Caribbean Sea	13	Police force
4	Nicolas Cage	14	Mole
5	Wendy Craig	15	Nick Cave
6	Crocodile (or alligator)	16	Chipping
7	Ice	17	USA
8	Glinda	18	The British Army
9	Othello	19	Queen Victoria
10	Liverpool FC	20	Austria

Easy

1   In volleyball, how many touches of the ball are allowed before a team must return it over the net?

2   Nadia Comăneci, who scored the first perfect 10 in an Olympic gymnastics event, represented which country?

3   As at 2019, who was the youngest person to have won the World Snooker championship?

4   In December 2019, Fallon Sherrock became the first woman to win a match in the World Championship of which indoor sport?

5   Who was the first snooker player to earn over £1 million pounds from the sport?

6   In which sport is the playing area bordered by two channels called gutters?

7   Which boxer (d.2011) was nicknamed "Smokin'"?

8   Which indoor sport is played on a surface measuring nine feet by five feet?

9   Pike and tuck are positions in which aquatic sport?

10 Amir Khan unified the WBA and IBF world titles at what boxing weight?

11 In squash, what is the minimum number of points required to win a game?

Medium

12 "Clean and jerk" and "snatch" are the two elements of which sport?

13 Ippon and waza-ari are scoring moves in which martial art?

14 What name is given to an individual game in a snooker match?

15 What is the maximum number of people allowed in a team in synchronised swimming?

16 Excluding points for a free throw, what two scores can be achieved by basketball moves?

17 In which variety of gymnastics would a hoop and ribbon be used?

18 Which indoor game was first played at the Gloucestershire country estate of the Duke of Beaufort?

19 Which country has won the most gold medals in table tennis at the Olympic Games?

20 How many outfield players are there in a handball team?

Hard

Answers to QUIZ 362 – Reading and Writing

1	*Pride and Prejudice* (1813)	11	Compare with
2	Brackets	12	*Silas Marner*
3	Below (ç)	13	Miranda Hart
4	Exclamation point	14	1960s (1969)
5	John Keats	15	Medicine (*The British Medical Journal*)
6	Greg Norman	16	2000s (2007)
7	1980s (1989)	17	John Bunyan
8	*Shoots*	18	Clive James
9	Index	19	Three
10	Trees	20	Bill Bryson

1 Woden is the Old English name for which Norse god?

2 Which duo, usually heard on Radio 5, presented the 2020 BBC4 series *Home Entertainment Service*?

3 For which English county cricket team did Michael Atherton play from 1987 to 2001?

4 Who played Henry Talbot in *Downton Abbey*?

5 What is the capital of Cuba?

6 The comedian John Bishop was born in which English city?

7 What word describing a chemical substance that can dissolve other substances can also mean "cruel"?

8 The name of which group of Greek islands means "twelve islands"?

9 The name of what dried fruit completes the title of a comedy-drama series starring Ashley Jensen, *Agatha ___*?

10 What does the word "mawkish" mean?

11 What was the subtitle of Guy Richie's 2011 sequel to the 2009 film *Sherlock Holmes*?

12 The title song of which musical begins with the line "What good is sitting alone in your room"?

13 What type of animal is Marley in the film *Marley & Me*?

14 A type of currant bun decorated with sugar is named after which area of London?

15 Which European language uses an upside-down question mark to indicate the beginning of a question?

16 Which of these is the correct spelling: profecy, propecy or prophecy?

17 On what part of a uniform is an epaulette worn?

18 What is a peony?

19 What name is given to a pipe in a street from which fire fighters can obtain water?

20 The Benetton clothing brand was founded in which country?

Easy

Medium

Hard

Answers to QUIZ 363 – Pot Luck

1	Ioan Gruffudd	11	Ireland
2	Three (Africa, Asia and South America)	12	Quarantine
3	Trousers (specifically jeans)	13	South Africa
4	A stone (launched from a sling)	14	Ricky Tomlinson
5	Tom Hanks	15	France
6	Anarchy	16	Eggshells
7	*Fawlty Towers*	17	A helicopter (helipad)
8	The sea	18	Hummus
9	Public speaking	19	Water
10	Wimbledon (1991)	20	Cornwall

Easy

1. *In the Morning* was a 2006 single by which rock band?
2. The UK newspaper *The Evening Standard* is distributed in which city?
3. In which decade was the TV series *The Hour* set?
4. What was the title of the 1990 sequel to the film *48 Hrs*?
5. Who was the main presenter of the radio show *Just a Minute* from its launch in 1967 until 2019?
6. What four words follow "Morning has broken" in the hymn?
7. How many hours behind GMT is Los Angeles?
8. The line "All those moments will be lost in time, like tears in rain" is from which 1982 sci-fi film?
9. Which type of meat is described as "minute" when thinly sliced and fried?
10. What is the name of the main character, played by Gary Cooper, in the 1952 film *High Noon*?

Medium

11. *Eight Days a Week* was a 1965 single by which band?
12. By what shorter name is the Greenwich Time Signal usually referred to?
13. Somebody said to have second sight appears to be able to do what?
14. Who played Dawn in the TV series *The Office*?
15. Which politician was the focus of the 2017 film *Darkest Hour*?
16. How many hours are there in five days?
17. Which singer presented the 1998-2001 game show *The Moment of Truth*?
18. Which song begins with the line: "Midnight, not a sound from the pavement"?
19. *The Waltz of the Little Dog*, usually referred to as *The Minute Waltz*, was written by which composer?
20. *Time (Clock of the Heart)* was a 1982 single by which band?

Hard

Answers to QUIZ 364 – Indoor Sports

1	Three	11	11 (or higher by two clear points)
2	Romania	12	Weightlifting
3	Stephen Hendry (aged 21)	13	Judo
4	Darts (PDC World Championship)	14	A frame
5	Steve Davis	15	Eight (minimum of four)
6	Ten-pin bowling	16	Two or three points
7	Joe Frazier	17	Rhythmic gymnastics
8	Table tennis	18	Badminton
9	Diving	19	China (28 as at 2020)
10	Light-welterweight	20	Six (and one goalkeeper)

1   Which TV sleuth has had sidekicks played by Caroline Quentin, Julia Sawalha and Sheridan Smith?

2   What two-word term is a score of two over par in golf?

3   Which Indian state has the shortest name?

4   In mathematics, what can be mean, median or mode?

5   The Drakensberg Mountains in South Africa are named after which mythical creature?

6   Which pop singer played Che Guevara in the original London production of *Evita*?

7   The character Hello Kitty originated in which country?

8   What type of food is Double Gloucester?

9   What two words, that differ only by their first letter, mean "brave man" and "nothing"?

10 Fez hats are usually what colour?

11 Is the Isle of Dogs peninsula in east, south or west London?

12 Who played the title character in the 1997 crime film *Donnie Brasco*?

13 The character Gru first appeared in which animated film?

14 Which old-fashioned laundry aid can also be used as a percussion instrument?

15 The LA Chargers compete in which sport?

16 What name is given to the study of families and their history?

17 What was the title of the 1991 no.1 by Vic Reeves and The Wonder Stuff?

18 In chess, a player can move either of which two pieces on their opening move?

19 Who created the children's TV series *Fraggle Rock*?

20 In which country was DJ Calvin Harris born?

Answers to QUIZ 365 – Pot Luck

1	Odin	11	*A Game of Shadows*
2	Mark Kermode and Simon Mayo	12	*Cabaret*
3	Lancashire	13	A dog (Labrador retriever)
4	Matthew Goode	14	Chelsea
5	Havana	15	Spanish
6	Liverpool	16	Prophecy
7	Caustic	17	The shoulder
8	Dodecanese	18	A flowering plant
9	*Raisin*	19	(Fire) hydrant
10	Sentimental	20	Italy

1   The capital of the US state of Wisconsin is named after which president?

2   In Greek legend, Paris was a prince of which ancient city?

3   How many Central American countries have capital cities which are the name of the country followed by "City"?

4   Which capital city in the southern hemisphere is named after the UK prime minister Arthur Wellesley (d.1852)?

5   How many of the vowels in the alphabet have an enclosed space when written in capital letters?

6   Proverbially, to which European capital city do all roads lead?

7   Which capital city is the UK's second-most popular tourist destination?

8   What type of drink is Fuller's London Pride?

9   In which European capital city is there a museum dedicated to the artist René Magritte?

10 How is Copenhagen described in the title of a song from the 1952 musical film Hans Christian Andersen?

11 The name of which European country completes the name of the capital of Trinidad and Tobago, Port of ___?

12 Which singer released the 1977 solo single *Tokyo Joe*?

13 The bank Capital One was founded in which country?

14 Santiago Cabrera played one of the title characters in which TV series broadcast from 2014 to 2016?

15 Which capital city is the most populous in the European Union?

16 Reykjavík is the capital city of which island country?

17 The name of which UK capital city featured in the title of a 1989 Simple Minds song?

18 Brussels is famous for what type of delicate cloth?

19 Which prime minister introduced the UK capital gains tax, in 1965?

20 The name of which European capital city is an anagram of "made smart"?

Answers to QUIZ 366 – Time

1	Razorlight	11	The Beatles
2	London	12	"The pips"
3	1950s	13	See the future
4	*Another 48 Hrs*	14	Lucy Davis
5	Nicholas Parsons	15	Sir Winston Churchill
6	"Like the first morning"	16	120
7	Eight hours	17	Cilla Black
8	*Blade Runner*	18	*Memory* (from *Cats*)
9	Steak	19	(Frédéric) Chopin
10	Will Kane	20	Culture Club

Easy

Medium

Hard

1   What was the subtitle of the 2019 Spider-Man film released in July 2019?

2   As at the end of 2019, who held the record for the most appearances for the Northern Ireland football team, with 119 caps?

3   In the USA, what type of clothing are sneakers?

4   Potsdam is a city in which European country?

5   How many of Henry VIII's wives were executed?

6   *Ladies' Night* (1979) was the first UK top ten single for which group?

7   What type of farm building might be built in a "Dutch" style?

8   To the nearest whole number, how many centimetres are there in four inches?

9   What is made by the Swiss company Raymond Weil?

10   Which UK political party has a yellow Welsh poppy as its logo?

11   Which Leonardo DiCaprio film was released first: *The Beach, The Departed* or *The Revenant?*

12   What is the name of the flag flown when the British monarch is in residence?

13   Joe Montana (b.1956) was a famous player in which American sport?

14   What is added to vodka and coffee liqueur to make a White Russian?

15   The TV series *The A Word* is set in which English county?

16   In which century did the Battle of Agincourt take place?

17   What were Miranda Richardson, Phyllis Logan and Zoë Wanamaker called in the title of a 2018 drama series?

18   What is the nickname of darts champion Martin Adams?

19   Who duetted with Roy Orbison on a 1987 version of *Crying?*

20   In the nursery rhyme *I Had a Little Nut Tree*, the daughter of the king of which country came to visit?

Answers to QUIZ 367 – Pot Luck

1	Jonathan Creek	11	East London
2	Double bogey	12	Johnny Depp
3	Goa	13	*Despicable Me*
4	Average	14	Washboard
5	Dragon	15	American football
6	David Essex	16	Genealogy
7	Japan	17	*Dizzy*
8	Cheese	18	Knight or pawn
9	Hero and zero	19	Jim Henson
10	Red	20	Scotland

What are the names of these African animals?

Easy

Medium

Hard

1

2

3

4

5

6

7

8

Answers to QUIZ 368 – Capital

1	(James) Madison	11	Spain
2	Troy	12	Bryan Ferry
3	Three (Guatemala, Mexico and Panama)	13	USA
4	Wellington (Duke of Wellington)	14	*The Musketeers*
5	Two (A and O)	15	Berlin (Germany)
6	Rome	16	Iceland
7	Edinburgh	17	Belfast (*Belfast Child*)
8	Beer	18	Lace
9	Brussels	19	James Callaghan (Baron Callaghan of Cardiff)
10	Wonderful (*Wonderful Copenhagen*)	20	Amsterdam (the Netherlands)

1   Baron Hardup appears in which pantomime?

2   The four elements associated with the zodiac are air, fire, water and which other?

3   On what is a fresco painted?

4   Which takeaway company advertises that it provides "The Official Food of Everything"?

5   Which two words that differ only by their first letter mean "feeling" and "nervous"?

6   SN is the international car registration for which country?

7   *Killing Me Softly* and *Ready or Not* were 1996 hits for which group?

8   Chuck is a cut of which type of meat?

9   The town of Formby lies in which metropolitan county?

10 Who played Mr Micawber in the 2019 film *The Personal History of David Copperfield*?

11 For which English football team did German striker Jürgen Klinsmann play on loan in the 1994-95 season?

12 If a situation goes wrong, with which fruit is it compared?

13 What name is given to the most senior diplomat in a Commonwealth country?

14 In which event did Tessa Sanderson compete for Britain?

15 Is Mn the chemical symbol for magnesium or manganese?

16 *Collision Course* (2016) was the fifth film in which animated series?

17 Lord Snooty is a character in which comic?

18 How many days are there in the month of May?

19 Wein is the name of which capital city in its own language?

20 What words complete the title of the Wham! hit, *Wake Me Up ___*?

Answers to QUIZ 369 – Pot Luck

1	*Far from Home*	11	*The Beach* (2000)
2	Pat Jennings (from 1964 to 1986)	12	The Royal Standard
3	(Casual) shoes	13	American football
4	Germany	14	Cream
5	Two (Anne Boleyn and Catherine Howard)	15	Cumbria
6	Kool & the Gang	16	15th century (1415)
7	A barn	17	*Girlfriends*
8	10 centimetres	18	Wolfie
9	Luxury watches	19	kd lang
10	Plaid Cymru	20	Spain

1   Which two London boroughs have names beginning with "L"?

2   Shenandoah National Park is in which country?

3   Which tourist attraction is described by its advertising slogan as "The happiest place on earth"?

4   In which country was Charlize Theron born?

5   Hillhead and Partick are areas in which Scottish city?

6   The Flemish Region is part of which European country?

7   The River Dart flows through which English county?

8   Do the Canary Islands lie north or south of Madeira?

9   At which venue was the 2019 Rugby Super League final held?

10 The Britannia Bridge joins which island to mainland Wales?

11 The Minneapolis Lakers basketball team changed their name when they moved to which city in 1960?

12 Something described as Provençal is from which country?

13 Is the republic of San Marino on the east coast or the west coast of Italy?

14 The followers of which religious denomination worship in a building called a Kingdom Hall?

15 Which constituency did David Cameron represent when he became the UK prime minister?

16 Which is the second-largest city in the Republic of Ireland?

17 The Derbyshire village of Eyam lies within which National Park?

18 The Krusty Krab restaurant features in which children's TV series?

19 At which English venue has the World Darts Championship taken place since 2008?

20 HD is the postcode area code for which English town?

Easy

Medium

Hard

1   What type of plant is comfrey?

2   What is nine multiplied by six?

3   Former boxer Evander Holyfield was born in which country?

4   Which of these singles was a no.1 earliest in the 1980s: *Caravan of Love, I'm Your Man* or *West End Girls*?

5   In which decade was *The Good Life* first broadcast?

6   What is the official language of Monaco?

7   Who starred in the 2020 film *Dolittle*?

8   What would you be doing if you were using rickrack?

9   Which comedian acts as Greg Davies' assistant on the TV game show *Taskmaster*?

10   In relation to education, for what do the letters GCSE stand?

11   In the English version of Scrabble®, how many "K" tiles are there?

12   What word for unimportant matters means "three roads" in Italian?

13   The country of Armenia lies on which continent?

14   Who wrote the 1973 song *Knockin' on Heaven's Door*?

15   In the name of the football club Sunderland AFC, for what does the "A" stand?

16   What name is given to both an expensive fungus and a type of chocolate?

17   Which US president owned a cat named Socks?

18   The Gorgons appear in which branch of mythology?

19   What linked items are made by bowyers and fletchers?

20   Madhur Jaffrey is associated with the cuisine of which country?

Answers to QUIZ 371 – Pot Luck

1	*Cinderella*	11	Tottenham Hotspur FC
2	Earth	12	A pear (go pear-shaped)
3	A wall	13	High Commissioner
4	Domino's®	14	The javelin
5	Sense and tense	15	Manganese
6	Senegal	16	*Ice Age*
7	The Fugees	17	*The Beano*
8	Beef (steak)	18	31
9	Merseyside	19	Vienna
10	Peter Capaldi	20	*Before You Go-Go*

Easy

1 Who voiced the character President Business in *The Lego Movie*?

2 In which decade did Mariah Carey release the albums *Butterfly* and *Rainbow*?

3 Bushy Park is on the banks of which major English river?

4 The *Carabinieri* are the official police force in which country?

5 What is a busy Lizzie?

6 What is the chemical symbol for carbon?

7 Bushido was the code of laws governing which group of Japanese fighters?

8 In what part of the body does a cardiologist specialise?

9 Who would wear a busby?

10 In which country is the medieval fortified city of Carcassonne?

11 Steve Buscemi played Nucky Thompson in which TV series, first broadcast in 2010?

12 The fruit of the carob tree is used as a substitute for what foodstuff?

13 What was the title of the only no.1 single by Kate Bush?

14 Carl XVI Gustaf became king of which European country in 1973?

Medium

15 A *Bushel and a Peck* is a song from which 1950 musical?

16 Famous for its rugby team, which is the largest town in Carmarthenshire?

17 The name of which creature completes the title of the 1931 Marx Brothers' film ___ *Business*?

18 Where in the human body are the carpal bones?

19 Which word meaning "to move in a busy manner" is also the name of an old-fashioned item of clothing?

20 Ellis Carver, played by Seth Gilliam, was a character in which US police drama of the 2000s?

Hard

Answers to QUIZ 372 – Locations

1	Lambeth and Lewisham	11	Los Angeles (LA Lakers)
2	USA	12	France
3	Disneyland	13	The east coast
4	South Africa	14	Jehovah's Witnesses
5	Glasgow	15	Witney (Oxfordshire)
6	Belgium	16	Cork
7	Devon	17	The Peak District
8	South	18	*SpongeBob SquarePants*
9	Old Trafford	19	Alexandra Palace
10	Anglesey	20	Huddersfield

ANSWERS ON PAGE 377

1   For which Coventry-based rugby union team did Joe Launchbury sign in 2010?

2   What is the English translation of the French phrase *hors de combat*?

3   Which operatic song provided Luciano Pavarotti with a top ten hit in 1990?

4   *How Will I Know* was a 1985 hit for which singer?

5   Which year saw Len Goodman's final appearance as Head Judge on *Strictly Come Dancing*?

6   The 1987 film *Cry Freedom* was set in which country?

7   What colour are the top and bottom stripes on the flag of Argentina?

8   What name is given to a large group of bees flying together?

9   Which of these cities lies furthest west: Coventry, Leicester or Manchester?

10 In which 2009 animated film are helium balloons used to move a house?

11 What name is given to wet sand into which you sink, if you try to walk on it?

12 The South Mimms services lie close to which motorway?

13 What word precedes "element" to refer to something that is found in very small amounts in living things?

14 In which century did Leonardo da Vinci paint the *Mona Lisa*?

15 Which UK prime minister created the Department for International Trade in 2016, following the vote to leave the European Union?

16 A fuselage is part of which form of transport?

17 What type of hat is an opera hat?

18 In relation to finance, the word "forex" is a combination of which two words?

19 What name is given to the primary place on a Formula 1 grid?

20 What is the one-word name of the campaign that encourages people to have a meat-free month at the beginning of the year?

Easy

Medium

Hard

Answers to QUIZ 373 – Pot Luck

1	A herb	11	One
2	54	12	Trivia
3	USA (Alabama)	13	Asia
4	*I'm Your Man* (November 1985)	14	Bob Dylan
5	1970s (1975)	15	Association
6	French	16	Truffle
7	Robert Downey Jr	17	Bill Clinton
8	Sewing (braided trim in a zigzag)	18	Greek mythology
9	Alex Horne	19	Bows and arrows
10	General Certificate of Secondary Education	20	India

Easy

1   George Best played for which football team from 1963 to 1974?

2   Who famously uttered the line "I want to be alone" in the 1932 film *Grand Hotel*?

3   What do the letters "GA" stand for in the netball position?

4   Gil Grissom was a character in which US series?

5   Galliano is a yellow liqueur from which country?

6   With what metal is something coated when it is galvanised?

7   "The boys of the NYPD choir were singing Galway Bay" is a line from which song?

8   Gareth Thomas played the title character in which TV sci-fi series, first broadcast in 1978?

9   Grace Poole is a character in which classic novel of 1847?

10 Who played Gregory in the 1981 film *Gregory's Girl*?

11 Where would a gauntlet be worn?

12 In North America, what is a gulch?

13 What was the first name of Naya Rivera's character in the TV series *Glee*?

14 Giovanni is the Italian equivalent of which English name?

Medium

15 Guernica, the subject of a painting by Picasso, is a village in which European country?

16 Which radio presenter (b.1984) is nicknamed "Grimmy"?

17 The village of Grasmere lies in which English National Park?

18 What type of creature is a goosander?

19 Grantham is a town in which English county?

20 Which drink did George Orwell consider tasted better when drunk from a china cup?

Hard

Answers to QUIZ 374 – Bus and Car

1	Will Ferrell	11	*Boardwalk Empire*
2	1990s (1997 and 1999)	12	Chocolate
3	The Thames	13	*Wuthering Heights*
4	Italy	14	Sweden
5	A plant (of the genus *Impatiens*)	15	*Guys and Dolls*
6	C	16	Llanelli
7	Samurai	17	*Monkey*
8	The heart	18	The wrist
9	A soldier (it is a tall hat)	19	Bustle
10	France	20	*The Wire*

ANSWERS ON PAGE 379

1   Who won the International Male Solo Artist Brit award in 2020?

2   With what is an Irish coffee topped?

3   Ganesh is a deity in which religion?

4   How many arrows are there in the standard recycling symbol?

5   In which county is the town of Cirencester?

6   The two-word name of which town in county Durham can be made from the name of a chess piece and a large city in New Zealand?

7   Who refused to accept the Best Actor Oscar for his role in a 1972 film?

8   Fort Lauderdale is a city in which US state?

9   Boyzone were formed in which decade?

10 What was the title of the prequel to *Last of the Summer Wine*?

11 What type of bird is a gannet?

12 What is the British equivalent of the American phrase "play hookey"?

13 In nature, what is a giant puffball?

14 Who hosted *Desert Island Discs* from 1985 to 1988?

15 County Wicklow is part of which province of the Republic of Ireland?

16 What is 40% of 120?

17 Which actress co-starred with Leslie Nielsen in *The Naked Gun* films?

18 In which century was Mohandas Gandhi born?

19 Who had a 1976 hit with *Love and Affection*?

20 What was the title of the 2019 film in which musician Jack Malik was the only person who could remember the Beatles?

Easy

Medium

Hard

Answers to QUIZ 375 – Pot Luck

1	Wasps	11	Quicksand
2	Out of the fight	12	M25
3	*Nessun Dorma*	13	Trace (element)
4	Whitney Houston	14	The 16th century (completed c.1517)
5	2016	15	Theresa May
6	South Africa	16	An aeroplane (its main body section)
7	(Light) blue	17	A (collapsible) top hat
8	A swarm	18	Foreign exchange
9	Manchester	19	Pole position
10	*Up*	20	Veganuary

Easy

1   What was the title of Nik Kershaw's first top five hit?

2   What is the first name of Kaye Wragg's *Holby City* character?

3   Who starred in the 1982 film *First Blood*?

4   Which legendary king featured in the 1995 film *First Knight*?

5   What is the first double-digit prime number?

6   In which branch of the arts would someone assume the first position?

7   Which of these judges did not appear in the first series of *The X Factor*: Cheryl, Louis Walsh or Simon Cowell?

8   What was the title of Kate Atkinson's first novel, published in 1995?

9   To what price did first-class stamps rise in March 2020?

10 What four words follow "The First Nowell" in the Christmas carol?

11 Tim Campbell was the first winner of which reality TV show?

12 Who became the US First Lady in January 2017?

13 On what day would a first-foot enter a house in Scotland?

14 If you have a female first cousin, what relation is she to your parents?

Medium

15 Which singer had a 1972 hit with *The First Time Ever I Saw Your Face*?

16 Which rock group's name is also the name of the first book of the Old Testament?

17 In which decade did Lee Westwood first represent Europe in the Ryder Cup?

18 The "first-past-the-post" system is used in which local and national events in the UK?

19 Who holds the position of First Lord of the Treasury in the UK?

20 *Love in the First Degree* was a 1987 hit for which group?

Hard

Answers to QUIZ 376 – G

1	Manchester United FC	11	On the hand
2	Greta Garbo	12	A narrow ravine or valley
3	Goal attack	13	Santana (Lopez)
4	*CSI: Crime Scene Investigation*	14	John
5	Italy	15	Spain
6	Zinc	16	Nick Grimshaw
7	*Fairytale of New York* (The Pogues featuring Kirsty McColl)	17	The Lake District
8	*Blake's 7*	18	Water bird (duck)
9	*Jane Eyre*	19	Lincolnshire
10	John Gordon Sinclair	20	Beer

1   What is the first name of Hermione Norris' *Cold Feet* character?

2   Where on the body would gaiters be worn?

3   Which 1989 song was Michael Bolton's highest-charting UK single?

4   The adjective "ducal" is connected with which level of the peerage?

5   Canal Turn and Foinavon are fences in which horse race?

6   Which fictional bear was found with the message "Please look after this bear" attached to his coat?

7   Tromsø is a town in which Scandinavian country?

8   What is the basis for the drink advocaat?

9   How many members were there in the group Girls Aloud?

10 What type of fruit is a Galia?

11 Midway Airport serves which US city?

12 Proverbially, what killed the cat?

13 In which century was Anton Chekhov's play *The Cherry Orchard* first performed?

14 How many letters prefix the six digits of a National Insurance number?

15 What name is given to a tennis shot in which the palm of the hand faces the direction in which the ball is being hit?

16 As at the end of 2019, which 2013 film and its 2019 sequel were amongst the top three highest-grossing animated films of all time?

17 *The Wilderness Years* (1993) and *The Cappuccino Years* (1999) are instalments in the life of which literary character?

18 Cathy Gale, played by Honor Blackman, was a character in which 1960s TV series?

19 Which car company made the Scirocco model?

20 Which Welsh city is alphabetically last?

Easy

Medium

Hard

Answers to QUIZ 377 – Pot Luck

1	Tyler, the Creator	11	A seabird
2	Cream	12	Play truant
3	Hinduism	13	A fungus (mushroom)
4	Three	14	Sir Michael Parkinson
5	Gloucestershire	15	Leinster
6	Bishop Auckland	16	48
7	Marlon Brando (*The Godfather*)	17	Priscilla Presley
8	Florida	18	19th century (1869)
9	1990s (1993)	19	Joan Armatrading
10	*First of the Summer Wine*	20	*Yesterday*

1   Which TV character, introduced on *Noel's House Party*, is pink with yellow spots?

2   A bruise is usually described as being what two colours?

3   What colour was the Rolling Stones' rooster?

4   Which organisation for girls was originally called Rosebuds?

5   Which rugby union team is nicknamed "the Cherry and Whites"?

6   How is potassium bitartrate referred to when it is used in baking?

7   What was the name of Violet Carson's character in *Coronation Street*?

8   What colour dresses are the girls wearing in the song *My Favourite Things*?

9   *Fields of Gold*, famously covered by Eva Cassidy, was written by which singer?

10   What type of fruit is a Pink Lady?

11   How many years of marriage are celebrated at a silver anniversary?

12   How many legs are there on a tripod?

13   What colour is the flag awarded to beaches that meet EU standards of cleanliness and water quality?

14   Jade Ewen was a member of which girl group from 2009 to 2011?

15   What colour is orange blossom?

16   What type of bird is a greylag?

17   In the TV series, what colour are the Clangers?

18   What colour is Sesame Street's *Oscar the Grouch*?

19   An image of which US president features on the Purple Heart medal?

20   What colour thoroughfare did Sir Elton John say goodbye to in the title of a song?

Answers to QUIZ 378 – First

1   What type of beer is Guinness®?

2   In which decade did Raúl Castro succeed Fidel Castro as First Secretary of the Communist Party in Cuba?

3   What was the name of Ted Danson's character in the TV series *Cheers*?

4   Which of these classic novels was published first: *Alice's Adventures in Wonderland*, *Black Beauty* or *Mary Poppins*?

5   The city of Sheffield is in which English county?

6   What was the title of the 2019 sequel to the film *It*?

7   What name for a charity fund-raising sale is taken from the Middle Eastern name for a market?

8   Peaches are native to which continent?

9   The name of which secretion produced by the liver is also used as a word for "anger"?

10 Which graffiti artist directed the 2010 film *Exit Through the Gift Shop*?

11 The song *Love Changes Everything*, a hit for Michael Ball, is from which musical?

12 In which sport might a longbow be used?

13 What does a town contain if it is referred to as a garrison town?

14 What is the nickname of the fictional pilot James Bigglesworth, created by WE Johns?

15 What number do the Roman numerals CCCVI represent?

16 Who starred in the title role in the 2010-12 TV series *Dirk Gently*?

17 The company Rimmel makes what type of product?

18 What word can refer to "a substance burned for its scent" and "to make extremely angry"?

19 In which decade did Swing Out Sister have top ten hits with *Breakout* and *Surrender*?

20 Which of the characters from the TV series *Friends* had a hairstyle named after her?

Easy

Medium

Hard

Answers to QUIZ 379 – Pot Luck

1	Karen	11	Chicago
2	The legs	12	Curiosity
3	*How Am I Supposed to Live Without You*	13	20th century (1904)
4	Duke	14	Two
5	The Grand National	15	Forehand
6	Paddington	16	*Frozen* and *Frozen II*
7	Norway	17	*Adrian Mole* (Sue Townsend)
8	(Raw) egg	18	*The Avengers*
9	Five	19	Volkswagen
10	A melon	20	Swansea

Easy

1 *Fünf* is German for which number?

2 What colour is Fungus the Bogeyman?

3 Which comedian released the 1975 single *Funky Moped*?

4 "Try now we can only lose and our love become a funeral pyre" is a lyric from which song?

5 What word completes the title of the musical *A Funny Thing Happened on the Way to the ___*?

6 The funny bone is just above which joint of the human body?

7 In 1964, who starred in the original Broadway production of *Funny Girl*?

8 The song *Funiculì, Funiculà* originated in which country?

9 Who played George Simmons in the 2009 film *Funny People*?

10 On what is a funicular railway situated?

Medium

11 Which English playwright wrote the 1994 farce *Funny Money*?

12 What type of creature is a funnel-web?

13 Which actor played Dick Harper in the 2005 film *Fun With Dick and Jane*?

14 Pippa Funnell has won Olympic medals in what form of sport?

15 Which circus performer can be referred to as a funambulist?

16 Which US singer released the 2008 album *Funhouse*?

17 Which actress starred as Jo Stockton in the 1957 film *Funny Face*?

18 How many funnels were there on the *RMS Titanic*?

19 What is the plural of "fungus"?

20 Which girl group teamed up with Fun Boy Three on the 1982 hit *It Ain't What You Do (It's the Way That You Do It)*?

Hard

Answers to QUIZ 380 – Colours

1	Mr Blobby	11	25
2	Black and blue	12	Three
3	Red (*Little Red Rooster*)	13	Blue
4	Brownies	14	Sugababes
5	Gloucester	15	White
6	Cream of tartar	16	A goose
7	Ena Sharples	17	Pink
8	White (with blue satin sashes)	18	Green
9	Sting	19	George Washington
10	An apple	20	Yellow (*Goodbye, Yellow Brick Road*)

1   What is the opposite of "concave"?

2   Russ Conway (d.2000) had chart hits in the 1950s and 1960s on which instrument?

3   The 1869 novel *War and Peace* was set in which country?

4   The Japanese dish sukiyaki is usually made with which meat?

5   Who is "nipping at your nose" in the song that begins "Chestnuts roasting on an open fire"?

6   In what field of study was JK Galbraith (d.2006) a famous name?

7   Hampshire has three cities: Portsmouth, Winchester and which other?

8   Which part of a central heating system controls the temperature?

9   Author JM Barrie was born in which century?

10 What colour is watercress?

11 What nationality was racing driver Ayrton Senna?

12 In which decade were photographs introduced on British passports?

13 Is an angle of 140 degrees an acute angle or an obtuse angle?

14 Geraldine Somerville played which character in the Harry Potter films?

15 In WWI, was Manfred von Richthofen a famous pilot, sailor or soldier?

16 The film *Apocalypse Now* is set during which conflict?

17 What is the first name of Patsy Palmer's *EastEnders* character?

18 What colour is Beaujolais Nouveau wine?

19 What is the official language of Mexico?

20 Which singer makes up a duo with Chaka Demus?

Easy

Medium

Hard

Answers to QUIZ 381 – Pot Luck

1	Stout	11	*Aspects of Love*
2	2010s (2011)	12	Archery
3	Sam Malone	13	A military base
4	*Alice's Adventures in Wonderland* (1865)	14	Biggles
5	South Yorkshire	15	306
6	*It Chapter Two*	16	Stephen Mangan
7	Bazaar	17	Cosmetics
8	Asia (China)	18	Incense
9	Bile	19	1980s (1986-87)
10	Banksy	20	Rachel ("The Rachel")

What are the names of these items of sports equipment?

Easy

Medium

Hard

1

2

3

4

5

6

7

8

Answers to QUIZ 382 – Fun

1	Five	11	Ray Cooney
2	Green	12	A spider
3	Jasper Carrott	13	Jim Carrey
4	*Light My Fire* (The Doors)	14	Equestrian sport (eventing)
5	*Forum*	15	A tightrope walker
6	The elbow	16	Pink
7	Barbra Streisand	17	Audrey Hepburn
8	Italy	18	Four
9	Adam Sandler	19	Fungi
10	A steep hill or side of a mountain	20	Bananarama

ANSWERS ON PAGE 387

1   Pauline Fowler was a character in which long-running series?

2   The Atlantic record label was founded in which country?

3   Which variety of cabbage shares its name with a London hotel, but is actually named after a region of France?

4   Which island is listed in the Guinness World Records as being the largest volcanic island in the world?

5   At which stadium did Tottenham Hotspur FC play until 2017?

6   How many leaves does a cinquefoil plant have?

7   Who had a 2017 top ten hit with *Blinded by Your Grace, Pt. 2*?

8   Which planet is the hottest in the solar system?

9   The Red Sea is an inlet of which ocean?

10   In which century was *The Wind in the Willows* published?

11   Flour, milk and which other ingredient are used to make Yorkshire pudding?

12   A dram is a small measure of which alcoholic drink?

13   What is sold in a French *poissonnerie*?

14   In the fairy-tale, what does Jack trade for a handful of magic beans?

15   Who co-presented the 2020 TV series *The Fantastical Factory of Curious Craft* with Anna Richardson?

16   "The rest is silence", spoken by the title character, are the final words in which play by Shakespeare?

17   In which decade did Suzi Quatro have hits with *Can the Can* and *Devil Gate Drive*?

18   Which country precedes the word "spruce" in the name of an evergreen tree popular at Christmas?

19   What type of bird is a stork?

20   In which decade was the BBC Sports Personality of the Year award first presented?

Answers to QUIZ 383 – Pot Luck

1	Convex	11	Brazilian
2	Piano	12	1910s (1915)
3	Russia	13	Obtuse
4	Beef	14	Lily Potter
5	Jack Frost	15	Pilot
6	Economics	16	The Vietnam War
7	Southampton	17	Bianca
8	Thermostat	18	Red
9	19th century (1860)	19	Spanish
10	Green	20	Pliers

Easy

1   The 2004 film *Million Dollar Baby* featured which sport?

2   How many *Psychopaths* were there in the title of the 2012 film?

3   The 1964 film *633 Squadron* was set during which conflict?

4   How many dresses are there in the title of the 2008 Katherine Heigl film?

5   What type of establishment was *84 Charing Cross Road* in the title of the 1987 film starring Anne Bancroft?

6   Howard Keel played Adam Pontipee in which 1954 musical film?

7   What number completes the title of the Kathryn Bigelow film, ___ *Dark Thirty*?

8   Which actress starred in the 1966 film *One Million Years B.C.?*

9   Which board game features in the 1957 fantasy film *The Seventh Seal?*

10 How many *Dalmatians* are there in the title of the 2000 sequel?

11 Who played Henry VIII in the 1969 film *Anne of a Thousand Days?*

Medium

12 In which decade was the original *The Dirty Dozen* film released?

13 How many monkeys are there in the title of the 1995 Bruce Willis sci-fi film?

14 Charles and Carrie are the main characters in which 1994 romcom?

15 The 1999 comedy film *Three Kings* was set in which country?

16 What was the title of the 1990 sequel to *Three Men and a Baby?*

17 What number completes the title of the 1988 film about a baseball scandal, ___ *Men Out?*

18 How many *Degrees of Separation* are there in the title of the 1993 film?

19 In which decade was the film *12 Angry Men* released?

20 Which 1975 film, set in a mental institution, won five Oscars, including Best Actor and Best Actress?

Hard

Answers to QUIZ 384 – Sports Equipment

1   Curling stone
2   (Ten-pin) bowling ball
3   Ice hockey stick
4   Tennis racket
5   Dumbbell
6   Shuttlecock
7   Golf clubs
8   Rugby ball

1   The food company Ginsters® is based in which English county?

2   *Blah Blah Blah* was a 2010 single by which US singer?

3   "Buck House" is the nickname of which London building?

4   In the TV series *The Sopranos*, what was the name of Tony's wife?

5   Which two countries have an estimated population of more than 1 billion?

6   Who had a hit in 1967 with *Something's Gotten Hold of My Heart*?

7   Which of these films won the Best Picture Oscar first: *Out of Africa*, *Platoon* or *Rocky*?

8   The variety of broccoli called calabrese is named after which region of Italy?

9   What is the name of the NFL team based in Dallas?

10 Which animal might be referred to as "a porker"?

11 What is the two-word term for consent that must be obtained before a building is constructed?

12 The name of which superhero completes the title of a play by George Bernard Shaw: *Man and ___*?

13 LL is the postcode area code for which Welsh town?

14 In which month does British Summer Time end?

15 What type of fish is a koi?

16 Which 1980s comedy series was written by Ben Elton, Lise Mayer and Rik Mayall?

17 How many Formula 1 World Championship titles did Michael Schumacher win?

18 In which type of building would an official wear a surplice?

19 Ingrid Kristiansen, four-times winner of the London Marathon, represented which country?

20 What is used as the outer coating on southern fried chicken?

Answers to QUIZ 385 – Pot Luck

1	*EastEnders*	11	Eggs
2	USA	12	Whisky
3	Savoy cabbage	13	Fish
4	Iceland	14	A cow
5	White Hart Lane	15	Keith Lemon
6	Five	16	*Hamlet*
7	Stormzy (featuring MNEK)	17	1970s (1973-74)
8	Venus	18	Norway
9	The Indian Ocean	19	A wader
10	20th century (1908)	20	1950s (1954)

Easy

1 The town of Andover is in which English county?

2 The name of which animal completes the title of the Aesop fable: *Androcles and the ___*?

3 Anderson shelters were constructed in the UK during which war?

4 In which decade was the children's TV programme *Andy Pandy* first broadcast?

5 The Andaman Islands are part of which continent?

6 Pamela Anderson played Casey Jean Parker in which 2017 film, based on a TV series?

7 *And I Am Telling You I'm Not Going* is a song from which 1981 stage musical, subsequently adapted into a film?

8 Is St Andrews on the east, north or west coast of Scotland?

9 The adjective "Andean" relates to a mountain range on which continent?

10 In which country was the singer Andrea Bocelli born?

11 Who wrote the 1742 novel *Joseph Andrews*?

Medium

12 "And did those feet in ancient time" are the opening words of which hymn?

13 The name "Andrew" is derived from the word for "man" in which ancient language?

14 How many times did Andy Roddick reach the Wimbledon men's singles final?

15 The San Andreas geological fault runs through which US state?

16 Eamonn Andrews presented people with a "big red book" on which TV series?

17 In music, at what pace should something marked as *andante* be played?

18 Andy Bell and Vince Clarke make up which pop duo?

19 Which type of dog is famously used to advertise Andrex® toilet paper?

20 What is the currency unit of Andorra?

Hard

Answers to QUIZ 386 – Numerical Films

1	Boxing	11	Richard Burton
2	*Seven*	12	1960s (1967)
3	WWII	13	12 (*12 Monkeys*)
4	27 (*27 Dresses*)	14	*Four Weddings and a Funeral*
5	A bookshop	15	Iraq
6	*Seven Brides for Seven Brothers*	16	*Three Men and a Little Lady*
7	*Zero*	17	Eight
8	Raquel Welch	18	*Six*
9	Chess	19	1950s (1957)
10	102	20	*One Flew Over the Cuckoo's Nest*

ANSWERS ON PAGE 391

1 *Be-Bop-A-Lula* was a 1956 hit for which singer?

2 Who played Kayleigh Kitson in *Peter Kay's Car Share*?

3 Which Hollywood actor married barrister Amal Alamuddin in 2014?

4 From which animal is gammon obtained?

5 The plot of which 1982 sci-fi film involved hunting down replicants?

6 What was the name of Craig Charles' character in *Coronation Street*?

7 Which of these countries does not play in the Six Nations rugby union tournament: France, Italy or Spain?

8 In the sitcom *Are You Being Served?*, what was Captain Peacock's occupation?

9 Slim Whitman (d.2013) was a famous name in which genre of music?

10 Lou Macari (b.1949) played international football for which team?

11 If someone's behaviour is described as "altruistic", are they being selfish or selfless?

12 Gascony is a historical region in which country?

13 An American student described as a sophomore is in which year at university?

14 What would someone be doing, if they were using a snorkel?

15 Which adjective relating to the British monarchs in the 18th and early 19th centuries also refers to a native of a US state?

16 The town of Aviemore is situated in which National Park?

17 *Feliz Navidad* means "Merry Christmas" in which language?

18 What was the setting for the 1973 film *Westworld*?

19 How many pints are there in five quarts?

20 Diana Ross was the lead singer of which 1960s group?

Easy

Medium

Hard

Answers to QUIZ 387 – Pot Luck

1	Cornwall	11	Planning permission
2	Kesha	12	*Superman*
3	Buckingham Palace	13	Llandudno
4	Carmela	14	October
5	China and India	15	A carp
6	Gene Pitney	16	*The Young Ones*
7	*Rocky* (1976)	17	Seven
8	Calabria	18	A church or cathedral
9	The Dallas Cowboys	19	Norway
10	A pig	20	Breadcrumbs

Easy

1   Which reality TV star had to drop out of the 2019 series of *Strictly Come Dancing* due to injury?

2   Who presented the travel programme *Wish You Were Here...?* from 1974 until 2003?

3   Forensic scientists Jack Hodgson and Clarissa Mullery are characters in which crime drama series?

4   What kind of establishment is the Woolpack in *Emmerdale*?

5   On the quiz show *The Chase*, which of the Chasers is nicknamed "The Dark Destroyer"?

6   Which character in *EastEnders* famously said: "You ain't my mother"?

7   Who created *Brookside* and *Hollyoaks*?

8   *River City* is set in which UK country?

9   Which character in the original series of *Dallas* was temporarily replaced by Donna Reed for one series?

10 James, Siegfried and Tristan were the main characters in which TV series, first broadcast in 1978?

Medium

11 The phrase "Tonight...I'm going to be" is associated with which talent show?

12 In which county is *Birds of a Feather* set?

13 In which decade was *Match of the Day* first broadcast?

14 What relation was Nell Mangel to Joe Mangel in *Neigbours*?

15 In which series was a central character famously shot in 1980?

16 Captain Jim Brass and Nick Stokes are characters in which US police procedural series?

17 What is the name of the taxi firm featured in *Coronation Street*?

18 Which series on astronomy broadcast its 800th episode in May 2020?

19 The phrase "Here's one I made earlier" is associated with which children's TV series?

20 What kind of establishment provided the setting for *Crossroads*?

Hard

Answers to QUIZ 388 – And

1	Hampshire	11	Henry Fielding
2	Lion	12	Jerusalem (William Blake)
3	WWII	13	Greek
4	1950s (1950)	14	Three (2004, 2005, 2009)
5	Asia (a territory of India)	15	California
6	*Baywatch*	16	*This Is Your Life*
7	*Dreamgirls*	17	Moderately slow
8	The east coast	18	Erasure
9	South America (Andes)	19	Labrador
10	Italy	20	The euro

1   In *Toy Story 4*, Forky has been made from which item of cutlery?

2   In which century was the writer Rudyard Kipling born?

3   What type of creature is a shubunkin?

4   In which year did WWII begin?

5   How many times did Sir Ian Botham win the BBC Sports Personality of the Year Award?

6   Which weather presenter took part in the 2015 series of *Strictly Come Dancing*?

7   In the traditional bingo call, what number is "One dozen"?

8   Which TV cook wrote the 2016 book *Foolproof Cooking*?

9   Which two singers duetted on the 2020 no.1 hit *Rain on Me*?

10 On which motorway are the Reading services?

11 Apart from the Commonwealth star, how many stars are there on the Australian flag?

12 In music, what symbol raises a note by a semitone?

13 What do you do if you mollify someone?

14 In Germany, what type of public building is a *Bibliothek*?

15 Is Ar the chemical symbol for argon or arsenic?

16 Which rugby league club is nicknamed "The Saints"?

17 The city of Albufeira is in which European country?

18 Who directed the 2019 film *1917*?

19 *Who's David* was a 2004 UK chart-topper for which band?

20 John Rocha is a famous name in which profession?

Easy

Medium

Hard

Answers to QUIZ 389 – Pot Luck

1	Gene Vincent	11	Selfless
2	Sian Gibson	12	France
3	George Clooney	13	Second year
4	Pig	14	Swimming (slightly underwater)
5	*Blade Runner*	15	Georgian
6	Lloyd Mullaney	16	The Cairngorms National Park
7	Spain	17	Spanish
8	Floorwalker	18	An amusement park
9	Country and western	19	Ten pints
10	Scotland	20	The Supremes

Easy

1 What colour is the central stripe on the French flag?

2 In the Spanish language, is a tilde mark placed above or below a letter?

3 What is the name of the main character, a former prisoner, in the musical *Les Misérables*?

4 Who was the second Spanish golfer to captain the European Ryder Cup team?

5 Who succeeded François Mitterrand as President of France?

6 *Cuatro* is the Spanish word for which number?

7 Which principality lies between France and Spain?

8 The Tour de France was first staged in which century?

9 The French Riviera is part of the coastline of which body of water?

10 Which Spanish region is alphabetically first?

11 Which French leader was nicknamed "Boney" by the British?

12 What type of shop is a Spanish *carnicería*?

13 What is the French equivalent of the English name Andrew?

Medium

14 Spanish footballer Fernando Torres transferred to Chelsea FC in 2011 from which other English club?

15 Which region of France is the furthest west?

16 What type of food is gazpacho?

17 Which Parisian square has a name that means "Place of peace"?

18 What stringed instrument traditionally accompanies a flamenco dance?

19 *Bateau* is the French word for which type of transport?

20 By what name is the top flight football league in Spain usually referred to?

Hard

Answers to QUIZ 390 – Long-running Series

1	Jamie Lang	11	*Stars in Their Eyes*
2	Judith Chalmers	12	Essex
3	*Silent Witness*	13	1960s (1964)
4	Pub	14	Mother
5	Shaun Wallace	15	*Dallas* (JR Ewing)
6	Zoe Slater	16	*CSI: Crime Scene Investigation*
7	Phil Redmond	17	Street Cars
8	Scotland	18	*The Sky at Night*
9	Miss Ellie	19	*Blue Peter*
10	*All Creatures Great and Small*	20	A motel

ANSWERS ON PAGE 395

1 Who wrote the 2009 children's book *Mr Stink*?

2 In which century did Botticelli paint *The Birth of Venus*?

3 What name is given to a bedcover made from lots of different-coloured pieces sewn together?

4 General Hux was a character in which series of sci-fi films?

5 What word is said in the Christian church at the end of a prayer?

6 Noel Gallagher played which instrument in Oasis?

7 JAL is the flag-carrier airline of which country?

8 What do Americans call braces?

9 Which leader was born earliest: Lawrence of Arabia, Napoleon Bonaparte or William Sherman?

10 In which decade were swimming races using the butterfly stroke introduced into the Olympic Games?

11 Doris Lessing was awarded which Nobel Prize in 2007?

12 What word precedes "cabinet" in the name of the senior group of Opposition ministers?

13 Which Scottish city is alphabetically first?

14 Which golf club is used to hit the ball furthest: an iron, a sand wedge or a wood?

15 Mosel wine is from which European country?

16 *A New Flame* (1989) and *Stars* (1991) were hit albums for which group?

17 Which Hollywood actress portrayed Cora's mother, Martha Levinson, in the TV series *Downton Abbey*?

18 The coastal town of Workington lies within which English county?

19 What animal's name is used to refer to a hard task or a boring job?

20 What name is given to the charge added to a restaurant bill where the customer has brought their own wine?

Easy

Medium

Hard

Answers to QUIZ 391 – Pot Luck

1	A spork	11	Five
2	19th century (1865)	12	Sharp
3	A fish (goldfish)	13	Placate them
4	1939	14	Library
5	Once (1981)	15	Argon
6	Carol Kirkwood	16	St Helens
7	12	17	Portugal
8	Mary Berry	18	Sam Mendes
9	Lady Gaga and Ariana Grande	19	Busted
10	M4	20	Fashion design

Easy

1 Who preceded Bill Clinton as US president?

2 What is the name of Benedict Cumberbatch's character in The Avengers series of films?

3 In which country are the Billboard music charts published?

4 In Scotland, a ben is what type of geographical feature?

5 In the film *The Lion King*, what is the name of the hornbill who advises Simba?

6 Which car company makes the Continental model?

7 How many pockets are there on a billiard table?

8 Is Benin in the east or the west of Africa?

9 "Every day we say a prayer – will they change our bill of fare" is a lyric from which 1960 song?

10 What is the first name of Ben Stiller's character in the 2000 film *Meet the Parents*?

Medium

11 How old was Billie Piper when she became the youngest person to have a single that went straight to no.1 in the UK?

12 Benidorm is situated on which Spanish coastal region?

13 Billingsgate is an area of which English city?

14 Ben Crenshaw is a former professional in which sport?

15 Bill Bixby starred as scientist Dr Banner in which TV series, first shown in 1978?

16 Darren Bent (b.1984) played international football for which team?

17 A billycan is usually used to hold what?

18 What is the official language of Bangladesh?

19 What do British people call an American billfold?

20 Benson was the butler to the Tates in which TV comedy series?

Hard

---

1 What was the title of the 1980s sitcom about the Porter family?

2 What was Freddie Mercury's real surname?

3 Which acting duo topped the UK charts in 1995 with *Up on the Roof*?

4 In which decade was the TV series *Ashes to Ashes* set?

5 What colour shirts do the British and Irish Lions rugby team wear?

6 Which fruit might be Barbados or maraschino?

7 What name was given to a Victorian institution for the destitute?

8 Does the word "splice" mean "to join" or "to separate"?

9 In the Middle Ages, what type of animal might have been referred to as a charger?

10 Which is the highest of these voice ranges: alto, mezzo-soprano or soprano?

11 The 1956 film *The Battle of the River Plate* was set during which conflict?

12 Who was the UK Home Secretary from May 2010 until July 2016?

13 In which field throwing event is the maximum weight of the object thrown 2kg for men and 1kg for women?

14 Daniel Quilp and Kit Nubbles are characters in which novel by Charles Dickens?

15 The town of Bannockburn lies just south of which Scottish city?

16 What substance is carried by a channel known as a sluice?

17 The Italian name Luigi corresponds to which French name?

18 What name is given to the liquid that surrounds an unborn baby?

19 What is seven multiplied by six?

20 Which of these is the correct spelling: tarpaulin, tarpaullin or tarrpaulin?

Answers to QUIZ 393 – Pot Luck

1	David Walliams	11	Nobel Prize in Literature
2	15th century (c.1485)	12	Shadow
3	Patchwork quilt	13	Aberdeen
4	Star Wars	14	A wood
5	Amen	15	Germany
6	Guitar	16	Simply Red
7	Japan (Japan Airlines Ltd)	17	Shirley MacLaine
8	Suspenders	18	Cumbria
9	Napoleon Bonaparte (1769)	19	Donkey (work)
10	1950s (1956)	20	Corkage

Easy

1   Volks Electric Railway, opened in 1883, is a feature of which seaside resort on the English south coast?

2   What name is given to the process of removing errors from a computer program?

3   To what did the cost of a colour TV licence rise in April 2020?

4   Daisy-wheel, dot matrix and thermal are types of what computer-related item?

5   What is the decimal equivalent of the binary number 100?

6   For what do the letters CCTV stand?

7   The Victorian model village of Saltaire is part of which English city?

8   In relation to computing, for what is the word "bot" short?

9   The Porsche car company was founded in which country?

10 On a standard keyboard, which letter is between Y and I?

11 White and which other colour are used on the WhatsApp logo?

12 The Tamagotchi™ toy first went on sale in which decade?

13 For what is the acronym OFCOM short?

14 What nationality was the inventor Charles Babbage?

15 Which was the first network to launch 5G technology in the UK, in May 2019?

16 What is the name of the BBC's online study support for UK school pupils?

17 Which of these scientific advances happened first: the discovery of radium, the formation of the theory of relativity, or the creation of the periodic table?

18 In which century was the mechanical cash register invented?

19 What name is given to the study of metals?

20 In relation to a business, for what do the letters R&D stand?

Answers to QUIZ 394 – Bill and Ben

1	George HW Bush	11	15
2	Dr (Stephen) Strange	12	The Costa Blanca
3	USA	13	London
4	A mountain	14	Golf
5	Zazu	15	*The Incredible Hulk*
6	Bentley	16	England
7	Six	17	Water (for heating over a campfire)
8	The west	18	Bengali
9	*Food, Glorious Food (Oliver!)*	19	A wallet
10	Greg (Focker)	20	*Soap*

QUIZ 397 – Pot Luck

ANSWERS ON PAGE **399**

1. Bergen is the second-largest city of which Scandinavian country?

2. The adjective "femoral" relates to which part of the human body?

3. Is Romania a monarchy or a republic?

4. Stan Butler and Jack Harper were characters in which comedy series, first shown in 1969?

5. The name of which type of pudding also means a stupid person?

6. The 1972 album *Liza with a "Z"* was the soundtrack of a concert by which singer?

7. Which Asian country is the world's largest producer of gold?

8. The town of Bury lies on which river?

9. How many Grand Slam doubles tennis tournaments did John McEnroe win during his career?

10. Which of the Great Lakes is the largest by volume?

11. What word can mean both "a small glass toy" and "a type of stone"?

12. In which English city does the supermarket Morrisons have its headquarters?

13. *Call Me Maybe* was a 2011 single by which US singer?

14. In poetry, for what is the word "morrow" short?

15. Who released the 1994 single *Cornflake Girl*?

16. The football team UC Sampdoria are based in which country?

17. In relation to geology, a tremor is a minor version of what event?

18. The shipping area of Cromarty lies off the coast of which UK country?

19. What is the main herb in a Lincolnshire sausage?

20. Who played Mike Barrett in the TV series *Casualty*?

Answers to QUIZ 395 – Pot Luck

1	*2point4 Children*	11	WWII
2	Bulsara	12	Theresa May
3	Robson & Jerome	13	The discus
4	1980s	14	*The Old Curiosity Shop*
5	Red	15	Stirling
6	Cherry	16	Water
7	A workhouse	17	Louis
8	To join	18	Amniotic fluid
9	A horse	19	42
10	Soprano	20	Tarpaulin

ANSWERS ON PAGE 400

1   The cover of which 1973 album by Pink Floyd featured a prism splitting light into a rainbow?

2   If someone is described as light-fingered, what do they do?

3   *The Light Fantastic*, the second novel in the Discworld series, was written by which author?

4   What is the middle colour on a traffic light?

5   "The feeling that I can't go on is light years away" is a lyric from which 1984 song?

6   Which group had a 2005 UK hit with *City of Blinding Lights*?

7   Who co-starred with Willem Dafoe in the 2019 film *Lighthouse*?

8   What two-word term is given to the glow from street lights that makes it difficult to see the stars?

9   By what acronym is a light-emitting diode usually referred to?

10 Which group had a 1976 UK hit with *Blinded by the Light*?

11 How many Oscars did the 2016 film *Moonlight* win?

12 In which type of building would you find footlights?

13 A light box is used to treat which winter condition?

14 Who wrote the 1854 poem *The Charge of the Light Brigade*?

15 "Your mind becomes fast as lightning" is a lyric from which 1974 song?

16 Melisandre of Asshai was a priestess of the Lord of the Light in which TV series?

17 What are you doing if you are "tripping the light fantastic"?

18 Who wrote the 1995 novel *Northern Lights*?

19 What is the full name of the group known as ELO?

20 "Rage, rage against the dying of the light" is a line from which poem by Dylan Thomas?

Answers to QUIZ 396 – Innovations and Inventions

1	Brighton	11	Green
2	Debugging	12	1990s (1996)
3	£157.50	13	Office of Communications
4	Printer	14	English
5	Four	15	EE
6	Closed-circuit television	16	BBC Bitesize
7	Bradford	17	The creation of the periodic table (1869)
8	Robot	18	19th century (1879)
9	Germany (Stuttgart)	19	Metallurgy
10	U	20	Research & Development

1   What fraction of a pint is a fluid ounce?

2   Singer Lulu was born in which country?

3   What shape is the ball in Australian rules football?

4   Which of these actors starred in *Doctor Who* first: Christopher Eccleston, Colin Baker or Peter Capaldi?

5   In the card game Happy Families, what is Mr Chip's occupation?

6   Which comedy series was set in the fictional Rudge Park Comprehensive?

7   What is a jonquil?

8   Which single by The Hollies originally reached the top five in 1969, and had further success in 1988 after being used in a TV advert?

9   Which vitamin is most prominent in blackberries?

10 Korky the Cat was a character in which comic?

11 Who had a hit in 1983 with *I'm Still Standing*?

12 What is 111 in Roman numerals?

13 Which rugby union club has a red star and crescent on its badge?

14 If something is described as "cumbersome", is it heavy or light?

15 Which annual sporting event finishes at Mortlake?

16 What two colours are the stripes on the flag of the USA?

17 In which century did Sir Thomas More write *Utopia*?

18 Ceylon is the former name of which country?

19 How many musicians play in a septet?

20 The African National Congress is a political party in which country?

Answers to QUIZ 397 – Pot Luck

1	Norway	11	Marble
2	The femur (the bone in the thigh)	12	Bradford
3	A republic	13	Carly Rae Jepsen
4	*On the Buses*	14	Tomorrow
5	Fool	15	Tori Amos
6	Liza Minnelli	16	Italy (Genoa)
7	China	17	An earthquake
8	River Irwell	18	Scotland
9	Nine (Wimbledon five times, US Open four times)	19	Sage
10	Lake Superior (2900 cubic miles)	20	Clive Mantle

What are the names of these TV presenters?

1    2    3

4    5    6

7    8    9

Easy

Medium

Hard

Answers to QUIZ 398 – Light

1	*The Dark Side of the Moon*	11	Three
2	Steal things	12	A theatre
3	Sir Terry Pratchett	13	Seasonal Affective Disorder (SAD)
4	Amber	14	Alfred, Lord Tennyson
5	*The Power of Love* (Jennifer Rush)	15	*Kung Fu Fighting* (Carl Douglas)
6	U2	16	*Game of Thrones*
7	Robert Pattinson	17	Dancing
8	Light pollution	18	Philip Pullman
9	LED	19	Electric Light Orchestra
10	Manfred Mann's Earth Band	20	*Do Not Go Gentle Into That Good Night*

1　Who wrote and originally recorded the song *Fool (If You Think it's Over)*, later a hit for Elkie Brooks?

2　Who wrote the 1946 novel *Titus Groan*?

3　Who provided the voice of Tigress in the film *Kung Fu Panda*?

4　In Greek mythology, Poseidon was the god of the sea and of what types of event?

5　To the nearest ten, how many episodes of *ER* were made?

6　As at 2020, *Voyager 2* is the only spacecraft to have visited which two planets?

7　Provoleta is an Argentinean variety of what food?

8　The Cheltenham Gold Cup-winning horse Kauto Star was bred in which country?

9　Before becoming president, Barack Obama served as a senator for which US state?

10　What word can mean both "a substance that fixes dye" and "sarcastic"?

11　In which European capital city did the 1919 Peace Conference take place?

12　Roald Dahl wrote the screenplay for which James Bond movie?

13　Which animal has a name that means "whalehorse" in Dutch?

14　What is the nickname of the Japanese rugby union team?

15　Which book of the Old Testament comprises three sermons delivered to the Israelites by Moses?

16　Silicon and lead belong to which chemical family?

17　Which fictional sci-fi hero was born on March 22, 2233, in Riverside, Iowa?

18　Which Commonwealth capital holds the record for being the world's windiest city?

19　In which country is the city of Mosul?

20　The heritage town of Adare lies in which Irish county?

Answers to QUIZ 399 – Pot Luck

1	1/20th	11	Sir Elton John
2	Scotland	12	CXI
3	Oval	13	Saracens
4	Colin Baker (1984)	14	Heavy
5	Carpenter	15	The Boat Race
6	*The Inbetweeners*	16	Red and white
7	A flower (of the narcissus family)	17	16th century (1516)
8	*He Ain't Heavy, He's My Brother*	18	Sri Lanka
9	Vitamin C	19	Seven
10	*The Dandy*	20	South Africa

ANSWERS ON PAGE 404

Easy

1   What nationality was the composer Jules Massenet (d.1912)?

2   Which George Gershwin opera features the characters Sportin' Life, Crown and Mingo?

3   Franz Schubert was originally buried alongside which other famous composer?

4   Which girl group had a hit with *Red Dress* in 2006?

5   What is the English translation of the movement in *Carnival of the Animals* entitled *Personnages à longues oreilles*?

6   By what title is Beethoven's *Piano Concerto No. 5* popularly known?

7   Which singer had top ten hits with *Shoulda Woulda Coulda* (2002) and *Come as You Are* (2004)?

8   Herb Alpert and Jerry Moss founded which record label in 1962?

9   The singing group Fisherman's Friends are from which English county?

10   Who said "I don't make music for eyes. I make music for ears."?

11   *Pilate's Dream* is a song from which musical?

12   As at 2020, which film holds the record for having the best-selling soundtrack of all time?

Medium

13   Which musical instruments are made by a founder?

14   What was the top-selling album of the 1970s in the UK?

15   For which song, released as a single in 1994, did Bruce Springsteen win an Oscar?

16   In which decade was the Royal Philharmonic Society formed?

17   "She's the one that keeps the dream alive" is a lyric from which 1997 song?

18   *Fluorescent Adolescent* was a 2007 single by which band?

19   A fanfare is traditionally played on what type of instrument?

20   Which dance act had UK top ten hits in 1992 with *Twilight Zone* and *Workaholic*?

Hard

Answers to QUIZ 400 – TV Presenters

1   Fiona Bruce
2   Naga Munchetty
3   Adrian Chiles
4   Richard Hammond
5   Steve Backshall
6   Gabby Logan
7   Matt Baker
8   Liz Bonnin
9   Ore Oduba

1. In the New Testament, from which city did Paul escape in a basket?

2. What is the name of the economic policy that is based on controlling the financial supply of a country?

3. In the video game series, what type of mythical creature is Spyro?

4. Which is the second-largest city in California?

5. As at 2019, how many gold medals had Peru won at the Olympic Games?

6. Which Special Administrative Region of China is a famed resort for gamblers?

7. In the film *Finding Nemo*, what type of animal is the character Bruce?

8. Which sport was popularised by Duke Kahanamoku (d.1968)?

9. Which spirit is used to make a mint julep cocktail?

10. Dr Max Liebermann was a character in which 2019 TV crime series?

11. What was the title of Marilyn Monroe's last feature film?

12. The village of Branston, famous for the pickle brand, lies in which English county?

13. Which Russian writer wrote the works *The Song of the Stormy Petrel* (1901) and *Children of the Sun* (1905)?

14. From which English port did the *RMS Lusitania* make her maiden voyage?

15. Which is the smallest species of tiger?

16. Who originally said "One swallow does not a summer make"?

17. Which US state has the nickname "the Land of Lincoln"?

18. Nereid is a moon of which planet?

19. Which type of apple did the Beatles use for the logo of their record label?

20. What does the name "Felix" mean in Latin?

Answers to QUIZ 401 – Pot Luck

1	Chris Rea	11	Paris
2	Mervyn Peake	12	*You Only Live Twice*
3	Angelina Jolie	13	Walrus
4	Earthquakes	14	The Cherry Blossoms
5	330 (331)	15	Deuteronomy
6	Uranus and Neptune	16	Carbon family
7	Cheese	17	Captain Kirk
8	France	18	Wellington
9	Illinois	19	Iraq
10	Mordant	20	County Limerick

1   A *galette des rois*, traditionally eaten to mark the end of the festive season, originated in which country?

2   *Nocciola* is the Italian for which nut?

3   The Clare Valley is a wine-producing region in which country?

4   What type of food is the Italian burrata?

5   What is the navy bean called in the UK?

6   The word "salary" is derived from the Latin name of which condiment?

7   In cooking, what is meant by the word "shuck"?

8   The alternative name of the custard tart called *pastel de nata* includes the name of which country?

9   What type of food is bucatini?

10   Which French word is used to describe a small independent winery or beer maker?

11   Barmbrack, a type of bread, is associated in Ireland with which annual event?

12   Malmsey is a sweet variety of which wine?

13   With what is *nero di seppia* pasta coloured?

14   In Sweden, tallstrunt tea is made with the leaves of which tree?

15   Which seafood can be served in Kilpatrick (or Kirkpatrick) style?

16   What is the "It" in a Gin and It cocktail?

17   Which alcoholic beverage can be described as Lambic?

18   The name for which perfume mixture can also be applied to a meat stew?

19   What type of meat is cured to make speck?

20   In which country is the nut-based liqueur Frangelico produced?

Answers to QUIZ 402 –Music

1	French	11	*Jesus Christ Superstar*
2	*Porgy and Bess*	12	*The Bodyguard*
3	Beethoven	13	Bells
4	The Sugababes	14	*Bridge Over Troubled Water* (Simon and Garfunkel)
5	Characters with long ears	15	*Streets of Philadelphia* (from *Philadelphia*)
6	*The Emperor*	16	1810s (1813)
7	Beverley Knight	17	*Brimful of Asha* (Cornershop)
8	A&M Records	18	The Arctic Monkeys
9	Cornwall	19	A trumpet
10	Adele	20	2 Unlimited

1   What type of insects are found in the family of creatures known as carabids?

2   Who won The Open golf championship in 2019?

3   Who recorded the 2018 country rap song *Old Town Road*?

4   The Peter and Paul Fortress is situated in which Russian city?

5   "Pack it up, pack it in, let me begin" is the opening lyric from which 1992 song?

6   *Tuskegee* was a 2012 album from which soul singer?

7   In which decade of the 20th century did Norway become a fully independent country?

8   What is the nickname of the Ireland national rugby league team?

9   Atlantis was first mentioned in the writings of which ancient Greek philosopher?

10 Chequers, the official residence of the UK Prime Minister, lies close to which range of hills?

11 Sheku Kanneh-Mason, who won the BBC Young Musician competition in 2016, plays which instrument?

12 Who stars in the sitcom *Sick of It*?

13 Which novel by Ernest Hemingway features a trip to Pamplona from Paris?

14 In which century was the first authorised English version of the Bible printed?

15 Dane Bowers was runner-up to which other contestant on *Celebrity Big Brother* in 2010?

16 Astronauts Fred Haise and Jack Swigert took part in which Apollo mission?

17 The Kenai Fjords National Park is in which US state?

18 Edward VII's coronation was delayed from June to August in which year as a result of him requiring surgery?

19 The shoebill stork is native to which continent?

20 In *The Princess Diaries* (2001), who played Queen Clarisse Renaldi of Genovia?

Answers to QUIZ 403 – Pot Luck

1	Damascus	11	*The Misfits*
2	Monetarism	12	Staffordshire
3	A dragon	13	Maxim Gorky
4	San Diego	14	Liverpool
5	One (in shooting, 1948)	15	Sumatran tiger
6	Macau	16	Aristotle
7	Great white shark	17	Illinois
8	Surfing	18	Neptune
9	Bourbon whiskey	19	Granny Smith
10	*Vienna Blood*	20	Happy

1 Which area in Lower Manhattan has a name derived from "Triangle Below Canal Street"?

2 Which common man's name comes from the Greek for "horse-loving"?

3 Which word can mean both a unit of measurement in chemistry and a burrowing animal?

4 The word "honcho", for a boss, derives from which language?

5 Which qualification has a name that comes from the Greek for "double folded" of paper?

6 Which keyboard character is called an octothorpe?

7 Agraphia is the inability to perform which task?

8 What does an antipyretic help prevent?

9 What does *avant* mean?

10 Which word for a festival is taken from an Italian word meaning "the removal of meat"?

11 The name of which Swiss city is also another name for alfalfa?

12 "Antediluvian" refers to a time before which Biblical event?

13 The Arctic takes its name from the Greek for which animal?

14 Which metallic element takes its name from the Greek word for "stone"?

15 Which board game was originally called Lexiko?

16 The annelid group of worms takes its name from the Latin for what shape?

17 Which French word for a bedroom means "a place to sulk"?

18 Which everyday food takes its name from the Aztec for "bitter water"?

19 What is the only country with a name that contains both the letters Q and Z?

20 Of what is ergophobia a fear?

Answers to QUIZ 404 – Food and Drink

1	France	11	Hallowe'en
2	Hazelnut	12	Madeira wine
3	Australia	13	Squid ink
4	Cheese	14	Pine
5	Haricot bean	15	Oysters
6	Salt	16	Sweet (Italian) vermouth
7	To remove an outer casing	17	Beer
8	Portugal (Portuguese egg tart)	18	Potpourri
9	Pasta	19	Pork
10	Boutique	20	Italy

1   Nijō and Gion are districts of which Japanese city?

2   Which author wrote the novels *Lie Down with Lions* (1985) and *Code to Zero* (2000)?

3   In relation to crime in the US, for what do the letters APB stand?

4   In which decade was Italy's Salvatore Schillaci the top scorer in a FIFA World Cup Finals tournament?

5   Which actress starred in the films *Water for Elephants* (2011), *Devil's Knot* (2013) and *Inherent Vice* (2014)?

6   US author Jeff Lindsay created which antihero, portrayed on television by Michael C Hall?

7   What was the full first name of lyricist Ira Gershwin?

8   By which more common name is woodbine known?

9   In the nursery rhyme, in what did the three wise men of Gotham go to sea?

10 In which decade did Kingston become the capital of Jamaica, taking over from Spanish Town?

11 Which is the second-largest German state, by land area?

12 To the nearest ten, how many countries are there in Asia?

13 What was the full name of the *Sex and the City* character usually referred to as "Mr Big"?

14 The powan fish is found in which European country?

15 Which inventor said "I failed my way to success"?

16 To the nearest five percent, what percentage of the human body is made up of hydrogen?

17 Jai alai is a version of which Basque ball game?

18 The Roman fort of Birdoswald is situated in which modern-day county?

19 Two outer rings were identified around which planet by the Hubble telescope in 2003-05?

20 The marasca is a type of which fruit?

Answers to QUIZ 405 – Pot Luck

1	(Ground) beetles	11	Cello
2	Shane Lowry	12	Karl Pilkington
3	Lil Nas X	13	*The Sun Also Rises*
4	St Petersburg	14	16th century (1539 – The Great Bible)
5	*Jump Around* (House of Pain)	15	Alex Reid
6	Lionel Richie	16	*Apollo 13*
7	1900s (1905)	17	Alaska
8	Wolfhounds	18	1902
9	Plato	19	Africa
10	The Chiltern Hills	20	Dame Julie Andrews

Easy

1   The flight between the islands of Westray and Papa Westray is only 1.5 minutes long. In which island group does it take place?

2   The Blasket Islands lie off the west coast of which country?

3   Which British Overseas Territory hosted the Island Games sporting competition in 2019, despite not being an island?

4   What is the common name of the plant, native to the Canary Islands, that has the Latin name *Dracaena Draco*?

5   How many major islands are there in the Ionian islands?

6   The rock known as the "Old Man of Storr" lies on which island?

7   Which is the largest of the Ionian islands?

8   The Little Green Train tourist service runs on which Mediterranean island?

9   The island of Rapa Nui (Easter Island) is a territory of which country?

10 Réunion island in the Indian Ocean is part of which country?

11 To which island group does Colonsay belong?

Medium

12 Samson is the largest uninhabited island in which UK island group?

13 Carrauntoohil is the highest mountain on which island?

14 The island of Lindau lies in which state of Germany?

15 What is the alternative name of the Hill of the Church of John on the Isle of Man, where the island's laws are proclaimed?

16 On which Mediterranean island would you find the Valley of the Temples?

17 Port Vila is the capital of which Pacific island nation?

18 What is the second-largest island in the world?

19 Which 115-island archipelago in the Indian Ocean has the capital Victoria?

20 On which UK island is there a pub that never closes?

Hard

Answers to QUIZ 406 – Words

1	Tribeca	11	Lucerne
2	Philip	12	The flood
3	Mole	13	Bear
4	Japanese	14	Lithium
5	Diploma	15	Scrabble®
6	Hash symbol (#)	16	Ring
7	Writing	17	Boudoir
8	A fever	18	Chocolate
9	Ahead of	19	Mozambique
10	Carnival	20	Work

1   Phnom Penh, the capital of Cambodia, lies on which river?

2   Trivandrum Airport is located in which Asian country?

3   Who played Dr Grace Augustine in the 2009 film *Avatar*?

4   In which decade did Manchester United FC win their first FA Cup?

5   Sergey Bubka (b.1963) was a world champion in which sport?

6   In 1813, Robert Southey became Poet Laureate after which Scottish poet declined the position?

7   Which band released the 1970s albums *Band on the Run* and *London Town*?

8   Which element has a name from the German for "copper demon"?

9   The USA's annexation of which state led to the Mexican-American War in 1846?

10 What word completes the title of the 2012 Justin Bieber and Nicki Minaj hit, *Beauty and a ___*?

11 In Roman mythology, who was the mother of Cupid?

12 Which country sent the rover *Yutu* to the Moon in 2013?

13 The Mahabodhi Temple in Bodh Gaya is a temple for which religion?

14 *Cichorium intybus* is the Latin name for which edible plant?

15 Under what name did the Labour Party win its seats as MPs in the 1900 and 1906 elections?

16 Na_2CO_3 is the formula for which chemical compound?

17 In which century was the Cistercian order of monks formed?

18 By what name is the Central Criminal Court of England and Wales better known?

19 Who co-created and starred in the 2020 TV series *Feel Good*?

20 In which country were football and golf banned in 1457?

Easy

Medium

Hard

Answers to QUIZ 407 – Pot Luck

1	Kyoto	11	Lower Saxony
2	Ken Follett	12	50 (48)
3	All points bulletin	13	John James Preston
4	1990s (1990)	14	Scotland
5	Reese Witherspoon	15	Thomas Edison
6	Dexter	16	10 (9.5%)
7	Israel	17	Pelota
8	Honeysuckle	18	Cumbria
9	A bowl	19	Uranus
10	1870s (1872)	20	Cherry

Easy

1   In which year was the Partition of India, creating India and the Dominion of Pakistan?

2   Which revolutionary died as a result of an assassination attempt by Ramón Mercader in 1940?

3   Which event marked the end of the Vietnam War in 1975?

4   The Battle of Antietam, or Sharpsburg, was a significant 1862 battle in which conflict?

5   In which country was the WWI Battle of Fromelles fought?

6   The capital city of which African country was named after US president James Monroe?

7   Who was the first European explorer known to have reached New Zealand?

8   Which airline flew the first commercial transatlantic flight, in 1938?

9   Who was king of the United Kingdom at the time of the American Revolution and Napoleon's defeat at Waterloo?

10 From which English airport did Amy Johnson begin her pioneering flight to Australia?

11 Which ship transported the Unknown Warrior from France to England?

Medium

12 The first man walked on the Moon in 1969. In which year did the last moonwalk of the 20th century take place?

13 The name of which geological age means "Old Stone Age"?

14 In which decade did Charles Darwin's expedition on *HMS Beagle* take place?

15 In which Caribbean country did the Six Years' War take place from 1868-74?

16 Which US president unveiled the Statue of Liberty?

17 Martin Luther King Jr's assassin, James Earl Ray, was arrested in which country?

18 In 1872, in which ocean was the *Mary Celeste* found drifting without a crew?

19 Which future US president was the youngest naval aviator of WWII?

20 The Battle of Long Tan was part of which conflict?

Hard

Answers to QUIZ 408 – Islands

1	The Orkney Islands	11	The Inner Hebrides
2	Ireland	12	The Isles of Scilly
3	Gibraltar	13	Ireland
4	Dragon tree	14	Bavaria
5	Seven	15	Tynwald Hill
6	Isle of Skye	16	Sicily
7	Kefalonia	17	Vanuatu
8	Sardinia	18	New Guinea
9	Chile	19	The Seychelles
10	France	20	Lundy (Marisco Tavern – but only serves during permitted hours!)

ANSWERS ON PAGE **413**

1 Who played the title role in the 2017 film *Lady Bird*?

2 Belvoir Castle lies in which English county?

3 In which decade was Dame Iris Murdoch born?

4 Who plays Anne in the TV series *The Windsors*?

5 Rh is the chemical symbol for which element?

6 Canberra, Nevada, and Snow Cap are varieties of which vegetable?

7 What is the pen name of thriller writer James Grant (b.1954)?

8 How is a plantar wart more commonly known?

9 Who is the lover of Orlando in Shakespeare's *As You Like It*?

10 Which of the bones in the human ear differs by one letter from the word for the members of a former South American empire?

11 Which Scottish football team is nicknamed "The Jags"?

12 The Sennheiser electronics company specialises in what type of equipment?

13 The Wollemi National Park lies in which Australian state?

14 What shape appears on the flag of Morocco?

15 What sport would you have been playing if you were using a Haskell ball?

16 Jim Toth is the second husband of which Hollywood actress?

17 Which group recorded a cover version of *West End Girls* in 1993?

18 Who took over from Phillip Schofield as the main *Children's BBC* presenter?

19 An Amok curry is steamed wrapped in what type of leaves?

20 In the name of the record label RCA, for what did the letters RCA originally stand?

Answers to QUIZ 409 – Pot Luck

1	River Mekong	11	Venus
2	India	12	China
3	Sigourney Weaver	13	Buddhism
4	1900s (1909)	14	Chicory
5	Pole vault	15	Labour Representative Committee
6	Sir Walter Scott	16	Sodium carbonate
7	Wings	17	11th century (1098)
8	Nickel	18	The Old Bailey
9	Texas	19	Mae Martin
10	*Beat*	20	Scotland

1   Detective Kenzo Mori featured in which 2019 TV series?

2   Who created the 2020 sci-fi TV series *Avenue 5*?

3   The TV series *Little House on the Prairie* was set in which US state?

4   Who joined the *Call the Midwife* cast in 2018 to play Sister Hilda?

5   Lauren Lee Smith plays the title role in which Canadian crime drama series?

6   Who took over as chief of the hunters in the TV series *Hunted* following the departure of Peter Bleksley?

7   Adam Frost is a presenter on which long-running TV series?

8   Who played Dorothea Brooke in the 1994 TV adaptation of *Middlemarch*?

9   Who joined the *Eggheads* team after winning the second series of *Are You an Egghead*?

10 Which former tennis player was runner-up to Joe Swash on the 2008 series of *I'm a Celebrity...Get Me Out of Here!*?

11 Who wrote the novels on which the 1970s TV series *The Pallisers* was based?

12 The Channel 4 sitcom *Home* is set in which Surrey town?

13 In 2003, Will Mellor won a celebrity edition of which singing talent show?

14 What was the profession of Patrick Glover in the TV series *Father, Dear Father*?

15 In which sitcom, shown from 2013 to 2016, did Mathew Baynton play an elf?

16 Who were the co-presenters of the 2020 series *Easy Ways to Live Well*?

17 Who played Detective Marty Hart in the series *True Detective*?

18 Ed Chigliak, played by Darren E Burrows, was a character in which 1990s TV series?

19 *The Mentalist* was set in which US state?

20 Cress Williams plays which DC superhero in a TV series of the same name?

Answers to QUIZ 410 – History

1	1947	11	*HMS Verdun*
2	Leon Trotsky	12	1972
3	The Fall of Saigon	13	Palaeolithic
4	American Civil War	14	1830s (1831-36)
5	France	15	Dominican Republic
6	Liberia (Monrovia)	16	Grover Cleveland
7	Abel Tasman	17	England
8	Lufthansa	18	The Atlantic Ocean
9	George III	19	George Bush Snr (aged 18)
10	Croydon Airport	20	Vietnam War

1   Which singer played Bombalurina in the 2019 film *Cats*?

2   In the children's series *Captain Scarlet and the Mysterons*, from which planet did the Mysterons arrive?

3   Detective Carrie Wells is the main character in which US crime series?

4   In which country is the Seto Inland Sea?

5   Which element makes up around 42% of Mercury's atmosphere?

6   Who wrote the children's novels *Birthday Boy* (2017) and *Head Kid* (2018)?

7   How old was Miley Cyrus when she was cast as Hannah Montana?

8   The dish of Poké bowl is central to which cuisine?

9   What was the name of Jafar's parrot in the 1992 animated film *Aladdin*?

10   Who wrote the screenplay for *Brief Encounter*?

11   For what type of music is John Philip Sousa (d.1932) best known?

12   What was the name of Melbourne's Docklands Stadium from 2009 to 2018, a name shared with an English football stadium?

13   Who composed the Oscar-winning score for the 1987 film *The Last Emperor*?

14   What is the name of Catalans Dragons' home stadium?

15   Coffee is believed to have originally been grown on which continent?

16   Before becoming president, Bill Clinton served as the governor for which US state?

17   The saying that "youth is wasted on the young" is attributed to which playwright?

18   Which US poet wrote *"Hope" is the Thing with Feathers* (c.1861)?

19   Which word describes cows and oxen?

20   Which band, formed in the 1970s, briefly changed their name to Morris and the Minors?

Easy

Medium

Hard

Answers to QUIZ 411 – Pot Luck

1	Saoirse Ronan	11	Partick Thistle FC
2	Leicestershire	12	Audio
3	1910s (1919)	13	New South Wales
4	Vicki Pepperdine	14	A star
5	Rhodium	15	Golf
6	Cauliflower	16	Reese Witherspoon
7	Lee Child	17	East 17
8	Verruca	18	Andy Crane
9	Rosalind	19	Banana leaves
10	Incus (Incas)	20	Radio Corporation of America

1   Which brand of motorcycles has the nickname "Hog"?

2   Billund Airport is located in which Scandinavian country?

3   In terms of vehicles, for what do the letters AWD stand?

4   Which car manufacturer has a name that translates as "I roll" in Latin?

5   In which country is the 140-mile-long scenic road called the Icefields Parkway?

6   Bristol Blenheim was the name of which two different forms of transport, one made from 1935, the other from 1976?

7   In which decade was the Trabant car first produced?

8   What was the name of the high-speed tilting train introduced in the UK in 1978?

9   Which three US automobile companies are collectively known as "the Big Three"?

10 Which old-fashioned word for a form of public transport is Latin for "for all"?

11 In which US state is the 125-mile long Seward Highway?

12 Which early form of transport with a French name derives from the term "swift foot"?

13 Which car manufacturer has a logo featuring a stylised image of a serpent eating a human?

14 What type of transport is produced by the Piaggio company?

15 In 1972, which UK city became the last to close its trolleybus system?

16 In which decade were double yellow lines introduced as a road marking in the UK?

17 What is used to measure a fuel's ability to resist engine knock?

18 Which sports car manufacturer makes the Gallardo?

19 DXB is the airport code for which Asian airport?

20 The Bradfield Highway crosses which famous bridge?

Answers to QUIZ 412 – Television

1	*Giri/Haji*	11	Anthony Trollope
2	Armando Iannucci	12	Dorking
3	Minnesota	13	*Fame Academy*
4	Fenella Woolgar	14	A novelist
5	*Frankie Drake Mysteries*	15	*Yonderland*
6	Ben Owen	16	Hugh Fearnley-Whittingstall and Steph McGovern
7	*Gardeners' World*	17	Woody Harrelson
8	Juliet Aubrey	18	*Northern Exposure*
9	Pat Gibson	19	California
10	Martina Navratilova	20	Black Lightning

1   Which actress wrote the 2019 novel *A Nice Cup of Tea*?

2   What was the name of James I's wife (d.1619)?

3   The Celebes Sea is part of which ocean?

4   *Trelawny* is a patriotic song from which English county?

5   Which sport is played by the Severn Stars?

6   In the Roman mythological story of Romulus and Remus, which of the twins committed fratricide?

7   What was the title of the first UK commercial breakfast television programme, which began broadcasting in 1983?

8   In relation to entertainment, for what does the acronym EGOT stand?

9   What are the names of the twins in the musical *Blood Brothers*?

10 For which Premier League football club did Tim Cahill play from 2004 to 2012?

11 In which US state was the novel *Gone With the Wind* set?

12 Which weapon was named after a large trumpet invented and played by 1930s US comedian Bob Burns?

13 Philosopher and author Albert Camus (d.1960) was born in which country?

14 A Shirley Temple cocktail traditionally consists of which soft drink with a splash of grenadine?

15 Which Hollywood actress starred in the 1944 film *Cover Girl*?

16 What is 3 factorial, written as 3!?

17 In which chapter of Genesis does the story of the Flood begin?

18 Which Radio 5 presenter was named Best Speech Presenter at the 2020 Audio and Radio Industry Awards?

19 What is the basis of a remoulade sauce?

20 Alberta, Saskatchewan and which other Canadian province are known as "the Prairie Provinces"?

Easy

Medium

Hard

Answers to QUIZ 413 – Pot Luck

1	Taylor Swift	11	Marches
2	Mars	12	Etihad Stadium
3	*Unforgettable*	13	Ryuichi Sakamoto
4	Japan	14	Stade Gilbert Brutus
5	Oxygen	15	Africa
6	David Baddiel	16	Arkansas
7	11	17	George Bernard Shaw
8	Hawaiian	18	Emily Dickinson
9	Iago	19	Bovine
10	Sir Noël Coward	20	Madness

What are these Greek letters?

1

2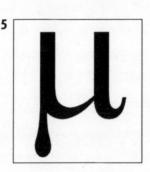

3

4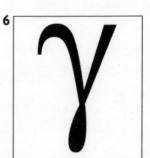

5

6

7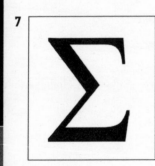

8

9

Easy

Medium

Hard

Answers to QUIZ 414 – Getting Around

1	Harley-Davidson (Harley Owners Group)	11	Alaska
2	Denmark	12	Velocipede
3	All-wheel drive	13	Alfa Romeo
4	Volvo	14	Motorbikes and scooters
5	Canada	15	Bradford
6	An aircraft (bomber) and a car	16	1960s (1960)
7	1950s (1957)	17	Octane rating
8	Advanced Passenger Train (APT)	18	Lamborghini
9	Fiat Chrysler, Ford and General Motors	19	Dubai
10	Omnibus	20	Sydney Harbour Bridge

1   The Snowbirds are the aerobatics team of the air force in which country?

2   What nationality was the composer Donizetti (d.1848)?

3   As at the end of 2019, which element in the periodic table was alphabetically last?

4   The Sun-Maid brand of raisins is associated with which US state?

5   What type of creature is a black-tailed godwit?

6   According to the 2019 Global Peace Index, what was the world's second most peaceful country?

7   In the TV series *The Simpsons*, who is the mayor of Springfield?

8   The Ocean of Storms can be found where in the solar system?

9   What is the name of the young teacup who befriends Belle in *Beauty and The Beast* (1991)?

10   Which instrument has a name that means "wooden sound" in Greek?

11   What is added to crème pâtissière to make crème diplomat?

12   What was the nickname of the Hughes H-4 Hercules aeroplane, which made its only flight in 1947?

13   In Greek mythology, Zeus turned his lover Io into what type of animal?

14   Who was King of the English from 929 to 939 AD?

15   What is the major religion in Ecuador?

16   The team mate of Graham Hill, which British driver was runner-up in the 1968 Formula 1 Championship?

17   As at end of 2019, Brian Lara held the record for the highest individual score in a Test Cricket match. What was his score?

18   In which decade did eligible UK citizens first receive an old age pension?

19   What nationality was Gertrude Ederle, the first woman to swim the English Channel?

20   Which band had a 1975 hit with *Fancy Pants*?

Easy

Medium

Hard

Answers to QUIZ 415 – Pot Luck

1	Celia Imrie	11	Georgia
2	Anne of Denmark	12	Bazooka
3	The Pacific Ocean	13	Algeria
4	Cornwall	14	Ginger ale
5	Netball	15	Rita Hayworth
6	Romulus	16	6 (3 x 2 x 1)
7	*TV-am*	17	Chapter six
8	Emmy, Grammy, Oscar and Tony (awards)	18	Emma Barnett
9	Eddie and Mickey	19	Mayonnaise (or sometimes aioli)
10	Everton FC	20	Manitoba

Easy

1   Which was the first thoroughfare in London to display Christmas lights?

2   In 1962, which type of transport had a trial period connecting Rhyl in North Wales with The Wirral?

3   The statue of *Boadicea and Her Daughters* is situated next to which bridge in London?

4   Which major city in the UK is built on two extinct volcanoes?

5   In which decade was the Advertising Standards Authority founded in the UK?

6   Which city is named after Lady Wulfruna?

7   In the RAF, what rank is immediately below squadron leader?

8   The Pontcysyllte Aqueduct, the highest aqueduct in the world, carries which waterway?

9   Which London Underground line was constructed in the 1960s?

10 Magdalen Bridge in Oxford spans which river?

11 The Hercules Garden is within the grounds of which Scottish castle?

12 The arts complex of Snape Maltings is in which English county?

13 Chiswick House in west London is an example of what type of architecture?

14 The Northampton Museum is particularly noted for its collection of which items of clothing?

Medium

15 What is the fourth-largest city in Scotland, by population?

16 What event was held in Bellahouston Park in Glasgow from May to December 1938?

17 Who, as well as in 2016-7, became the First Minister of Northern Ireland in January 2020?

18 The ruins of Waverley Abbey, the first monastery to be founded in the British Isles, lie in which county?

19 Which Pembrokeshire seaside town has a Welsh name that means "Fortlet of the fish"?

20 Ten of the Red Arrows' team of mechanics and a photographer are collectively referred to by what name, that also refers to a style of entertainment?

Hard

Answers to QUIZ 416 – Greek Letters

1   Theta
2   Epsilon
3   Beta
4   Lambda
5   Mu
6   Gamma
7   Sigma
8   Omicron
9   Delta

ANSWERS ON PAGE 421

1   What is the largest member of the gull family?

2   What is Brad Pitt's real first name?

3   Who is Steve Rogers' superhero alter ego?

4   How are the two institutions The International Bank for Reconstruction and Development and the International Development Association referred to?

5   In 1961, who became the first golfer from outside of the USA to win the US Masters?

6   The 2001 film *The Score* was the last film to feature which Hollywood great?

7   Bono and the Edge wrote the song to which 1990s Bond film?

8   Imperial Airways became part of which airline in 1939?

9   Who duetted with Michael McDonald on the 1986 single *On My Own*?

10 Conisburgh Castle is located in which metropolitan county?

11 How many Punic Wars were fought between Rome and Carthage?

12 What is the longest distance race over which the women's speed skating Olympic event takes place?

13 Which bakery item can also refer to the winning of a tennis set 6-0?

14 Rosalind is a moon that orbits which planet?

15 Galileo Galilei Airport serves which Italian city?

16 Which road connects The Mall with Hyde Park Corner?

17 Which English novelist was awarded the Nobel Prize in Literature in 1932?

18 What might be referred to as a libation?

19 The Kikuyu is the largest group of people in which country?

20 Which fruit has the Latin name *Olea europaea*?

Easy

Medium

Hard

Answers to QUIZ 417 – Pot Luck

1	Canada	11	Chantilly cream (whipped cream)
2	Italian	12	The Spruce Goose
3	Zirconium	13	Cow
4	California	14	Aethelstan
5	A bird	15	Christianity (Catholicism)
6	New Zealand	16	Sir Jackie Stewart
7	Joe Quimby	17	400
8	On the Moon	18	1900s (1909)
9	Chip	19	American
10	Xylophone	20	Kenny

1 In which city is the Whitney Museum of American Art?

2 In which UK city is the mosaic sculpture known as *The Big Fish*?

3 Which artist painted *Benefits Supervisor Sleeping* (1995)?

4 *The Studio Boat* (1876) and *Snow at Argenteuil* (1874-75) are works by which artist?

5 *View of Toledo* (c.1600) is a famous work by which artist?

6 Queen Maria Luisa of Spain was the patroness of which artist?

7 What word completes the title of a 1912 work by Marcel Duchamp, ___ *Descending a Staircase, No.2*?

8 In which European capital was Gustav Klimt born?

9 *Beautiful Inside My Head Forever* was a two-day auction in 2008 of which artist's work?

10 Who painted a famous version of Van Gogh's *Bedroom at Arles* in 1992?

11 *Chelsea Girls* was a 1966 film produced by which artist?

12 What does the name of the art movement De Stijl mean in English?

13 Futurism was a 20th-century movement based primarily in which country?

14 Which red pigment was originally made from the powdered mineral cinnabar?

15 The statue *Pietà*, housed in the Vatican City, is the only piece that was signed by which artist?

16 By what nickname was US artist Anna Mary Robertson Moses better known?

17 Titian was the most important member of which 16th-century school of painting?

18 In which city is the Munch Museum?

19 Who painted the 17th-century work *Girl Interrupted at Her Music*?

20 Who presented the 2020 BBC Four series *The Art Mysteries*?

Answers to QUIZ 418 – The UK

1	Regent Street (1954)	11	Blair Castle
2	Hovercraft	12	Suffolk (near Aldeburgh)
3	Westminster Bridge	13	Palladian
4	Edinburgh	14	Footwear
5	1960s (1962)	15	Dundee
6	Wolverhampton	16	The Empire Exhibition
7	Flight lieutenant	17	Arlene Foster
8	The Llangollen Canal	18	Surrey (near Farnham)
9	The Victoria Line	19	Tenby (Dinbych-y-pysgod)
10	The River Cherwell	20	Circus

1 In which county is the National Trust property of Anglesey Abbey?

2 Which metallic element has a name from the Greek word for "smell"?

3 Who said "I have no special talent. I am only passionately curious"?

4 Kanō Jigorō created which martial art, in 1882?

5 Which novel and film series takes place on the fictional Isla Nublar?

6 *Who's Sorry Now* (1984) was an autobiography by which US singer?

7 The flag of Indonesia (red band on top and white on the bottom) is a reverse of which country's flag?

8 What is a gudgeon?

9 Sir Bertram Ramsay was responsible for which major operation during WWII?

10 In Norse mythology, who were the parents of Baldur?

11 In which modern-day country did the poet Shelley die in 1822?

12 In which year was AP McCoy named BBC Sports Personality of the Year?

13 Which dance duo recorded the 1994 single *I Like to Move It*?

14 Louis Botha (d.1919) was the first prime minister of which country?

15 In which decade was *Reader's Digest* first issued?

16 What was the real first name of actress Bette Davis?

17 Which Mediterranean island is known as "The Scented Isle"?

18 Who presents the Radio 4 documentary series *Short Cuts*?

19 The loris is native to which continent?

20 In which year was golf reinstated as an Olympic sport, after an absence of 112 years?

Easy

Medium

Hard

Answers to QUIZ 419 – Pot Luck

1	The great black-backed gull	11	Three
2	William	12	5,000m
3	Captain America	13	A bagel
4	The World Bank	14	Uranus
5	Gary Player	15	Pisa
6	Marlon Brando	16	Constitution Hill
7	*GoldenEye*	17	John Galsworthy
8	British Overseas Airways Corporation (BOAC)	18	A drink
9	Patti LaBelle	19	Kenya
10	South Yorkshire	20	Olives

Easy

1   From what natural substance is the feature that scientists call the Great Atlantic Sargassum Belt formed?

2   The Cerrado is an important ecoregion in which country?

3   In relation to weather, what is a downburst?

4   Which five-letter term is given to a major ecological community that extends over a large area?

5   The Harmattan is a dry wind from which desert?

6   On a weather map, what do areas have equal amounts of, if they are connected by an isohyet?

7   Which wood is harvested from the tropical hardwood tree species *Tectona grandis*?

8   Which continent experiences the least rainfall?

9   Which natural property does a lodestone display?

10 The Aeolian process involves which natural phenomenon's ability to change the surface of the Earth?

Medium

11 The world's largest crater lake, Lake Toba, lies in which country?

12 In geography, what is a ria?

13 Which African country has the longest coastline?

14 The island of Ischia lies in which sea?

15 Tasmania and New Zealand are located in which band of strong winds?

16 Which country has the greatest number of active volcanoes?

17 The word "maelstrom", used to describe a violent and confused situation, is named after a strong current off the coast of which country?

18 What, in Scotland, is a corrie?

19 What six-letter word of Spanish origin refers to a dry stream bed with steep sides?

20 The Eisriesenwelt, near Salzburg, is the largest cave in the world of what type?

Hard

1 What is the English name of the South American river Rio de la Plata?

2 The Eagles hit *Lyin' Eyes* was taken from which studio album?

3 Which waterbird has a Slavonian species?

4 Which comedian is a co-host on *The Big Narstie show*?

5 In which decade was Joan of Arc canonised?

6 Who became the controller of Radio 4 in 2019?

7 How long is a term served by someone elected to the US Senate?

8 Which 1959 film is set in the fictional European Duchy of Grand Fenwick?

9 A chattering is the collective noun for which members of the crow family?

10 What shape is a bacillus bacterium?

11 How old was Lottie Dod (d.1960) when she became the youngest winner of the Wimbledon women's singles tennis championship in 1887, a record that still stood in 2020?

12 As at 2020, which two teams have won the most Copa America football tournaments?

13 Which driver was runner-up in both the 1983 and 1984 Formula 1 seasons?

14 What word completes the title of the 1922 silent film, *Nanook of the ___*?

15 Who was the father of Vanessa Redgrave?

16 Who recorded the 1993 album *The Colour of My Love*?

17 The ancient city of Nineveh lay on which river?

18 In which decade was Philip K Dick's novel *Do Androids Dream of Electric Sheep?* published?

19 Blenheim Palace in Oxfordshire was designed in which architectural style?

20 The Hoover Institution is part of which US university?

Answers to QUIZ 421 – Pot Luck

1	Cambridgeshire	11	Italy
2	Osmium	12	2010
3	Albert Einstein	13	Reel 2 Real
4	Judo	14	South Africa
5	Jurassic Park	15	1920s (1922)
6	Connie Francis	16	Ruth
7	Poland	17	Corsica
8	A fish	18	Josie Long
9	The Dunkirk evacuation	19	South America (Brazil)
10	Odin and Frigg	20	2016

ANSWERS ON PAGE 426

1 In which century did William Harvey publish his work *On the Motion Of the Heart and Blood in Animals*?

2 Which metallic element is named after the Greek god Iris?

3 Rhea is a moon of which planet?

4 What does a renogram show?

5 A fullerene molecule consists of which element?

6 What is the axis of rotation of the Earth, in degrees (allow five degrees either way)?

7 In which decade was penicillin first mass-produced?

8 What is the term for the family of five elements: fluorine, chlorine, bromine, iodine and astatine?

9 What crosses a Wheatstone bridge?

10 What is produced by the human body's eccrine glands?

11 What is the medical term for an artificial body part?

12 Which infectious human disease was certified as eradicated in 1980?

13 In terms of light, what does Snell's law formulate?

14 Which parts of the body are made of osteons?

15 The element ruthenium is named after which country?

16 The brain activity monitoring method electroencephalography is commonly abbreviated to which three letters?

17 Roughly what percentage of the human body is blood: 8%, 18% or 28%?

18 What colour is liquid oxygen?

19 Which sugar is released in the digestion of starch in the human body?

20 Carbohydrates are formed of which three chemical elements: hydrogen, oxygen and which other?

Answers to QUIZ 422 – Natural World

1	Seaweed	11	Indonesia (Sumatra)
2	Brazil	12	A narrow coastal inlet
3	A strong current of air	13	Madagascar
4	Biome	14	The Tyrrhenian Sea
5	The Sahara	15	The Roaring Forties
6	Rainfall	16	Indonesia
7	Teak	17	Norway
8	Antarctica	18	A valley (formed by glacial erosion)
9	Magnetism	19	Arroyo
10	Wind	20	Ice (cave)

1   Which is the slowest land mammal species on earth?

2   Which *Game of Thrones* actress married singer Joe Jonas in Las Vegas in May 2019?

3   Who was the runner-up in the 2020 Masters Snooker Championship?

4   What compound gives Mars its reddish appearance?

5   Which US city is nicknamed "the City of Brotherly Love"?

6   For which 1945 film did Joan Crawford win her only Oscar?

7   Which protest song, written by Abel Meeropol, was recorded by Billie Holiday in 1939?

8   What is the more common name for the laryngeal prominence?

9   For what do the initials AT&T stand in the name of the US company?

10 How many times did Jim Clark win the Mexican Grand Prix, a record as of 2019?

11 Which musician was crowned King of the Jungle in the 2011 series of *I'm a Celebrity…Get Me Out of Here!*?

12 The three main ingredients of the dish Scotch woodcock are toast, anchovy paste and which other item?

13 What was the real surname of the actor Richard Burton?

14 Who was the first president of the Fifth Republic of France?

15 The Thames Flood Barrier has one bank in the borough of Newham and the other bank in which borough?

16 The area known as "the Valley of the Volcanoes" lies in which South American country?

17 In which century did the philosopher John Stuart Mill live and die?

18 The condition spondylosis affects which specific part of the human body?

19 What colour arrow featured in the title of an 1888 novel by Robert Louis Stevenson?

20 *Songs Our Daddy Taught Us* (1958) was an album by which singing duo?

Easy

Medium

Hard

Answers to QUIZ 423 – Pot Luck

1	River Plate	11	15
2	*One of These Nights*	12	Uruguay (15) and Argentina (14)
3	The grebe	13	Alain Prost
4	Mo Gilligan	14	*North*
5	1920s (1920)	15	Sir Michael Redgrave
6	Mohit Bakaya	16	Céline Dion
7	Six years	17	River Tigris
8	*The Mouse That Roared*	18	1960s (1968)
9	Choughs	19	Baroque
10	Rod-shaped	20	Stanford University

1 ZSL stands for what, in relation to conservation?

2 Zion National Park lies in which US state?

3 The Spanish city of Zaragoza lies on which river?

4 What type of creature is a zander?

5 Which car company manufactured the Zephyr from 1950 to 1972?

6 In the New Testament, Zebedee was the father of which two apostles?

7 Zac Efron was born in which decade?

8 *Zadok the Priest* was written by which composer?

9 The island of Zanzibar lies in which ocean?

10 Who became the oldest ever winner of the FIFA World Cup when he captained the Italy side to victory in 1982?

11 Zandvoort is a racing circuit in which country?

12 General Zod is a particular enemy of which superhero?

13 Who composed the soundtracks to *Inception* (2010) and *Interstellar* (2014)?

14 Where is a zuchetto worn?

15 ZA is the car registration code for which country?

16 Which children's author created the world of Zafrica?

17 The name of the fictional vigilante Zorro is the Spanish for which animal?

18 Dr John Zoidberg was a character in which animated sci-fi series?

19 The Ziller Valley lies in which European country?

20 In a Mexican town or city, what is the zócalo?

Answers to QUIZ 424 – Science

1	1620 (1628)	11	Prosthesis
2	Iridium	12	Smallpox
3	Saturn	13	Refraction
4	The kidneys	14	Bones
5	Carbon	15	Russia
6	23.45 degrees	16	ECG
7	1940s (1944)	17	8%
8	Halogens	18	(Pale) blue
9	Electricity	19	Maltose
10	Sweat	20	Carbon

1 What is the medical name for the navel?

2 *(Your Love Keeps Lifting Me) Higher and Higher* was a 1967 hit for which singer?

3 The title of the novel *The Fault in Our Stars* is taken from a quote from which play by Shakespeare?

4 Who co-starred with Matthew Goode in the 2010 film *Leap Year*?

5 The juice of which fruit is used in a rickey cocktail?

6 What is Taylor Swift's middle name?

7 The Weight Watchers diet was devised by New Yorker Jean Nidetch in which decade?

8 Who played lawyer Henry Drummond in the 1960 film *Inherit the Wind*?

9 Who collaborated with Jack White on *Another Way to Die*, the theme song to the Bond film *Quantum of Solace*?

10 Bolsover Castle lies in which English county?

11 Who stars as Geralt of Rivia in the Netflix series *The Witcher*?

12 Greg Louganis (b.1960) was a world and Olympic champion in which sport?

13 In which year was the tie-break in the final set introduced at the Wimbledon tennis championships?

14 Which two European countries received aid under the 1948-49 Truman Doctrine?

15 The 18th-century Cavendish Experiment investigated which force?

16 The name of the city Chicago is derived from a word for which wild vegetable?

17 Which of these English monarchs reigned earliest: Mary I, Henry IV or Richard II?

18 In the New Testament, which of the twelve apostles is alphabetically last?

19 The song *With a Flair* is from which musical film?

20 In 1963, who became the first person to renounce a peerage so that he could stand as an MP?

Easy

Medium

Hard

Answers to QUIZ 425 – Pot Luck

1	(Three-toed) sloth	11	Dougie Poynter
2	Sophie Turner	12	Scrambled eggs
3	Ali Carter	13	Jenkins
4	Iron oxide	14	Charles de Gaulle
5	Philadelphia	15	Royal Borough of Greenwich
6	*Mildred Pierce*	16	Peru
7	*Strange Fruit*	17	19th century (1806-73)
8	Adam's apple	18	The vertebrae
9	American Telephone and Telegraph	19	Black (*The Black Arrow*)
10	Three	20	The Everly Brothers

Easy

1. What is the name of the farm that is home to the character of Worzel Gummidge?

2. What is the surname of Arrietty and Pod in the children's novel *The Borrowers*?

3. Mary Lennox is the main character in which early 20th-century children's novel?

4. Who created the character of Tom Gates?

5. Who wrote the 2018 children's novel *The Ice Monster*?

6. In the novel by SF Said, what type of cat is Varjak Paw?

7. What is the surname of Matilda in the novel by Roald Dahl?

8. Who replaced Severus Snape as Professor of Potions at Hogwarts?

9. What was the pen name of Theodor Geisel, creator of a famous feline in striped headwear?

10. Which TV cartoon character has a best friend called Boots the Monkey?

11. Dutch artist Dick Bruna created which enduring children's character?

12. What was the name of Shari Lewis' most famous sock puppet?

Medium

13. In *The Gruffalo*, the main character of the mouse meets a fox, an owl, and which other carnivorous creature?

14. What was the name of Bilbo and Frodo's house in the Shire?

15. What is the name of Alvin and the Chipmunks' adoptive father and manager?

16. Which Disney character takes his name from the Swahili for "lion"?

17. Pidsley, a farmer's cat, features in which TV series?

18. What is the name of the hound in the 1981 film *The Fox and the hound*?

19. What was the subtitle of the 2011 film *The Adventures of Tintin*?

20. Who wrote the 1965 fantasy novel *Elidor*, featuring the Watson children?

Hard

---

1 In which decade did the first women's cricket Test match take place?

2 Who plays pathologist Fleur Perkins in the TV series *Midsomer Murders*?

3 What is the name of the fictional Roman detective created by Lindsey Davis?

4 Orzo, or risoni, is what type of food?

5 Who played the inspector in the 1954 film *An Inspector Calls*?

6 Who wrote the 2019 novel *The Second Sleep*?

7 Which Japanese city has a name that translates as "East Capital"?

8 Which was the only singles Grand Slam title that tennis player Gabriela Sabatini won?

9 *The Phantom Menace* was released how many years after *Return of the Jedi*?

10 Which band recorded the 2002 album *Songs About Jane*?

11 The world's largest book fair is held in which German city?

12 Which post-Impressionist artist said "Everything in nature takes its form from the sphere, the cone and the cylinder"?

13 Charles Brandon, First Duke of Suffolk, was the brother-in-law of which English king?

14 In which country was the actress Audrey Hepburn born?

15 The opening shot in which war was referred to as "the shot heard around the world"?

16 Who succeeded Robert Runcie (Baron Runcie) as Archbishop of Canterbury in 1991?

17 How is the Shakespearean character Robin Goodfellow better known?

18 Which singer/songwriter released the 1983 album *An Innocent Man*?

19 What is the capital city of El Salvador?

20 Maximilian I served as Holy Roman Emperor in which century?

Easy
Medium
Hard

Answers to QUIZ 427 – Pot Luck

1	The umbilicus	11	Henry Cavill
2	Jackie Wilson	12	Diving
3	*Julius Caesar*	13	2019
4	Amy Adams	14	Greece and Turkey
5	Lime juice	15	Gravity
6	Alison	16	Onion (shikaakwa in the Algonquin language)
7	1960s (1963)	17	Richard II (1377-99)
8	Spencer Tracy	18	Thomas
9	Alicia Keys	19	*Bedknobs and Broomsticks*
10	Derbyshire	20	Anthony Wedgwood Benn

What are the names of these dog breeds?

1

2

3

4

5

6

7

8

Answers to QUIZ 428 – Children's Characters

1	Scatterbrook Farm	11	Miffy
2	Clock	12	Lamb Chop
3	*The Secret Garden*	13	A snake
4	Liz Pichon	14	Bag End
5	David Walliams	15	Dave
6	A Mesopotamian Blue	16	Simba
7	Wormwood	17	*Shaun the Sheep*
8	Horace Slughorn	18	Copper
9	Dr Seuss	19	*The Secret of the Unicorn*
10	Dora the Explorer	20	Alan Garner

1 What was the subtitle of the 2015 film in the Mad Max series?

2 The sinking of which ocean liner by the Germans in 1915 contributed to the USA entering WWI?

3 In the famous American folk song, what was the name of the elder daughter of the "miner forty-niner"?

4 Which country was scheduled to host the cancelled 1940 summer Olympic Games?

5 In the 1966 sci-fi film *Fantastic Voyage*, where does the voyage take place?

6 A sugar cube and Angostura bitters form the base of which cocktail, made with whiskey or brandy?

7 In the Old Testament, Rachel died following the birth of which son?

8 Of what is a comet mostly composed?

9 The Rosa Khutor resort was a venue for Alpine skiing at which Winter Olympic Games?

10 What sport do the Sydney Roosters play?

11 What sort of kisses did Mac and Katie Kissoon sing about in 1975?

12 What was the name of the publishing house founded in 1917 by Leonard and Virginia Woolf?

13 In which decade was the ENIAC computer built?

14 The Timor Sea is part of which ocean?

15 Whom did Konstantin Chernenko succeed as leader of the Soviet Union?

16 Boogie-woogie is a style of which music genre?

17 How many counties are there in the Republic of Ireland?

18 A famous diet of the 1970s was named after which New York town and village?

19 Which is the oldest independent country in Africa?

20 What was the name of Audrey Hepburn's princess in the film *Roman Holiday*?

Easy

Medium

Hard

Answers to QUIZ 429 – Pot Luck

1	1930s (1934)	11	Frankfurt
2	Annette Badland	12	Paul Cézanne
3	Marcus Falco	13	Henry VIII
4	Pasta	14	Belgium
5	Alastair Sim	15	The American War of Independence
6	Robert Harris	16	George Carey (Baron Carey of Clifton)
7	Tokyo	17	Puck
8	The US Open (1990)	18	Billy Joel
9	16 (1999 and 1983)	19	San Salvador
10	Maroon 5	20	16th century (1508-19)

1 The Circumlocution Office features in which Charles Dickens novel?

2 For what do the letters "AW" stand in the name of the organisation IFAW?

3 In which decade was the Fabian Society founded?

4 NICE sets guidelines for funding of medicines in England and Wales. What is the Scottish equivalent?

5 By which nickname was the Central Overland California and Pikes Peak Express Company better known?

6 Which UK charity was founded in 1889 as the Plumage League?

7 In which decade was the Save the Children fund founded?

8 Land at Brandelhow was the National Trust's first purchase in which modern-day National Park?

9 Which organisation began in the Canadian community of Stoney Creek in 1897?

10 In which decade was the British Library created as a separate entity from the British Museum?

11 For what do the initials ATS stand in relation to the WWII organisation?

12 In which decade was the Guide Dogs for the Blind Association formed?

13 Which organisation runs the Nature's Calendar citizen science project?

14 In which two oceans does the International Ice Patrol monitor the presence of icebergs?

15 Which organisation founded the "Woman's Guild" in 1887, opening up membership to men in 1997?

16 The RNLI's busiest lifeboat station is on the River Thames next to which bridge?

17 Which new country joined the United Nations in 2011?

18 In which city is the World Health Organization based?

19 For which organisation does Johnny English work in the film series?

20 What is the French name of the organisation often referred to in English as Doctors Without Borders?

Easy

Medium

Hard

1   In which Australian state was Qantas Airways founded?

2   Who starred as Katherine Lester in the 2016 film *Lady Macbeth*?

3   Which of the planets is the second-largest of the "gas giants"?

4   *Castor* is the genus name for which animal?

5   What name is given to a coin that is struck especially for collectors?

6   How many teams played in the 1934 FIFA World Cup?

7   *Mylo Xyloto* was a 2012 hit album for which band?

8   In which decade was the Terracotta Army discovered in China?

9   What travels through substances by convection?

10 Who portrayed Jay Gatsby in the 1974 film *The Great Gatsby*?

11 In which decade was the comic strip *Peanuts* first published?

12 What is a highly prized Blue Mauritius?

13 The Oscar-winning film *The Pianist* was set during which conflict?

14 Yale University is situated in which US state?

15 Who became Radio 3's youngest presenter when she joined the station in 2019 to present *This Classical Life*?

16 The name of which art movement, which was chosen at random, means "hobby horse"?

17 Which Irish singer, with Carrie Crowley, hosted the 1997 Eurovision Song Contest?

18 The word "electric" is derived from the Greek for what substance used in jewellery?

19 By what acronym was the Council for Mutual Economic Assistance (1949-91) better known?

20 Who was the runner-up in the BBC Sports Personality of the Year poll in 2019?

Answers to QUIZ 431 – Pot Luck

1	*Fury Road*	11	*Sugar Candy Kisses*
2	*The Lusitania*	12	Hogarth Press
3	Clementine	13	1940s (1945)
4	Japan	14	Indian Ocean
5	Inside the human body	15	Yuri Andropov
6	Old fashioned	16	Jazz
7	Benjamin	17	26
8	Ice (mixed with dust)	18	Scarsdale (The Scarsdale Diet)
9	2014 (Sochi)	19	Ethiopia
10	Rugby league	20	Ann

1   The 1993 film *The Joy Luck Club* was based on a novel by which author?

2   Which two actresses co-starred in the 1998 film *Stepmom*?

3   Billy Casper is the main character in which 1969 film?

4   Which two actors played the title roles in the 2019 film *The Two Popes*?

5   Which Oscar-winning film was an adaption of Indian author Vikas Swarup's book *Q & A*?

6   Who played the male lead alongside Dame Elizabeth Taylor in *Giant* (1956)?

7   In which 1942 film did Sir Noël Coward play Captain EV Kinross?

8   Which 2018 documentary film told the story of triplets separated at birth?

9   Mac, a hotshot executive, is the leading character in which 1983 film?

10 To which country is James Bond sent in the opening part of *Dr No*?

11 Which film tells the true story of Operation Chastise?

12 Which film won the Best Cinematography Oscar at the 2020 award ceremony?

13 Danny and his father Frank Butterman feature in which Simon Pegg film?

14 Which future star of Doctor Who appeared in the 1963 film *This Sporting Life*?

15 The characters of Tuffnut, Fishlegs and Snotlout featured in which animated film series?

16 Ralph Fiennes played Count László Almásy in which film?

17 *The Founder* (2016), starring Michael Keaton, was about which restaurant chain?

18 Which actress featured in the films *We Bought a Zoo* (2011), *Hitchcock* (2012), and *Her* (2013)?

19 George Clooney and Julia Roberts starred in which 2016 crime thriller about a TV financial reporter?

20 Who played the wife of Jack Nicholson's character in the horror film *The Shining*?

Answers to QUIZ 432 – Organisations

1	*Little Dorrit*	11	Auxiliary Territorial Service
2	Animal Welfare	12	1930s (1934)
3	1880s (1884)	13	The Woodland Trust
4	The Scottish Medicines Consortium	14	The Atlantic and Antarctic Oceans
5	Pony Express	15	The Church of Scotland
6	The RSPB	16	Waterloo Bridge (Tower Station)
7	1910s (1919)	17	South Sudan
8	The Lake District	18	Geneva
9	The Women's Institute	19	MI7
10	1970s (1973)	20	*Médecins Sans Frontières*

1. "You made the wine now drink a cup" is a lyric from which 1975 song?

2. In which decade did the US Open tennis championship change from a grass surface to a clay surface?

3. Who played Max in the 2008 film *Get Smart*?

4. Who adapted and directed the 2019 film *Little Women*?

5. Which British sea captain founded the area of New Albion in 1579?

6. Eltham Palace lies in which borough of London?

7. What is the major religion in Algeria?

8. Who wrote the 1924 play *The Vortex*?

9. What is described by the attributes of brightness, hue and saturation?

10. The Itaipu hydroelectric dam is located on the border of Paraguay and which other country?

11. Where in the solar system would you find The Sea of Islands?

12. In which decade did the Cannes Film Festival first take place?

13. What word, meaning to move towards war without actually starting it, is associated with US Secretary of State John Dulles?

14. Who was the world heavyweight boxing champion from 1937 to 1949?

15. Released in 1975, what was the Altair 8800?

16. Which early computer shares its name with one of the Ancient Wonders of the World?

17. What name is given to the showjumping competition that involves clearing a small number of large obstacles?

18. In which decade was the Aldeburgh Festival founded?

19. Who played DI Rachel Carey in the 2019 TV series *The Capture*?

20. Who wrote the 1912 tone poem *On Hearing the First Cuckoo in Spring*?

Answers to QUIZ 433 – Pot Luck

1	Queensland	11	1950s (1950)
2	Florence Pugh	12	An 1847 postage stamp
3	Saturn	13	WWII
4	The beaver	14	Connecticut
5	Proof coin	15	Jess Gillam
6	16	16	Dadaism
7	Coldplay	17	Ronan Keating
8	1970s (1974)	18	Amber
9	Heat	19	COMECON
10	Robert Redford	20	Lewis Hamilton

Easy

Medium

Hard

ANSWERS ON PAGE 438

Easy

1   What is the most populous landlocked country in the world?

2   Which New Zealand city is nicknamed "the City of Sails"?

3   Which is the largest city in Africa?

4   Trench Town is a famous area of which city?

5   Which currency did Ecuador adopt in 2000?

6   Which country's flag consists of a red circle on a green background?

7   The Alentejo is a region of which European country?

8   Which region of China has a name that translates as "Fragrant Harbour"?

9   The ruins of the ancient city of Troy are in which modern-day country?

10 Which country was formerly known as Portuguese East Africa?

11 Which US state has a name that means "snow covered" in Spanish?

12 Cape Agulhas is the most southerly tip of which continent?

13 The Labrador Sea is part of which ocean?

14 Spandau is a borough in which European city?

Medium

15 Which US state is closest to Cuba?

16 What is the most populous city in the Southern Hemisphere?

17 How many hours is New York ahead of Los Angeles?

18 The Red River Delta is part of which country?

19 The capital of the Canadian province British Columbia is situated on which island?

20 Which island's name is the Portuguese for "wood"?

Hard

Answers to QUIZ 434 – Film

1	Amy Tan	11	*The Dam Busters*
2	Julia Roberts and Susan Sarandon	12	*1917*
3	*Kes*	13	*Hot Fuzz*
4	Sir Anthony Hopkins and Jonathan Pryce	14	William Hartnell
5	*Slumdog Millionaire*	15	*How to Train Your Dragon*
6	Rock Hudson	16	*The English Patient*
7	*In Which We Serve*	17	McDonald's
8	*Three Identical Strangers*	18	Scarlett Johansson
9	*Local Hero*	19	*Money Monster*
10	Jamaica	20	Shelley Duvall

ANSWERS ON PAGE 439

1 Which planet has an average temperature of 462 degrees Celsius?

2 Who wrote the novel series on which the 2017 film *Dark Tower* was based?

3 Which dog, also known by a different country's name, takes its name from a historical region of France?

4 *Stadium Arcadium* was a 2006 hit album for which band?

5 Who played Sid Luft, Judy Garland's third husband, in the 2019 *Judy* biopic?

6 In *Les Misérables*, what is Éponine's surname?

7 The Ishihara test is used to diagnose which disorder?

8 What name is given to a letter that can be pronounced with more than one sound?

9 What is the lowest commissioned rank in the US navy?

10 Which of these kings of England reigned first: Edward I, John or Richard I?

11 What was the name of the first permanent English settlement in North America, established in 1607?

12 Crab the dog appears in which Shakespeare play?

13 In which 1985 film did John Huston direct his daughter, Anjelica, to a supporting role Oscar?

14 On a precious metal hallmark, the head of which creature is used to identify the London Assay Office?

15 The head of which mythical creature is depicted on the Sicilian flag?

16 Whose first UK no.1 hit was *Yeh Yeh* in 1964?

17 Domino is the main Bond girl in which Ian Fleming novel and film?

18 Spraints refers to the droppings of which creature?

19 Which TV series of 2019 featured the characters of Julia Day and Benjamin Greene?

20 In which county is the town of Royston?

Easy

Medium

Hard

Answers to QUIZ 435 – Pot Luck

1	*Evil Woman* (ELO)	11	The Moon
2	1970s (1975)	12	1940s (1946)
3	Steve Carell	13	Brinkmanship (or Brinksmanship)
4	Greta Gerwig	14	Joe Louis
5	Sir Francis Drake	15	A microcomputer
6	Royal Borough of Greenwich	16	Colossus
7	Islam	17	Puissance
8	Sir Noël Coward	18	1940s (1948)
9	Colour	19	Holliday Grainger
10	Brazil	20	Frederick Delius

1   Which HE Bates novel of 1958 took its title from a line in William Shakespeare's Sonnet 18?

2   *The Coral Island* (1857) was a novel by which author?

3   In which decade was *The Prime of Miss Jean Brodie* first published?

4   Who wrote *Goodbye Columbus* (1959) and *Portnoy's Complaint* (1969)?

5   In printing, what is standardised using the Pantone system?

6   *Wives and Daughters* and *Cousin Phillis* were 1860s works by which author?

7   Which Roman writer and thinker wrote the early encyclopedic work *Natural History*?

8   The novel *A Brief History of Seven Killings* by Marlon James won which major literary prize in 2015?

9   Which Dickens novel satires America?

10   Which William Makepeace Thackeray novel has the subtitle *A Novel without a Hero*?

11   Who wrote the 2020 crime novel *The Night Fire*?

12   *A Tale of the Christ* (1880) is the subtitle to which Lew Wallace novel, made into an epic film?

13   Which famous novel of 1960 is set in Maycomb, Alabama?

14   Who wrote the 1969 memoir *As I Walked Out One Midsummer Morning*?

15   What form of transport features in Jerome K Jerome's *Three Men on the Bummel*?

16   Which journalist (d.2019) wrote the posthumously-published autobiography *Motherwell*?

17   Scottish furniture maker and burglar William "Deacon" Brodie was the inspiration behind which Robert Louis Stevenson book?

18   Who wrote the novels *After You'd Gone* (2000) and *Hamnet* (2020)?

19   The 19th-century book *The Mysterious Island* was written by which French novelist?

20   Which term to describe Australia comes from the title of a 1964 book by academic Donald Horne, which the author intended to be ironic?

ANSWERS ON PAGE 441

1   *Someone to Watch Over Me* (2011) was the third album by which singer?

2   The name of which city completes the title of the 2019 novel, *The Beekeeper of* ___?

3   The notorious highwayman Dick Turpin was born in which English county?

4   The prefix "glosso" refers to which part of the body?

5   As well as the Assassins, which other secret society features in the video game series *Assassin's Creed*?

6   Who played Oz in the 2013 film *Oz the Great and Powerful*?

7   The Java Sea is part of which ocean?

8   What name is given to a baby koala?

9   Actress Sally Lindsay was a member of which school choir, that had a 1980 Christmas hit with *There's No-one Quite Like Grandma*?

10   In which country was singer Keith Urban born?

11   Charlie Chaplin was the co-founder of which film studio?

12   In which decade was the modern British Commonwealth formed by the London Declaration?

13   Which was the first US state to ratify the constitution?

14   During which year of World War I did the Germans launch the Spring Offensive?

15   In which decade was the FBI created in the US?

16   Which of these scientists was born first: Albert Einstein, Marie Curie or Michael Faraday?

17   In the Star Wars films, Anakin Skywalker is brought over to the dark side by which character?

18   Which chemical element has the atomic number 28?

19   In the New Testament, which of the apostles had a name beginning with "B"?

20   Which singer/songwriter lived at 251 Menlove Avenue in Liverpool, now owned by the National Trust?

Answers to QUIZ 437 – Pot Luck

1	Venus	11	Jamestown
2	Stephen King	12	*The Two Gentlemen of Verona*
3	Alsatian (Alsace)	13	*Prizzi's Honor*
4	Red Hot Chili Peppers	14	A leopard
5	Rufus Sewell	15	Medusa (Gorgon)
6	Thénardier	16	Georgie Fame (and the Blue Flames)
7	Colour blindness	17	*Thunderball*
8	Polyphone	18	An otter
9	Ensign	19	*Gold Digger*
10	Richard I (1189-99)	20	Hertfordshire

1 Who served as the US Secretary of Defense from 1975 to 1977 and 2001 to 2006?

2 What was Eva Perón's occupation before going into politics?

3 Which political leader was born in the city of Gori, now part of the country of Georgia?

4 Alexander Lukashenko became the first president of Belarus in which decade?

5 From 2001 to 2009, Hillary Clinton was a senator for which state?

6 Who was elected President of the EU Commission in December 2019?

7 Who was the first US president to be impeached?

8 Sir John Key was prime minister of which country from 2008 to 2016?

9 Which US president was nicknamed "the Great Communicator"?

10 Goodluck Jonathan was the president of which African country from 2010 to 2015?

11 In 1997, Jenny Shipley became the first female prime minister of which country?

12 The prime minister of which European country was forced to resign in 2016 as a result of the Panama Papers leak?

13 Which football club did Silvio Berlusconi own from 1986 until 2017?

14 Which former prime minister was portrayed by Jason Watkins in the TV series *The Crown*?

15 Who preceded David Lloyd George (First Earl Lloyd-George of Dwyfor) as UK prime minister?

16 Josip Tito served as president of which former country from 1953 to 1980?

17 In which decade was Sir John Major born?

18 What is the minimum age at which someone can become president of the USA?

19 Édith Cresson was the prime minister of which country from 1991 to 1992?

20 Who was first elected Member of Parliament for Islington North in 1983?

Answers to QUIZ 438 – Books

1	*The Darling Buds of May*	11	Michael Connelly
2	RM Ballantyne	12	*Ben-Hur*
3	1960s (1961)	13	*To Kill A Mockingbird*
4	Philip Roth	14	Laurie Lee
5	Colour	15	The bicycle
6	Elizabeth Gaskell	16	Deborah Orr
7	Pliny the Elder	17	*Strange Case of Dr Jekyll and Mr Hyde*
8	Man Booker Prize	18	Maggie O'Farrell
9	*Martin Chuzzlewit*	19	Jules Verne
10	*Vanity Fair*	20	The Lucky Country

1 Marche is a region of which European country?

2 Who wrote and starred in the TV series *Ladhood*?

3 Claes Bang played the supernatural title role in which 2020 television series, adapted by Steven Moffat and Mark Gatiss?

4 What is Egypt's second-largest city?

5 The title of the Duke of Wellington was derived from a town in which county?

6 What is the distinguishing feature of a pinniped animal?

7 In *Measure for Measure*, the lead character is the duke of which city?

8 Which gas forms the primary composition of Mars' atmosphere?

9 Which girl group released the 1963 song *He's So Fine*?

10 In which New York borough was the 2019 film *21 Bridges* set?

11 Where is a hydrophone designed to be used?

12 Which European monarchs were the first parents-in-law of Henry VIII?

13 Who co-starred with Ryan Reynolds in the 2012 film *Safe House*?

14 The second-largest constellation gives its name to which sign of the zodiac?

15 In which decade did the Spanish-American war take place, following an explosion on the *USS Maine* in Havana Harbour?

16 Who played John Wayne's niece in *The Searchers* (1956)?

17 In which decade was Amnesty International founded?

18 Which of these metals is the best conductor of electricity: aluminium, copper or silver?

19 Kombu and wakame are what type of food?

20 How is oil of vitriol more commonly known?

Easy

Medium

Hard

Answers to QUIZ 439 – Pot Luck

1	Susan Boyle	11	United Artists
2	*Aleppo*	12	1940s (1949)
3	Essex	13	Delaware
4	Tongue	14	1918
5	Knights Templar	15	1900s (1908)
6	James Franco	16	Michael Faraday (1791)
7	The Pacific Ocean	17	Palpatine
8	Joey	18	Nickel
9	St Winifred's School Choir	19	Bartholomew
10	New Zealand	20	John Lennon

Easy

1 Myrtha is the Queen of the Wilis in which ballet?

2 Who composed the score for the 1993 film *Schindler's List*?

3 The carioca dance originated in which country?

4 Which US composer wrote *Alexander's Ragtime Band*, first recorded in 1911?

5 In which country of the UK is the ballet *La Sylphide* set?

6 Which US singer (d.1996) was known as "the First Lady of Song"?

7 What is the approximate translation of *demi-plié*?

8 Carly Simon's Oscar-winning song *Let the River Run* was used in which 1988 film?

9 Where does Act One of *Swan Lake* take place?

10 What was the full first name of US musician and actor Hoagy Carmichael?

11 Which Russian impresario commissioned Stravinsky's famous ballet scores?

12 In which capital city is the Teatro Colón opera house?

13 In which decade was Anna Pavlova born?

Medium

14 Who wrote the WWI song *Keep the Home Fires Burning*?

15 Who choreographed the ballet *The Rite of Spring*?

16 Blue Note Records is famous for which genre of music?

17 The 1958 ballet *Ondine* was intended to showcase which ballerina?

18 In which Midwest US state was Fred Astaire born?

19 Which three jewels featured in the 1967 ballet choreographed by George Balanchine?

20 Which character in Puccini's *La bohème* is described as a poet?

Hard

Answers to QUIZ 440 – Politicians

1	Donald Rumsfeld	11	New Zealand
2	Actress	12	Iceland (Sigmundur Davíð Gunnlaugsson)
3	Joseph Stalin	13	AC Milan
4	1990s (1994)	14	Harold Wilson (Baron Wilson of Rievaulx)
5	New York	15	Herbert Asquith (First Earl of Oxford and Asquith)
6	Ursula von der Leyen	16	Yugoslavia
7	Andrew Johnson (1868)	17	1940s (1943)
8	New Zealand	18	35
9	Ronald Reagan	19	France
10	Nigeria	20	Jeremy Corbyn

1   Who co-starred with Fred Astaire in the 1948 film *Easter Parade*?

2   What type of animal is the inland taipan?

3   The 1992 novel *The Way Through the Woods*, later adapted for television, featured which fictional detective?

4   Which singer released the albums *Illuminations* (2010) and *All That Echoes* (2013)?

5   What is the capital and largest city of Bahrain?

6   The ruins of Warkworth Castle are situated in which county?

7   How many realms of existence are there according to Buddhism?

8   Miley Cyrus played Missi in series ten of which long-running TV series?

9   In which film did Mae West say, "Why don't you come up sometime and see me?"

10   In the King James Bible, what is the tenth Commandment?

11   Which Scottish football team plays home games at Fir Park Stadium?

12   In which English county is the town of Selby?

13   What type of creature is a brown recluse?

14   Which of these rivers is the longest: the Danube, the Rhine or the Mississippi?

15   What is the legal minimum age for driving in Japan?

16   How many toes does an ostrich have on each foot?

17   The Hume Highway links which two major Australian cities?

18   Which chemical element is represented by the symbol Sr?

19   What are the question and answer doctrines used in the teaching of Christian religions?

20   What is affected by the disorder aphasia?

Easy

Medium

Hard

Answers to QUIZ 441 – Pot Luck

1	Italy	11	Underwater (microphone)
2	Liam Williams	12	Ferdinand and Isabella
3	*Dracula*	13	Denzel Washington
4	Alexandria	14	Virgo
5	Somerset	15	1890s (1898)
6	It has flippers (seal)	16	Natalie Wood
7	Vienna	17	1960s (1961)
8	Carbon dioxide	18	Silver
9	The Chiffons	19	Seaweed
10	Manhattan	20	Sulphuric acid

What are the names of these World Heritage Sites?

Easy

1

2

3

4

Medium

5

6

7

8

Hard

Answers to QUIZ 442 – Music and Dance

1	*Giselle*	11	Sergei Diaghilev
2	John Williams	12	Buenos Aires
3	Brazil	13	1880s (1881)
4	Irving Berlin	14	Ivor Novello
5	Scotland	15	(Vaslav) Nijinsky
6	Ella Fitzgerald	16	Jazz
7	Half-bend	17	Margot Fonteyn
8	*Working Girl*	18	Nebraska
9	A park (in front of a palace)	19	Emeralds, rubies and diamonds
10	Hoagland	20	Rodolfo

1   Caerhays Castle lies in which English county?

2   What was the name of Danny Walters' character in *EastEnders*?

3   Where in the human body is the tricuspid valve?

4   Who directed the 1950 film *Sunset Boulevard*?

5   What characteristic of materials is measured by the Brinell scale?

6   How many original members were there in Steely Dan?

7   In which decade did women's ice hockey make its debut at the Winter Olympic Games?

8   Which of these moons of Neptune is the largest: Nereid, Proteus or Triton?

9   Thomas Jefferson was elected as president of the USA in which decade?

10 Who played Captain Queeg in the 1954 film *The Caine Mutiny*?

11 The adjective of which country is often used to describe the large exercise balls used in gyms?

12 The Ashoka Chakra is on the centre stripe of the flag of which country?

13 What is the full name of the instrument usually referred to as a cello?

14 What colour is the circle used as the international sign for diabetes?

15 Asunción is the capital of which country?

16 Which term is used to describe ink-producing sea creatures such as octopuses, squid, and cuttlefish?

17 What is used to make bonito flakes in Japanese cuisine?

18 How many Apollo missions landed on the moon?

19 What is the title of the spin-off series from the TV programme *Narcos*, first aired in 2018?

20 The Dungeness crab is named after a port in which US state?

Easy

Medium

Hard

Answers to QUIZ 443 – Pot Luck

1	Judy Garland	11	Motherwell FC
2	A snake	12	North Yorkshire
3	Inspector Morse	13	A spider
4	Josh Groban	14	The Mississippi (2,320 miles)
5	Manama	15	18
6	Northumberland	16	Two
7	Six	17	Sydney and Melbourne
8	*Two and a Half Men*	18	Strontium
9	*She Done Him Wrong*	19	Catechisms
10	Thou shalt not covet	20	Speech

Easy

1   Which aviator won the Orteig Prize in 1927 for flying non-stop between New York and Paris?

2   The Stirling Prize is awarded for excellence in which discipline?

3   Who was the first person to be awarded a second Nobel Prize?

4   In which year did the Turner Prize become open to artists of any age?

5   Which singer was awarded the Presidential Medal of Freedom by Ronald Reagan in 1985?

6   In 2014, who became the youngest person to be awarded the Nobel Peace Prize?

7   In which decade was the Pulitzer Prize first presented?

8   Which Russian author declined the Nobel Prize in Literature in 1958?

9   As at 2020, for how many Oscars had Glenn Close been nominated, without having won an award?

10 Which snakes appear on the Calcutta Cup trophy?

Medium

11 The Norman Brookes Challenge Cup is awarded to the winner of which sporting event?

12 Who received the Special Recognition Award at the 2020 National Television Awards?

13 Which Take That single won the BRIT Award for Best Single in 1994?

14 In 1907, who became the first woman to receive the Order of Merit?

15 The Marcel Benoist Prize is awarded annually to the scientist of which European country who has made the most useful scientific discovery?

16 In which decade was the Rhodes Scholarship established?

17 In which sport is the Albert Goldthorpe Medal presented?

18 US scientist Richard Feynman (d.1988) was jointly awarded which Nobel Prize in 1965?

19 Which 2019 prize was jointly awarded to all four shortlisted nominees, after they requested to be considered as a collective?

20 As at 2020, who is the only US president to have been awarded the Purple Heart medal?

Hard

Answers to QUIZ 444 – World Heritage Sites

1   Machu Picchu (Peru)
2   The Alhambra Palace (Spain)
3   Skellig Michael (Republic of Ireland)
4   Petra (Jordan)
5   The Forbidden City (China)
6   Salzburg (Austria)
7   New Lanark (Scotland)
8   Rapa Nui (Easter Island)

1   Who presents the TV series *A House through Time*?

2   In which decade was the financial company Goldman Sachs founded?

3   Which dance developed in the 1890s along the Argentine-Uruguay border?

4   What was the title of the last novel completed by Charles Dickens?

5   Which UEFA Champions League-winning football club did Frank Rijkaard manage from 2003 to 2008?

6   To the nearest minute, how long is the Meat Loaf song *Bat out of Hell*?

7   Which book appears latest in the Old Testament: Ecclesiastes, Exodus or Ezra?

8   The X Games annual extreme sports event was founded in which decade?

9   How is US human rights activist Malcolm Little better known?

10 Which is the largest constellation?

11 What does a person suffering from trichotillomania feel compelled to do?

12 Native to New Zealand, what type of creature is a tuatura?

13 Who won her first singles title at the 2020 Australian Open tennis championships?

14 Ralph Fiennes made his film debut in 1992 playing which famous literary character?

15 Who was the US Secretary of State from 2013 to 2017?

16 Which bone in the human body is named after the ancient Greek word for cuckoo?

17 Which Renaissance-period woodwind instrument is bent like the letter J?

18 Mataram is the largest city on which Indonesian island?

19 What is the name of the wolfdog in the title of a 1906 novel by Jack London?

20 What is the official language of Grenada?

Easy

Medium

Hard

Answers to QUIZ 445 – Pot Luck

1	Cornwall (near St Austell)	11	Switzerland (Swiss balls)
2	Keanu Taylor	12	India
3	The heart	13	Violoncello
4	Billy Wilder	14	Blue
5	Hardness	15	Paraguay
6	Two	16	Cephalopods
7	1990s (1998)	17	Fish (tuna)
8	Triton	18	Six
9	1800s (1801)	19	*Narcos: Mexico*
10	Humphrey Bogart	20	Washington

1   The 2015 fight between Manny Pacquiao and which boxer was described as the "Fight of the Century"?

2   In 1872, the first FA Cup took place at which London location?

3   The Hopman Cup is contested in which sport?

4   The Alpine Club, founded in London in 1857, was the first club devoted to which sport?

5   In 1936, George Nissen and Larry Griswold built the first modern example of which gymnastic apparatus?

6   In which decade was the Olympic Games first televised in colour?

7   Which country beat Canada in both the 2018 and 2019 men's World Curling Championships?

8   What is the nickname of Huddersfield's rugby league team, first used in 1996?

9   Which England footballer (b.1941) made one appearance for the Essex first-class cricket team?

10 In which country is the largest cricket ground in the world, opened in February 2020?

11 How many times did Tom Watson win the Open during his golfing career?

12 At which Olympic Games did Eric Moussambani set a record slow time in a heat for the 100m freestyle swimming?

13 In which decade did seeding first take place at the Wimbledon tennis championships?

14 Arlington International Racecourse is located in which US state?

15 The Uber Cup is the women's world championship competition in which sport?

16 In which decade did the British Empire Games add "and Commonwealth" to its name?

17 Fouls in which winter sport include cross-checking and spearing?

18 Which retired professional skateboarder is nicknamed "The Birdman"?

19 Christian Coleman won which men's event in the 2019 World Athletics Championship?

20 Which US city does the Celtics basketball team call home?

Answers to QUIZ 446 – Awards and Prizes

1	Charles Lindbergh	11	Men's singles tennis title at the Australian Open
2	Architecture	12	Sir Michael Palin
3	Marie Curie	13	*Pray*
4	2017	14	Florence Nightingale
5	Frank Sinatra	15	Switzerland
6	Malala Yousafzai	16	1900s (1902)
7	1910s (1917)	17	Rugby league
8	Boris Pasternak	18	Nobel Prize in Physics
9	Seven	19	The Turner Prize
10	(King) cobras	20	John F Kennedy

1   Which is the fifth-largest planet in the solar system?

2   What is the name of Kacey Ainsworth's character in the TV series *Grantchester*?

3   In which decade was Brooklands, the first British motor racing circuit, opened?

4   What are stored in an ossuary?

5   Which king ordered the building of Hurst Castle in Hampshire?

6   Who played the title character in the 1933 film *The Private Life of Henry VIII*?

7   In the Bible, what is the name of the tent used by the Israelites to house the Ark of the Covenant?

8   Which news network was founded by the ruling family of Qatar?

9   Which remote part of the Edwards Air Force Base in Nevada is synonymous with UFO conspiracy theories?

10 How many days are there in 14 weeks?

11 What nationality is tennis player Daniil Medvedev (b.1996)?

12 In 1311, which English cathedral replaced the Great Pyramid of Giza (Pyramid of Cheops) as the world's tallest man-made structure?

13 Which of these countries has the largest area: Chad, Chile or Cuba?

14 In which decade did Superman first appear in a comic?

15 As at 2020, how many recognised states are there in Africa?

16 What does a frugivore eat?

17 The Queen of the Night is a major character in which Mozart opera?

18 How many standard periods are there in an ice hockey match?

19 What measure of gold is 75% pure?

20 A tallit is a prayer shawl worn in which religion?

Easy

Medium

Hard

Answers to QUIZ 447 – Pot Luck

1	David Olusoga	11	Pull out their hair
2	1860s (1869)	12	Reptile
3	The tango	13	Sofia Kenin
4	*Our Mutual Friend*	14	Heathcliff (*Wuthering Heights*)
5	Barcelona	15	John Kerry
6	Ten minutes	16	Coccyx
7	Ecclesiastes	17	Crumhorn
8	1990s (1995)	18	Lombok
9	Malcolm X	19	*White Fang*
10	Hydra	20	English

1   The monkey puzzle tree is also known as a pine from which country?

2   Who wrote the 1995 novel *Enigma*, adapted into a film released in 2001?

3   Which group released the 1991 single *Mysterious Ways*?

4   The lines "A paradox, a paradox, a most ingenious paradox" appear in which Gilbert and Sullivan operetta?

5   In the TV series *Captain Scarlet*, what was the name of the Mysteron's human intermediary?

6   What word completes the title of the 2018 sci-fi film, *The ___ Paradox*?

7   The TV series *Murdoch Mysteries* is set in which country?

8   In which county is the ancient woodland site of Puzzlewood?

9   *The Mysterious Affair at Styles* was the first novel by which author?

10 Which game show features a "Teatime Teaser" before advertisement breaks?

11 Who co-starred as Nick and Audrey Spitz in the 2019 film *Murder Mystery*?

12 Which children's author wrote *The Mystery of the Burnt Cottage* (1943) and *The Mystery of Holly Lane* (1953)?

13 "You took a mystery and made me want it" is a lyric from which 1985 song?

14 Which actor carried the famous Doctor Who umbrella with a question-mark handle?

15 In the TV series *Gotham*, what was the Riddler's real name?

16 *The Mystery of Edwin Drood* (1870) was the last novel by which author, unfinished?

17 Who starred as Detective Inspector Rebecca Flint in the 2009 TV drama series *Paradox*?

18 Elgar's *Enigma Variations* were composed in which decade?

19 "Life is a mystery, everyone must stand alone" are the opening lines of which 1989 song?

20 Which comedian featured mix and match jigsaws in an episode of his *Modern Life is Goodish* TV series?

Answers to QUIZ 448 – Sport

1	Floyd Mayweather Jr	11	Five (1975, 1977, 1980, 1982, 1983)
2	(Kennington) Oval	12	2000 (Sydney)
3	Tennis	13	1920s (1924)
4	Mountaineering	14	Illinois
5	Trampoline	15	Badminton
6	1960s (1968)	16	1950s (1952)
7	Sweden	17	Ice Hockey
8	Huddersfield Giants	18	Tony Hawk
9	Sir Geoff Hurst	19	100m
10	India (Sarda Patel Stadium, 110,000 capacity)	20	Boston

1   What was the title of the 2019 TV series in which Martin Clunes portrayed DCI Colin Sutton?

2   What type of food is fattoush?

3   The 2011 period drama film *Anonymous* featured which English monarch?

4   *Word Gets Around* was the 1997 debut album by which Welsh band?

5   What is the longest distance race over which the men's speed skating Olympic event takes place?

6   The song *In the Ghetto*, a hit for Elvis Presley, is set in which city?

7   Which of these emperors reigned first: Claudius, Caligula, or Tiberius?

8   Which county cricket side did Dom Sibley join in 2018 following a spell on loan?

9   Peshawar is a major city in which country?

10 Kenny Wormald starred in the 2011 remake of which 1984 musical film?

11 What name is given to one of two or more existing forms of an element?

12 Coalville is a town in which English county?

13 Who played the lead female role in the 2012 film *This Means War*?

14 The Treaty of Manila (1946) recognised the independence of the Philippines from which country?

15 What type of craft is a Maori waka?

16 What type of animal is *Dora the Explorer* baddie Swiper?

17 The FIM is the governing body of which sport?

18 Who was the first king of Israel?

19 The dance troupe Tap Dogs was founded in which country?

20 Which pastime did Sherlock Holmes take up in his retirement?

Answers to QUIZ 449 – Pot Luck

1	Earth	11	Russian
2	Cathy Keating	12	Lincoln Cathedral
3	1900s (1907)	13	Chad (496,000 square miles)
4	Bones	14	1930s (1938)
5	Henry VIII	15	54
6	Charles Laughton	16	Fruit
7	The tabernacle	17	*The Magic Flute*
8	Al Jazeera	18	Three
9	Area 51	19	18 carat gold
10	98	20	Judaism

1   Which duo wrote the Dionne Warwick hit *Do You Know the Way to San Jose*?

2   Where in Paris is the tomb of the French Unknown Soldier?

3   Which actor starred in the 2009 sci-fi film *Knowing*?

4   The Tree of Knowledge appears in which book of the Bible?

5   The ABBA hit *Does Your Mother Know* was taken from which 1979 album?

6   Which scientist said "Knowledge of what is does not open the door to what should be"?

7   "Well I know 'cause I think about it all the time" is a lyric from which 1985 song?

8   In which European capital city was the 2011 Liam Neeson film *Unknown* set?

9   "When the wind is southerly, I know a hawk from a handsaw" is a quote from which Shakespeare play?

10 The 2013 documentary film *The Unknown Known* was about which former US Secretary of Defense?

11 *Into the Unknown* was a song from which 2019 animated film?

12 Which Greek philosopher said "All men by nature desire knowledge"?

13 Which vegetables are you said to know if you are well-versed in a subject?

14 In which decade was Beyoncé Knowles born?

15 Which actress co-starred with Paul Rudd in the 2010 film *How Do You Know*?

16 Which band had a 1989 hit with *If You Don't Know Me By Now*?

17 In which decade was "the knowledge" first required of London taxi drivers?

18 *Mr Know It All* was a 2011 song by which US artist?

19 Which US inventor said "An investment in knowledge pays the best dividend"?

20 In which year did Nick Knowles take place in *I'm a Celebrity…Get Me Out of Here!*?

Easy

Medium

Hard

1 Which Paralympian was presented with the Lifetime Achievement Award at the BBC Sports Personality awards in 2019?

2 Which is the largest town in the Irish county of Donegal?

3 The Husqvarna Group, which produces chainsaws and other outdoor power products, is based in which country?

4 What was the nickname of James Bond's autogyro in the film *You Only Live Twice*?

5 Michael Douglas found fame on which 1970s crime drama series?

6 What is the title of the Michelangelo fresco painted on the altar wall of the Sistine Chapel?

7 What is New Zealand's second-largest city?

8 How many circles of hell are there in Dante's *Inferno*?

9 Who played detective Benoit Blanc in the 2019 comedy drama film *Knives Out*?

10 How was the religious leader Karol Wojtyła better known?

11 Which Hollywood actor hosts the interview-based podcast *Here's the Thing*?

12 Which Pacific republic was formerly known as Pleasant Island?

13 In Vietnamese cuisine, what is pho?

14 What do you lose if you suffer exsanguination?

15 Which event is the first to be held in a decathlon?

16 What is the title of the cookery programme, first aired in 2020, presented by Henry Firth and Ian Theasby?

17 An area of New Delhi is named after which English architect, responsible for much of its design?

18 Which is the second-smallest US state, by area?

19 *A Walking Miracle* and *You Can Do Magic* were 1970s hits for which group?

20 Which citrus fruit is used in the gin-based Tom Collins cocktail?

Easy

Medium

Hard

---

1   In 1986, which flower was designated the national flower of the USA?

2   On what does an epiphytic plant grow?

3   What is the common name for the mostly red-flowering shrubs of the genus *Callistemon*?

4   Which plant takes its name from the Latin for "prickly plant"?

5   Which trees make up the genus *Salix*?

6   What is the more common name for rose mallow?

7   What colour are the flowers on a Judas tree?

8   A plant that is experiencing virescence is becoming what colour?

9   What type of tree is the banyan?

10 The famous tree known as the Major Oak is situated in which English forest?

11 Who was the Roman goddess of flowers?

12 What adjective describes a plant that has a green stem rather than a woody stem?

13 Tea trees and eucalyptus are part of which family?

14 What is the name of the 19th-century US pioneer who planted fruit trees across wide parts of Ohio, Pennsylvania, Indiana, and Illinois?

15 What is the maidenhair tree also called?

16 What type of plant is bamboo?

17 Orris root comes from which plant?

18 The Monterey cypress and Monterey pine are native to which US state?

19 Which part of a tree can also be called a bole?

20 How does an anemochore plant disperse its fruit or seeds?

Answers to QUIZ 452 – I Know

1	Burt Bacharach and Hal David	11	*Frozen II*
2	Under the Arc de Triomphe	12	Aristotle
3	Nicolas Cage	13	Your onions
4	Genesis	14	1980s (1981)
5	*Voulez-Vous*	15	Reese Witherspoon
6	Albert Einstein	16	Simply Red
7	*A Good Heart* (Feargal Sharkey)	17	1860s (1865)
8	Berlin	18	Kelly Clarkson
9	*Hamlet*	19	Benjamin Franklin
10	Donald Rumsfeld	20	2018

1   Which comic actor starred in the 1953 film *Trouble In Store*?

2   In the RAF, what rank is immediately above squadron leader?

3   What is Australia's third-most populous city?

4   Shoe salesman Al Bundy was the lead character on which long-running US comedy series?

5   The term "Gonzo" was first used to describe the writing style of which journalist and author?

6   Who played the lead role in the 1968 film *Planet of the Apes*?

7   Which Japanese form of entertainment has a name that means "sing, dance, skill"?

8   In 1944 Iceland became a republic, breaking a union with which country?

9   Who wrote the *The Courtney Novels* and *The Ballantyne Novels*?

10 Which Italian greeting translates into English as "at your service"?

11 The Livingstone Falls are a series of rapids on which African river?

12 Where in the human body is the philtrum?

13 Who played Mr Rochester in the 1943 film *Jane Eyre*?

14 Which bodily gland produces T cells?

15 The Prague Spring uprising took place in which year?

16 Which religious leader had a horse called Kanthaka?

17 In Greek mythology who was the mortal lover of Selene, the goddess of the moon?

18 Which winter sport was transferred from the Summer Olympics to the Winter Olympics in 1924?

19 In Indian cuisine, what are kofta?

20 Opened in 2009, which Welsh racecourse was the first new National Hunt racecourse to be built in the UK in 80 years?

Answers to QUIZ 453 – Pot Luck

1	Baroness Tanni Grey-Thompson	11	Alec Baldwin
2	Letterkenny	12	Nauru
3	Sweden	13	Soup
4	Little Nellie	14	Blood
5	*The Streets of San Francisco*	15	100m
6	*The Last Judgment*	16	*Living on the Veg*
7	Christchurch	17	Edward Lutyens (Lutyens' Delhi)
8	Nine	18	Delaware
9	Daniel Craig	19	Limmie & the Family Cookin'
10	Pope John Paul II	20	Lemon

Easy

1 In Denmark, it is traditional to pelt an unmarried person on their 25th birthday with which spice?

2 Which blue-flowered herb has a taste that is very similar to cucumber?

3 The flag of which country features the spice nutmeg?

4 What seasoned salt is added to a Bloody Mary cocktail?

5 Which herb takes its name from the Latin for "dew of the sea"?

6 What is the name of the sweet syrup used in cocktails that is made from almonds, sugar and rose water?

7 Garlic is native to which continent?

8 Which micronutrient is commonly added to salt?

9 Which cuboid, hard yellow/amber seeds are commonly used in Indian cuisine?

10 Which Italian city is particularly famous for producing balsamic vinegar?

11 How many herbs and spices does KFC boast in its secret recipe?

12 Malabar black is a form of which seasoning?

13 After cinnamon and clove, what is the world's third-most expensive spice by weight?

14 Which herb is sometimes referred to as gourmet's parsley?

15 Which common condiment is rich in the antioxidant lycopene?

16 Which rhizome is used in Indian cuisine for its flavour and bright yellow colour?

17 The mustard brand Maille originated in which country?

18 Stevia is used as a substitute for which common foodstuff?

19 Tamari is a Japanese variety of which flavouring?

20 Which US drink is traditionally flavoured with sarsaparilla?

Answers to QUIZ 454 – Trees and Plants

1	Rose	11	Flora
2	Another plant	12	Herbaceous
3	Bottlebrush	13	Myrtles
4	Cactus	14	Johnny Appleseed
5	Willow trees	15	Ginkgo (*Ginkgo biloba*)
6	Hibiscus	16	Grass
7	Pink	17	The iris
8	Green	18	California
9	Fig tree	19	The trunk
10	Sherwood Forest	20	By the wind

1   "I'd rather be liberated, I find myself captivated" is the opening line from which 1998 song?

2   What is 13 squared?

3   Constanze Weber (d.1842) was the wife of which composer?

4   In which year did Serbia and Montenegro make their debuts in the Eurovision Song Contest?

5   *Alejandro* was a 2010 hit single by which singer?

6   What is a yuzu?

7   Which New Zealand city suffered a severe earthquake in February 2011?

8   In terms of the human knee, for what do the letters ACL stand?

9   "Moonies" is a term used to describe members of which religious organisation?

10   Fremantle lies at the mouth of which river?

11   In which country did the wooden sandals called "geta" originate?

12   Which top Hollywood actor's father played Frank Costanza on *Seinfeld*?

13   Who was the first fictional female character to get a star on the Hollywood Walk of Fame?

14   What type of food is a merguez?

15   In which country is the football club AZ Alkmaar based?

16   To what do "majuscule" and "minuscule", meaning large and small, specifically refer to?

17   Which Australian actor played Perseus in the 2010 film *Clash of the Titans*?

18   Narendra Modi became the prime minister of which country in 2014?

19   In which 2014 film did Channing Tatum and Mark Ruffalo play Olympic wrestling champions?

20   To which bird family do canaries belong?

Easy

Medium

Hard

Answers to QUIZ 455 – Pot Luck

1	Sir Norman Wisdom	11	Congo
2	Wing commander	12	Under the nose (the vertical cleft)
3	Brisbane	13	Orson Welles
4	*Married... with Children*	14	The thymus
5	Hunter S Thompson	15	1968
6	Charlton Heston	16	Buddha
7	Kabuki	17	Endymion
8	Denmark	18	Ice hockey
9	Wilbur Smith	19	Meatballs
10	*Ciao*	20	Ffos Las (north of Llanelli)

1   A statue of which king on horseback occupies one of the plinths in Trafalgar Square?

2   Who wrote the 1926 novel *The Castle*?

3   In which London square are there statues of Christopher Columbus and Simón Bolivar, amongst others?

4   In which decade did the Golden Gate Bridge open?

5   Which museum was built as a result of Sir Hans Sloane leaving a large collection of objects to King George II for the nation?

6   Which of these structures is the tallest: the CN Tower, the Eiffel Tower or the St Louis Gateway Arch?

7   The world's largest surviving Victorian glasshouse is situated in which botanic garden?

8   In which South African city is the Soccer City Stadium?

9   The Scott Monument in Edinburgh is an example of what architectural style?

10   Which architect remodelled Kenwood House in London in the 18th century?

11   What type of character is the famous Las Vegas neon sign Vegas Vic?

12   How many pods are there on the London Eye?

13   On a precious metal hallmark, an image of what type of building is used to identify the Edinburgh Assay Office?

14   The stadium of Croke Park is located in which country?

15   Which Hampshire castle is the country seat of the Earl of Carnarvon?

16   The ancient Great Library was built in which Egyptian city?

17   Which monarch commissioned the Greenwich Royal Observatory?

18   The flag of which British Overseas Territory depicts a red castle with a yellow key?

19   The Bahá'í House of Worship known as the Lotus Temple lies in which capital city?

20   Who was the Roman emperor when construction began on the Colosseum?

Answers to QUIZ 456 – Flavourings

1	Cinnamon	11	Eleven
2	Borage	12	Pepper
3	Grenada	13	Cardamom
4	Celery salt	14	Chervil
5	Rosemary	15	Tomato ketchup
6	Orgeat	16	Turmeric
7	Asia	17	France
8	Iodine	18	Sugar
9	Fenugreek	19	Soy sauce
10	Modena	20	Root beer

Easy

Medium

Hard

1. To the nearest ten, how many Earth days does it take for Venus to orbit the Sun?

2. What was the subtitle of the second film in the Transformers series, released in 2009?

3. In 1911, the world's oldest known wooden implement was discovered in which English county?

4. Who had a 1977 hit with *Don't it Make My Brown Eyes Blue*?

5. What is the major religion in Mexico?

6. Which of these is not one of the "Galilean Moons" of Jupiter: Ganymede, Io or Metis?

7. In which 1978 film did Sir Peter Ustinov first play Hercule Poirot?

8. *Rhapsody on a Theme of Paganini* (1934) was written by which Russian pianist and composer?

9. Which sea creatures feature on the flag of Anguilla?

10. Who wrote the 1939 novel *Coming Up for Air*?

11. Aluminium is part of which group of elements?

12. The novels *Freedom* (2010) and *Purity* (2015) were written by which American author?

13. Who had a 1960 hit with *Chain Gang*?

14. In which English county is the earthwork statue known as *The Lady of the North* situated?

15. Which band teamed up with Sir Tom Jones in 2000 to record *Mama Told Me Not to Come*?

16. What sport is played by the Cleveland Cavaliers?

17. Harriet Tubman was a noted name in which American conflict?

18. Which African country is the most populous?

19. What was the first name of the 16th-century Italian artist known as Caravaggio?

20. Before making cars, Henry Ford worked as an engineer for a company founded by which famous inventor?

Answers to QUIZ 457 – Pot Luck

1	*Mulder and Scully* (Catatonia)	11	Japan
2	169	12	Ben Stiller's father (Jerry)
3	Mozart	13	Snow White
4	2007	14	A spicy sausage
5	Lady Gaga	15	The Netherlands
6	A citrus fruit	16	Letters (upper and lower case)
7	Christchurch	17	Sam Worthington
8	Anterior cruciate ligament	18	India
9	The Unification Church (of the United States)	19	*Foxcatcher*
10	The Swan River	20	Finches

What are the names of these guitarists?

Easy

1

2

3

Medium

4

5

6

7

8

9

Hard

Answers to QUIZ 458 – Buildings and Structures

1	George IV	11	Cowboy
2	Franz Kafka	12	32
3	Belgrave Square	13	A castle
4	1930s (1937)	14	Republic of Ireland (Dublin)
5	The British Museum	15	Highclere Castle
6	The CN Tower (1815 feet)	16	Alexandria
7	Kew Gardens (The Temperate House)	17	Charles II
8	Johannesburg (Nasrec)	18	Gibraltar
9	(Victorian) Gothic	19	Delhi (India)
10	Robert Adam	20	Vespasian (AD 22)

1 Cassius Marcellus Coolidge painted famous pictures of which animals playing poker?

2 Who played the lead female role in the 2010 film *Rabbit Hole*?

3 In the 1930s, cartoonist Alex Raymond created which sci-fi character?

4 What type of animal is a caracal?

5 In which Star Wars film was the character of Count Dooku killed?

6 Which was the only major golfing tournament won by Greg Norman, a feat he achieved twice?

7 *Flowers in The Window* was a 2002 single by which Scottish band?

8 Which Italian pastries of stuffed fried pastry dough has a name that means "little tubes"?

9 Who duetted on the 2014 single *Up* with Olly Murs?

10 Which chemical element has the atomic number 5?

11 Milwaukee is the largest city in which US state?

12 Who produced the drawing *Vitruvian Man* (c.1490)?

13 Juba is the capital and largest city of which African republic?

14 A Foucault pendulum, named after French physicist Léon Foucault, demonstrates which natural phenomenon?

15 Pam Dawber played one of the title characters in which 1970s-80s sitcom?

16 Which famous Victorian novelist published the weekly magazine *Master Humphrey's Clock*, featuring his novels and short stories?

17 In the Marx Brothers film *Duck Soup*, which of the brothers played the leader of the fictional country Freedonia?

18 As at 2020, which is the only South American country that is a member of OPEC?

19 What is usually put in a jardinière?

20 Prospero is a moon that orbits which planet?

Answers to QUIZ 459 – Pot Luck

1	220 days (224 days)	11	The boron group
2	*Revenge of the Fallen*	12	Jonathan Franzen
3	Essex (the Clacton Spear)	13	Sam Cooke
4	Crystal Gale	14	Northumberland
5	Christianity (Catholicism)	15	The Stereophonics
6	Metis	16	Basketball
7	*Death on the Nile*	17	American Civil War
8	Sergei Rachmaninoff	18	Nigeria
9	Dolphins	19	Michelangelo
10	George Orwell	20	Thomas Edison

Easy

1   Which US city holds a "Peach Drop" on New Year's Eve?

2   Waitangi Day is a public holiday held each year on February 6 in which country?

3   Charles Darwin was born on the same day as which US president, on February 12, 1809?

4   Which day was celebrated as a public holiday in England on May 29 from 1660 to 1859?

5   Which US federal holiday is celebrated annually on the third Monday of January?

6   In which year did the famous *EastEnders* Christmas Day scene take place when Den served Angie with divorce papers?

7   The Groundhog Day ceremony is held in which US state?

8   Earth Day, celebrating support for environmental causes, celebrated which anniversary in 2020?

9   What is the more common name for the Christian festival of Three Kings' Day?

10 What name is given to October 12 in Italy, Spain, and many countries of the Americas?

11 Which English county celebrates St Piran's Day on March 5?

12 The Day of the Sun, marked on April 15, is an annual celebration of the birthday of which Asian country's founder?

13 Which European country has an annual holiday known as "King's Day" on April 27?

14 In which month does International Left Handers Day take place?

15 Which former stadium hosted the US Live Aid concert in 1985?

16 Which country holds a National Day of Commemoration on the nearest Sunday to July 11?

17 On May 25, 1935, who set three world track and field records in the space of 45 minutes?

18 Which ship arrived in the UK on June 21 1948?

19 What name is given to the day, usually in March, when the greatest number of US party members vote for their presidential candidate?

20 Which US holiday was first celebrated in 1621?

Medium

Answers to QUIZ 460 – Guitarists

1   PJ Harvey
2   Eddie Van Halen
3   Eric Clapton
4   Carlos Santana
5   BB King
6   Jimmy Page
7   Orianthi
8   Joe Perry
9   KT Tunstall

Hard

ANSWERS ON PAGE 465

1 Actor Bryan Cranston first found fame playing the father on which family comedy?

2 Which gaseous element is named after the Greek word for "idle"?

3 In which decade was Sir Arthur Conan Doyle born?

4 Yellow-eyed and little blue are types of which animal?

5 What shape is a coccus bacterium?

6 Which of the following geological periods was the earliest: the Cretaceous, the Devonian or the Triassic?

7 Who directed the 1948 western *Fort Apache*?

8 *Makes Me Wonder* was a 2007 single by which band?

9 What do HG Wells' initials stand for?

10 Which Hindu deity is portrayed with a serpent around his neck?

11 Which *Seinfeld* actress also starred in the TV series *Veep*?

12 What does a styptic substance stop?

13 Michael Douglas and Diane Keaton co-starred in which 2014 romantic comedy film?

14 What is the occupation of the Shakespearean character Nick Bottom?

15 Southern Jutland is an area spanning which two countries?

16 James Comey Jr was the head of which US organisation from 2013 to 2017?

17 The black Périgord is a type of which prized foodstuff?

18 The airport in which US city is often referred to as Sea-Tac Airport?

19 Whom did actor Ryan Reynolds marry in 2012?

20 Who starred in the 2019 film *Uncut Gems*?

Easy

Medium

Hard

Answers to QUIZ 461 – Pot Luck

1	Dogs	11	Wisconsin
2	Nicole Kidman	12	Leonardo da Vinci
3	Flash Gordon	13	South Sudan
4	A large wildcat	14	Earth's rotation
5	*Revenge of the Sith*	15	*Mork & Mindy*
6	The Open (1986 and 1993)	16	Charles Dickens
7	Travis	17	Groucho Marx
8	Cannoli	18	Venezuela
9	Demi Lovato	19	A plant
10	Boron	20	Uranus

Easy

1   The dialogue in which 2004 film directed by Mel Gibson was in Aramaic, Hebrew and Latin?

2   Who directed the 1992 film *The Last of the Mohicans*?

3   How many Oscars did the 1982 film *Gandhi* win from its 11 nominations?

4   Which 1968 sci-fi film centres around an alien monolith?

5   In which decade was the film *How the West Was Won* released?

6   Who played Ashley Wilkes in the 1939 film *Gone with the Wind*?

7   Which 2003 film was the first fantasy film to win the Best Picture Oscar?

8   Who starred as Marcellus Gallio in the 1953 film *The Robe*?

9   The character of Lara Antipova appears in which 1965 film?

10 Which epic 1960 film was based on a 1951 novel by Howard Fast?

11 Who produced and directed the 1956 film *The Ten Commandments*?

Medium

12 *Braveheart* (1995) was mainly set in which century?

13 Who directed the 2000 film *Gladiator*?

14 Which 1963 historical film, winner of four Oscars, was the highest-grossing film of that year?

15 Who played King Leonidas in the 2007 film *300*?

16 In the 1998 film, what is the first name of Private Ryan?

17 Which fictional mineral was being mined in the 2009 film *Avatar*?

18 Who starred as Balian of Ibelin in the 2005 film *Kingdom of Heaven*?

19 Who directed the 1962 film *Lawrence of Arabia*?

20 What was the name of Kate Winslet's necklace in the film *Titanic*?

Hard

1   Michael McDonald is the lead singer with which band?

2   In 2020, which comedian briefly changed his name by deed poll to Hugo Boss?

3   *Yankee Doodle* is the anthem of which US state?

4   Which artist was knighted by both Philip IV of Spain and Charles I of England?

5   In classical Greek mythology, where is the abode of the blessed after death?

6   Which famous cartoon character was created by Mary Tourtel in 1920?

7   What nationality is tennis player Dominic Thiem (b.1993)?

8   County Sligo lies in which province of Ireland?

9   What is a saltine?

10 In what decade did Abraham Lincoln become US President?

11 *I Will Wait* was a 2012 single by which British group?

12 What term describes a written work that is of doubtful origin, particularly in the Christian religion?

13 In which decade was the British Army Parachute Regiment founded?

14 What type of creature is a lilac point?

15 How many "Jewels" are there in the Buddhist tradition?

16 The football club Helsingborgs IF is based in which country?

17 Which prefix, indicating 10^{12}, derives from the Greek word for "monster"?

18 Who presented the 2020 series of *Your Home Made Perfect*?

19 Who played Khan in the 2013 film *Star Trek into Darkness*?

20 The Egyptian city of Ismailia lies on which waterway?

Answers to QUIZ 463 – Pot Luck

1	*Malcolm in the Middle*	11	Julia Louis-Dreyfus
2	Argon	12	Bleeding
3	1850s (1859)	13	*And So It Goes*
4	Penguin	14	Weaver (*A Midsummer Night's Dream*)
5	Spherical (or nearly spherical)	15	Denmark and Germany
6	Devonian	16	FBI
7	John Ford	17	Truffle
8	Maroon 5	18	Seattle (Seattle-Tacoma)
9	Herbert George	19	Blake Lively
10	Shiva	20	Adam Sandler

1. In Elizabethan times, what name was given to a member of the audience standing near the stage in a theatre?

2. Who wrote the play *Leopoldstat*, which received its premier in London in 2020?

3. The Duchess of Berwick and Lord Darlington are characters in which play by Oscar Wilde?

4. The Royal Exchange Theatre lies in which English city?

5. Which 1947 musical is about an Irishman who moves to the US to bury a pot of gold?

6. Who wrote the three-play series *Mourning Becomes Electra*?

7. The Teatro Alcázar is located in which Spanish city?

8. *The School for Wives* and *The Misanthrope* were written by which 17th-century French playwright?

9. The song *A Little Bit of Good* is from which musical, first performed in 1975?

10. In the Shakespeare play, who kills Macbeth?

11. The musical *Come from Away* is set in which country?

12. What was the stage name of theatre impresario Frederick Westcott (d.1941)?

13. Which term for an attempt to manipulate a person by making them doubt their sanity is taken from a 1938 play by Patrick Hamilton?

14. The Yvonne Arnaud theatre is in which English county?

15. Which former *Sherlock* actor won the Evening Standard Best Actor award in 2019 for his role in *Present Laughter*?

16. What word refers to the slope of a stage away from the audience?

17. Who wrote the play *Medea*, first performed in 431 BC?

18. In what century did Christopher Marlowe live and die?

19. Who is considered the father of Greek drama and has lent his name to a general term for actors?

20. The 1996 film *The Birdcage* was based on which French play?

Answers to QUIZ 464 – Epic Films

1	*The Passion of the Christ*	11	Cecil B DeMille
2	Michael Mann	12	13th century
3	Eight	13	Sir Ridley Scott
4	*2001: A Space Odyssey*	14	*Cleopatra*
5	1960s (1962)	15	Gerard Butler
6	Leslie Howard	16	James
7	*The Return of the King*	17	Unobtanium
8	Richard Burton	18	Orlando Bloom
9	*Doctor Zhivago*	19	Sir David Lean
10	*Spartacus*	20	Heart of the Ocean

QUIZ 467 – Pot Luck

ANSWERS ON PAGE 469

1. Along with Stheno and Euryale, who was the other snake-haired Gorgon sister?
2. What ten-letter term sums up the change in society due to the influence of younger people?
3. What is the shortest distance over which a speed skating Olympic event takes place?
4. Who played Haymitch Abernathy in the Hunger Games series of films?
5. *It* was the 1983 debut album by which band?
6. The Brighton-based detective Roy Grace was created by which author?
7. In which Tom Clancy novel did the character Jack Ryan first appear?
8. Which limestone gorge on the border of Derbyshire and Nottinghamshire is noted for its cave art, discovered in 2003?
9. In law, what is the term given to the right of the first-born child to inherit his or her parents' main estate?
10. White Windsor is a variety of which vegetable?
11. Where does the fourth act of *Swan Lake* take place?
12. Which film studio uses the female personification of the US as its logo?
13. How much of the Moon is visible if it is described as "gibbous"?
14. Jason Atherton (b.1971) is a well-known name in which profession?
15. The Fountain of the Four Rivers and the Fountain of the Triton, located in Rome, were designed by which sculptor and architect?
16. Which geometrical shape is also the name of a bone in the wrist?
17. In 1978, which South American capital city became the first UNESCO World Cultural Heritage site?
18. Who played Ted Case in the TV series *New Tricks*?
19. On a plant, what is a cotyledon?
20. In which decade was Yahoo! founded?

Answers to QUIZ 465 – Pot Luck

1	The Doobie Brothers	11	Mumford & Sons
2	Joe Lycett	12	Apocryphal
3	Connecticut	13	1940s (1940)
4	(Sir Peter Paul) Rubens	14	(Siamese) cat
5	Elysium	15	Three (Buddha, Dharma and Sangha)
6	Rupert Bear	16	Sweden
7	Austrian	17	Tera
8	Connacht	18	Angela Scanlon
9	(Soda) cracker	19	Benedict Cumberbatch
10	1860s (1861)	20	The Suez Canal

467

1   What name is given to a prime number that is two less or two more than another prime number?

2   What is 260 multiplied by 5?

3   If two-sevenths of a number is 72, what is the number?

4   What name is given to the term for the numeracy equivalent of dyslexia?

5   How many cubic centimetres are in one cubic metre?

6   Which 1960s TV series famously had a lead character called Number Six?

7   Starting at one, what is the first number to include the letter B?

8   How many prime numbers are there between 1 and 30?

9   How many ounces are there in nine pounds?

10 What is 15 squared?

11 How many microns are there in a metre?

12 By what three letters is the food additive number E621 better known?

13 What is 5 factorial, written as 5!?

14 In the UK, how many zeros follow the number one in a traditional British quintillion?

15 What is the sum of all the numbers between 1 and 100?

16 What is the atomic number of calcium?

17 In Roman numerals, what is XVII multiplied by V?

18 What is the term for an equation that can be expressed as $ax^2 + bx + c = 0$?

19 How many hours are there in a week?

20 Who said "All things are numbers"?

Answers to QUIZ 466 – Theatre

1	Groundling	11	Canada
2	Sir Tom Stoppard	12	Fred Karno
3	*Lady Windermere's Fan*	13	Gaslighting (*Gas Light*)
4	Manchester	14	Surrey (Guildford)
5	*Finian's Rainbow*	15	Andrew Scott
6	Eugene O'Neill	16	Rake
7	Madrid	17	Euripides
8	Molière	18	16th century (1564-93)
9	*Chicago*	19	Thespis (Thespian)
10	Macduff	20	*La Cage aux Folles*

1   Which is the most northerly of the RHS gardens?

2   Who was Imogen Poot's co-star in the 2019 film *Vivarium*?

3   Rae's Creek can be found at which famous US golf course?

4   Who played Mata Hari in the 1931 film of the same name?

5   What word completes the title of the debut single by The Wanted, *All Time ___*?

6   What is the name of the wellness podcast broadcast by Tim Samuels?

7   *Eye of the Needle* was a 1978 novel by which author?

8   Bronze is traditionally associated with which wedding anniverary?

9   Which of these military figures was born first: Douglas MacArthur, Dwight D Eisenhower, or George Patton III?

10 In which decade was the photocopier invented?

11 By what means do fungi reproduce?

12 What is the 12-letter word for a long piece of formal writing required for a university degree?

13 Which 2004 film starring Denzel Washington was a remake of a 1962 film starring Frank Sinatra?

14 What was a London Particular?

15 In which decade was the Vienna Philharmonic Orchestra formed?

16 In Greek mythology, what musical instrument was associated with Orpheus?

17 Which gas is the primary component of Jupiter's atmosphere?

18 The title of which member of the Rat Pack's autobiography was *Yes I Can* (1965)?

19 What type of dish is cozido à Portuguesa?

20 In which county is the town of Caterham?

Medium

Hard

Answers to QUIZ 467 – Pot Luck

1	Medusa	11	Beside a lake
2	Youthquake	12	Columbia
3	500m	13	Half of it (but less than 75%)
4	Woody Harrelson	14	He is a chef
5	Pulp	15	(Gianlorenzo) Bernini
6	Peter James	16	Trapezium
7	*The Hunt for Red October*	17	Quito
8	Creswell Crags	18	Larry Lamb
9	Primogeniture	19	A leaf
10	Broad bean	20	1990s (1994)

Easy

1   Which is the third-largest lake in Italy?

2   In which country is there a mountain called Mount Disappointment?

3   Which lake contains approximately 20% of the world's fresh water?

4   Lake Ohrid straddles North Macedonia and which other country?

5   The Luberon Mountains lie in which European country?

6   Lake Ashi lies on which Japanese island?

7   The mountain goat is particularly associated with which range?

8   Which is England's deepest lake?

9   The Albula Tunnel is one of the highest tunnels in which mountain range?

10 In Greek mythology who was turned into mountains by Perseus using Medusa's head?

11 Lake Chucuito and Lake Pequeño make up which larger South American lake?

12 Which European mountain range is also known as "The Pale Mountains"?

13 Greater Ararat is the highest peak in which country?

14 Thunder Bay lies on which Great Lake?

15 Which dog breed is named after a water spirit said to inhabit Scottish lochs and pools?

16 The Black Mountains are part of which UK National Park?

17 Malcesine is a resort on which Italian lake?

18 The shape of an oxbow lake resembles which letter of the alphabet?

19 The Great Smoky Mountains lie along the border of North Carolina and which other US state?

20 The Snowy Mountains is the highest range in which country?

Answers to QUIZ 468 – Numbers

1	Twin prime	11	Million
2	1300	12	MSG (monosodium glutamate)
3	252	13	120 (5x4x3x2x1)
4	Dyscalculia	14	30
5	One million	15	5050
6	The Prisoner	16	20
7	Billion	17	LXXXV (17x5=85)
8	Ten	18	Quadratic equation
9	144	19	168
10	225	20	Pythagoras

ANSWERS ON PAGE **473**

1   The writer Deborah Moggach was born in which country?

2   As at 2019, which US president had served the shortest term?

3   In which year was Justin Timberlake born?

4   Who played Colonel Allen Faulkner in the 1978 film *Wild Geese*?

5   Which Swiss resort hosted the 1948 Winter Olympics?

6   What is the major religion in Somalia?

7   Since 1993, how many teams from outside South America have been invited to compete in the Copa America football tournament each year?

8   How many brothers formed Warner Bros?

9   The village of Porthcurno in Cornwall is home to a museum of what form of communication?

10 Who released the 2020 chart-topping album *Future Nostalgia*?

11 Which of these George Clooney films was released first: *One Fine Day, Out of Sight* or *Syriana*?

12 What is farmed in pisciculture?

13 Popular in the USA, what is a Russet Burbank?

14 Which direction is referred to by the word "boreal"?

15 The Farnese Palace lies in which European capital city?

16 What is the title of the BBC comedy series starring Guz Khan?

17 What term is used to refer to the presence of glucose in blood?

18 In 1949, who became the youngest cricketer to make an England Test debut, at the age of 18?

19 The island of Bora Bora lies in which body of water?

20 What was the county town of the former county of Anglesey?

Easy

Medium

Hard

Answers to QUIZ 469 – Pot Luck

1	Harlow Carr	11	Spores
2	Jesse Eisenberg	12	Dissertation
3	Augusta	13	*The Manchurian Candidate*
4	Greta Garbo	14	Thick fog (pea-souper)
5	*Low*	15	1840s (1842)
6	*All Hail Kale*	16	The lyre
7	Ken Follett	17	Hydrogen
8	Eighth anniversary	18	Sammy Davis Jr
9	Douglas MacArthur (1880)	19	A (meat) stew
10	1930s (1938)	20	Surrey

Easy

1 The legend of the Pied Piper of Hamelin took place in which German state?

2 Frederiksberg is a part of which European capital city?

3 In which decade did Switzerland become a full member of the United Nations?

4 What is the second-largest city in Belgium?

5 What is the alternative name for the Spire of Dublin, completed in 2003?

6 In the Mediterranean, what is the Ostro?

7 What are the main two colours on the flag of Liechtenstein?

8 Which of these famous Greeks was born first: Alexander the Great, Archimedes or Aristotle?

9 Which Mediterranean island and German river have a four-letter name that differs only by the last letter?

10 In 2014, how old was Francesco Totti when he became the oldest person to score in a UEFA Champions League football match?

11 The abbreviation for the Foreign and Commonwealth Office is the same as the three-letter code for an airport in which Italian city?

Medium

12 Frank-Walter Steinmeier became president of which country in 2017?

13 In which European city did the word "ghetto" originate?

14 Which Frenchman won the French Open tennis singles title in 1983?

15 Almuñécar is a popular tourist destination in which Spanish province?

16 In ancient Rome, how many cohorts formed a legion of soldiers?

17 What was the official name of Romania between 1965 and December 1989?

18 The TV series *Beck* is set in which European country?

19 To the nearest ten, how many inhabited Greek islands are there?

20 The 2011 French film *The Artist* was nominated for ten Oscars. How many did it win?

Hard

Answers to QUIZ 470 – Lakes and Mountains

1	Lake Como	11	Lake Titicaca
2	Australia	12	The Dolomites
3	Lake Baikal	13	Turkey
4	Albania	14	Lake Superior
5	France	15	Kelpie
6	Honshu	16	Brecon Beacons National Park
7	The Rocky Mountains	17	Lake Garda
8	Wast Water	18	U
9	The Alps	19	Tennessee
10	Atlas	20	Australia

ANSWERS ON PAGE 475

1 Who played the title characters in the 1974 film *Thunderbolt and Lightfoot*?

2 Which of these scientists was born first: Charles Darwin, Sir Isaac Newton or Nicolaus Copernicus?

3 How many known natural satellites does Mercury have?

4 What word completes the title of the 1995 Garbage hit, *Only Happy When It* ___?

5 Gauchito was the official FIFA World Cup mascot in which year?

6 Which technology company produces the Pentium brand of microprocessors?

7 Which Parks and Recreation star's voice features in the animated TV series *Duncanville*?

8 Which company invented the name "aspirin"?

9 What is a brambling?

10 What type of weather is described by the word "hoar"?

11 The site of the city of Tenochtitlan lies in which modern-day capital city?

12 Who starred as Lorraine Broughton in the 2017 film *Atomic Blonde*?

13 The name of which unit of length derives from the distance of outstretched arms?

14 In physics, what name is given to the deviation in the direction of a wave when it meets an obstacle?

15 By population, what is the second-largest city in Canada?

16 The BWF is the international regulatory body of which sport?

17 Cheam and Carshalton are both within which London borough?

18 For what was Arthur Rackham (d.1939) famous?

19 In 1906, the first ever motor-racing Grand Prix took place in which country?

20 Which creature is nicknamed the "vampire deer" because of its prominent tusks?

Easy

Medium

Hard

Answers to QUIZ 471 – Pot Luck

1	England	11	*One Fine Day* (1996)
2	William Henry Harrison (31 days in 1841)	12	Fish
3	1981	13	A potato
4	Richard Burton	14	North
5	St Moritz	15	Rome
6	Islam	16	*Man Like Mobeen*
7	Two	17	Glycaemia
8	Four (Harry, Albert, Sam and Jack)	18	Brian Close
9	The telegraph	19	The Pacific Ocean
10	Dua Lipa	20	Beaumaris

Easy

1   Which country hosted the World Alpine Ski championships in 2019?

2   The Shed End is part of which football stadium?

3   Which Scottish football team plays home games at Dens Park (Kilmac Stadium)?

4   What is the nickname of the Argentinian rugby union team?

5   In which year did Juan Manuel Fangio win his last Formula 1 World Championship?

6   What is Canada's national summer sport?

7   What grade of horse race is the Hennessy Gold Cup?

8   Which major golf tournament did Phil Mickelson win for the first time in 2004?

9   Hank Aaron (b.1934) was a record-setting player in which US sport?

10 Whom did Boris Becker beat to win his first Wimbledon title in 1985?

11 In which decade was the biathlon re-introduced to the Winter Olympic Games?

12 Which water sport does the IRF administer?

13 By what score did Uruguay beat Argentina in the first ever FIFA World Cup Final?

14 Norwegian Grete Waitz (d.2011) was a world champion in which athletics event?

15 In 1930, at 52 years of age, Wilfred Rhodes became the oldest person to play which sport for England?

16 In which country was the first zorbing site established in 1994?

17 K-90 and K-120 are terms used in which winter sport?

18 To the nearest ten feet, how far is it between the first and second base on a baseball diamond?

19 As at 2020, who is the only male athlete to have won both the 200m and 400m gold at the same Olympics?

20 In which country did the game of stoolball originate?

Medium

Hard

Answers to QUIZ 472 – Europe

1	Lower Saxony	11	Rome (FCO-Fiumicino)
2	Copenhagen	12	Germany
3	2000s (2002)	13	Venice
4	Antwerp	14	Yannick Noah
5	The Monument of Light	15	Granada
6	A (southerly) wind	16	Ten (nine after AD 50)
7	Blue and red	17	Socialist Republic of Romania
8	Aristotle (384 BC)	18	Sweden
9	Elba and Elbe	19	230 (227)
10	38	20	Five

ANSWERS ON PAGE 477

1 How many goals did Just Fontaine score at the 1958 FIFA World Cup Finals to win the Golden Boot?

2 As at the end of 2019, who was the youngest person to have assumed the office of US president without having been elected?

3 Which political party was led by George Lansbury from 1932 to 1935?

4 Which automobile company was founded in the US by William Durant in 1908?

5 The 1958 film *Carve Her Name with Pride* was set during which conflict?

6 Which country won the Olympic gold medal in men's field hockey six times in a row from 1928 to 1956?

7 Which European capital city lies on the river Manzanares?

8 Who sang the theme to the Bond film *You Only Live Twice*?

9 What name is given to the attempt to modify weather by dropping substances into clouds?

10 Jennifer Lopez had a 2003 hit with the single *All I Have* that featured which rapper?

11 Rami Malek played cybersecurity engineer Elliot Alderson in which TV series?

12 In 1993 who became the first golfer to win BBC Overseas Sports Personality for the Year for a second time?

13 Which US singer featured on Ed Sheeran's 2019 hit *Beautiful People*?

14 Gerhard Berger (b.1959) made his Formula 1 debut in which decade?

15 Which of the following geological periods was the earliest: the Cambrian, the Jurassic or the Triassic?

16 The first US vending machine, installed in stations in the 1880s, sold what product?

17 Which 2018 novel by Sally Rooney, featuring the characters of Connell and Marianne, was adapted for television in 2020?

18 What genus of plant is often referred to as a Guernsey lily?

19 To what did New Zealand increase its minimum driving age in 2011?

20 Who hosted the series of Radio 4's *The News Quiz* that began in April 2020, following on from Nish Kumar?

Easy

Medium

Hard

Answers to QUIZ 473 – Pot Luck

1	Clint Eastwood and Jeff Bridges	11	Mexico City
2	Nicolaus Copernicus (1473)	12	Charlize Theron
3	None	13	Fathom (six feet)
4	Rains	14	Diffraction
5	1978 (in Argentina)	15	Montreal
6	Intel	16	Badminton
7	Amy Poehler	17	Sutton
8	Bayer	18	Illustrating books
9	A bird	19	France
10	Frost	20	Chinese water deer

Easy

1   What is the married name of the title character of the play *Hedda Gabler*?

2   What was Tom Good's original occupation in the TV series *The Good Life*?

3   In 1661, who founded the dance school Académie Royale de Danse?

4   Which sitcom was adapted from the stage play *The Banana Box*?

5   Who wrote the play *The Father* (*Le Père*), on which the 2020 film starring Sir Anthony Hopkins was based?

6   Jahméne Douglas was runner-up to which winner of *The X Factor*?

7   What is comedian Bill Bailey's real first name?

8   Which musical, with lyrics written by Stuart Brayson and Tim Rice, closed in March 2014 after a 22-week run?

9   Which playwright was born Tomáš Straussler in 1937?

10   *All is True* was the original title for which Shakespeare play?

11   Who played Sally Smedley in the TV series *Drop the Dead Donkey*?

12   The early ballet, *Le Ballet des Polonais*, has what English title?

13   The theme tune from which TV series was covered by Paul McCartney and Wings on the 1975 album *Venus and Mars*?

14   Who wrote the plays *Far Away* (2000) and *A Number* (2002)?

15   In which decade did the first Royal Variety Performance take place?

16   How many of the 123 plays written by Sophocles have survived?

17   The tradition of water puppetry originated in which Asian country?

18   What was the name of Jean Marsh's character in the 1970s TV series *Upstairs, Downstairs*?

19   *Why She Would Not* was the final uncompleted work by which playwright?

20   Richard Park (b.1948) was a judge on which musical talent show?

Answers to QUIZ 474 – Outdoor Sports

1	Sweden	11	1960s (1960)
2	Stamford Bridge (Chelsea FC)	12	Rafting
3	Dundee FC	13	4-2
4	Los Pumas	14	The marathon
5	1957	15	(Test) cricket
6	Lacrosse	16	New Zealand
7	Grade 3	17	Ski jumping
8	The US Masters	18	90 feet
9	Baseball	19	Michael Johnson (1996)
10	Kevin Curren	20	England

1   Peneda-Gerês is the only National Park in which European country?

2   Which poet's first collected works was entitled *Poems, Chiefly Lyrical* (1830)?

3   The 1905 Treaty of Portsmouth concluded which war?

4   Aubrey Graham is the real name of which rapper?

5   Ole Einar Bjørndalen (b.1974) won 13 Olympic medals in which sport?

6   At the time of its opening in 2016, the Gatimaan Express was the fastest train in which country?

7   In the run-up to St Nicholas Day in early December, children in the Netherlands traditionally leave out wooden shoes filled with carrots and what else?

8   Stanley Holloway played Arthur Pemberton in which 1949 comedy film?

9   Who wrote the Barry Manilow song *Weekend in New England*?

10 In which car did James Hunt win his only Formula 1 World Championship?

11 Joan I of Navarre was the second wife of which English king?

12 Who won the Golden Boot at the 1950 FIFA World Cup?

13 What name is given to a sentence that includes every letter of the alphabet?

14 Canon Hardwicke Rawnsley (d.1920) and Robert Hunter (d.1913) were two of the founders of which organisation?

15 In which country is the Golden Bridge, which passes through a giant pair of stone hands?

16 Whale island lies in which English harbour?

17 In Roman times, what was a pilum?

18 Who played Gary Scant in the 2004 TV series *A Thing Called Love*?

19 "Out of Darkness Cometh Light" is the motto for which English city?

20 In Japan, what is *kaiseki*?

Answers to QUIZ 475 – Pot Luck

1	13	11	*Mr Robot*
2	Theodore Roosevelt (42 years old)	12	Greg Norman
3	The Labour Party	13	Khalid
4	General Motors	14	1980s (1984)
5	WWII	15	The Cambrian
6	India	16	Chewing gum
7	Madrid (Spain)	17	*Normal People*
8	Nancy Sinatra	18	Nerine
9	Seeding	19	16 (from 15)
10	LL Cool J	20	Angela Barnes

ANSWERS ON PAGE 480

Easy

1 What is the name of the branch of soil science that deals with crop production?

2 What does an areologist study?

3 Of what is metrology the scientific study?

4 What term is given to the study of friction between moving parts and ways of reducing it?

5 A tocologist works in which area of medicine?

6 Which branch of horticulture is concerned with the study and cultivation of fruit?

7 What type of creatures are studied by a carcinologist?

8 What term is given to the study of light rays and their chemical effects?

9 What is studied by a caliologist?

10 Of what is anemology the study?

Medium

11 In zoology, what is studied by a malacologist?

12 What types of plant does a pteridologist study?

13 What process is studied by a zymologist?

14 In physics, what is studied by a rheologist?

15 Where would an ethologist study animals?

16 What is studied in algology, also known as phycology?

17 What type of creature does a limacologist study?

18 Of what is sphygmology the study?

19 A batologist is a botanist who specialises in which type of plant?

20 What does a sitologist study?

Hard

Answers to QUIZ 476 – Stage and Screen

1	Tesman	11	Victoria Wicks
2	Draughtsman	12	*The Polish Ballet*
3	Louis XIV	13	*Crossroads*
4	*Rising Damp*	14	Caryl Churchill
5	Florian Zeller	15	1910s (1912)
6	James Arthur	16	Seven
7	Mark	17	Vietnam
8	*From Here to Eternity*	18	Rose (Buck)
9	Sir Tom Stoppard	19	George Bernard Shaw
10	*Henry VIII*	20	*Fame Academy*

Easy

Medium

Hard

1   In Norse mythology, what type of creatures are Huginn and Muninn?

2   Which author wrote the 1892 fairytale *The Brown Owl?*

3   Nicky Gore was the central character in which dystopian children's TV series, first broadcast in the 1970s?

4   In which country is the Bodbe Monastery situated?

5   Which Australian football club is nicknamed "The Dockers"?

6   In which decade did the Greek War of Independence begin?

7   What is the collective noun for a group of ferrets?

8   Mallam Aminu Kano International Airport is located in which African country?

9   *September of My Years* (1965) was a retrospective album by which singer?

10 In 1978, Michael Hext became the first winner of which competition?

11 The Similan islands lie in which sea?

12 Which empire was founded by Tughril and Chaghri Beg in 1037?

13 Who won the women's 400m gold medal at the 2019 World Athletics Championships?

14 What were the real first names of Rab Butler (Baron Butler of Saffron Walden)

15 Elberta is a variety of which fruit?

16 Who directed the 2001 film *The Royal Tenenbaums?*

17 "I watch you cry But you don't see I'm the one by your side" is a lyric from which 2012 song?

18 *Les Demoiselles d'Avignon* (1907) was painted by which artist?

19 Who was the first wife of Robert the Bruce, who died before her husband became King of Scotland?

20 The 1997 film *L.A. Confidential* was based on a novel by which author?

Answers to QUIZ 477 – Pot Luck

1	Portugal	11	Henry IV
2	Alfred, Lord Tennyson	12	Ademir de Menezes
3	The Russo-Japanese War	13	Pangram
4	Drake	14	The National Trust
5	Biathlon	15	Vietnam
6	India	16	Portsmouth Harbour
7	Hay	17	A type of javelin
8	*Passport to Pimlico*	18	Paul Nicholls
9	Randy Edelman	19	Wolverhampton
10	McLaren-Ford	20	A traditional dinner

1   In which decade did Vincent Van Gogh die?

2   Which writer was born in 1819 at South Farm on the Arbury Hall estate in Nuneaton?

3   Tracy Tupman is a character in which novel by Charles Dickens?

4   Which artist painted *Orange, Red and Yellow* (1961)?

5   What nationality was the poet Gabriela Mistral, who was awarded the Nobel Prize in Literature in 1945?

6   In *Nineteen Eighty-Four*, what was the first name of Winston Smith's wife?

7   What colour is the dog in the title of the 2003 novel by Martin Amis?

8   The 1919 play *Mr Pim Passes By* was written by which author, best known for his works for children?

9   The controversial 19th-century painting *Christ in the House of His Parents* was by which artist?

10 Which sci-fi author created the character of Elric of Melniboné?

11 What was the title of the 1942 epistolary novel by CS Lewis that he dedicated to JRR Tolkien?

12 *The Enigma of Arrival* by VS Naipaul is written in how many sections?

13 Which artist (d.1904) lived at Limnerslease near Guildford in Surrey, which is now part of an artists' village?

14 As at 2019, who is the only Nobel Literature laureate to have played first-class cricket (whilst at university)?

15 *American Gothic* (1930) is a famous painting by which artist?

16 Which author (d.2000) wrote the memoirs *To Keep The Ball Rolling*?

17 In which district of London did Liza live in the title of the debut novel by W Somerset Maugham?

18 What is Tom's surname in the children's novel *Tom's Midnight Garden*?

19 Who founded the 20th-century art movement known as Suprematism?

20 What was the title of the 2019 novel by Richard Powers that won the Pulitzer Prize for Fiction?

Answers to QUIZ 478 – Ologies

1	Agrology	11	Molluscs
2	The planet Mars	12	Ferns and similar plants
3	Measurements	13	Fermentation
4	Tribology	14	The flow and shape of matter
5	Obstetrics (childbirth)	15	In their own environment
6	Pomology	16	Algae
7	Crustaceans	17	Slugs
8	Actinology	18	The pulse
9	Birds' nests	19	Brambles
10	The movement of winds	20	Diet and nutrition

ANSWERS ON PAGE 483

1   The legendary Japanese sword Kusanagi is commonly associated with which virtue?

2   Which former WWE wrestler, now a commentator, graduated from Harvard Law School in 2006?

3   The 1918 Armistice of Salonica was between the Allied powers and which country?

4   Count Bertram of Roussillon appears in which Shakespeare play?

5   In which country did loquats originate?

6   Lake Elementaita and Lake Naivasha lie in which country?

7   On which course did Paul Lawrie win the 1999 Open golf championship?

8   In which 1950 film did Judy Garland perform the song *Get Happy*?

9   Which rock band released the albums *Stars of CCTV* (2005) and *Killer Sounds* (2011)?

10 Which city's coat of arms features a blue background with three crowns?

11 Which poet published the collection entitled *All Religions are One* (1788)?

12 The word "carr", meaning a waterlogged wooded terrain, derives from the word *kjarr* in which language?

13 Who succeeded Joyce Banda as President of Malawi in 2014?

14 What is the name given to the rectangular area used for fencing bouts?

15 Who played DI Harry Naylor in the 1990s drama series *Between the Lines*?

16 In which decade was René Descartes born?

17 Who released the song *There She Goes* in 1988?

18 The Caloris Basin can be found on which planet?

19 A pysanka is a traditionally decorated Easter egg from which country?

20 What is the surname of Amelia in the novel by Henry Fielding?

Easy
Medium
Hard

Answers to QUIZ 479 – Pot Luck

1	Ravens	11	The Andaman Sea
2	Ford Madox Ford	12	The Seljuk Empire
3	*The Changes*	13	Salwa Eid Naser
4	Georgia	14	Richard Austen
5	Fremantle	15	Peach
6	1820s (1821)	16	Wes Anderson
7	A business (or busyness)	17	*Picking Up the Pieces* (Paloma Faith)
8	Nigeria	18	Pablo Picasso
9	Frank Sinatra	19	Isabella of Mar
10	BBC Young Musician (of the Year)	20	James Ellroy

1   *Suze*, a French brand of bitters, is flavoured with the root of which plant?

2   *Changua* is a Colombian soup made from what two chief ingredients?

3   Which type of pasta derives its name from the Italian word for "twins"?

4   Imperial Star and Purple Sicilian are varieties of which vegetable?

5   What type of food is the Middle Eastern *ackawi*?

6   What is the main constitutent of the Chinese dish *Zhajiangmian*?

7   In which European country did Hasselback potatoes originate?

8   Caboc is a cream cheese from which country?

9   What is the Australian Burger King franchise called?

10 The first electrical advertisement in Piccadilly Circus was displayed in 1908, advertising which brand of drink?

11 Which seasoning is also known as myrtle pepper?

12 Which tropical fruit takes its name from the Latin for "sole of the foot"?

13 The dobos torte cake originated in which country?

14 What name is given to a dish of lobster that is cooked in a rich cream sauce flavoured with brandy or sherry?

15 What is a crubeen, in Ireland?

16 What is the name of the small bowl originating in China, in which tea is traditionally served?

17 *Nasturtium officinale* is the Latin name for which salad vegetable?

18 The Thai drink Krating Daeng was the origin of which worldwide drink brand?

19 What type of foodstuff is the Russian *pelmeni*?

20 *Heuriger* is the name given to wine taverns in which European country?

Answers to QUIZ 480 – Art and Literature

1	1890s (1890)	11	*The Screwtape Letters*
2	George Eliot	12	Five
3	*The Pickwick Papers*	13	George Watts
4	Mark Rothko	14	Samuel Beckett
5	Chilean	15	Grant Wood
6	Katharine	16	Anthony Powell
7	Yellow	17	Lambeth
8	AA Milne	18	Long
9	Sir John Everett Millais	19	Kazimir Malevich
10	Michael Moorcock	20	*The Overstory*

1 The Fono is the legislative assembly of which Pacific island nation?

2 For what do the initials stand in the title of the Black Eyed Peas' album *The E.N.D.?*

3 What type of creature is a deathstalker?

4 What is the profession of John Cusack's character in the 1997 film *Grosse Pointe Blank?*

5 Which old name for a Japanese shogun is used to describe a wealthy person in business?

6 "So stay there, 'Cause I'll be coming over" is a lyric from which 2008 song?

7 The Elaphiti Islands lie in which sea?

8 Which driver was runner-up in the Formula 1 World Championship in 1969 and 1970, but never won the title?

9 Minho is a historic wine-growing region of which country?

10 Guangzhou is the capital of which Chinese province?

11 Mound Metalcraft, founded in 1946, was the original name of which toy company?

12 What fraction of a gram is a picogram?

13 In legend, who was said to have been fatally wounded or killed at the Battle of Camlann?

14 At its completion in 2012, the Russky Island Bridge became the world's longest example of what type of bridge?

15 Adrian Mills and Kevin Devine were amongst the co-presenters of which TV programme, first broadcast in 1973?

16 The football team Shakhtar Donetsk is based in which country?

17 The Kuiper Belt lies how many astronomical units away from the Sun?

18 Norma Delores Ergstrom was the birth name of which singer (d.2002)?

19 Tai Woffinden was the world champion in which sport in 2013, 2015 and 2018?

20 Who wrote the 1967 crime novel *Endless Night?*

Easy
Medium
Hard

Answers to QUIZ 481 – Pot Luck

1	Courage or valour	11	William Blake
2	David Otunga	12	Old Norse
3	Bulgaria	13	Peter Mutharika
4	*All's Well That Ends Well*	14	Piste
5	China	15	Tom Georgeson
6	Kenya	16	1590s (1596)
7	Carnoustie	17	The La's
8	*Summer Stock*	18	Mercury
9	Hard-Fi	19	Ukraine
10	Kingston-upon Hull	20	Booth

QUIZ 484 – History

ANSWERS ON PAGE 486

Easy

1 Cecilio Báez and Benigno Ferreira were leaders of which country during the early 20th century?

2 In which decade was the Chinese Manchu dynasty overthrown?

3 Pons Aelius was the Roman name for the settlement that became which city?

4 In what decade was the Treaty of Nanking signed which ceded Hong Kong to the British?

5 Which English philosopher became Lord Chancellor in 1617?

6 Sauromates II (d.210) was a ruler of which ancient kingdom?

7 Opened in 1872, the first railway in Japan ran between which two locations?

8 What was the name of John Cabot's ship in which he reached North America in 1497?

9 In which decade was the position of Lord Mayor of London first recorded?

10 What was the name of the daughter of King Alfred who became known as "The Lady of Mercia"?

Medium

11 Which king did the Greeks defeat in the Battle of Marathon?

12 The WWI Battle of Coronel took place off the coastline of which country?

13 Which French prime minister shared the 1926 Nobel Peace Prize with the German foreign minister Gustav Stresemann?

14 In 1549, which resident of Wymondham in Norfolk led a rebellion against the monarchy?

15 Fidel Castro's revolutionary movement was named after which date?

16 Which spy was the last person to be executed at the Tower of London?

17 Who led the victorious army at the 329BC Battle of Jaxartes?

18 Which king died at the 1632 Battle of Lützen?

Hard

19 Atahualpa, the last Inca emperor, died in which decade?

20 Which three countries were involved in the Kalmar Union?

Answers to QUIZ 482 – Food and Drink

1 Gentian
2 Milk and eggs
3 Gemelli
4 Artichoke
5 Cheese
6 Noodles
7 Sweden
8 Scotland
9 Hungry Jack's
10 Perrier water
11 Allspice
12 Plantain
13 Hungary
14 Lobster Newburg
15 A pig's trotter
16 Chawan
17 Watercress
18 Red Bull
19 Dumplings
20 Austria

1   The triquetral bones are located in which part of the human body?

2   In which country are the Butchart Gardens, designated as a national site of historic interest?

3   In which decade was the National Hockey League's inaugural season?

4   What nationality was heavyweight boxing champion Tommy Burns? (d.1955)

5   What does the verb "to cachinnate" mean?

6   How is British singer Tahliah Barnett better known?

7   What is the unit of currency in Cambodia?

8   In Norse mythology, who was the Queen of the Underworld?

9   To the nearest ten million miles, how far is the Earth from the Sun?

10   Who had a 2005 hit with *Dance Dance*?

11   Sir William Thomson (First Baron Kelvin) asserted that which medical discovery of 1895 would prove to be a hoax?

12   Who plays Kate in the TV series *This is Us*?

13   In which decade did the Year of the Three Emperors occur in the German Empire?

14   The brothers Sirrus and Achenar, sons of Atrus, were characters in which 1993 video game?

15   What was the name of Jim Broadbent's character in the 2001 film *Moulin Rouge!*?

16   In sport, for what was AW Tillinghast (d.1942) famous?

17   The World Heritage Site of Rila Monastery lies in which European country?

18   If a ship is careened, what happens to it?

19   Which Roman emperor succeeded Titus and preceded Nerva?

20   What item of clothing was awarded to the winners of the Open golf championship between 1860 and 1870?

Answers to QUIZ 483 – Pot Luck

1	Samoa	11	Tonka
2	*Energy Never Dies*	12	One trillionth
3	Scorpion	13	King Arthur
4	An assassin	14	Cable-stayed
5	Tycoon	15	*That's Life!*
6	*Sweet Disposition* (The Temper Trap)	16	Ukraine
7	The Adriatic Sea	17	50
8	Jacky Ickx	18	Peggy Lee
9	Portugal	19	Speedway
10	Guangdong	20	Dame Agatha Christie

What are the names of these New York landmarks?

Easy

1

2

3

4

Medium

5

6

7

8

Hard

Answers to QUIZ 484 – History

1	Paraguay	11	Darius I
2	1910s (1912)	12	Chile
3	Newcastle-upon-Tyne	13	Aristide Briand
4	1840s	14	Robert Kett
5	Francis Bacon	15	26th of July
6	The Bosporan Kingdom	16	Josef Jakobs
7	Tokyo and Yokohama	17	Alexander the Great
8	*The Matthew*	18	Gustavus Adolphus of Sweden
9	1180s (1189)	19	1530s (1533)
10	Æthelflæd	20	Denmark, Norway and Sweden

ANSWERS ON PAGE 489

1   *Battle Cry*, used in the Transformers film series, was recorded by which band?

2   Félix Savón (b.1967) competed for Cuba in which sport?

3   Dr Max Goodwin, played by Ryan Eggold, is the central character in which TV series?

4   The rufiyaa is the unit of currency of which island nation?

5   Bangor International Airport is located in which US state?

6   How many wooden blocks are there in a game of *Jenga®*?

7   What is the national animal of Jordan?

8   Which actress (b.1973) was originally named Amanda Rogers?

9   In which sport are the Brownlow Medal and the Leigh Matthews Trophy awarded annually?

10 *Over You* and *Same Old Scene* were tracks on which Roxy Music album?

11 The 1909 oil drop experiment to measure the charge of the electron was carried out by which two scientists?

12 Weston Loomis were the middle names of which American poet?

13 Which spring flower shares its name with a variety of the mineral zircon?

14 In which country is the Murchison Falls National Park?

15 *Pastinaca sativa* is the Latin name for what vegetable?

16 The Chicago Cubs baseball team play their home games at which stadium?

17 Which Disney film was inspired by the works of Carlo Collodi?

18 In December 1902 until February 1903, which South American country had its ports blocked by the UK and other countries for failing to repay loans?

19 Narayana is another name for which god?

20 By area, which is the largest South African province?

Easy

Medium

Hard

Answers to QUIZ 485 – Pot Luck

1	The wrists	11	X-rays
2	Canada	12	Chrissy Metz
3	1910s (1917)	13	1880s (1888)
4	Canadian	14	*Myst*
5	To laugh loudly	15	Harold Zidler
6	FKA Twigs	16	He designed golf courses
7	The riel	17	Bulgaria
8	Hel	18	It is turned on its side
9	90 million miles (93 million)	19	Domitian
10	Fall Out Boy	20	A red leather belt

1   What was the name of the icy planet on which the rebels made their base in *The Empire Strikes Back*?

2   Rob Grant and Doug Naylor created which long-running sci-fi series?

3   Who wrote the novel on which the 1955 film *This Island Earth* was based?

4   What was the name of James Callis' character in the 2004 TV remake of *Battlestar Galactica*?

5   Which author was also the editor of the sci-fi magazine *New Worlds* in the 1960s?

6   The 2004 film *The Chronicles of Riddick* was a sequel to which 2000 film?

7   Moonbase Alpha featured in which TV series?

8   Who wrote the novel *Rosewater*, which won the 2019 Arthur C Clarke prize for science fiction?

9   What was the subtitle of the pilot film for the TV series *Babylon 5*?

10   In the Guardians of the Galaxy films, what is the first name of Peter Quill's mother?

11   Which US sci-fi author (d.2016) also wrote under the names AJ Orde and BJ Oliphant?

12   Wikus van de Merwe is the leading character in which 2009 film?

13   How is Mr Griffin referred to in the title of an early sci-fi novel?

14   *The Commuter* and *Human Is* were episodes of which 2017 TV series?

15   Who directed the 2019 film *Terminator: Dark Fate*?

16   Who played the character known as Cigarette-Smoking Man in *The X Files*?

17   The novels *Earth Hive* (1992) and *Nightmare Asylum* (1993) by Steve Perry were based on which film franchise?

18   Who wrote the 1998 novella *Story of Your Life*, the basis for the 2016 film *Arrival*?

19   What was the title of the *Doctor Who* spin-off that was broadcast on BBC Three in 2016?

20   Which 2005 sci-fi novel is narrated by Kathy H?

Answers to QUIZ 486 – New York Landmarks

1   Central Synagogue
2   Grand Central Terminal
3   Flatiron Building
4   St Patrick's Cathedral
5   The Eldorado (apartments)
6   The Met Life Tower
7   The Plaza Hotel
8   The Woolworth Building

1 Which volcano takes its name from the Greek god of darkness?

2 What is the third-smallest country in the world, by area?

3 In which 2020 TV series did Robert Carlyle play prime minister Robert Sutherland?

4 *Mellon Collie and the Infinite Sadness* was a 1995 album by which band?

5 Which horse, ridden by Liam Treadwell, won the 2009 Grand National?

6 What was the title of James Callaghan's (Baron Callaghan of Cardiff's) memoirs, published in 1987?

7 Which actor (b.1995) won the Rising Star Award at the 2020 BAFTA Film awards?

8 The Finnish name for January is "tammiku", named after which tree?

9 What is the name given to the point in the Moon's orbit when it is closest to the Earth?

10 What type of creature is a dowitcher?

11 Lake Pichola lies in which country?

12 What is the name of the 51-mile route that links Nether Stowey in Somerset to Lynmouth in Devon?

13 Which US city is home to The Rockets basketball team?

14 What name is given to a six-sided prism with sides that are parallelograms?

15 Edward Weston and the Murray family are characters in which novel of 1847?

16 Who wrote and directed the 2018 film *Life Itself*?

17 Which city hosted the 1912 Summer Olympic Games?

18 Which type of bird has species including laggar, lanner and prairie?

19 In Japanese cuisine, what is meant by the word *shun*?

20 Who succeeded Pope Leo IV and preceded Pope Nicholas I?

Medium

Hard

Answers to QUIZ 487 – Pot Luck

1	Imagine Dragons	11	Robert Millikan and Harvey Fletcher
2	Boxing	12	Ezra Pound
3	*New Amsterdam*	13	Hyacinth
4	The Maldives	14	Uganda
5	Maine	15	Parsnip
6	54	16	Wrigley Field
7	The Arabian oryx	17	*Pinocchio*
8	Portia de Rossi	18	Venezuela
9	Australian football	19	Vishnu
10	*Flesh + Blood* (1980)	20	Northern Cape

1 What was the title of Psy's follow-up to *Gangnam Style*?

2 *Carry You* (2013) was a single from which group who appeared on *The X Factor*?

3 What nation did Cascada represent in 2013 in the Eurovision Song Contest?

4 Who became the drummer for the Foo Fighters in 1997?

5 The Grease Band formed as the backing group for which singer?

6 Who wrote the 1977 Rita Coolidge hit *We're All Alone*?

7 The band Audioslave was formed by members of which two other bands?

8 Guy Berryman is the bass player for which band, formed in the 1990s?

9 *Maria Maria* was a 2000 hit for which band?

10 What is the stage name of Rodrick Wayne Moore Jr (b.1998)?

11 Colby O'Donis featured on which Lady Gaga hit?

12 Which band released the 2007 album *Minutes to Midnight*?

13 Danny Wood is an original member of which vocal group?

14 In which country was the video of Katy Perry's 2014 single *Dark Horse* set?

15 John Rzeznik was the lead singer with which 1990s band?

16 Which English band formed in 1988 under the name Seymour?

17 Which US band released the 2018 album *Cage to Rattle*?

18 "I've been dancing on top of cars and stumbling out of bars" is a lyric from which 2019 song?

19 Which rock band performed the "Monolith" tour in 2018-19?

20 In which European country was the singer Gotye born?

Answers to QUIZ 488 – Science Fiction

1	Hoth	11	Sherri S Tepper
2	*Red Dwarf*	12	*District 9*
3	Raymond F Jones	13	*The Invisible Man*
4	Dr Gaius Baltar	14	*Electric Dreams*
5	Michael Moorcock	15	Tim Miller
6	*Pitch Black*	16	William B Davis
7	*Space: 1999*	17	*Alien*
8	Tade Thompson	18	Ted Chiang
9	*The Gathering*	19	*Class*
10	Meredith	20	*Never Let Me Go*

QUIZ 491 – Pot Luck

ANSWERS ON PAGE 493

1   The 1940s painting *Self Portrait: Between the Clock and Bed* was the work of which artist?

2   In which sport was the Windisch technique previously used?

3   "Ferntickles" is an old dialect word for what physical feature?

4   The Seven Valleys is a key text in which religion?

5   What is the name of the lead singer of KC and the Sunshine Band?

6   *The Name of Action* (1930) was the second published novel by which author?

7   Turicum was the Roman name for which European city?

8   In the Star Wars films, what is the name of Rey's home planet?

9   The city of Madurai lies in which Indian state?

10 Located in Malmö, what is the Turning Torso?

11 "This royal throne of kings, this scepter'd isle" is spoken by which Shakespearean character?

12 In Roman times, what were equites?

13 In 1985, Richard Bass became the first person to achieve what feat?

14 Henri Matisse was particularly associated with which artistic style?

15 In which decade did the Gunfight at the OK Corral take place?

16 *Vicia Faba* is the Latin name for which edible item?

17 Who provided the voice of Simba in the 1994 film *The Lion King*?

18 Where in the human body is the rhomboid minor muscle located?

19 "The Truth is Strong" is the motto of which English city?

20 Who was the Greek equivalent of the Norse god Týr?

Easy

Medium

Hard

Answers to QUIZ 489 – Pot Luck

1	Mount Erebus	11	India
2	Nauru	12	The Coleridge Way
3	*Cobra*	13	Houston
4	The Smashing Pumpkins	14	Rhombohedron
5	Mon Mome	15	*Agnes Grey*
6	*Time and Chance*	16	Dan Fogelman
7	Micheal Ward	17	Stockholm
8	Oak	18	Falcon
9	Perigee	19	Seasonality
10	A bird	20	Pope Benedict III

1. How many players are on each team in a game of Canadian football?

2. In which country was the footballer Enner Valencia born in 1989?

3. English businessmen Alfred Edwards and Herbert Kilpin were among the founders of which European football club in 1899?

4. Which country took the bronze medal in the men's 4x100m relay at the 2019 World Athletics Championships?

5. How many races were there in the first Formula 1 season in 1950?

6. What is the name of the foothold from which a player pushes off in curling?

7. The IWRF governs which Paralympic sport?

8. As at 2019, in which year did cricket make its only appearance in the Summer Olympics?

9. How high, in feet or metres, is the post that holds the basket on a korfball court?

10. Joe Montana spent the majority of his US National Football League career with which team?

11. As at 2020, Lothar Matthäus holds the record for appearances in the most number of FIFA World Cup Finals matches. How many did he play in?

12. Los Teros is the nickname given to the national rugby union team of which country?

13. Which country won the women's water polo silver medal at the 2019 World Aquatic Championships?

14. Over what distance is the team pursuit event held in cycling?

15. In which American state did the first ever Ryder Cup take place in 1927?

16. From what is the ball made in the Asian game of sepak takraw?

17. What is the alternative name of the sport Octopush, which was invented in the 1950s?

18. Which team won the Superbowl in both 1993 and 1994?

19. Ferenc Puskás played for which national football team from 1945 to 1956?

20. William Beers (d.1900) was instrumental in setting up the modern version of which team sport?

Answers to QUIZ 490 – Rock and Pop Music

1	*Gentleman*	11	*Just Dance*
2	Union J	12	Linkin Park
3	Germany	13	New Kids on the Block
4	Taylor Hawkins	14	Egypt
5	Joe Cocker	15	Goo Goo Dolls
6	Boz Scaggs	16	Blur
7	Soundgarden and Rage Against the Machine	17	Daughtry
8	Coldplay	18	*Sucker* (Jonas Brothers)
9	Santana	19	Thirty Seconds to Mars
10	Roddy Ricch	20	Belgium

QUIZ 493 – Pot Luck

ANSWERS ON PAGE 495

1 Who was the first female photographer (d.1976) to be awarded a Royal Warrant?

2 Which 2001 film was inspired by the Brian Aldiss short story *Supertoys Last All Summer Long*?

3 In which country is the area known as the Bay of Islands?

4 What does an actinometer measure?

5 Who was the Greek equivalent of the Roman God Vesta?

6 Which 1967 novel, set in the fictitious town of Macondo, told the story of the Buendía family?

7 The Château de Chambord in the Loire Valley was built for which French king?

8 On which island is the Teide Astronomical Observatory?

9 The Athabasca Valles can be found on which planet?

10 Who hosted the 2011 TV game show *Epic Win*?

11 Which track on Kanye West's 2007 album *Graduation* was dedicated to Jay-Z?

12 Which team won the first ever Formula 1 Constructors Championship in 1958?

13 *In the End* was a 2002 hit for which band?

14 Who won the Man of the Tournament award in the 2019 Cricket World Cup?

15 Which instrument did Alan Rickman's character play in the 1990 film *Truly, Madly, Deeply*?

16 In which decade did the Glasgow Subway open?

17 Sandra Goodrich (b. 1947) is better known by what stage name?

18 In which country was philosopher Peter Singer born?

19 Hathor was a major goddess in which religion?

20 Bourbon Street is a tourist attraction in which US city?

Easy

Medium

Hard

Answers to QUIZ 491 – Pot Luck

1	Edvard Munch	11	John of Gaunt (*Richard II*)
2	Ski jumping	12	Knights
3	Freckles	13	Climb the tallest mountain on every continent
4	Bahá'í	14	Fauvism
5	Harry Wayne Casey	15	1880s (1881)
6	Graham Greene	16	Broad bean
7	Zürich	17	Matthew Broderick
8	Jakku	18	Top of the back
9	Tamil Nadu	19	Oxford
10	A skyscraper	20	Ares

Easy

1 The writer Patricia Highsmith was born in which US state?

2 Which band released the 1994 single *Dry County*?

3 Sir George Reid was the first High Commissioner to the United Kingdom from which country?

4 In Greek mythology, the Meliae were dryads associated with which tree?

5 Which bird features on the coat of arms of High Wycombe in Buckinghamshire?

6 In 1963, in which town was the UK's first permanent dry ski slope opened?

7 Who directed the 2000 film *High Fidelity*?

8 The Gibson cocktail, made with gin and dry vermouth, has what food item as a garnish?

9 Dame Penelope Keith and Sir Richard Stilgoe have both served as High Sheriff of which county?

10 In which decade was the poet John Dryden born?

Medium

11 What was the name of the fictional town featured in the 1973 film *High Plains Drifter*?

12 What word indicates "dry" on a bottle of Portuguese wine?

13 Sir Matthew Bourne's ballet *Highland Fling* is a reworking of which classical work?

14 Who wrote the novel on which the 1989 film *A Dry White Season* was based?

15 The fictional highwayman Captain Macheath first appeared in which musical work of 1728?

16 The 1991 Marillion single *Dry Land* was taken from which album?

17 In which decade did Highgate Cemetery open?

18 What was the original UK title of the 1954 Ealing comedy that was released in the US as *High and Dry*?

19 Who won the gold medal in the women's high jump at the 2016 Olympic Games?

20 Which writer (1771-1832) was buried at Dryburgh Abbey?

Hard

Answers to QUIZ 492 – Team Sports

1	12	11	25
2	Ecuador	12	Uruguay
3	AC Milan	13	Spain
4	Japan	14	4 km
5	Seven	15	Massachusetts
6	Hack	16	Rattan
7	Wheelchair rugby	17	Underwater hockey
8	1900	18	The Dallas Cowboys
9	11.5 feet (3.5 metres)	19	Hungary
10	San Francisco 49ers	20	Lacrosse

1 By what other name is the 1952 Sino-Japanese Peace Treaty known?

2 Which South American species of penguin was named after a Portuguese explorer (d.1521)?

3 What term is given to the unintentional repetition of words or phrase by a copyist?

4 In which country is the Thian Hock Keng temple, dedicated to the sea goddess Mazu?

5 What shape is something that is described as "annular"?

6 Alex MacMorrow, played by Alex Etel, was the main character in which 2007 fantasy film?

7 The 1957 novel *The Sandcastle* was written by which author?

8 Which 1980s singer subsequently became a gardener and won a Gold Medal at the Chelsea Flower Show in 2005?

9 The chiffon cake originated in which country?

10 The Karaiskakis Stadium is home to which successful football club?

11 What nationality was the composer Ole Bull (d.1880)?

12 John Dawes, Shane Williams and which other Welsh player (d.1919) were inducted into the Rugby Hall of Fame in 2016?

13 Which 1970s TV series featured the fictional band "The Little Ladies"?

14 Opened on Oxford Street in 1864, what type of shop was John Lewis' first store?

15 Of what is orology the study?

16 Mik Kaminski played what instrument in the ELO?

17 How is the fruit of the plant *Solanum lycopersicum* more commonly known?

18 Who was the original presenter of the 1990s interior design series *Homefront*?

19 What type of creature is a pale tussock?

20 What type of foodstuff is lavash?

Answers to QUIZ 493 – Pot Luck

1	Dorothy Wilding	11	*Big Brother*
2	*AI: Artificial Intelligence*	12	Vanwall
3	New Zealand	13	Linkin Park
4	The intensity of radiation	14	Kane Williamson
5	Hestia	15	The cello
6	*100 Years of Solitude* (Gabriel Garcia Márquez)	16	1890s (1896)
7	Francis I	17	Sandie Shaw
8	Tenerife	18	Australia
9	Mars	19	Ancient Egyptian
10	Alexander Armstrong	20	New Orleans

Easy

1   The town of Oudtshoorn in South Africa is particularly associated with which bird?

2   Which creature has the world's heaviest brain?

3   Wallace's giant bee, the largest known living species of bee, is native to which country?

4   "Hirundine" is an adjective referring to which type of bird?

5   What is the name given to the sharp edge of a bird's beak?

6   As at 2020, which museum in China holds the Guinness World Record for the largest collection of dinosaur eggs?

7   Which bird has the taxonomical name *Coturnix coturnix*?

8   What name is given to the markings on a jaguar or leopard?

9   "Leopard" and "Yellow Cellar" are types of which garden creature?

10 What primitive type of creature was an archaeopteryx?

Medium

11 On which plant do cinnabar moths usually lay their eggs?

12 What does a xylophagous organism eat?

13 What type of creatures gather at an *arribada*?

14 The town of Kikinda, nicknamed "the owl capital of the world" because of the numbers that roost there, is in which country?

15 What musical name is given to the species of pipistrelle bat that emits calls at a higher frequency than the common pipistrelle?

16 The coquí species of frogs are native to which country?

17 What is the collective noun for a group of pine martens?

18 What is the fastest species of shark?

19 Sloths and which other type of creature make up the order of mammals called *Pilosa*?

20 What type of creature is an Arabian Mau?

Hard

Answers to QUIZ 494 – High and Dry

1	Texas	11	Lago
2	Bon Jovi	12	Seco
3	Australia	13	*La Sylphide*
4	The ash tree	14	André Brink
5	A swan	15	*The Beggar's Opera* (John Gay)
6	Torquay	16	*Holidays in Eden*
7	Stephen Frears	17	1830s (1839)
8	A pickled onion	18	*The Maggie*
9	Surrey	19	Ruth Beitia
10	1630s (1631)	20	Sir Walter Scott

1   The author Kenneth Grahame spent his working life at which organisation?

2   The Welsh name for which English city translates as "old road"?

3   Iceland lies on the boundary of which two tectonic plates?

4   Which boxer (d.2019) was nicknamed "Sweet Pea"?

5   Which Austrian village became a global tourist attraction after being rumoured to be the basis for Arendelle in the Frozen films?

6   *Morus nigra* is the Latin name for which berry?

7   Which Asian capital city has a name that means "stone village"?

8   Which National Hockey League team is nicknamed "The Ducks"?

9   For which 1933 film did Katherine Hepburn win her first Best Actress Oscar?

10   Punch Bowl features at which British golf course?

11   What type of creature is a Bagot?

12   Ranthambhore National Park lies in which country?

13   What is impignoration?

14   The *testudo* defensive formation used by the Roman army took its name from which animal?

15   Who was the Greek equivalent of the Roman goddess Proserpina?

16   Who played the title role in the 1970s TV series *Petrocelli*?

17   The Stanley Spencer Gallery, opened in 1962, is situated in which English village?

18   In which decade was the Workers' Educational Establishment formed?

19   What was the title of the 2009 film, starring Jamie Foxx and Robert Downey Jr, that was based on the true story of musician Nathaniel Ayers?

20   How many seats did the Labour Party win in the 2019 UK General Election?

Easy

Medium

Hard

Answers to QUIZ 495 – Pot Luck

1	The Treaty of Taipei	11	Norwegian
2	The Magellanic penguin	12	Arthur Gould
3	Dittography	13	*Rock Follies*
4	Singapore	14	A draper's
5	Ring-shaped	15	Mountains
6	*The Water Horse*	16	The violin
7	Dame Iris Murdoch	17	The tomato
8	Kim Wilde	18	Tessa Shaw
9	The USA	19	A moth
10	Olympiakos	20	(Unleavened) flatbread

Easy

1 Which French writer (d.2005) coined the term "ecofeminism" in 1974?

2 What was the name of the first female MP elected to the UK House of Commons in 1918?

3 In which year did the Peace Camps protesting against nuclear weapons begin at Greenham Common in Berkshire?

4 Founded in 2009, after whom is the second Tuesday of October named to celebrate the achievements of women in STEM subjects?

5 Who was the first US Women's Open golf champion?

6 Who was appointed the second UK Minister for Women in 1998?

7 Which 2016 film told the story of NASA employees Katherine Johnson, Dorothy Vaughan and Mary Jackson?

8 Which figure of the French Renaissance wrote the collection of short stories called the *Heptaméron*, published posthumously in 1558?

9 In which decade did management consultant Marilyn Loden coin the phrase "glass ceiling"?

10 As at 2020, who held the record for the most Grammy Awards won by a female artist?

Medium

11 In 1993, who became the first female winner of the Turner Prize?

12 Adelaide Hoodless (d.1910) was the founder of which women's organisation?

13 Who won the women's doubles title at the 2020 Australian Open tennis championships?

14 In 1910, Elise (Raymonde) de Laroche became the first woman to receive what licence?

15 Which abbess (d.1179) who was also a composer and writer, was known as "the Sybil of the Rhine"?

16 In which year was the Equal Pay Act first introduced in the UK?

17 In 2015, who became the Church of England's first female bishop?

18 Who was elected as the prime minister of Finland in December 2019, heading a coalition of parties all led by women?

19 Who was the first African woman to be awarded a Nobel Prize (the Peace Prize)?

20 Who played Emily Davison in the 2015 film *Suffragette*?

Hard

Answers to QUIZ 496 – Animal World

1	The ostrich	11	Ragwort
2	Sperm whale	12	Wood
3	Indonesia	13	Sea turtles (to lay eggs)
4	Swallow	14	Serbia
5	Tomium	15	Soprano pipistrelle
6	Heyuan Museum	16	Puerto Rico
7	Quail	17	A richness
8	Rosettes	18	The shortfin mako shark
9	Slug	19	Anteaters
10	Bird	20	A cat

ANSWERS ON PAGE 251

1   Phil Hill won the 1961 Formula 1 World Championships driving which make of car?

2   A "bellowing" is the collective noun for a group of which bird?

3   *Because of the Times* was a 2007 chart-topping album by which band?

4   Depicted on the modern flag of Argentina, who was the ancient Inca sun god?

5   What is the first name of the children's character Dr Dolittle?

6   The artist Rosalba Carriera (d.1757) was particularly noted for working in which medium?

7   What was the family surname in the 1970s TV drama series *The Brothers*?

8   Arlanda Airport is located in which Scandinavian city?

9   What was the name of Felicity Jones' character in the 2019 film *The Aeronauts*?

10   To the nearest hour, how many hours does it take for the planet Uranus to complete one full rotation?

11   What is the occupation of Calchas, Cressida's father, in Shakespeare's *Troilus and Cressida*?

12   What can be arranged using the Goldschmidt classification?

13   Cole Sear was the main character in which 1999 film?

14   The Gallatin National Forest lies in which US state?

15   What is the currency unit of Mauritius?

16   What was the full first name of author W Somerset Maugham?

17   For which football club did Denis Law play between leaving Manchester City and joining Manchester United?

18   Who was elected President of the European Parliament in July 2019?

19   The 17th-century work *The World, or Treatise on the Light* was a major work by which philosopher?

20   The River Neretva flows through which two countries?

Answers to QUIZ 497 – Pot Luck

1	The Bank of England	11	A goat
2	Hereford	12	India
3	The Eurasian plate and the North American plate	13	The state of being mortgaged or pawned
4	Pernell Whitaker	14	Tortoise
5	Hallstatt	15	Persephone
6	Black mulberry or blackberry	16	Barry Newman
7	Tashkent (Uzbekistan)	17	Cookham, Berkshire
8	Anaheim	18	1900s (1903)
9	*Morning Glory*	19	*The Soloist*
10	Royal Liverpool	20	202

Easy

1 Which 2018 film starring Jesse Eisenberg, Alexander Skarsgård and Salma Hayek was set in the world of high-frequency trading?

2 What was the name of Stephen Rea's character in the 1992 film *The Crying Game*?

3 For which 1966 film did Steve McQueen (d.1980) receive his only Oscar nomination?

4 Which actress voiced Jane in the 1999 *Tarzan* film?

5 Who played dressmaker Reynolds Woodcock in the 2017 film *Phantom Thread*?

6 What was the name of Helen Bertinelli's alter-ego in the 2020 film *Birds of Prey*?

7 Which character did Sophie Thompson play in *Harry Potter and the Deathly Hallows - Part 1*?

8 *A Dame to Kill For* (2014) was a sequel to which 2005 film?

9 Henry Holland is the leading character in which 1951 film?

10 What was the title of the 2000 film based on the real-life African-American football coach Herman Boone?

Medium

11 Richard Griffiths played Uncle Monty in which 1987 film?

12 Who composed the music for the 1956 film *The Ten Commandments*?

13 What is the surname of the twins Cameron and Tyler, portrayed in *The Social Network* by Armie Hammer?

14 Em Reed, Finn Dodd and Sophia Darling were characters in which 1995 film based on a Whitney Otto novel?

15 What was the name of Sir Dirk Bogarde's character in *The Servant* (1963)?

16 In the 2014 film *Noah*, who played the wife of the title character?

17 *Zero to Hero* was a straight-to-video sequel to which 1997 animated film?

18 What was the title of the first film to be released featuring the Marx Brothers?

19 Which 2002 film directed by David Fincher centres on the character of Meg Altman?

20 Who wrote the 1905 novel *Where Angels Fear to Tread*, which was made into a film in 1991?

Hard

Answers to QUIZ 498 – Women

1	Françoise d'Eaubonne	11	Rachel Whiteread
2	Constance Markievicz	12	The Women's Institute
3	1981	13	Timea Babos and Kristina Mladenovic
4	Ada Lovelace	14	Pilot's licence
5	Patty Berg	15	Hildegard of Bingen
6	Margaret Jay (Baroness Jay of Paddington)	16	1970
7	*Hidden Figures*	17	Libby Lane
8	Marguerite de Navarre	18	Sanna Marin
9	1970s (1978)	19	Wangari Maathai
10	Alison Krauss	20	Natalie Press